A Concise Companion to
Chaucer

Blackwell Concise Companions to Literature and Culture

General Editor: David Bradshaw, University of Oxford

This series offers accessible, innovative approaches to major areas of literary study. Each volume provides an indispensable companion for anyone wishing to gain an authoritative understanding of a given period or movement's intellectual character and contexts.

Chaucer	Edited by Corinne Saunders
English Renaissance Literature	Edited by Donna Hamilton
The Restoration and Eighteenth Century	Edited by Cynthia Wall
Shakespeare on Screen	Edited by Diana E. Henderson
The Victorian Novel	Edited by Francis O'Gorman
Modernism	Edited by David Bradshaw
Postwar American Literature and Culture	Edited by Josephine G. Hendin
Twentieth-Century American Poetry	Edited by Stephen Fredman
Contemporary British Fiction	Edited by James English
Feminist Theory	Edited by Mary Eagleton

A Concise Companion to
Chaucer

Edited by Corinne Saunders

Blackwell
Publishing

BLACKWELL PUBLISHING
350 Main Street, Malden, MA 02148-5020, USA
9600 Garsington Road, Oxford OX4 2DQ, UK
550 Swanston Street, Carlton, Victoria 3053, Australia

First published 2006 by Blackwell Publishing Ltd

1 2006

Library of Congress Cataloging-in-Publication Data

A concise companion to Chaucer / edited by Corinne Saunders.
   p. cm.—(Blackwell concise companions to literature and culture)
Includes bibliographical references and index.
 ISBN-13: 978-1-4051-1387-8 (hardcover: alk. paper)
 ISBN-10: 1-4051-1387-1 (hardcover: alk. paper)
 ISBN-13: 978-1-4051-1388-5 (pbk. : alk. paper)
 ISBN-10: 1-4051-1388-X (pbk. : alk. paper) 1. Chaucer, Geoffrey, d.
1400—Criticism and interpretation—Handbooks, manuals, etc.
I. Saunders, Corinne J., 1963–   II. Series.

 PR1924.C59 2006
 821'.1—dc22

                                             2005019821

A catalogue record for this title is available from the British Library.

Set in 10 on 12.5 pt Meridian
by SNP Best-set Typesetter Ltd, Hong Kong
Printed and bound in the United Kingdom
by TJ International, Padstow, Cornwall

For further information on
Blackwell Publishing, visit our website:
www.blackwellpublishing.com

Contents

Contents

vi

Illustrations

Acknowledgements

My greatest debt is to the contributors to this volume, whom I should like to thank for their generosity in writing a series of original essays, which so elegantly balance scholarship and approachability, and from which I have learned much. I am most grateful for the consistent good humour and helpfulness of contributors at all stages in the making of this book. I am grateful too to my colleagues in the Department of English Studies at the University of Durham for their continued support, and to my fellow medievalists and friends across the University and at other institutions.

I should like to thank especially Emma Bennett of Blackwell for inviting me to devise and edit this volume, and all the staff of Blackwell, in particular Karen Wilson, for their invaluable assistance. I have benefited greatly too from the care and efficiency of my copy-editor, Sandra Raphael.

I am grateful to my parents and friends for their interest and support in yet another project, and especially to David Fuller, who has, once again, offered intellectual stimulus and unfailing engagement and encouragement.

Notes on Contributors

Julia Boffey is Professor of Medieval Studies at Queen Mary, University of London.

Neil Cartlidge is Lecturer in Old and Middle English at University College Dublin. He is also the author of two books, *Medieval Marriage: Literary Approaches 1100–1300* (1997) and *The Owl and the Nightingale: Text and Translation* (2001).

A. S. G. Edwards is currently Professor of English at the University of Glamorgan.

Judith Ferster has taught at Colby College, Brandeis University, and North Carolina State University. Her books are *Chaucer on Interpretation* (1985), *Fictions of Advice: The Literature and Politics of Counsel in Late Medieval England* (1996), and *Arguing through Literature: A Thematic Anthology and Guide to Academic Writing* (2005).

Richard Firth Green is Humanities Distinguished Professor of English at Ohio State University. He is the author of *A Crisis of Truth: Literature and Law in Ricardian England* (1998), *Poets and Princepleasers: Literature and the English Court in the Late Middle Ages* (1980), and of numerous articles in such journals as *Speculum, Medium Ævum, Chaucer Review* and *Studies in the Age of Chaucer*.

David Fuller is Emeritus Professor of English in the University of Durham and the University's Public Orator. He is the author of *Blake's Heroic Argument* (1988), *James Joyce's Ulysses* (1992) and (with David Brown) *Signs of Grace: Sacraments in Poetry and Prose* (1995); and editor of Marlowe's *Tamburlaine the Great* (1998), *Blake: Selected Poetry and Prose* (2000), with Patricia Waugh, *The Arts and Sciences of Criticism* (1999) and with Victor Watts and Corinne Saunders a modernized version of *Pearl* (2005).

John C. Hirsh is Professor of English at Georgetown University, with a special interest in late medieval literature and religion. His recent books include *The Boundaries of Faith: The Development and Transmission of Medieval Spirituality* (1996), *Chaucer and the Canterbury Tales* (2003) and *Medieval Lyric: Middle English Lyrics, Ballads and Carols* (2005).

Norm Klassen is Associate Professor of English at St Jerome's University in the University of Waterloo, Ontario, Canada. Subsequent to his first book, *Chaucer on Love, Knowledge, and Sight* (D. S. Brewer), he has published articles on medieval English and French literature as well as the Italian reformer Peter Martyr Vermigli, part of whose Latin commentary on Romans he is translating for the Peter Martyr Library project.

Steven F. Kruger is Professor of English and Medieval Studies at Queens College and the Graduate Center, City University of New York. His books include *Dreaming in the Middle Ages* (1992), *AIDS Narratives: Gender and Sexuality, Fiction and Science* (1996), *Approaching the Millennium: Essays on Angels in America* (1997, co-edited with Deborah R. Geis), *Queering the Middle Ages* (2001, co-edited with Glenn Burger) and *The Spectral Jew: Conversion and Embodiment in Medieval Europe* (forthcoming 2006).

Andrew Lynch teaches in English, Communication and Cultural Studies at the University of Western Australia, and writes on medieval and medievalist literature. He has a particular interest in the medieval literary tradition of war and peace, including its modern reception and adaptation in Britain and Australia.

Corinne Saunders is Reader in the Department of English Studies at the University of Durham. She is the author of *The Forest of Medieval*

Romance (1993) and *Rape and Ravishment in the Literature of Medieval England* (2001). She has edited *Chaucer* (Blackwell Guides to Criticism, 2001); *A Companion to Romance: From Classical to Contemporary* (2004); *Cultural Encounters in Medieval Romance* (2005); (with Françoise Le Saux and Neil Thomas), *Writing War: Medieval Literary Responses* (2004); and (with Jane Macnaughton) *Madness and Creativity in Literature and Culture* (2005). She is English editor of the journal *Medium Ævum*.

Marion Turner is Lecturer in Medieval Literatures at King's College London. She has published several articles on Chaucer and on late fourteenth-century London. Her book on Chaucer and conflict is forthcoming.

Barry Windeatt is Professor of English in the University of Cambridge, and a Fellow of Emmanuel College. His books include a parallel-text edition of *Troilus and Criseyde* (1984; 2nd edition 1990) and an edition of the poem for Penguin (2003), an Oxford critical guide to *Troilus and Criseyde* (1992), an annotated edition of *The Book of Margery Kempe* (2000; 2004) and a translation of the same work for Penguin (1985). He has edited *English Mystics of the Middle Ages* (1994) and (with Ruth Morse) *Chaucer Traditions: Studies in Honour of Derek Brewer* (1990).

R. F. Yeager is Professor of English at the University of West Florida. His most recent book is *Who Murdered Chaucer? A Medieval Mystery* with Terry Jones, Terry Dolan, Alan Fletcher and Juliette Dor.

Note on Edition

Unless otherwise specified, all quotations of Chaucer's writings in this volume are taken from *The Riverside Chaucer*, edited by Larry D. Benson, 3rd edition (Boston: Houghton Mifflin, 1987; Oxford: Oxford University Press, 1988). They are cited by titles of individual works and line numbers. The Introduction and explanatory material are cited as Benson 1987.

Introduction

Corinne Saunders

'The lyf so short, the craft so long to lerne . . .'

This, the opening line of Geoffrey Chaucer's poem the *Parliament of Fowls*, refers to the difficulty of learning to love, with all that that entails – the difficulty of learning the conventions and behaviours of love, but also of the pursuit and winning of the beloved, as well as of the complex negotiation between individual, chance and destiny in loving, and between secular and sacred love. All these aspects of love recur as subjects right across Chaucer's writings, treated in a startling range of perspectives and voices – human, animal and divine, tragic and comic, male and female. Chaucer's sense of the complexity of love is clear in the *Parliament of Fowls*, in which we are offered the contrasting perspectives of Nature and Venus, as well as of courtly and uncourtly birds, and in which the choice between suitors is deferred at the end of the poem, while the narrator is himself an unsuccessful lover. Yet the 'craft' he finds it painful to learn is not just love, but writing itself, and this too is a recurrent theme across Chaucer's oeuvre, often interwoven with that great subject of love. Chaucer is peculiarly aware of the craft of writing – the delicate relation of sophisticated art and artifice to inspiration and imagination, the varied possibilities of form and genre, the creative potential of narrative voice, and the different levels of reading and meaning. The postmodern emphases on the unreliability of the narrator, the

1

uncertainties of interpretation, the shifting truths of fiction are all already present in Chaucer's writing – in his use of multiple voices and his polyvalent narratives, in the tension between received authority, classical or Christian, and individual experience in his work, and in his fashioning of 'old stories' into newly subjective tellings.

Perhaps Chaucer's self-conscious awareness of the craft of writing is clearest in his repeated play with the notion of the uncertain, naïve narrator, a rich source of comedy and irony across his work: the first audience must have been acutely aware of the contrast between Chaucer the author and the unworldly, frequently bumbling tellers of his tales. In both the *Book of the Duchess* and the *Parliament of Fowls*, the narrator is a disappointed lover, often comically misguided. In the *House of Fame* he is the naïve 'Geffrey', who, caught up in the claws of a giant eagle, responds that he would prefer to read about the stars rather than look so closely upon them. In the *Legend of Good Women* too he searches for truth among old books, chastised by the god of Love for his unfair treatment of women in *Troilus and Criseyde*, in which he presents himself as only the servant of lovers, not daring to love. In the *Canterbury Tales*, he becomes the overly trusting pilgrim reporter and failed storyteller, whose abortive romance of Sir Thopas is such appalling doggerel that he is eventually silenced by the Host, 'Thy drasty rymyng is nat worth a toord!' (VII, 930), and whose second attempt is not a poem at all, but a lengthy prose moral treatise, 'The Tale of Melibee'. None of these figures reflect the actuality of Chaucer's life as courtier, diplomat and civic officer, nor his writerly fame. The gap between the writerly and the actual self serves to remind us of the artifice and self-consciousness of Chaucer's writing, and of his ready irony, as well as of the difficulty of pinning down the Chaucerian voice.

Yet perhaps there is truth too in the bookishness of his narrators, such as the teller of the *Book of the Duchess*, who reads his 'romaunce' (48) deep into the night to counter insomnia, and in the repeated images of reading 'olde bokes' (*Legend of Good Women*, 25). To some extent, Chaucer's literary practice must indeed have occurred late in the night and depended on an insistence on bookishness in the interstices of his working life. Whereas he was evidently recognized as a writer by his contemporaries, and his fame contrasts strikingly with the anonymity of many medieval authors, he was not a writer by profession. Born in the early 1340s, Chaucer belonged to a new upper middle class: his father was a successful vintner in London, who had served as deputy chief butler to Edward III; the young Chaucer probably attended a grammar school in London, and his writings reflect a knowledge not only of Latin literature, but also of history, theology, natural philosophy, astrology and law. He was attached first to the household of Elizabeth, Countess of Ulster (1357), and his various travels in her employ included a military campaign in France (1359–60), when he was captured and ransomed. Chaucer's links with the court were both public and personal: in 1366 he married a knight's daughter and lady-in-waiting, Philippa de Roet, whose sister was to become the third wife of one of the king's sons, John of Gaunt; the next year, Chaucer became a member of the royal household of Edward III. As one of perhaps forty men in the king's service, his duties would have ranged from household tasks to diplomatic missions, and his numerous journeys to the Continent provided access to the literatures that were to be so formative in his writing. While Chaucer's early dream-vision poems, particularly the *Book of the Duchess* (1368–72), reflect the influence of French poetry, and he translated part of the *Romance of the Rose* before 1372, the later dream-vision poems, the *House of Fame* (1378–80), the *Parliament of Fowls* (1380–2) and the *Legend of Good Women* (1380–7), draw on Italian writing, in particular the poetry of Dante, Petrarch and Boccaccio; *Troilus and Criseyde* (1382–6) translates Boccaccio's *Il Filostrato* (*c*.1335).[1]

In 1374 Chaucer was given the important public office of comptroller of the custom house, and made responsible for the collection of an export tax and other taxes. His diplomatic missions also continued. Eventually he left London for Kent, where he was made a Justice of the Peace and Member of Parliament; he then became Clerk of the King's Works, responsible for the construction and repair of all the royal residences and the king's holdings; finally he became overseer of the royal forest in Somerset. It was during this later period that he undertook the *Canterbury Tales* (*c*.1387 onwards). Chaucer's numerous appointments suggest his rare success as diplomat and civil servant in a turbulent political world; his friend Thomas Usk, by contrast, was beheaded for treason. A royal protection issued for Chaucer describes him as 'our beloved esquire going about divers parts of England on the king's arduous and pressing business' (1398).[2] Despite our considerable knowledge of Chaucer's life, however, there are many gaps, such as the mysterious record of his release from *raptus*, a charge that can mean either rape or abduction, by one Cecily Champain: the record is connected with other legal accusations brought against Chaucer by two London citizens, so it may well have been part of a financial dispute of some sort. Chaucer appears to have had two sons, 'little Lewis', to whom his *Treatise of the Astrolabe* (*c*.1391) is dedicated, but about whom we know nothing else, and Thomas, who like his father led a highly successful public life, and one of whose daughters married the powerful Duke of Suffolk. For the Middle Ages, Chaucer's life was relatively long: his tomb records the date of his death as 25 October 1400. In the last year of his life, Chaucer leased a house in the parish of Westminster Abbey, and thus was buried there – the beginning of Poets' Corner.

If in one sense Chaucer seems wonderfully at ease in his practice of his writerly craft from his earliest works, in another his learning of it was indeed long, stretching across his life and drawing on the shifting literary and cultural influences of a varied and well-travelled existence. His writings are multifaceted, often evoking a world far distant from our own – a world of surreal dreams, talking beasts, gods and goddesses, miracles and marvels, knights and ladies – a world of romance rather than realism. Yet they can also depict in minute detail the idiosyncrasies of the medieval social estates, the nobility, Church and peasantry, and of the various strands of bourgeois society that made up the great city of London. Perhaps Chaucer is best remembered for the comic realism of, for instance, 'The Miller's Tale' with its robust evocation of the play between the lusty Alisoun, the clever clerk Nicholas, the foolish cleric Absolon, and Alisoun's deceived carpenter husband, all hinging on an open casement window in medieval Oxford, ' "Tehee!", quod she, and clapte the wyndow to' (I, 3740). But such gifts of earthy social comedy and realism are balanced by the extraordinary poetic heights of *Troilus and Criseyde*, with its exploration of the sublimity and the agony of love, and its questions concerning the possibility of faithfulness, free will and happiness, and by the lofty ideals of 'The Knight's Tale' and 'The Franklin's Tale', which probe the limits of human generosity and perfection. In something of the same way, the vibrantly three-dimensional, bourgeois figure of the Wife of Bath, rejoicing in her sexuality, is balanced by the ideal of the courtly lady Emilye in 'The Knight's Tale', her beauty an embodiment of the Maytime garden she strolls in, and by the passionate saint and martyr Cecilia, subject of 'The Second Nun's Tale' – all three figures weave together different literary conventions and traditions, whether in the service of realism or idealism. Chaucer was above all a consummate artist, and he demonstrated his artistry in his ability to span those two poles, to write in all available medieval genres from the robust, low-life *fabliau* to the high-flown tragedy and romance, from the secular tale to the saint's life. He was as skilled in lyric poetry as in dramatic narrative, and his canvas was as easily the individual psyche as the gamut of medieval society.

In his own time, Chaucer was viewed as one of the great 'makars', in whose footsteps writers such as Lydgate, Henryson and Dunbar followed, and later, Shakespeare and Spenser. Although we retain only a few medieval references to Chaucer, these celebrate his poetry: the French courtly poet Deschamps refers to him as 'grant translateur, noble Geffroy Chaucier' ('Ballade' to Chaucer, *c*.1386); his English contemporary John Gower writes of England as full of his songs of love, 'of ditees and of songes glade' (*Confessio Amantis, c*.1390); and Thomas Usk calls him 'the noble philosophical poete in Englissh' (*Testament of Love, c.* 1387).[3] His popularity is attested too by the existence of some fifty manuscripts of his complete works, a very large number for this period and indicative of a wide circulation. Deschamps' phrase, 'grant translateur', also indicates that Chaucer may have been perceived as differently great in the medieval period: great for his ability to translate, to make old stories new, to reinvent and to infuse old traditions with new life. He himself was perhaps most concerned to be seen as following in the footsteps of the classical writers, rather than as shaping a new English tradition – although he has so often since been seen as the 'father of English literature'. Indeed, Chaucer's relation with literary fame is an uneasy one, as his characterization of storytellers suggests, and his writing is full of mocking yet self-conscious references to his own reputation. The polyvalent, shifting quality of his voice underpins his enduring appeal, for his writing has signified in dramatically different ways to different individuals and cultures: he has been the translator, the philosopher, the moralist, the comedian, the realist, the tragedian and the absurdist. The readers of the past have produced one Chaucer after another according to the *Zeitgeist* of the age, and no doubt will continue to do so. This study adds one more collection of voices to the many that have engaged with Chaucer, but it also aims to allow Chaucer to speak for himself, through the illumination of some of the shaping ideas, political, cultural and literary, of his time, and of his poetic and intellectual emphases.

A Concise Companion to Chaucer provides an introduction to a writer who, even in the twenty-first century, is still studied in some form by a majority of students of English literature, as well as by those in other areas of medieval studies. Unlike other *Companion* volumes, this one is structured according to Chaucer's major works, and is broadly chronological, so that appropriate critical essays may be read alongside individual texts. All essays have been newly commissioned and are intended both to be accessible to those exploring Chaucer for the first time and of interest to those returning to Chaucer. Contributors combine contemporary historical and cultural scholarship with a variety of recent critical emphases. The volume as a whole aims to open out the Middle Ages by situating Chaucer in political, social, intellectual and literary terms, and thus to shape an awareness of the discourses of the medieval thought world that underlie its cultural difference. This book plays a role complementary to the extensive Blackwell *Companion to Chaucer* edited by Peter Brown (2000), a compendious collection of essays on contextual topics and an invaluable reference tool, and to my own Blackwell Guide to Criticism, *Chaucer* (2001), which surveys the history of Chaucer criticism and presents a range of extracts from definitive twentieth-century critical works on Chaucer, with introductions and commentary.

The first section of this volume offers several contextual essays on general topics. Marion Turner treats politics and London life, looking at Chaucer's own experience as courtier and diplomat, both in London and on the Continent. London life, with its interrelated courtly, intellectual and civic spheres, is explored with special reference to Chaucer's intellectual circle and his contemporaries, and is placed in the larger context of the politics of medieval England, its changing notions of kingship and rule, and its fluid and formative social structures. Julia Boffey and A. S. G. Edwards probe the cultural context of Chaucer's writings in terms of manuscripts and textual transmission in this period before printing, considering ownership of manuscripts and book production, the ways in which Chaucer's works circulated, the possible contexts of their composition and their probable readers, and different ways of reading. They call attention too to the assumptions of modern editors, and the differences between medieval and modern ideas of books and reading. The literary and intellectual context is further elaborated by R. F. Yeager, who explores the distinctive medieval view of the authority of books, and the idea of literary sources, addressing questions of convention and originality in writing, and tracing Chaucer's several literary heritages – classical, Continental (French and Italian) and English – with an emphasis on his earlier poetry.

Two further essays focus particularly on the earliest narrative poems composed by Chaucer, the *Book of the Duchess*, the *House of Fame* and the *Parliament of Fowls*, and more generally on the mode of these poems, that of the dream vision. Steven F. Kruger places Chaucer's dream visions in the context both of the literary tradition of the dream vision (courtly and philosophical) and of medieval dream theory, particularly that of Macrobius. Kruger illuminates Chaucer's play on notions of different categories of dreams, and the recurrence of dreams in his later writing, not only in his later dream vision the *Legend of Good Women* but also in *Troilus and Criseyde* and the *Canterbury Tales*. For Chaucer dreams provide key narrative devices, evoking the ideas of prophecy and the otherworld, but are also profoundly linked to notions of the psyche and creativity. Barry Windeatt explores further Chaucer's unique use of the dream vision in his analysis of the ways Chaucer infuses the conventions of courtly writing with imaginative power. While Chaucer's early writing is deeply rooted in French courtly tradition, employing its tropes and forms with easy elegance, it also treats courtly ideals with acute realism and the questioning, often ironic tone so characteristic of Chaucer.

The third group of essays focuses on Chaucer's greatest narrative achievement, *Troilus and Criseyde*. Andrew Lynch traces the relation of the poem to its various sources, in particular classical accounts of the Trojan war, placing special emphasis on the notion of the Trojans as the legendary ancestors of the British, and on the idea of London as the New Troy, as well as on the medieval understanding of history and legend. My own essay begins with the problematic idea of 'courtly love', setting this against the more fluid notion of *fin'amors* or refined love. The essay explores Chaucer's shaping of his sources and the conventions associated with love in *Troilus and Criseyde*, as well as his interweaving of romance and realism in order to portray the several faces of love, the ways in which the process of love constructs and deconstructs the self, and the complex dynamics of social and gender relations. Finally, Norm Klassen considers the interweaving of the genres of romance and tragedy in the poem, with particular attention to the emerging idea of tragedy and Chaucer's understanding of generic conventions. He probes the ways these shape the structure of the poem, and mesh with some of its central themes.

The fourth section of the volume focuses on the *Canterbury Tales*. Judith Ferster introduces the ideas of a story collection and of an 'encyclopaedia of kinds', a collection that presents a range of different literary genres. She surveys the different medieval genres used by Chaucer, the idea of estates satire, the drama of the Canterbury pilgrimage and also the ways in which Chaucer's tellers intersect with the tales they tell. Richard Firth Green approaches the tales in terms of the ideas of morality and immorality, setting these against the conventional religious model of the seven deadly sins, and showing that Chaucer develops his own notion of morality rooted in the medieval concept of 'trouthe', an ideal that echoes through the discourses of kingship, justice, law, chivalry, friendship, moral responsibility and good governance. Neil Cartlidge treats these two poles of morality and immorality from a different perspective in his consideration of marriage, sexuality and the family in the *Canterbury Tales*. He places each of these topics in the context of medieval clerical teachings, looking at how Chaucer calls these into question, and considering the nexus of explicit sexuality and immorality, by contrast to idealized portrayals of marriage and desire, as well as the treatment of familial bonds. Finally, John Hirsh addresses the subject of Christianity and the Church, arguing for the importance in the *Canterbury Tales* of the ideas of pilgrimage and the common good. He places Chaucer's writings in terms of the religious ideals and flawed actualities of the medieval Church and its practices, and explores the power of the drive towards spiritual perfection.

The final essay, by David Fuller, reanimates Chaucer in a different way, by considering the importance of reading his poetry aloud and the various modes in which this may be done. The essay addresses the different topics inherent in reading poetry aloud – sound, metre, syntax, poetic language, voice and emphasis – and surveys the range of readings available, in both reconstructed and modern pronunciation, to show the ways in which they illuminate Chaucer's poetry. Indeed, the overall aim of this volume is to open up new ways of reading Chaucer, whether silently or aloud, by indicating some of the subtleties and richness of his art, with its play between creative imagination and sophisticated literary inheritance, and its participation in a complex network of social, cultural and intellectual discourses.

Notes

1 In general, Chaucer's works cannot be dated precisely, and there has been much debate about chronology; these are the approximate dates adopted in Benson (1987), whose notes include full discussion.
2 Quoted in Benson (1987), xxi; documents pertaining to Chaucer's life may be found in Martin M. Crow and Clair C. Olson, *Chaucer Life-Records* (1966).
3 For these and other early references (up to 1930) see J. A. Burrow's anthology, *Geoffrey Chaucer* (1969). See also Caroline F. E. Spurgeon's three volumes, *Five Hundred Years of Chaucer Criticism and Allusion* (1914–22, reprinted 1960), Derek S. Brewer, *Chaucer: The Critical Heritage* (1978), and Corinne Saunders (ed.), *Chaucer*, Blackwell Guides to Criticism (2001).

References and Further Reading

There are a great many introductions to Chaucer and to his individual poems; the following does not pretend to be comprehensive but is a selection of some of the most influential or most recent ones. For further bibliography, see in particular the ongoing series *The Chaucer Bibliographies* (Toronto: University of Toronto Press, 1983–) and G. A. Rudd (ed.), *A Complete Critical Guide to Chaucer* (New York: Garland, 2001). Further reading may also be found in the two journals devoted to Chaucer, *Chaucer Review* and *Studies in the Age of Chaucer*. The latter offers annotated bibliography on relevant publications.

Aers, David (1986). *Chaucer*. Brighton: Harvester.

Anderson, J. J. (ed.) (1974). *Chaucer:* The Canterbury Tales*: A Casebook*. London: Macmillan.

Allen, Valerie and Ares Axiotis (eds) (1997). *Chaucer*. New Casebooks Series. Basingstoke: Macmillan; New York: St Martin's Press.

Ashton, Gail (1998). *Chaucer:* The Canterbury Tales. Basingstoke: Macmillan; New York: St Martin's Press.

Blamires, Alcuin (1987). *The Canterbury Tales*. The Critics Debate. Basingstoke: Macmillan.

Boitano, Piero and Jill Mann (eds). (2004). *The Cambridge Companion to Chaucer*. 2nd edn. Cambridge Companions to Literature. Cambridge: Cambridge University Press.

Burrow, J. A. (ed.) (1969). *Geoffrey Chaucer: A Critical Anthology*. Harmondsworth: Penguin.

Brewer, Derek (ed.) (1978). *Geoffrey Chaucer: The Critical Heritage*. London: Routledge.

Brewer, Derek (1998). *A New Introduction to Chaucer*. 2nd edn. London: Longman.

Brown, Peter (1994). *Chaucer at Work: The Making of the Canterbury Tales*. London: Longman.

Brown, Peter (ed.) (2000). *A Companion to Chaucer*. Blackwell Companions to Literature and Culture. Oxford: Blackwell.

Cooper, Helen (1989). *The Canterbury Tales*. Oxford Guides to Chaucer. Oxford: Clarendon Press.

Crow, Martin M. and Clair C. Olson (1966). *Chaucer Life-Records*. Oxford: Clarendon Press.

Dillon, Janette (1993). *Geoffrey Chaucer*. Writers in their Time. Basingstoke: Macmillan Press.

Donaldson, E. Talbot (1970). *Speaking of Chaucer*. London: Athlone Press.

Ellis, Steve (ed.) (2005). *Chaucer: An Oxford Guide*. Oxford: Oxford University Press.

Hirsh, John (2002). *Chaucer and the* Canterbury Tales*: A Short Introduction*. Blackwell Introductions to Literature. Oxford: Blackwell.

Knight, Stephen (1986). *Geoffrey Chaucer*. Oxford: Blackwell.

Minnis, A. J. (1995). *The Shorter Poems*. Oxford Guides to Chaucer. Oxford: Clarendon.

Pearsall, Derek (1985). *The Canterbury Tales*. London: George Allen and Unwin.

Phillips, Helen (2000). *An Introduction to the* Canterbury Tales: *Reading, Fiction, Context*. Basingstoke: Macmillan.

Saunders, Corinne (ed.) (2001). *Chaucer*. Blackwell Guides to Criticism. Oxford: Blackwell.

Spurgeon, Caroline F. E. (ed.) (1960). *Five Hundred Years of Chaucer Criticism and Allusion: 1357–1900*. 3 vols. New York: Russell and Russell. [First published in 1914–22.]

Windeatt, Barry (1992). *Troilus and Criseyde*. Oxford Guides to Chaucer. Oxford: Clarendon Press.

Part One

Chaucer in Context

The frontispiece of an early fifteenth-century manuscript of *Troilus and Criseyde*, depicting Chaucer reading to a courtly audience (The Master and Fellows of Corpus Christi College, Cambridge MS 61, fol. 1b).

Chapter One

Politics and London Life

Marion Turner

Chaucer made a reasonable amount of money in his life but, as far as we know, he never earned a penny from his writing. Instead, he held a variety of jobs: he was a pageboy, a customs officer, a Member of Parliament, a diplomat, a soldier, Clerk of the King's Works and (probably) a spy. As a player in the political world of the late fourteenth century, his name frequently occurs in legal and political documents. 'Galfrido Chaucer Londonie' – as he is termed in the household accounts of Elizabeth, Countess of Ulster, in 1357 – is a familiar presence in the archives (Crow and Olson 1966: 13). The records tell us, for example, that in 1359–60 he fought at the siege of Reims and was captured and ransomed, that in 1374 Edward III granted him a gallon of wine daily for life, that in 1376 he was sent on journeys to further the secret business of the king, that in 1388 he was twice sued for debt, and that in 1399 he took a fifty-three-year lease of a house in the precincts of Westminster Abbey (Crow and Olson 1966: 24, 112, 42–3, 384–91, 535–6). His career, his marriage and his private actions are all revealed to some extent in surviving documents. We know who his father was (a well-off London wine merchant) and who his wife was (Philippa de Roet, daughter of a knight from Hainault). Chaucer was a man who always needed to earn his own living, and he therefore occupied a social position far from the top of medieval society. However, he was very well connected and had the favour of influential figures in the court. His wife's sister (Kathryn Swynford) was the long-term mistress, and later the wife, of John of Gaunt, one of the most important men in England, uncle of Richard II and father of the usurper Henry IV. Chaucer's earliest long poem – the *Book of the Duchess* – was written on the occasion of the death of John's first wife (Henry's mother) Blanche of Lancaster. Many of Chaucer's friends were men of power and influence at court, and he himself had the political acumen to make himself agreeable to different political groups, receiving grants from both Richard and Henry in the mid and late 1390s. Chaucer always managed to stay out of political trouble, absenting himself from London when times were particularly turbulent, and somehow staying on good terms with everyone who mattered in a time of great political unrest (Strohm 1990).

The second half of the fourteenth century was a period dominated by upheaval and conflict. The Black Death and the beginning of the Hundred Years' War in the middle of the century ushered in an increasingly problematic era. Europe was split by the Great Schism: between 1378 and 1417 there were two popes, one at Rome and one at Avignon. One of the most dramatic revolts in English history took place in 1381, when rebelling peasants (and others) entered London and slaughtered immigrants, the Chief Justice, and the Archbishop of Canterbury. An extremely powerful heretical movement, Lollardy, arose in the 1380s, inspired by the teachings of John Wycliffe. The king lost power to a coalition of nobles in 1388, won it back, but became increasingly tyrannical and was deposed in 1399 by his cousin. The city of London was torn apart by factional disputes so vicious that one mayor was executed in 1388. While this extraordinary political maelstrom was taking place, literature in English was rising to greater prominence than ever before, as writers such as John Gower, William Langland, the anonymous *Gawain*-poet and Geoffrey Chaucer used the language in novel and exciting ways. As someone who lived at the heart of contemporary political life – who was living on the walls when the peasants stormed them, whose friends were closely associated with Lollardy, who was dangerously linked with those purged in 1388 – Chaucer was perfectly placed for writing about his times. Yet to do so could also be risky, particularly for someone whose livelihood depended on the favour of the king. As a result, Chaucer generally talks about politics in oblique and subtle ways, and makes few overtly political statements. Even when he does directly address contemporary events, his meaning tends to remain ambiguous and double-edged.

Politics and Discourses

Politics are refracted in manifold ways in Chaucer's poetry. His most direct political statements are reserved for his short poems. 'Lak of Stedfastnesse' is a ballad in the form of a complaint, echoing the ideas of Boethius' *Consolation of Philosophy*. The first three verses lament the degeneracy of contemporary society, characterizing it as 'fals' (3) and 'variable' (8), dominated by the breakdown of truth (personal integrity) and by the separation between word and deed. It is a world 'turned up-so-doun' (5), a time of political and social darkness. In the final stanza, Chaucer proposes a solution, in 'Lenvoy to King Richard':

> O prince, desyre to be honourable,
> Cherish thy folk and hate extorcioun.
> Suffre nothing that may be reprevable
> To thyn estat don in thy regioun.
> Shew forth thy swerd of castigacioun,
> Dred God, do law, love trouthe and worthinesse,
> And wed thy folk agein to stedfastnesse.
>
> (22–8)

On one level, this is typical 'advice to princes' material, encouraging and supporting the king. The poet suggests that the solution to social problems lies in strong kingship. The father-like king must subdue and control his errant subjects through a benign assertion of his power, acting firmly and fairly. This could be read as a decidedly royalist poem with the message that Richard's 'swerd of castigacioun' is the country's only hope. On the other hand, the verse could imply that the king has irresponsibly allowed his country to degenerate appallingly; that so far he has not been honourable, has not cherished his people, has not hated extortion and so on. The penultimate line is particularly damning, as it suggests that the king needs to be reminded to dread God, administer justice, love truth and worthiness – behaviour that should be fundamental to kingship. The lines perhaps suggest that Richard himself needs to be wed to 'stedfastnesse'. Chaucer could thus be making either a pro- or an anti-Ricardian statement in this poem – or both. As usual, he hedges his bets.

In other short poems, political comments are buried beneath complex aesthetics and displays of learning. 'Fortune: Balades de

Visage sans Peinture' ['Ballads on a Face without Painting'] is a skilful triple ballade, ending with an envoy in rime royal. It too is strongly influenced by Boethius' *Consolation of Philosophy*, and also draws on the *Romance of the Rose* and on Dante. It is also, however, firmly rooted in the here and now, and reveals Chaucer's knowledge of contemporary law and politics. A dialogue between 'le pleintif' and Fortune, in the form of a legal debate, structures the poem. Terms such as 'statut' (43) and 'ordinaunce' (44) are scattered throughout the poem, and the final lines locate it firmly in the early 1390s. The envoy addresses three princes, begging either two or three of them to relieve the plaintiff by asking (the plaintiff's) best friend to give him a better position. After 1390, all royal gifts had to be authorized by at least two of the Dukes of York, Lancaster and Gloucester. The delicate Boethian complaint thus proves to be a specific, political plea for preference, couched in precise and striking legal terms.

Chaucer is usually reluctant about discussing the politics of the 1380s and 1390s in such an open way. Yet contemporary politics infuse all his writings. For example, his writings often reflect and comment on contemporary political systems, albeit in subtle ways. By criticizing political structures or satirizing kings in an abstracted setting such as ancient Athens ('The Knight's Tale') or Troy (*Troilus and Criseyde*), Chaucer secures himself from potential accusations of sedition. The *House of Fame* could be read as a searing indictment of the shallow sycophancy and arbitrary advancement of the contemporary court, but it could easily be defended – or dismissed – as an abstruse, non-political piece occupied solely with the world of literature and art. Similarly, a scene in the *Prologue to the Legend of Good Women* paints a highly critical picture of court life, but the court described is that of the god of Love. Alceste declares:

> The god of Love hereth many a tale yfeyned.
> For *in youre court is many a losengeour**,   *flatterer
> And many a queynte* totelere* accusour*,   *crafty tattling
>   slanderer
>
> That tabouren* in youre eres many a thynge   *drum
> For hate, or for jelous ymagynyng,
> And for to han with you som dalyaunce.
> Envye – I preye to God yeve hire myschaunce! –
> Is lavender* in the grete court alway [. . .]   *laundress
> This shulde a ryghtwys lord han in his thought,
> And *not ben lyk tyrants of Lumbardye,*
> *That usen wilfulhed and tyrannye.*

For he that kyng or lord is naturel,
Hym oughte nat be tyraunt and crewel.
(G 327–34, 353–7, emphasis mine)

This passage claims to be about the god of Love, and the flatterers and liars that surround him, but the language is highly political, suggesting a less abstract relevance. Terms such as 'grete court', 'ryghtwys lord', 'tyraunts' and 'kyng' clearly speak to political life. Furthermore, although Alceste begins by talking specifically about the god of Love, she has certainly moved into the world of the fourteenth century by the time she refers to 'tyraunts of Lumbardye' – the Visconti despots of Milan, whom Chaucer visited and negotiated with in 1378 and to whose notorious behaviour he refers elsewhere in his work (Wallace 1997). By lines 356–7 Alceste is making a general comment about the responsibilities of any ruler. The passage both warns against the lies of chattering courtiers ('For in youre court is many a losengeour / And many a queynte totelere accusour') and urges the ruler to reasonable behaviour, seeming most concerned about tyranny – mentioned three times in four lines. Such concerns are particularly relevant to Richard II and his court. In the Merciless Parliament of 1388, Richard's favourites were dismissed (some were executed) as the culmination of powerful lords' anxieties about the kind of people whom Richard raised to high honour. Richard's dependence upon faction remained a cause for criticism throughout his reign (Saul 1997). He was also strongly criticized for his tyrannical tendencies: he did not want to take the advice of the great landowners of the realm, he removed the traditional liberties of the city from London in 1392, and he insisted on promoting an image of himself as a semi-divine figure (Barron 1971; Saul 1997). One chronicler writes that, after dinner, Richard would sit on a throne gazing around the room, and anyone on whom his eyes fell had to kneel down immediately (Saul 1997: 342). Alceste's criticisms of the god of Love are thus particularly appropriate for Richard – and in their intimations of irresponsibility they echo 'Lak of Stedfastnesse'. Yet Chaucer says nothing directly; rather, in a move that we might describe as characteristically Chaucerian, he leaves the reader to draw his or her own conclusions, to decide for him or herself whether the poet is talking about the god of Love, Richard, neither or both.

Parliament is given similar treatment in his work. Chaucer does not talk explicitly about a contemporary parliament – in which he himself sat – but he stages crucial parliament scenes, most notably in the

Marion Turner

Parliament of Fowls and in Book IV of *Troilus and Criseyde*. Although the latter scene is set in Troy, and deals with a specific situation in the Trojan war, the parliament is recognizable as a medieval English parliament. It is called by the king, combines lords and more common people, and has the power to make legally binding decisions ('it moste ben and sholde, / For substaunce of the parlement it wolde' [216–17]) that cannot be overruled by the king. Even the subject which this parliament is discussing – a truce and an exchange of prisoners with the enemy – is relevant to late fourteenth-century England, in which the war with France was frequently discussed in parliament. The 'cloude of errour' (200) of the Trojans might well refer to a contemporary parliament as well as to a fictional past. The *Parliament of Fowls* is, on the surface, a fairly frivolous poem about birds debating issues of love and sex. Its parliament setting gives it greater political resonance. The 'lower-class' birds contradict the voices of authority in this poem, and they prove to have a great deal more common sense than their social superiors have. Their interruptions, their refusal to agree with the higher-class birds, and their intrusion into Nature's plan for the parliament calls to mind the English parliament's actual ability to curb the power of the king. This poem is also a good example of how Chaucer uses genre and discourse in such a way as to suggest broader political points (Strohm 1989: 151–7, 163–8). The lower-class birds' attack on the discourse of courtly love as a genre that goes nowhere could be read as a political statement about the vitality of the common people as opposed to the decaying aristocracy. The goose, cuckoo and duck all secure their partners and get on with procreation while the tercel eagles remain trapped in their own longing. The superior pragmatism and argumentative ability of the direct, plain-speaking common birds serve as an onslaught on the irrelevant values of the royal and aristocratic birds. The common birds' ability to use legal language ('I wol seye my verdit' [503]), and their determination to speak on their 'owene autorite' (506), constructs a picture of a confident, able group of people emerging in parliamentary and city life, challenging the hegemony of the inward-looking aristocracy.

Similar points could be made about the Miller's interruption of the Knight in the *Canterbury Tales*, a moment which some critics have termed a literary peasants' revolt (David 1976: 92). The Peasants' Revolt itself was devastating to the mindset of the ruling classes, many of whom thought it must be a punishment from God. Utter confusion and terror are evident in accounts written by chroniclers and by Chaucer's contemporary, John Gower. Artisans and tradespeople, as well as peasants, rose in protest against a plethora of wrongs, most notably poll taxes and the intrusion of legal, written culture on the traditional rights of the people. Londoners opened the city gates to the rebels, and they flowed in at Aldgate, above which Chaucer resided at the time. Their activities included burning down John of Gaunt's palace (the Savoy), taunting the queen mother in her own bedroom, beheading important officials and massacring Flemish immigrants. Reputedly led by Jack Straw and Wat Tyler, these rebels were effective and powerful. Although they were eventually persuaded to disperse, their actions had been terrifying indeed. Chaucer has almost nothing to say about these extraordinary events. At one point he refers to the 'cherles rebellyng' ('The Knight's Tale', I, 2459) at another to the 'blase of strawe' (*Troilus and Criseyde*, IV, 184) spreading through the people of the city, both of which phrases might or might not refer to the revolt. Only once does he make an unequivocal reference to the rebels; in 'The Nun's Priest's Tale', when describing a cacophonous barnyard chase, the narrator declares:

> So hydous was the noyse – a, benedicitee! –
> Certes, he Jakke Straw and his meynee*   *company
> Ne made nevere shoutes half so shrille
> Whan that they wolden any Flemyng kille,
> As thilke day was maad upon the fox.
>   (VII, 3393–7)

It is difficult to know what to make of these lines. Certainly, the peasants are being compared to shrieking animals, but they are animals with a legitimate target, the fox, who is the evil predator of the tale. Moreover, the target is an animal often used to represent lawyers, and the lawyer was one of the principal hate-figures of the revolt. The flippancy of the comment makes the tone hard to read, and it is, of course, spoken not in an authorial voice, but in the voice of one of the unreliable pilgrims.

In some ways, the dramatic and prominent interruption of the order of tale-telling by the Miller makes a much clearer point about contemporary politics, social hierarchy and the rights of the non-aristocratic classes, but does so in an indirect way. When the Miller insists upon his right to tell a tale early on in the pilgrimage, and goes on to tell a fabliau that brilliantly parodies 'The Knight's Tale' and exposes the pretensions of the high-flown discourse of courtly love, he participates in the *Tales'* more general assertion that the middle classes have just as much right to voice their opinions as their social superiors. This in itself is a radical point. By upsetting the order of tales, the Miller rebels against oppressive social and political structures, and strikes a blow for the less important people in society (although the lowly Plowman remains silent in the *Tales*). It is also worth noting that millers were particularly prominent in the Peasants' Revolt itself. In the *Canterbury Tales*, then, as in the *Parliament of Fowls*, political points are made through the celebration of polyphony. Both texts are marketplaces, packed with competing voices and jostling discourses, places in which political hierarchies struggle to maintain their structure, and discourses interrupt and contradict each other (Strohm 1989: 168–72). But Chaucer is careful to say nothing directly, and never commits himself openly to a political point of view.

The variety of discourses that Chaucer employed reveals his interesting (and precarious) social and political position: he straddled court and city. He was undoubtedly the most skilled poet of his day. He understood Latin, French and Italian, introduced the pentameter into English, wrote in rhyming couplets, rime royal and prose, wrote romance, fabliaux, saints' lives, sermons, parodies, complaints, dream poetry and translations. This virtuosity was partly enabled by his social flexibility. The example of Chaucer's interaction with Italy and Italian is instructive. His writing was heavily influenced by Italian literature; without texts such as Dante's *Divine Comedy* and Boccaccio's *Il Filostrato [The One Prostrated by Love]*, Chaucer's major works could not have been written. One recent critic has suggested that the politics of the *Canterbury Tales* are consistently shaped by Chaucer's engagement with contrasting Italian political forms: the polity of the city-state, represented by Dante and Boccaccio, and the hierarchical horrors of tyranny, represented by the poet of the Visconti, Petrarch (Wallace 1997). Chaucer probably acquired his excellent understanding of Italian through his mercantile background and childhood in the Vintry ward of the City of London (Pearsall 1992: 18). His father certainly did business with Italian merchants. Chaucer was then able to go to Italy because he had the favour of the court and was a trusted royal servant. (He was sent there on a trading mission and on the private business of the king in 1372, and again to negotiate for alliances in 1378.) Chaucer's trade background *and* his acceptability to the royal family thus both contributed to his opportunity to gain Italian manuscripts and to engage fully with Italian literature.

Chaucer's literary abilities were similarly various: he was just as competent at deploying bourgeois language or at inventing conversation as he was at writing stylized courtly verse and formal rhetorical speeches. He was familiar with the courtly language of love and romance, and wrote his most courtly poem – the *Book of the Duchess* – for a courtly occasion, the death of a member of the royal family. Some of his friends at court wrote poetry that imitated Chaucer's dream poetry – most notably Sir John Clanvowe's *Boke of Cupide* quotes from 'The Knight's Tale' and takes the form of a bird debate like the *Parliament of Fowls*. At the same time, the legal training that Chaucer may have received at the Inns of Court (anecdote has it that he was fined by the Inns for beating up a friar in Fleet Street), and his immersion in city life, enabled him to use 'city' discourses with ease. 'The Tale of Melibee,' for example, is written in a watered-down form of curial prose, an elaborate prose style common in legal and political documents. All his life Chaucer had close connections with the law courts. He appeared in court as a witness to the Scropes' right to bear a certain coat of arms, as a Justice of the Peace, as surety for his friends, to take wardships of the property of minors, to be released from further actions concerning the rape of Cecily Champain, and as a victim of robbery (Crow and Olson 1966: 370–1, 348–54, 276–91, 294–302, 343–5, 477–86). Legal scenes are important in texts such as 'The Wife of Bath's Tale' and 'The Man of Law's Tale', and the *House of Fame* could be read as a parody of a judge and court. Short poems such as the 'ABC' and the 'Complaint unto Pity' reveal Chaucer's confident deployment of the language of the law courts. In this social sphere we find readers quite different from the chamber knight, Clanvowe. These readers include men such as Thomas Usk, the first known reader of *Troilus and Criseyde*, a lowly scribe who wrote a long tract called the *Testament of Love*, and who was executed by the Merciless Parliament of 1388 (Strohm 1990).

Chaucer's writings can be set in many literary contexts: the vernacular poetry that was developing all over Europe in the fourteenth century, contemporary English poetry or generic traditions. For the purposes of considering Chaucer's engagement with London life, his writings need to be considered in the context of textual production in London in the 1380s and 1390s. England was still very much a trilingual country at this time, and English remained the poor relation of French and Latin. Times were changing, however: in 1362 a statute was passed prescribing the use of English in court, and by the 1380s English documents were being entered into the Rolls of Parliament, although this was very unusual. The language gained more status in the fifteenth century as the usurping kings – Henry IV and then his son Henry V – emphasized their patriotism through an increased use of English (Lindenbaum 1999; Ormrod 2003). In Chaucer's time, writing in English was a conscious choice. Writing in the vernacular remained a suspicious activity as it inevitably invited a wider audience and made literature available to a more socially diverse group of people. Writing and reading in English was a potentially liberating act and could therefore be viewed with distrust: in England, the heresy of the day was characterized by the heretics' belief in the importance of translating the Bible into English. Usk, one of Chaucer's first readers, repeatedly tried to use textual culture to save his own skin. First, he turned traitor to his erstwhile master, John Northampton (mayor of London), and betrayed him in his *Appeal*. Languishing in disgrace as a traitor – though in a better position than the exiled Northampton – he wrote the *Testament of Love* in self-justification: it is heavily influenced by Chaucer and cites him admiringly. Usk's writings seem to have helped him to gain promotion, but ultimately they could not save him from the executioner's axe when his new patrons fell from power (Strohm 1990; Turner 2002). He is a good example, however, of a low-class man attempting to use vernacular writing and documentary culture for his own ends – he saw writing in English as a way to shape his own fate. Yet others saw such writing as incriminating. Usk's own new patron, Nicholas Brembre, had in the past shown great suspicion of clerkly writing, in particular the Jubilee Book, a compendium of laws and city regulations put together by Northampton. Brembre's ally, Nicholas Exton, who became mayor in 1386, had the book burnt. Set in this kind of context, Chaucer's reluctance to make direct political statements seems extremely sensible. His brilliant use of unreliable narrators is a device that silences the authorial voice, enabling him to distance himself from whatever views his texts express. 'Blameth nat me' ('The Miller's Prologue', 3181) is a mantra for Chaucer. But his writings everywhere reveal their provenance in the London of the late fourteenth century.

London Life and Chaucer's Poetry

Snapshots of London are peppered throughout the 'General Prologue' to the *Canterbury Tales*, which as a whole reflects the burgeoning 'middle-class' life that developed in the cities with particular force after the Black Death. We hear of the self-important guildsmen whose wives want to be first in church processions, of the London ale favoured by the Cook, of the Manciple who cheats his employers at an Inn of Court, of the immoral Pardoner based in the suburbs at Charing Cross. Harry Bailly is compared to city officials – 'A fairer burgeys was ther noon in Chepe' (754) – as Chaucer mentions the most famous commercial street in London, evoking an atmosphere of trade, power and energy. Harry himself, of course, resides in Southwark, and prospers through his Tabard Inn. Southwark, just over the river from the City proper, was notorious for prostitution, tavern life and unsavoury trades, a profoundly appropriate place for the motley crew of Canterbury pilgrims to assemble and to begin their unruly journey.

A brief examination of one of Chaucer's London pilgrim portraits reveals Chaucer's perceptive understanding of the world of the city. He writes:

A Sergeant of the Lawe, war and wys,	
That often hadde been at the Parvys,	
Ther was also, ful riche of excellence.	
Discreet he was and of greet reverence –	
He semed swich, his wordes weren so wise.	
Justice he was ful often in assise*,	*court of assizes
By patente* and by pleyn commissioun.	*king's letter of appointment
For his science and for his heigh renoun,	
Of fees and robes hadde he many oon.	
So greet a purchasour* was nowher noon:	*land-buyer
Al was fee symple* to hym in effect;	*unrestricted possession
His purchasyng myghte nat been infect*.	*invalidated
Nowher so bisy a man as he ther nas,	
And yet he semed bisier than he was.	
In termes* hadde he caas and doomes* alle	*Year Books; *decisions
That from the tyme of kyng William were falle.	
Therto he koude endite* and make a thyng*,	*draft; *legal document
Ther koude no wight pynche* at his writyng;	*find a flaw in
And every statut koude* he pleyn* by rote*.	*knew entirely *by heart
He rood but hoomly* in a medlee* cote,	*simply; *parti-coloured
Girt with a ceint* of silk, with barres* smale;	*belt; *stripes
Of his array telle I no lenger tale.	
('General Prologue', I, 309–30)	

The Man of Law is immediately established as a London man: he has often been at the Parvys, the porch of St Paul's Cathedral, where lawyers hawked their services. St Paul's was the greatest church in the walled city – in other contemporary poems such as *St Erkenwald* it functions as a kind of symbol of London – and so this reference firmly locates the Man of Law in an urban context. Chaucer shows off his familiarity with legal discourse in this portrait as the description is dripping with legal language: 'By patente and by pleyn commissioun', 'fee symple', 'statut', 'assise'. The Man of Law is a lawyer of lawyers – he knows all the cases and judicial decisions from 1066 to the present day, and knows every statute by heart. The description also reveals Chaucer's awareness of the degeneracy of the city and of lawyers as he evokes the grasping, semi-criminal atmosphere of capitalist life. The Man of Law knows how to keep just on the right side of public opinion without sacrificing his suspect activities. We are told: 'Discreet he was and of greet reverence – / He semed swich, his wordes weren so wise' and then 'Nowher so bisy a man as he ther nas, / And yet he semed bisier than he was.' Both couplets follow the same formula: in the first line we are told of an admirable quality of the Man of Law that is undercut in the subsequent line by the use of the word 'semed'. He seems discreet, but he might not be; he seems busy, but in fact he is less so than he appears. The taint of dishonesty hangs over all of the Man of Law's attributes. The fact that 'Al was fee symple*' (*unrestricted possession) emphasizes his acquisitive desires. Overall, we are given an impression of a grasping man of deceptive appearance, a man fully representative of the wiliness of contemporary London.

This wiliness is particularly well demonstrated at the end of the spectacular first fragment of the *Canterbury Tales* in 'The Cook's Tale', a stunning street narrative that lasts for fewer than sixty lines. Promoting the story that he is about to tell, the Cook terms it, 'A litel jape that fil in oure citee' (I, 4343). His use of the word 'oure' situates not only himself and the Host, but also the other pilgrims – and perhaps even the wider audience of the tale – in a London ambience. The first line of the tale repeats this phrase – 'oure citee' (I, 4365) – again placing those listening to the tale in a London context. The Cook's initial description of the tale as a 'litel jape' constructs an image of the city as young, playful and fond of playing tricks. He then tells a story of a wild, exuberant apprentice who dances, gambles, drinks and robs his master, until finally he is sacked and moves in with a fellow rioter whose wife is a prostitute. The tale mentions specific London locations: Perkyn Revelour is sometimes 'lad with revel to Newegate' (I, 4402) – led to Newgate prison on the city walls. He also leaps out of the shop 'whan ther any ridyng was in Chepe' (I, 4377) – whenever a procession goes along Cheapside, the heart of the city of London. Here we might think of the lavish entry for King John of France when he arrived as a prisoner of the Black Prince in 1357, or of the series of pageants that were staged in the city to celebrate Richard's reconciliation with it in 1392. These pageants depicted tableaux of the biblical wilderness and of the New Jerusalem. Cheapside was adorned with rich ornaments and angelic actors, and the guildsmen themselves dressed up as angels (Barron 1971: 190–1; Federico 2003: 18–28). It is easy to imagine crowds of city-dwellers thronging the streets to participate in these elaborate displays of wealth and civic importance.

'The Cook's Tale' also evokes the atmosphere of the contemporary city more generally. It is high-spirited and entertaining – Perkyn is always dancing, hopping, singing, loving, disporting himself and playing. It is also seedy: Perkyn and his friends spend their time in the 'taverne' rather than working in the 'shoppe' (I, 4376), and they seem obsessed with dice-playing, gambling and overspending at their masters' expense. Perkyn's liking for the tavern would have had particular resonance at a time when there were regulations against forming confederacies in a tavern, and when tavern life was regularly associated with deadly sins and immoral behaviour. We might also think of the uncertain morality of another group who came together in a tavern – the Canterbury company itself.

The imagery of the short tale conjures up a picture of a marketplace. Perkyn is compared to the 'goldfynch' (I, 4367) and to the 'berye' (I, 4368), he is as full of sexual love as the hive is of honey (I, 4373) and, when his master decides to sack him, he compares the apprentice to a 'roten appul' (I, 4406). These terms evoke an image of the countryside in the city, reminiscent both of the immigrant labour that flooded into London from the countryside in the fourteenth century, particularly in the wake of the plague, and of the produce and goods that were sold in London, in the markets and shops. The rottenness of the apple emphasizes the fact that goods were not always worth buying. In almost every line of this tale we learn something about perceptions of London life. Perkyn's disreputable 'meynee' (I, 4381) reminds us of contemporary suspicions of tavern associations and confederacies; the reference to his 'craft of vitailliers' (I, 4366) reminds us of the importance of guild associations. The description of his playing dice in the street, leaping and dancing in the road, or being forcibly led down to prison evokes a lively, busy picture of the bustling streets of London (which Chaucer must often have watched from the windows of his house on the walls). The mention of the frustrated shop-owner, who must in his own 'shoppe abye' (I, 4393) because Perkyn's laziness and dishonesty is losing him so much money, neatly describes the put-upon master, while the depiction of the apprentice moving his possessions to his friend's house when he is thrown out of his work-lodgings illustrates the casual lifestyle of a carefree young man. The statement that 'Revel and trouthe, as in a lowe degree, / They been ful wrothe al day' ('revelling and truth are always fighting with each other in a man of low class' [I, 4397–8]) both emphasizes Perkyn Revelour's dishonesty and invites some sympathy for him – it is hard utterly to condemn youthful play. The Cook here suggests that the excitement of London life goes hand in hand with its disreputable criminality. Chaucer's other London tale emphasizes this disreputable criminality as the city's defining trait: 'The Canon's Yeoman's Tale' depicts London as a place of lies, tricks and treachery, a place where the servant betrays his criminal master and that master makes his living from betraying his victims. The description of the Canon and his Yeoman 'lurkynge' alongside 'thise robbours and thise theves' in company with those who 'holden his pryvee fereful residence' memorably evokes the dark corners of London life ('The Canon's Yeoman's Prologue', VIII, 658–60).

The intense aggression and vicious competitiveness of London life is encapsulated in the encounter between the Cook and the Host that precedes 'The Cook's Tale'. After the Reeve has told his tale of a cuckolded miller, the Cook (identified here as the 'Cook of Londoun') immediately interprets the tale as a joke about hosts, about those who allow others to lodge in their houses. He thus implies that the tale is an attack on the Host himself, asserting that 'herberwynge by nyghte is perilous' (I, 4332). This comment has particular resonance in the context of late fourteenth-century London. In 1381 a regulation was passed that a hosteler must allow no one for whom he would not answer to lodge in his inn, and in 1384 the mayor and aldermen blamed innkeepers' harbouring of criminals for an upsurge in criminal activity in London and the suburbs (Riley 1868: 453; Cartin 1996: 194). The Cook implies that Harry Bailly is potentially criminal, and that he participates in activities that could come back to haunt him. The Host replies in similar vein, by accusing the Cook of reheating his pies too often, and of selling unhygienic food in his shop – activities that were strictly legislated against at this time. Many people, Harry claims, curse the Cook because of his ruthless and dangerous practices. The fact that the two men insult each other in this familiar, trade-centred way locates them in a London-based linguistic community – a place, incidentally, where slander was a very serious matter (Lindahl 1987: 115–18). Chaucer may even have been referring to a real rivalry here: the two people involved in this exchange were both historical personages living in Chaucer's London – Harry Bailly and Roger de Ware (Pearsall 1992: 232). The atmosphere of the exchange between the two men is thick with distrust, anger and competition: we sense incipient violence ready to explode if given the chance.

The trade squabbling between the Cook and the Host, the Man of Law's suspect business practice, and the image of Perkyn stealing, rioting and periodically spending time in prison are vignettes that fit in well with the turbulent London that Chaucer knew (Bird 1949). City-dwellers were strongly implicated in the 'revelry' of the Peasants' Revolt, and comparisons have been drawn between 'The Cook's Tale' and such social insurgence (Strohm 2000: 51–64). In the 1380s the government of the city was profoundly unstable and disreputable. Control of the mayoralty ricocheted between two rival groups, factions dominated by Nicholas Brembre and John Northampton. The antagonisms between these groups led to a state of open warfare in the city, which often manifested itself in disputes between different trades. When elections were held, the dominant group would prevent their opponents from voting; murders were openly carried out in the street and went unpunished (Strohm 2000: 112–31). Laws were quickly passed and as quickly repealed. After the election of 1383, which Brembre won, probably by force, Northampton's supporters protested in the streets, and a cordwainer, John Constantyn, who urged his associates to close their businesses and support Northampton, was summarily executed and his head displayed at Newgate (Barron 2004: 24). The London streets and the prison described in 'The Cook's Tale' were often the scenes of real political tragedies.

Northampton – the champion of the small man, but also the protégé of the immensely influential John of Gaunt – was sentenced to death in 1384, but the sentence was commuted to exile. When the political tide turned, Nicholas Brembre (with whom Chaucer had worked at the customs house) was not so lucky. In 1388 the Merciless Parliament, dominated by the Lords Appellant, sought to curb Richard's powers and strip his favourites of office. One of those favourites was the erstwhile mayor, Brembre, who was executed at the same time as Usk. Even those of high status were vulnerable to attack; another one of the victims of the Appellants' purge was Richard de Vere, Duke of Ireland and Earl of Oxford. Nine years later, when Richard took his revenge, the victims were of even greater status – they included the Earl of Arundel and the Duke of Gloucester (Saul 1997).

Such high-stake treachery and intrigue are reflected in Chaucer's greatest urban poem, *Troilus and Criseyde*. The city – Troy – depicted in this poem is strikingly similar to London (known as New Troy at this time). Its palaces, gardens, parliament, walls and architecture are recognizable as those of the medieval city. Furthermore, like London, Troy is a site of urban betrayal and conflict (Turner 2003). In the opening verses of the poem we are told of the traitor Calchas, who abandons the city for the invading Greeks. This 'lord of gret auctorite' (I, 65) creeps out of the city 'ful pryvely' (I, 80) and goes over to the besieging Greek camp. London too was beset by betrayal: Thomas Usk betrayed his master (Northampton), London aldermen were accused of opening the gates of the city to the peasants in 1381, Richard's closest advisers were beheaded for treason. In *Troilus and Criseyde*, the city reacts with horror to Calchas' actions:

> Gret rumour gan, whan it was first aspied
> Thorugh al the town, and generaly was spoken,
> That Calkas traitour fled was and allied
> With hem of Grece, and casten* to be wroken*   *plotted; *avenged
> On hym that falsly hadde his feith so broken,
> And seyden he and al his kyn at-ones
> Ben worthi for to brennen, fel* and bones.   *skin
>
> (I, 85–91)

This stanza emphasizes many of the defining characteristics of Troy. Rumour, a destructive force that spreads panic and whips up outrage, runs through the city, and incites mob violence. Calchas' treason encourages bloody revenge in those left behind – they plot revenge not only on him but also on his relations, wanting to burn them 'fel and bones'. These lines reveal the thought processes of the townspeople, dwelling on the fact that Calchas is defined as a 'traitour', as one 'that falsly hadde his feith so broken'. Having established the enormity of what Calchas has done, the people move on to thoughts of 'righteous' revenge, and 'al his kyn' are casually included in their hatred without comment. The final line closes not only the stanza but also the judgement on Calchas and his family – they are condemned to be burnt, skin and bones, a detailed image of vengeance that is then starkly contrasted with the description of the terrified Criseyde that fills the next three stanzas. The city is depicted as a frightening place of treachery and mob rule, self-interest and anger. London too frequently saw scenes of mob rule and unruliness – most notably in the Peasants' Revolt, when the Flemings were slaughtered *en masse*, but also in the factional disputes that surrounded the mayoral elections and often spilled over into street-fighting, assassinations and riots.

High-level treason and the folly of the common people are also prominent themes later in Chaucer's poem. In Book IV, the Trojan parliament is a scene of chaos and uproar: the people are dominated by 'errour' (IV, 200), argue with Hector and beg for the return of someone who will be their downfall. This parliament decides to exchange Criseyde for Antenor who 'was after traitour to the town' (IV, 204). This detail is not in Chaucer's source; the poet seems particularly concerned to stress the treacherous nature of this Trojan, and the misguided nature of those in parliament. Again, a great man in the city is revealed to be a traitor, and the masses are unthinking and foolish. The parliament scene also strongly reveals the split between those of different social groups and with different agendas as the authoritative prince, Hector, argues with the common people of the city. Shortly after the parliament Troilus attests to his own treacherous desires when he begs the gods to kill his 'fader, kyng of Troye' (IV, 276) or his brothers, rather than take Criseyde away from him. In *Troilus and Criseyde* the city is portrayed as a place informed by betrayal and self-interest, and dominated by a chaotic mob. Troy thus appears to be an arresting refraction of the city that Chaucer knew so well.

Chaucer's Social Circles

Chaucer's ability to write convincingly about diverse aspects of politics and London life, from the disreputable taverns of Southwark to parliament, from the shops of Cheapside to the courtly chambers of Westminster, using discourses of legal life alongside those of courtly love, reflects his own versatile social position. His own self-presentations in his poems illustrate his chameleon nature. In the *House of Fame*, his persona is stolidly bourgeois – he spends his day at his 'labour' (652) and must do the accounts – the 'rekenynges' (653) – before he can go home to read his book. He lives in a world so urban that his neighbours are almost at his 'dores' (650). But in the *Prologue to the Legend of Good Women* he is a courtly supplicant in a world of kings and gardens, who is ultimately ordered to write his book and 'yive it the quene, / . . . at

Eltham or at Sheene' (F 496–7) – that is, at one of the royal residences near London. This is an altogether more socially elevated sphere. Those of his contemporaries to whom Chaucer refers also reflect the diversity of his audience and companions (Strohm 1989: 47–83). In three of his short poems Chaucer mentions courtiers who seem to have been his friends: Sir Philippe de la Vache (in 'Truth'), Henry Scogan (in 'Lenvoy de Chaucer a Scogan') and Sir Peter Bukton (in 'Lenvoy de Chaucer a Bukton'). Vache was a chamber knight who served under Edward III, Richard II and Henry IV, Scogan a squire in the king's household who later became tutor to the sons of Henry IV, and Bukton a steward to Henry of Derby (later Henry IV) (Pearsall 1992: 181–5). All were well-off men, socially above Chaucer, who managed to have successful careers both before and after the usurpation. The familiar addresses to the men and the casual reference to the Wife of Bath in 'Lenvoy de Chaucer a Bukton' suggest that they participated in a textual community in which Chaucer's writings were familiar. The setting of 'The Summoner's Tale', in obscure Holderness, might even have been suggested to Chaucer by Bukton's official responsibility for dykes and ditches in that Yorkshire town (Pearsall 1992: 184). In these short poems the topics are quite conventional: love is the subject of the two envoys, and 'Truth' deals with the vagaries of court life and the need to turn to God. But the poems are also personal, each one referring to a specific situation in which the addressee finds himself, and also occasionally referring to contemporary political events. 'Lenvoy de Chaucer a Bukton', for example, mentions those taken 'in Frise' (23), probably a reference to the Frisian expedition of 1396, a reference that also might remind us of Chaucer's personal experience of captivity in war. We might also remember that Bukton and Chaucer served together on campaign with John of Gaunt in 1369 (Pearsall 1992: 184). The short poems are packed with references that we cannot fully understand, private jokes and comments that were probably comprehensible only to Chaucer's coterie. 'Lenvoy de Chaucer a Scogan', for instance, describes Scogan as one who 'knelest at the stremes hed' (43) (the head of the Thames, Windsor) and exhorts him to remember Chaucer, who is at 'th'ende of which strem' (45) (probably Greenwich), languishing away 'in solytarie wildernesse' (46). He seems to be asking Scogan to help him, to exert his patronage somehow, but the exact situation is lost to us.

In *Troilus and Criseyde*, Chaucer lauds two men of a different stamp: 'O moral Gower, this book I directe / To the and to the, philosophical Strode' (V, 1856–7). John Gower was a lawyer, a minor landholder and a poet, who resided over the river in Southwark. He wrote long poems in the three languages of the day, most notably the Latin *Vox Clamantis [The Voice of One Crying]*, which opens with an explicit, passionate discussion of the Peasants' Revolt, and the English *Confessio Amantis [Confession of the Lover]*. Ralph Strode was an Oxford philosopher and colleague of Wycliffe's who then became a London lawyer and lived, like Chaucer, over one of the city's gates, in his case Aldersgate. These two men were renowned for their learning and bookishness, and were associated very much with the city, rather than with the court (Strode in particular). Finally, Chaucer's shortest poem is 'Chaucer's Wordes Unto Adam, His Owne Scriveyn' (the scribe recently identified as Adam Pynkhurst). These lines are filled with anxiety about the reliability of scribal transmission. They remind us that Chaucer's readers included this relatively lowly class of men – Thomas Usk, scrivener, is one of Chaucer's most interesting and acute early readers (Turner 2002). The community of scribes probably knew Chaucer's poetry very well – indeed, as Chaucer himself suggests in this short poem, some of the words that we read today as Chaucer's might in fact be scribal interpolations.

Conclusions

Chaucer was fully engaged with the political life of his day. He was a man who lived through great political upheavals, which are refracted in his extraordinary writings. He went about on the king's secret business, he was a prisoner of war, he saw colleagues executed, he travelled all over the continent, he spent years immersed in the mundanity of the customs and he did not always manage to stay out of debt. His posthumous elevation to the position of national poet, father of English literature, has served to remove him from the world that he inhabited with such vigour. In the fifteenth century he came to be seen as a patriotic court poet, a man of great morality and sagacity. Later generations of readers emphasized his transcendence, his ability to write about 'God's plenty', about a transhistorical 'human nature' (Trigg 2002). Such readings elided his reliance upon his own historical moment for subject-matter and for discourse, taking him out of fourteenth-century London and constructing him as a magisterial figure who could somehow rise above history. Yet Chaucer's greatest poetic achievements could – of course – be accomplished only because he harnessed the resources available to him. In the 'General Prologue' he used his unparalleled poetic ability to set up a *Decameron*-like tale collection, uniting his personal knowledge of the emerging middle classes and of Southwark tavern life with the genre of estates satire (Mann 1973). In *Troilus and Criseyde* he yoked together his detailed knowledge of contemporary London life with his impressive understanding of recent Italian poetry by Boccaccio, Dante and Petrarch. Everything that Chaucer wrote was firmly rooted in the world in which he lived: Chaucer embraced the life of his times, and his poetry opens up fourteenth-century urban life to us in all its disreputable diversity.

See also chapter 2, MANUSCRIPTS AND AUDIENCE; chapter 3, BOOKS AND AUTHORITY; chapter 6, LOVE IN WARTIME, *TROILUS AND CRISEYDE* AS TROJAN HISTORY.

References and Further Reading

Barron, Caroline M. (1971). 'The Quarrel of Richard II with London 1392–7'. In F. R. H. Du Boulay and Caroline M. Barron (eds), *The Reign of Richard II: Essays in Honour of May McKisack*. London: Athlone, pp. 173–201.

Barron, Caroline M. (2004). *London in the Later Middle Ages: Government and People 1200–1500*. Oxford: Oxford University Press.

Bird, Ruth (1949). *The Turbulent London of Richard II*. London: Longmans, Green.

Braswell, Mary Flowers (2001). *Chaucer's 'Legal Fiction': Reading the Records*. London: Associated Universities Press.

Butterfield, Ardis (ed.) (2006). *Chaucer and the City*. Woodbridge, Suffolk: Boydell and Brewer.

Carlin, Martha (1996). *Medieval Southwark*. London: Hambledon Press.

Crow, Martin and Clair C. Olson (1966). *Chaucer Life-Records*. Oxford: Clarendon Press.

David, Alfred (1976). *The Strumpet Muse: Art and Morals in Chaucer's Poetry*. Bloomington: Indiana University Press.

Federico, Sylvia (2003). *New Troy: Fantasies of Empire in the Later Middle Ages*. Minneapolis: University of Minnesota Press.

Knight, Stephen (1986). *Geoffrey Chaucer*. Oxford: Blackwell.

Lindahl, Carl (1987). *Earnest Games: Folkloric Patterns in the Canterbury Tales*. Bloomington: Indiana University Press.

Lindenbaum, Sheila (1999). 'London Texts and Literate Practice'. In David Wallace (ed.), *The Cambridge History of Medieval English Literature*. Cambridge: Cambridge University Press, pp. 284–309.

Mann, Jill (1973). *Chaucer and Medieval Estates Satire: The Literature of Social Classes and the General Prologue to the Canterbury Tales*. Cambridge: Cambridge University Press.

Middleton, Anne (1978). 'The Idea of Public Poetry'. *Speculum* 53, 94–114.

Ormrod, W. M. (2003). 'The Use of English: Language, Law, and Political Culture in Fourteenth-century England'. *Speculum* 78, 750–87.

Pearsall, Derek (1992). *The Life of Geoffrey Chaucer.* Oxford: Blackwell.

Riley, H. T. (1868). *Memorials of London and London Life.* London: Longmans.

Saul, Nigel (1997). *Richard II.* New Haven and London: Yale University Press.

Strohm, Paul (2000). *Theory and the Premodern Text.* Minneapolis: University of Minnesota Press.

Strohm, Paul (1990). 'Politics and Poetics: Usk and Chaucer in the 1380s'. In Lee Patterson (ed.), *Literary Practice and Social Change in Britain, 1380–1550.* Berkeley, Los Angeles, Oxford: University of California Press, pp. 82–112.

Strohm, Paul (1989). *Social Chaucer.* Cambridge, Mass.: Harvard University Press.

Trigg, Stephanie (2002). *Congenial Souls.* Minneapolis: University of Minnesota Press.

Turner, Marion (2003). '*Troilus and Criseyde* and the "treasonous aldermen" of 1382: Tales of the City in Late Fourteenth-century London'. *Studies in the Age of Chaucer* 25, 225–57.

Turner, Marion (2002). ' "Certaynly his noble sayenges can I not amende": Thomas Usk and *Troilus and Criseyde*'. *Chaucer Review* 37, 26–39.

Wallace, David (1997). *Chaucerian Polity: Absolutist Lineages and Associational Forms in England and Italy.* Stanford, Calif.: Stanford University Press.

Chapter Two

Manuscripts and Audience

Julia Boffey and A. S. G. Edwards

Near the end of the F version of the *Prologue to the Legend of Good Women*, the narrator/poet is given his instructions. The goddess of Love, Queen Alceste, tells him that he must write 'a glorious legende / Of goode wymmen . . . That were trewe in lovyng al hire lyves' (F 483–5). Alceste is equally clear in telling him what he is to do with this 'legende':

> And whan this book ys maad, yeve it to the quene,
> On my byhalf, at Eltham or at Sheene.
>
> (F 496–7)

The specificity of reference here provides a clear indication of the audience for which Chaucer's poem was envisioned. Both Eltham and Sheen were royal palaces, and 'the quene' is therefore Anne of Bohemia, wife of Richard II.

This passage is one of the clearest indications we have in Chaucer's poems of his sense of his audience. It situates the poet/narrator in a courtly environment, one in which he is both sufficiently valued to be charged with the commission of writing a poem, and also a sufficiently familiar presence to be humorously mocked as lower than 'a worm' (F 318), and characterized as the enemy of good women everywhere.

Indeed, the *Prologue* as a whole can be read as reflecting the rather uneasy relationship that is likely to exist between court poet and the milieu in which he must operate. The fact that Chaucer makes a nar-

34

rative butt of his own comic self-representation while simultaneously taking the opportunity to offer a lengthy enumeration of his own works emphasizes the terms of this relationship (see Boffey and Edwards 2003). The poetic construct entails a form of social representation that renders Chaucer subservient and allows the very topic of his verse to be dictated by his social superiors. But the humiliation he endures within the poem carries the possibility of potential rewards outside it, charged as he is with a royal commission at the end of the *Prologue*. And the wider context of the *Prologue*, with its references to the courtly game of the flower and leaf (cf. e.g. F 186–90), makes clear the playful, courtly context of such humiliation. Social pain nonetheless leads to poetic gain and promises tangible benefit in both the material and literary senses.

Some of Chaucer's other poems similarly hint at a complex social connection between poet and milieu. His earliest major work, the *Book of the Duchess*, seems to have been composed at the prompting of John of Gaunt, Duke of Lancaster and eldest son of Edward III, to create some form of memorial for his dead wife, Blanche, Duchess of Lancaster (d. 1368). The *Parliament of Fowls*, like the *Prologue to the Legend of Good Women*, probably originated in some form of seasonal courtly game. And the narrative voice in *Troilus and Criseyde* seeks to establish a direct relationship with those auditors who are in 'this compaignye' (I, 450) or 'this place' (II, 30, 43). It is tempting – and not unreasonable – to identify those auditors with the aristocratic world evoked in the *Prologue to the Legend of Good Women*, a world given visual form in the famous miniature that prefaces *Troilus* in one manuscript, Cambridge, Corpus Christi College 61 (see p. 12 and Pearsall 1977).

Yet any such attempts at identification, however general, serve to remind us of the difficulties involved in attempts to explore Chaucer's audience. All these works seem to belong to the first part of Chaucer's poetic career, which largely precedes the composition of the *Canterbury Tales*. But there are important historical gaps in our knowledge. We lack any physical evidence of the original circulating forms of these early works that would give us a clearer understanding of who was reading them in Chaucer's lifetime and what their views on his poems might have been. The earliest surviving manuscript of the *Book of the Duchess* dates from more than seventy years after its postulated date of composition. For the *House of Fame* the gap is more than sixty years. For the *Parliament*, the *Legend of Good Women* and *Troilus and Criseyde* it is between thirty and forty years (information on the manuscripts and their dating is available in Benson 1987). What may have happened to the texts and circulation of these poems during these long intervals is unknowable.

The situation is more or less the same for Chaucer's most important later work, the *Canterbury Tales*. It is just conceivable that the textually significant Hengwrt and Ellesmere manuscripts of it (Aberystwyth, National Library of Wales MS Peniarth 392, and San Marino, California, Huntington Library MS EL 26 C 9* respectively) were prepared while Chaucer was still alive. And it seems virtually certain that some of the *Tales* circulated separately during Chaucer's lifetime. The *Prologue to the Legend* indicates the existence in the mid-1380s of versions of 'The Knight's Tale' and 'The Second Nun's Tale' (see F 420–1, 426), and the casual invitation to Chaucer's close friend, Bukton, 'The Wyf of Bathe, I pray yow that ye rede' (29), shows that Bukton was expected to have some version of it close to hand. But we have no knowledge of the nature or extent of Chaucer's personal involvement in these instances of the transmission of his writings: we do not know how much he actively sought on his own behalf to disseminate his work – or if he did so at all.

Indeed, Chaucer's own words reveal a degree of scepticism about the transmission of his works. Near the end of *Troilus and Criseyde* he includes this prayer for his book:

> And for ther is so gret diversite
> In Englissh and in writyng of oure tonge
> So prey I God that non myswrite the,
> Ne the mysmetre for defaute of tonge;
> And red wherso thow be, or elles songe,
> That thow be understonde, God I biseche!
>
> (V, 1793–8)

His words recognize the reality of late fourteenth-century English as a dialectal language, varying in forms from region to region in ways that raise uncertainty about whether it will be 'understonde'. And such uncertainty is seen as having textual implications: scribes could 'myswrite' or 'mysmetre' his work because of their linguistic ignorance ('defaute of tonge'). The prayer acknowledges the powerlessness of the author to ensure that his work is preserved as he might wish.

At the heart of this uncertainty is the fact of Chaucer's consciousness of writing within a manuscript culture where his works were spread by scribal transmission, that is, copying by hand. Manuscript transcription is both labour-intensive and highly fallible (for descriptions of the physical processes involved see Shailor 1989). Chaucer himself understood the problems and has left his own strikingly pessimistic testimony to the textual instability manuscript copying creates in his shortest surviving poem, addressed to his 'own scriveyn' or scribe, Adam. This poem offers a unique insight into the practicalities of composition in a manuscript culture and the problems of textual fidelity:

> Adam scriveyn, if ever it thee bifalle
> Boece or Troylus for to wryten newe,
> Under thy long lokkes thou most have the scalle*,   *scaly rash
> But* after my makyng thow wryte more trewe;   *unless
> So ofte adaye I mot thy werke renewe.
> It to correcte and eke to rubbe and scrape,
> And al is through thy negligence and rape*.   *carelessness

The act of scribal transmission is seen by Chaucer as an impediment to the faithful preservation of his text. It requires of him more labour of correction ('to rubbe and scrape') in order to correct Adam's 'negligence' and 'rape'.

Chaucer's complaints raise questions. In what sense was Adam his 'own' scribe? Was he a retainer within Chaucer's household or a trained copyist he regularly used to copy his literary works? In what form did Chaucer transmit his original texts of 'Boece' or 'Troylus' to Adam? And what happened to these texts after Chaucer had corrected them?

These questions cannot be answered confidently. They serve only to remind us, once again, of how little we really know about the manuscript culture in which Chaucer wrote. Living as we do in a culture where the technology of writing is so advanced as to make pen and paper close to obsolete, it requires a considerable effort of historical adjustment to remind ourselves that Chaucer lived in a world where paper or parchment (a form of treated membrane) were very expensive, and pens hand-made and not necessarily reliable. We cannot even say with certainty that Chaucer employed such materials when he wrote his initial drafts. It is quite likely that he wrote them with a stylus on wax tablets that could be scraped clean and reused after their content was transferred to some more permanent medium. It was presumably at this stage that the draft was transferred to a trained scribe, like Adam, to prepare a fair copy. This copy was evidently then returned to Chaucer for further correction. But what happened after that poses another series of unanswerable questions. Who did Chaucer intend these manuscripts for? Were they for his own further use or for presentation to friends or prospective patrons, or were they for release into some form of commercial manuscript circulation where they would be copied by professional scribes?

Only a very small amount of evidence can be gleaned about Chaucer's working practices as a poet and his own expectations of the forms in which his works would find an audience. The depiction of 'Chaucer at work' given by the eagle in the *House of Fame* seems to underline the equation of authorial composition with the physical act of writing:

> thou wolt make
> A-nyght ful ofte thyn hed to ake
> In thy studye, so thou writest,
> And ever mo of love enditest*. *compose
> (631–4)

Yet Chaucer's own references to some of his works as 'songes' suggest that they circulated in forms that were (at least in part) orally transmitted, and could be taken to indicate that written copies were not necessary. One of the lines from *Troilus* quoted above – 'red wherso thow be, or elles *songe*' – gives further weight to the likelihood that oral performance and thus oral transmission may have been a factor in the dissemination of what we now think of as Chaucer's 'writings'. Nonetheless, Chaucer's habitual reference to his works in the materially recorded form of 'books' does seem to indicate a conception of literary production in which written copies played a vital part. Just as the penance imposed by Alceste in the *Prologue to the Legend of Good Women* is envisaged as generating a 'book', so the *Legend* is itself invoked as a 'large volume' in the list of Chaucer's works which prefaces 'The Man of Law's Tale' (II, 57–76). Other works are listed as 'books' at further points in the *Legend* (e.g. F 417 and G 264, G 405) and in the 'Retractions' which conclude the *Canterbury Tales* (X, 1081–94).

The forms in which Chaucer's compositions were first recorded no doubt varied in nature according to the circumstances which generated them. As the anxious dream of the *Legend*'s prologue makes clear, the activities of many medieval authors were governed by complex factors of service and obligation intimated in the excuses Alceste makes to Cupid on the dreamer's behalf. He may have written the works to which Cupid objects, she says, simply because his position required him to write something ('for he useth thynges for to make / Hym rekketh* noght of what matere he take' [*cares], F 364–5). On the other hand he might have been writing to commission, and unable to disobey a command ('Or him was boden make thilke tweye [commanded to make those two works to which Cupid objects] / Of som persone, and durste yt nay withseye', F 364–7). Each of these sets of circumstances might have significantly determined the way in which works were recorded, generating on the one hand hurried copies preserving the regular output of the court retainer and on the other more lavish productions designed to honour a particular commissioner. Other, different forms of presentation copy might have been produced for those invoked or acknowledged in Chaucer's works outside the context of the *Legend*: the 'Lyte Lowys my sone', to whom *A Treatise on the Astrolabe* is addressed; 'moral Gower' and 'philosophical Strode', named in *Troilus and Criseyde*; even the French knight and poet Oton de Grandson, praised in 'The Complaint of Venus', with whom Chaucer may have exchanged samples of work.

Along with the likelihood of formally produced presentation volumes, there exists the probability that some works circulated in Chaucer's lifetime in more ephemeral forms. The first 'publication' of some of the short, occasional poems in particular must have necessitated little more than a single sheet or 'lytel writ' such as that mentioned in the final stanza of 'Lenvoy de Chaucer a Bukton'. That a number of these poems are explicitly and sometimes familiarly addressed to individuals (Bukton, Scogan, 'thou Vache', 'Prince', 'Conquerour of Brutes Albyon* [*Brutus' Albion, England]') would seem to locate their origins in social networks and occasions in which the retention of formal copies may not have seemed either appropriate or important. The patchiness which characterizes the later transmission of these short poems during the fifteenth century may well underline the special circumstances of their composition and early circulation: few survive in early fifteenth-century copies, and the witnesses overall vary widely in number, from twenty-two surviving manuscripts of 'Truth' to only single ones of 'To Rosemounde' and the 'Envoy to Bukton' and 'Adam Scriveyn'.

Whatever forms these copies may have taken, they seem to reflect problems in the processes of faithful textual transmission held up as an ideal by Chaucer in his words to Adam. Chaucer may have taken care to oversee and correct copies of his works in the primary stages of their transmission, but there are no indications that he sought or was able to extend authorial supervision beyond this point. Once his writings were in wider circulation, the contexts in which they were successively copied must anyway have been so various that it is hard to imagine how textual consistency might have been preserved. Some manuscripts (particularly of the longer works such as *Troilus and Criseyde* and the *Canterbury Tales*, and particularly those produced in London) seem to have been the work of commercial scribes, perhaps working in the loosely associated networks of which examples have recently been reconstructed (Doyle and Parkes 1977). But others were produced by individuals working for themselves, or by groups of scribes linked by household or community affiliations. The working methods operating in these different contexts must have varied considerably, determined by variable factors like the kind of exemplars available and the proficiency of the copyists involved.

There is furthermore much evidence to support the hypothesis that Chaucer engaged in what has been termed 'rolling revision', returning to compositions with modifications and adaptations as they suggested themselves over the course of time, but taking no pains to ensure that these were incorporated into versions of his works already in circulation (see Hanna 1988 for further discussion of this). Among the shorter lyrics, 'Truth' survives in two distinct states and, like 'Fortune' and 'The Complaint of Chaucer to his Purse', apparently circulated both with and without an envoy, as if possibly used for different contingencies at different moments. Marked variations in some of the manuscripts of *Troilus* suggest that it was modified over time by the serial insertion of 'blocks' of text that heightened the Boethian implications of the narrative. The addition of such philosophical material is so systematic in those manuscripts in which it occurs as to suggest a programme of authorial revision (Windeatt 1979).

The most extreme example of this apparent revision to produce different 'states' of the text is the *Prologue to the Legend of Good Women*, which survives in two forms. One is an early-fifteenth-century manuscript that contains a version of the *Prologue* so different from the other extant copies that it has conventionally been given its own distinct status by modern editors, and termed the 'G-text' (so called because of its inclusion in Cambridge University Library MS Gg. 4. 27) in order to distinguish it from the F-text (named after a textually important copy which survives in Oxford, Bodleian Library MS Fairfax 16). It has been assumed that Chaucer returned to the work some years after its initial completion and transmission, instituting changes which, for whatever combination of reasons, have been preserved in only one copy.

These issues of textual fluidity are particularly complex in relation to the *Canterbury Tales*. To the evidence of its manifestly unfinished state can be added the fact that the two very early, authoritative copies now generally known as the Hengwrt and Ellesmere manuscripts appear to be in the hand of the same single scribe. Yet these manuscripts present the text in very different orders and vary in content, most notably in Hengwrt's omission of 'The Canon's Yeoman's Tale'. They also contain variant readings that can be seen as authoritative. Whether Chaucer was involved directly in the preparation of either manuscript is unclear. What is clear is that ordering the *Tales* remained a problem for a number of later copyists and that the ordering adopted by modern editors is not necessarily a reflection of Chaucer's own intentions (see Owen 1990 for further discussion).

The scribes of copies made later than Hengwrt and Ellesmere were also conscious of the broader issue of incompleteness, which they sought to conceal to various degrees by adding spurious links between *Tales* or by adjusting endings to incomplete ones. The most striking demonstration of such an adjustment is the incorporation of the romance *Gamelyn*, not by Chaucer, but appended to the fragmentary 'Cook's Tale' in over twenty manuscripts of the *Canterbury Tales*. Less frequently other tales were added, like the spurious 'Tale of Beryn', which appears in one manuscript of the *Tales* at Alnwick Castle (in the library belonging to the Duke of Northumberland). In the mid-fifteenth century, Lydgate's *Siege of Thebes*, written explicitly as a continuation of the *Tales*, is added to some manuscripts. These additions suggest, among other things, the perceived potential of Chaucer's poem as an open-ended collection.

Other textual aspects of the *Tales* are equally confused. In some instances there seem no obvious reasons for Chaucer to have assigned a particular tale to a particular pilgrim. Thus, the opening lines of 'The Shipman's Tale' (VII, 1–19) clearly indicate that it was intended for a female narrator, most likely the Wife of Bath, in view of its subject-matter. We do not know whether Chaucer made the odd-seeming decision to allocate it to its received narrator, or whether this was taken on grounds of expediency by an early posthumous editor of Chaucer's *Tales*. But it is assigned to the Shipman in all manuscripts in which it appears. The Second Nun's reference to herself as an 'unworthy son of Eve' (VII, 62) has been interpreted as another anomaly deriving from textual confusion. Perhaps most problematic for successive editors have been the difficulties posed by attempting to reconcile the order of tales in different manuscripts with the order of places and times specified on the journey towards Canterbury.

These points are worth stressing because they remind us that the form in which we read Chaucer in modern editions is one far removed from the manuscript forms in which his works survive. In important respects the modern forms of Chaucer give his poems an appearance of order that they have not historically possessed. No single manuscript, for example, comprises the totality of Chaucer's works that are included in the modern standard edition, the *Riverside Chaucer*. No manuscript has a layout that corresponds to its carefully set out pages, with line numbers, glosses, running heads and carefully regularized punctuation and orthography. Even forms of titles that we accept as standard are often modern inventions: no edition before the twentieth century seems to have called the Prologue to the *Canterbury Tales* the 'General Prologue', for instance.

It seems to have been the case that Chaucer had little interest in such questions of order and regularity. Furthermore he seems to have been little preoccupied with larger questions that have concerned posterity, like the idea of canonizing his oeuvre through the assembling of his 'collected works'. He does talk, notably in the *Prologue to the Legend* and in the Prologue to 'The Man of Law's Tale' (II, 57–76), about the range of his works, but these enumerations seem to be attempts to make his audience conscious of the scope of his poetic achievement, an establishing of credentials among those in a position to commission similar works. There is no evidence that Chaucer ever sought to bring his works together in any systematic way.

Nor did posterity feel much need to remedy this lack. There is one early attempt, some time in the first quarter of the fifteenth century, to assemble a large number of Chaucer's works in a single manuscript collection: the *Canterbury Tales, Troilus and Criseyde*, the *Legend of Good Women*, the *Parliament of Fowls*, and a number of lyrics – the 'ABC', the 'Envoy to Scogan', 'Lak of Stedfastnesse'. This manuscript, now Cambridge University Library Gg. 4. 27, also reveals a degree of concern with physical presentation that is untypical of the majority of Chaucer manuscripts: it is carefully decorated and illustrated. Yet although the collection seems informed by some attempt at canonical comprehensiveness, it stretches beyond Chaucer's works to include, for example, a poem by Chaucer's follower, John Lydgate (*The Temple of Glass*), as well as other works of unknown authorship. While Chaucer's poetic achievement seems to be a controlling principle in the assemblage of works for inclusion in the manuscript, it does not amount to a principle of exclusivity.

There is only one comparable attempt to bring Chaucer's major works together on any scale. It comes at the very end of the fifteenth century, in a manuscript that is now Oxford, Bodleian Library, Arch. Selden. B. 24. Here a number of the poems in Gg. 4. 27 reappear together: *Troilus and Criseyde*, the *Legend of Good Women*, the *Parliament of Fowls*, together with the Complaints of Mars and Venus, and the lyric 'Truth'. But to an even greater degree the Chaucerian contents are blended with other fifteenth-century materials: poems by Lydgate, Hoccleve and Walton, and a number of further items with Scottish connections. The Chaucerian core of the collection seems to have been seen as one that could be enlarged by the inclusion of what were felt to be cognate although uncanonical works.

These two collections are unusual in their scope. The inclusion together in CUL MS Gg. 4. 27 of the *Canterbury Tales* and *Troilus and Criseyde* is particularly noteworthy since these two works (unlike most of Chaucer's output) achieved an autonomous identity and tended to circulate in manuscripts on their own. Of the sixteen complete manuscripts of *Troilus and Criseyde* that survive, in the substantial majority it is the primary or sole content (see Root 1914). Of the fifty-five manuscripts that seem to have included some approximation to the full text of the *Canterbury Tales*, forty-six contain only this work.[1] Such numbers indicate the extent to which these works were seen as sufficiently substantial to circulate separately, and to establish their own distinct literary identities in the minds of both manuscript producers and readers.

The circulation of Chaucer's other poems, even his longer ones, was rather different. There is no clear evidence that his dream visions, the *Book of the Duchess*, the *House of Fame* and the *Parliament of Fowls*, circulated separately, nor did the *Legend of Good Women*. These works were instead incorporated into larger collections, usually conjoined with the verse of others. The clearest testimony to this is provided by the manuscripts of the 'Oxford group', so called because all of the relevant manuscripts are in the Bodleian Library, Oxford: Fairfax 16, Tanner 346 and Bodley 638. These three manuscripts, copied over a period of about fifty years, show considerable similarities in content. They all include the *Legend* and the *Parliament*; two of them also include the *House of Fame* and the *ABC*; Fairfax 16 includes the largest number of Chaucer's lyrics, some of which also appear in either or both of the other manuscripts. The correspondences and variations among these volumes, and the further relationships to other manuscripts implied by their contents and textual affiliations, suggest that large collections like these were assembled out of smaller groupings of material, now termed 'booklets' (Brusendorff 1925; Boffey and Thompson 1989).

It is only with the advent of print that we perceive the first attempts to assemble Chaucer into forms that correspond to our modern reading experience. When William Caxton set up the first printing press in England in Westminster about 1476 he chose the *Canterbury Tales* as his first major book; he produced a second edition, with illustrations, in about 1483, and in the same year printed the first edition of *Troilus and Criseyde*. Other early English printers were quick to follow his example. It was not, however, until 1532 that William Thynne produced the first comprehensive edition of Chaucer, the first edition of any English writer to be characterized as 'the works.' It was largely in this form that Chaucer was subsequently presented to new readers until the latter part of the eighteenth century when the first attempts at critical editing of Chaucer began (the essays in Ruggiers 1984 survey the printed editions).

Our understanding of Chaucer's relationship to his earliest audiences is in part determined by information provided in his own writings and in the works of others who responded to them (Lerer 1993). The material forms in which his texts circulated during the fifteenth century, however, have an important role in the body of evidence about reception and response. Information of this sort to be gleaned from the manuscripts is inevitably rather fragmentary, but it does offer grounds for some provisional conclusions, particularly to do with the composition of Chaucer's audience. It seems that Chaucer's fifteenth-century audience was much wider than the courtly milieu invoked in the *Prologue to the Legend of Good Women* would lead us to suppose. Indeed, there is surprisingly little evidence from Chaucer's surviving manuscripts to associate his writings with the top levels of medieval society. Few of them can be linked with the ranks of the nobility. The most distinctive association of any of his writings with a noble audience is embodied in the readership of *Troilus and Criseyde*. One manuscript of it contains the arms of the future Henry V, whose interest in vernacular poetry was to develop after he became king, through his patronage of Lydgate and Hoccleve. Another important manuscript of this poem, now Cambridge, Corpus Christi College MS 61, may have been commissioned by Henry, Lord Scrope (d. 1415). And a late copy of this and other Chaucerian poems was executed for Henry, Lord Sinclair; it is now Bodleian Library MS Arch. Selden. B. 24.

In contrast, few of the far larger number of *Canterbury Tales* manuscripts can be associated with the nobility.[2] Some, like the famous Ellesmere manuscript, invite the supposition of a noble patron in their lavishness; and it is possible that this was owned, if not commissioned by, a member of the de Vere family, the Earls of Oxford. The former Devonshire manuscript of the *Canterbury Tales*, now in a private collection in Japan, a very large and elaborately decorated copy, invites the same assumption; it has been argued that it was owned by Margaret Beaufort, the mother of Henry VII. Walter, Lord Hungerford, was probably a very early owner of Cambridge University Library Dd. 4. 24. Paris, Bibliothèque Nationale fonds anglais 39 was written for John, Duke of Angoulême. But in general *Canterbury Tales* manuscripts do not lend themselves to a hypothesis that links physical form to social class.

Few other manuscripts can be linked very securely to any particular group or social category. Some manuscripts do have affiliations to religious houses or individual religious. For example, London, British Library MS Harley 7333, a large collection that unites the *Canterbury Tales* with a number of other works, was evidently prepared in the Augustinian house of St Mary le Pratis, in Leicestershire, in the mid-fifteenth century. Geneva, MS Bodmer 48 was possibly owned by the priory of Christchurch, Canterbury. And Manchester, Chetham's Library MS 6709, a collection of religious verse in English, largely saints' lives, contains Chaucer's 'The Second Nun's Tale' and 'The Prioress's Tale', copied by William Cotson, who describes himself as 'canonicus'.

In general though, it is not possible to establish with certainty very much about the earliest owners or readers of manuscripts of the *Canterbury Tales*. In so far as their provenance can be established, they seem to have been owned by a relatively wide social spectrum in the fifteenth century. This spectrum included a number of members of the gentry, as demonstrated by London, British Library MS Sloane 1685, which seems to have been in the possession of the family of Sir Thomas Neville (d. 1460), or Oxford, Bodleian Library MS Bodley 414, owned by a member of the East Anglian Paston family. The different dialects of their copyists indicate that while many of these manuscripts were prepared within London or its environs, their geographical origins spread over a wide area.

Other aspects of the body of surviving manuscripts offer different kinds of information about early readers, although it is worth stressing that such features do not often permit secure generalizations. While the numbers of copies in which individual works have survived may seem likely to serve as some index of their popularity, for example, any such statistics are obviously bound to be distorted by unquantifiable and random accidents of time. Some of Chaucer's early dream visions, the *Book of the Duchess* and the *House of Fame*, survive in only three copies each. Of the later ones, in contrast, there are sixteen copies of the *Parliament of Fowls*, and the *Legend of Good Women* survives complete (or approximately so) in ten manuscripts. It may be that Chaucer had access to production networks that enabled relatively widespread dissemination of his works only when his career was somewhat advanced – a situation that would have favoured the noticeably wider circulation of copies of the *Canterbury Tales*. But such an argument is speculative, like much else to do with textual transmission.

It is equally hard to make sense of the evidence of the layout and appearance of particular texts when so many unknowable but doubtless influential factors – precedent, available labour, the requirements of specific commissioners – may distort our understanding of its relationship to reception. Some general tendencies can, however, be signalled. Many of the manuscripts of *Troilus* and/or the *Canterbury Tales* are large, well-produced volumes, with text supplied by competent scribes and enhanced by various forms of ornamentation or decoration. The same can be said of some of the collections of Chaucer's shorter poems, such as Fairfax 16, which contains all of his dream visions and many of his lyrics. But a number of manuscripts containing Chaucer's works are relatively undistinguished in material terms, and sometimes include his works in contexts of strikingly miscellaneous collections. Copies of the lyrics 'Gentilesse', 'Lak of Stedfastnesse', 'Truth' and 'Against Women Unconstant' are, for example, in London, British Library MS Cotton Cleopatra D. vii tucked together, with no reference to Chaucer's name, among contents which include a Latin prose life of the Three Kings, a French *Brut* chronicle and English prose religious writings. The manuscript is made of parchment, but its texts are not specially enhanced (beyond the provision of coloured initials), and it does not appear to have been conceived as a *de luxe* volume. In collections of this sort it is impossible to attempt assessments of 'value' based on physical evidence.

Not a great deal can be said about the form of response constituted by the provision of illustration with the texts, since little of this is present in the surviving manuscripts of Chaucer's works. The famous series of pilgrim 'portraits' in the Ellesmere manuscript, one of the earliest copies of the *Canterbury Tales*, seems not to have prompted much in the way of a tradition; even the Hengwrt manuscript, apparently copied by the same scribe at approximately the same time, is unillustrated. But it is worth noting that where evidence of illustration remains it follows Ellesmere's strategy of depicting pilgrim-narrators rather than the content of the tales themselves: fragmentary remains of such a programme survive in the large anthology of Chauceriana which is now Cambridge, University Library MS Gg. 4. 27, and when Caxton produced an illustrated edition of the *Canterbury Tales* he followed this convention. Little can be said about the illustration of *Troilus and Criseyde* and the shorter poems. Of the extensive programme of miniatures planned for Cambridge, Corpus Christi College MS 61, only the famous *Troilus* frontispiece was completed, while the single surviving attempt to illustrate the minor poems – a tripartite picture of Mars, Venus and Jupiter in Bodleian Library MS Fairfax 16 – is markedly all-purpose, and seems more a statement of the volume's claim to aesthetic quality than an attempt to elucidate or emphasize any aspects of its content.

Activities of selection and excerption invite some conclusions about the tastes and preferences of Chaucer's early readers, although evidence in this area too needs to be treated with caution. Reasoning that a manuscript-compiler who selected a single Canterbury tale for inclusion in his or her book must have preferred this one to all the others is not entirely convincing unless it can be demonstrated that an active choice was made from the collection as a whole. The sixteen or so manuscripts that contain what seem to be deliberate selections do nonetheless suggest interesting patterns, including a clear preference for religious and moral tales over *fabliaux* (which do not appear in selected form at all), pointing to particular interest in 'The Clerk's Tale' and 'The Prioress's Tale', and demonstrating intriguing choices in certain individual compilations (see Silvia 1974). Longleat House MS 257, for example, a volume signed by Richard III as Duke of Gloucester, includes 'The Knight's Tale' and 'The Clerk's Tale'; London, British Library MS Harley 2382, whose contents seem to display a marked appropriateness for the needs of female readers, includes 'The Second Nun's Tale' and 'The Prioress's Tale'; and British Library MS Harley 1704 sets 'The Prioress's Tale' in the company of prose works known in other contexts to have served the needs of devout women. Particular tastes may also have influenced the two instances in which individual narratives from the *Legend of Good Women* are extracted from their usual surroundings. 'Thisbe' appears in the anthology known as the Findern manuscript (Cambridge, University Library MS Ff. 1. 6), a collection with a marked interest in women's voices which was seemingly put together by or for a group of social intimates; 'Dido' is incorporated in the vastly comprehensive Oxford, Bodleian Library MS Rawlinson C. 86, the other Chaucerian contents of which include 'The Clerk's Tale' and 'The Prioress's Tale'.

Signs of annotation in some manuscripts offer a rather complicated range of information, not always as clearly related to readers' responses as scholars and critics might wish. Marginal notes supplied by scribes (like many other forms of scribal apparatus, such as headings, titles, or colophons) may in some cases derive from Chaucer's working drafts – perhaps supplying information about or quotations from sources, or elsewhere indicating an insertion or a second thought – and it is not usually possible to interpret them as straightforward evidence of intelligent scribal analysis or commentary. The Latin quotation from Statius which prefaces 'The Knight's Tale', like the programmes of Latin glosses which occasionally accompany 'The Wife of Bath's Prologue' and 'The Man of Law's Tale', or some of the regularly recurring marginal notes to *Troilus and Criseyde*, may have their origin in Chaucer's own working drafts (see Boffey 1995). From time to time, though, scribes (or their directing editors) do enter into dialogue with the material they copy and leave some trace of a response to it. The most famous examples are the Latin notes made by the scribe Duxworth, who, copying the *Canterbury Tales* for the French nobleman John, Duke of Angoulême, during his lengthy house arrest after the French defeat at Agincourt, abandons transcribing 'The Squire's Tale' on the grounds that it is 'absurd' and offers pungent comments on other tales. Elsewhere other scribes insert remarks perhaps less swingeing but still pointed: one of a number of collaborating scribes responsible for the copy of *Troilus and Criseyde* in Oxford, Bodleian Library MS Rawlinson poet. 163, for example, adds his own retort to Criseyde's playful threat to beat Troilus (III, 1168–9) – 'ye with a ffether'. Signs of readers' engagement with the texts they encountered in manuscripts are generally less explicit, but their own often cryptic forms of annotation (underlining, pointing hands, and a range of other signs) are worth scrutiny.

Bridging the distance that separates us, as modern readers, from Chaucer and his original audience involves complex exercises in historical reconstruction. Embedded in that distance is a range of unfamiliar cultural and literary paradigms that we can barely glimpse, let alone confidently understand. We have tried here to stress the highly provisional nature of any conclusions about the environments in which Chaucer's works were written and circulated. Evidence is fragmented and at times susceptible to divergent interpretations. But any consideration of the material forms of Chaucer's poetry can at least serve to remind us of some of the essential differences between medieval and modern modes of literary production, and of the role these differences might play in our practices as readers.

See also chapter 1, POLITICS AND LONDON LIFE; chapter 3, BOOKS AND AUTHORITY; chapter 13, READING CHAUCER ALOUD.

Notes

1 Numbers of surviving manuscripts, here and elsewhere in the discussion, are derived from Julia Boffey and A. S. G. Edwards, *A New Index of Middle English Verse* (British Library: London, 2005).
2 *Canterbury Tales* manuscripts are described in Manly and Rickert (1940), volume 1.

References and Further Reading

Manuscript facsimiles: a number of the important manuscripts of Chaucer's works are now available in modern facsimiles; we do not list them here for reasons of limited space. Those interested in pursuing them will find a helpful listing in Richard Beadle (1998). 'Facsimiles of Middle English Manuscripts', in Vincent McCarren and Douglas Moffat (eds), *A Guide to Middle English Editing*. Ann Arbor: University of Michigan Press, pp. 319–31.

Boffey, Julia (1995). 'Annotation in Some Manuscripts of *Troilus and Criseyde*'. *English Manuscript Studies, 1100–1700* 5, 1–17.
Boffey, Julia and A. S. G. Edwards (2003). 'The *Legend of Good Women*'. In Piero Boitani and Jill Mann (eds), *The Cambridge Companion to Chaucer*. 2nd edn. Cambridge: Cambridge University Press, pp. 112–26.
Boffey, Julia and John J. Thompson (1989). 'Anthologies and Miscellanies: Production and Choice of Texts'. In Griffiths and Pearsall (eds), *Book Production and Publishing in Britain, 1375–1475*, pp. 279–316.
Brusendorff, Aage (1925). *The Chaucer Tradition*. London: Oxford University Press.
Doyle, A. I. and M. B. Parkes (1977). 'The Production of Copies of the *Canterbury Tales* and the *Confessio Amantis* in the Early Fifteenth Century'.

In M. B. Parkes and Andrew G. Watson (eds), *Medieval Scribes, Manuscripts and Libraries: Essays presented to N. R. Ker*. London: Scolar Press, pp. 163–212.

Edwards, A. S. G. and Derek Pearsall. 'The Manuscripts of the Major English Poetic Texts'. In Griffiths and Pearsall (eds), *Book Production and Publishing in Britain, 1375–1475*, pp. 257–69.

Griffiths, Jeremy and Derek Pearsall (eds) (1989). *Book Production and Publishing in Britain, 1375–1475*. Cambridge: Cambridge University Press.

Hammond, Eleanor P. (1904). *Chaucer: A Bibliographical Manual*. New York: Macmillan.

Hanna, Ralph (1988). 'Authorial Versions, Rolling Revision, Scribal Error? Or, the Truth about Truth'. *Studies in the Age of Chaucer* 10, 23–40.

Lerer, Seth (1993). *Chaucer and his Readers: Imagining the Author in Late-Medieval England*. Princeton, NJ: Princeton University Press.

Manly, John M. and Edith Rickert (eds) (1940). *The Text of the Canterbury Tales*. 8 vols. Chicago: University of Chicago Press.

Owen, Charles A., Jr. (1990). *The Manuscripts of the Canterbury Tales*. Cambridge: D. S. Brewer.

Pearsall, Derek (1977). 'The *Troilus* Frontispiece and Chaucer's Audience'. *Yearbook of English Studies* 7, 68–74.

Root, R. K. (1914 for 1911). *The Manuscripts of Chaucer's* Troilus, *with Collotype Facsimiles of the Various Handwritings*, Chaucer Society Publications, First Series, 98. London: Kegan Paul, Trench, Trübner and Oxford University Press.

Ruggiers, Paul G. (ed.) (1984). *Editing Chaucer. The Great Tradition*. Norman, Okla.: Pilgrim Books.

Shailor, Barbara A. (1989). *The Medieval Book*. New Haven: Yale University Press.

Silvia, Daniel S. (1974). 'Some Fifteenth-century Manuscripts of the *Canterbury Tales*'. In Beryl Rowland (ed.). *Chaucer and Middle English: Studies in Honour of Rossell Hope Robbins*. London: George Allen and Unwin, pp. 153–63.

Windeatt, Barry (1979). 'The Scribes as Chaucer's Early Critics'. *Studies in the Age of Chaucer* 1, 119–42.

Windeatt, Barry (1979).'The Text of the *Troilus*'. In M. Salu (ed.), *Essays on Troilus and Criseyde*. Woodbridge, Suffolk: Boydell and Brewer, pp. 1–22.

Chapter Three

Books and Authority

R. F. Yeager

Chaucer was a reader. When famously he says of the Clerk of Oxenford

> al that he myghte of his freendes hente*,   *gain
> On bookes and on lernynge he it spente.
> (*Canterbury Tales* I, 299–300)

no doubt he struck rather close to home, approximating himself. Like the rail-thin Clerk, in whom, he implies, the bibliophilic appetite was stronger than the instinct to eat, Chaucer seems to have read with both esurience and gusto – at once for knowledge, and for joy *simpliciter*. Reading Chaucer is to read about reading: the sleepless narrator of the *Book of the Duchess* seeks solace in 'a romaunce . . . / To rede and drive the night away' (48–9); the opening of the *Parliament of Fowls* is all about books, one – 'Tullyus of the Drem of Scipioun' [Cicero's *Dream of Scipio*] – providing the guide (Scipio Africanus himself) who conveys the dreaming narrator to the garden where the fowls meet and mate (10–15, 19ff.), unnamed others informing 'ful ofte' the poem's 'I' with all he knows about the god of Love; in *Troilus and Criseyde*, when Pandarus finds his niece, Criseyde and her ladies are gathered 'withinne a paved parlour' listening as 'a mayden reden hem the geste* / Of the siege of Thebes' (*tale: II, 81–4); the *Legend of Good Women* is all a congeries of stories derived from 'olde bokes' by its narrator, who confesses in the *Prologue* that 'On bokes for to rede I me delyte,

Prologue/ . . . So hertely, that ther is game noon/ That fro me bokes maketh me to goon' (F 25, 30, 33–4); the Monk boasts of 'tragedies' he owns, 'an hundred in my celle' (VII, 1971–2); the Wife of Bath's fifth husband Jankyn torments her, reading aloud to her his 'book of wikked wyves' (III, 685); in 'The Merchant's Tale' Old January, fortifying himself on his wedding night, follows the advice of 'daun Constantyn, / . . . in his book *De Coitu* [Constantinus Africanus' medical treatise *Concerning Coitus*]' (IV, 1810–11); 'hende' Nicholas of 'The Miller's Tale' has in his chamber 'his bookes grete and smale' (I, 3208) and on and on.

These and the other readers Chaucer creates have much to tell us about his attitudes toward books and authority. For books to play so prominently throughout his work their equivalent centrality in his own day-to-day life must surely be inferred. One thing to notice is their variety: reading is an activity that, without apparent self-consciousness, Chaucer locates in all 'three Estates' and their late medieval derivatives. January, thoroughly reprehensible though he may be, is nevertheless a knight. Criseyde and her companions (save, perhaps, for the 'mayden' who actually reads the book) are Trojan aristocracy, comparable to English ladies with direct access to court circles. Possibly a bit lower down in the social scale, but inferentially still of the first Estate, is the narrator of the *Book of the Duchess*, who chats as an equal with the Black Knight of his dream, and seems to have had an attendant servant in his bedchamber to 'reche me a book' (48) when he can't sleep. Churchmen, of course, we might expect to have been readers (although in reality, on that score we would have guessed wrong more often than right about clerics in Chaucer's day), so to find 'second Estaters' like the Clerk and even the Monk, or Alysoun of Bath's clerkly husband Jankyn, or the Oxford student Nicholas of 'The Miller's Tale' possessed of books seems – at least on the face of it – unsurprising. More intriguing, of course, is when we reckon the social reach of some of those readers and their books. Nicholas, lodging with the clearly labouring-class John the carpenter in Oseney, and Jankyn, who meets the Wife in a village where, despite her hard-earned mercantile status, she clearly had her roots, extend their books and their literacy into the lives of the lowest Estate. One might argue that some responsibility for the tales' violence is owed precisely to this intrusion of an unfamiliar book culture and its values into the bottom social third, to which it was 'unnatural'. (We have, after all, the anti-intellectualism of the 'riche gnof*' John – 'blessed be alwey a lewed* man' [*churl;

*unlearned: I, 2, 3455] – and the Wife's book-burning to confront and consider.)

But what strikes one on second glance is how *naturally* Chaucer *himself* finds a place for reading in all of these loci. In this he clearly reflects both his society at large and his own experience. At the end of the fourteenth century half at least of the population of all status groups could read in some measure, many, like Chaucer, in more than one language. John of Gaunt not only read and wrote himself, but also saw to it that his children (including his daughters) did; nor was his a completely unusual baronial household in this regard. Illiterate or semi-literate clergy were common enough, but so were their better-educated counterparts, like Chaucer's Parson – 'a lerned man, a clerk' (I, 480) – despite the fact that his 'toun' and parish must have been rustic indeed. He is mistaken by the Host as a 'Lollere' (II, 1173) or Lollard, a sect much represented among labouring-class men and women (as well as knights of Chaucer's intimate acquaintance), whose emphasis on individual Bible study hints at downward literate extension by 1400. Chaucer's own originary social group, the mercantilists and upwardly mobile bourgeoisie, were most of them lettered by the century's end, particularly in London and important commercial cities like York, Norwich and Bristol. Correspondence and documents were a part of routine business life. Nor is it impossible to think of such men truly as readers, in the sense of one who turned to books for pleasure and recreation as well as trade. Middle-class habits aped aristocratic practice in this as much as in other areas, such as dress and household ostentation. A thriving book-production industry in London during Chaucer's latter years is well documented, turning out both 'bespoke' and 'spec' copies of popular literature. (Judging from extant examples, romances seem to have sold particularly well.) Among the buyers of such volumes of varying elaborateness we can assuredly number a strong percentage of the kind of men in whose company in the Vintry young Geoffrey Chaucer grew up.

In assessing the near-omnipresence of books in his writings, it is helpful to take stock of what we know of Chaucer's biography too. The son of a well-to-do family in the wine business, Chaucer benefited both from paternal ambition and his father's connections as a purveyor of drink to the court, both of which fortuities doubtless placed him, at least by 1357, when he was perhaps 17, in the service of Elizabeth, Countess of Ulster, wife of Prince Lionel, eldest of the younger brothers of Edward, the Black Prince and royal heir. Precisely what Chaucer was doing prior to 1357 is uncertain – the record of payment in the

Countess's books for a page's paltok, or short cloak, is the earliest evidence we have of Chaucer's life – but no doubt the accomplishments sufficient to lend him appeal as a page in a princely household included literate (not yet necessarily literary) promise. Like most boys of merchant families, Chaucer would have learned his ABC and how to write in English at home, from a primer. (Also at home, in the give and take of the Vintry, a linguistic polyglot of wine traders and their families, some from Spain and Italy, he probably got a start as well in 'foreign' languages to complement his English and domestic French 'of Stratford atte Bowe', like that of the Prioress [I, 125].) In his seventh year he would have been sent to a grammar school to learn Latin. Closest to his parents' house in Thames Street was the Almonry school in St Paul's Cathedral, just minutes' walk away. Surviving lists of gifts to the school's libraries by almoners in 1328 and 1358 testify to an extensive holding available to the students and masters – over a hundred works, and there may have been more if other benefactors were as generous over the years. Itemized volumes included reference works (grammars, encyclopaedias, classical *florilegia* or anthologies), Roman authors (Virgil, Statius, Ovid, Claudian and Maximian), legal tomes and others on philosophy and law. We don't know, of course, that the boy Geoffrey attended the school at St Paul's (as we *can* be sure that he did not study at the Inns of Court, as once was thought), but the Almonry's rich library nonetheless suggests a level of opportunity at once available and proximate. We may assume with confidence that young Chaucer arrived in the Countess's halls fully able to take advantage of chances for further reading and for listening with an initiated, if not yet quite sophisticated, ear.

What works was young Chaucer likely to have known when he entered service? Latin grammar and composition were customarily taught by reading and imitating standard literary texts – Aesop's fables, Cato's *Distichs*, Virgil's first *Eclogue*, various excerpts from major writers collected in special anthologies designed for students. Never in his life was Chaucer a scholar per se (for which, no doubt, we should all be glad!), and often enough his apparent familiarity with Latin authors is traceable to such school anthologies: allusions to Claudian's *De raptu Proserpinae (The Rape of Proserpina: Houre of Fame,* 449, 1511) and his collection of laws, *De IV Consulatu Honorii (Parliament of Fowls,* 99–105), for example, have their origin in the collection *Liber Catonianus (Book of Cato the Orator),* a standard in the schools. Moreover, throughout his career Chaucer frequently relied on his French, turning more often to the *Ovide moralisé* than to *Metamorphoses* itself, or following Jean de

Meun's translation of Boethius' *Consolation of Philosophy* for the *Boece* whenever possible.

Once employed by the Countess of Ulster, Chaucer's education could only have bloomed. Magnate households seem not to have made schooling of pages systematic, but down the line there was work for secretaries or diplomatic go-betweens, towards which careers young men of lettered promise were selected and brought on, sometimes informally by a conscientious clerk. Perhaps this happened to Chaucer. In any case, his training would have included the usual graces – the etiquette of politic attention to the social needs of one's betters – and a chance as well to acquire full French fluency and probably polish his *Latinitas*. Unfortunately no evidence remains to establish the existence of a library for the Countess, not that this was unusual: the concept of 'a library' as we think of it was barely taking hold in the fourteenth century. Books were commonly stored not on shelves but in chests, along with the other valuables – a practice no doubt dictated in part by the peripatetic lives led by great magnates who followed the available provender from venue to venue to keep their subordinates honest and their retinues fed. Necessity had a hand in postponing the widespread acquisition of immobile book collections of any size until well after Chaucer's death. (In England, the first official royal library was Henry VII's.) Nonetheless, the few surviving lists from households comparable to the Countess's suggest that there Chaucer might have come into contact with popular religious manuals, for example, the *Somme le Roy [Summa of the King]*, the *Pèlerinage de la vie humaine [Pilgrimage of the Life of Man]*, advice books for proper chivalric and social behaviour (along the lines of the *Boke of the Ordre of Chyualry*), romances, ballades, virelais, rondeaux (the *formes fixes* of poetry) and love allegories like the *Roman de la Rose* and the *dits* of Machaut and Froissart.

But in any case, Chaucer wasn't limited to the Countess's books for long. On 20 June 1367 he was granted 20 marks as a life annuity by Edward III for his performance as a royal *valettus* or esquire. Although we have scant record of Chaucer's whereabouts between 1360 and then, it would be unusual if such a grant were issued upon his entry into the king's service. The Countess of Ulster died in 1363, and perhaps that was the year Chaucer was transferred to Westminster, where still wider opportunities for reading doubtless opened for him. It was a good time to come there as a *valettus*, a solid step up from a page in terms of responsibility and access. The Treaty of Brétigny, signed in October 1360 at Calais (with Chaucer present, probably still among Prince Lionel's men), put a pause to the war with France and made for a quieter decade than those on either side of it. Edward III was at home for the most part, putting money toward refitting his residences in London and close by, at Moor End, Sheen, Eltham, Langley and Havering. This meant bureaucracy moved less often as well, Chancery, Exchequer and Wardrobe finding themselves able to accommodate the king's needs without following him about. Court life was stabilized, and sophisticated culture along with it. Chaucer, no longer a page predominantly waiting on tables but a *valettus*, with more time and a mandate to polish the gentler skills he claims for the Squire of the 'General Prologue' ('He koude songes make and wel endite, / Juste and eek daunce, and weel purtreye* and write' [*draw: I, 95–6]), would have been in a good position to benefit from such literate localization.

He was not always there to take advantage of these chances. The latter 1360s found Chaucer much on the road. Even such incomplete records as exist put him abroad at least twice on the king's business: to Navarre and probably Galicia in early 1366; through Dover and Calais to somewhere (possibly Milan, where Prince Lionel married the daughter of Galeazzo Visconti) in 1368. In 1370 he had royal letters of protection to cross the Channel again, probably to northern France or Flanders. What task he accomplished we do not know, but his performance may have earned him a promotion. From 1371 to 1373 Chaucer is listed as an 'esquire of the king's chamber' (*scutiferis camere regis*), an office to which Edward III appointed only sixty-two men. Commensurate with this greater level of trust, his next mission was to Genoa, part of a team negotiating trading rights in Italy and at home. On this trip Chaucer may have gone through Germany to avoid France, the war having broken out again; we have no precise proof of his route. However, we do know he went to Florence in the spring of 1373 before turning back to England and joining quite a different branch of the civil service, as controller of the wool subsidy and wool and petty customs for the port of London, beginning in 1374.

This shift in Chaucer's *modus vivendi* should be appreciated for what it is – much more than a mere reversion out of the court and into the city whence sprang his roots. Its impact on Chaucer's reading opportunities should not be underestimated. Busy as he was – his duties called for attention to approximately a thousand documents annually, and much record-keeping and first-hand examination of the goods – he was nevertheless at no one's immediate beck and call, and the work was lighter between May and November. Then there would have been time to catch up on texts he might have missed, both new and old.

Chaucer's position in the custom house did not keep him altogether at home. He continued to travel on Crown business, making several trips to France between 1377 and 1381, presumably related to various proposals for marriage with Richard II, and an end to the renewed hostilities with France. In 1377 we know he went to Paris and to Montreuil, where his presence was noted by Froissart. In Paris he surely must have heard about the magnificent library of Charles V, numbering above a thousand volumes, and perhaps he used it. (Charles maintained a generous loan policy for favoured courtiers, like Christine de Pisan, and diplomatic guests as well.) If on this same trip he did meet Froissart in Montreuil, did they talk about recent poetic trends? The point about Chaucer's many travels, relevant to understanding his reading and his attitudes towards literary authority, is encapsulated precisely in such a trip as this – in the broadening of his acquaintance, the currency of his access to significant literatures both classical and vernacular, the enriching of his vision provided by his experiences outside England.

Of these journeys, very likely the most influential, took place between May and September 1378, when Chaucer visited Italy for the second time, as one of the party sent with royal greetings to Bernabò Visconti, ruler of Milan – or 'God of delit and scourge of Lumbardye', as Chaucer describes him in 'The Monk's Tale' (VII, 2400). Among the greatest delights undoubtedly for Chaucer, whose party stayed six weeks in Milan, was the large library Bernabò maintained. (Even more impressive was that of Bernabò's brother Galeazzo, patron of Petrarch, in Pavia, where Chaucer might have gone as well.) On this and his earlier Italian journey in 1368, language skills picked up as a boy in the Vintry would have stood him in good stead; indeed, a reasonable capacity to speak and read Italian could only have recommended him for such assignments. If in 1368 Chaucer discovered Dante, whose influence seems strong in poems usually dated 1373–8, on his second trip he found Petrarch and Boccaccio. We can safely assume that, with a bit more money in his pocket from his customs position than he had as a page, Chaucer added to his own library, collecting some of the books he was to mine so fruitfully during the next twenty years.

But what did Chaucer think of the books he read? After even so brief an overview of his reading, roughly to mid-life, the question is appropriate and potentially illuminating. It cuts directly to the heart of his entire enterprise as a writer of poems. In the minds of most literate Englishmen when Chaucer was born, verse could be effectively divided into two kinds – that produced by writers of Latin, and what came from others in (commonly) vernacular French or English. Although there was available to readers of Latin plenty of light, not to say scurrilous, work, it is safe to state broadly that Latin was considered the language for serious writing and that the vernaculars in general accommodated more frequently entertaining voices. Chaucer, of course (along with Langland, Gower and the author of *Pearl* and *Sir Gawain and the Green Knight*, to name three of the best) had a shaping hand in changing all of this in England – clearly on purpose, since had he wished to compose in Latin and French as well as English, as did his friend John Gower, he probably would have. So it is quite legitimate to inquire after what might have been Chaucer's attitudes towards letters and the writing that he would make his life's project.

Central to the question is the concept of literary 'authority' – *auctoritas* – as it was understood in the fourteenth century. *Auctores* were those possessed of this quality, and none of them had been alive for centuries. Virgil was one, Homer, as presented by the Latin chronicler Dares Phrygius, another; so were Aesop (in the version of Avianus primarily), Ovid, Statius, Lucan, Horace, Juvenal, Cicero, Livy, Sallust, Seneca, Quintilian, Suetonius, Boethius, Maximianus, Prudentius, Persius and – in a different way – the Church Fathers and subsequent theologians. (In this last category, a somewhat special case, by the fourteenth century even relative newcomers like Alain of Lille, Peter Riga, Matthew of Vendôme, Martianus Capella, Alexander of Villedieu and Bernard Silvestris could be included in the education of most readers. A true scholar, such as John of Salisbury, read more *auctores* and passed at least their names into the general pool, and perhaps a curiosity to investigate further: Apuleius, Hyginus, Pliny, Gellius, Ausonius, Vegetius, Orosius, Macrobius.) Literary *auctoritas* was a keystone of humanist Latin instruction as it developed under Charlemagne and spread outward through the rest of western Europe. In both the schools and later in the universities, scant significant distinction existed of the kind that we make now, between 'gold' and 'silver' Roman writers; indeed, the notion of the 'classical' itself wasn't invoked. Ethical venerability counted most in the establishment of an *auctor*, followed closely by the quantity of information present of a technical or practical kind. To some degree, this latter species of *auctoritas* could be occupation-specific, as the Physician's reading list of medical writers and natural philosophers attests:

Wel knew he the olde Esclapius,
And Deyscorides, and eek Rufus,
Olde Ypocras, Haly, and Galyen,
Serapion, Razis, and Avycen,
Averrois, Damscien, and Constantyn,
Bernard, and Gatesden, and Gilbertyn.

(I, 429–34)

Important as well was an imitable Latin writing style.

To be an 'author' when Chaucer was growing up was thus not an occupation, like a vintner, to which an ambitious young man might confidently aspire. Englishmen could be versifiers, of course, but then they were considered to be minstrels, or 'makers' – an indigenous term with the hands-on ring of artisan rather than artist about it. Nor was language the sole issue involved: authorship from ancient times came packaged with extraordinary powers to perceive the future, to do wonders. Greek *poiesis* meant 'creation' in the fullest sense, and *poietes* 'a creator'. Poets, in the example of Homer, the delineations of Plato and subsequent followers like Philo Judaeus, were uncommon men, uniquely touched by the gods. Although Greek was largely lost to Chaucer and his contemporaries, Greek ideas lived to be transmitted to them through their influence on the Romans, who picked this magical element up in the overlapping meanings of *vates* – at once a prophet, a seer, and an inspired bard. Hence the surprising (to us) medieval tradition that held Virgil to be a master magician, possessed of supernatural powers. It comes as a natural outgrowth of how *auctores* were understood: Statius, who called the *Aeneid* 'divine', doubtless thought little of the epithet beyond its aptness; but he opened a door for Boccaccio 1300 years later to add 'divine' to Dante's *Commedia* – a gesture received in Chaucer's lifetime not as blasphemous, but as acceptable because traditional. Hence also, *mutatis mutandis*, it is easier to place properly the veneration of the Church Fathers, and later theologians, as *auctores*. Their works were in their own way undeniably inspired, and their *auctoritas* – coming, as it did, from the highest power – was not to be questioned. Poetic achievement and divine intercession coalesced for the Middle Ages in the concept of *auctoritas*: Dante, always attuned to the intellectual trend, himself made Statius a Christian.

Offsetting the weight of such a formidable tradition sufficiently to clear a little space for himself as a writer must, therefore, have seemed to Chaucer a daunting task, at least at times. The sequence of his works shows him struggling with the problem, just as his contemporaries did, with various degrees of success and originality. One favourite method has already been mentioned – his continual naming of books, from which his narrative *personae*, acting as mere 'compilers' or recorders, reproduce stories written (usually) 'long ago'. The dodge – that nothing of an authorial sort is taking place – is of course just that, a dodge, but it is one of Chaucer's favourites. He works it from first to last, from the *Book of the Duchess* straight through to the *Canterbury Tales*, where written *auctoritas* gives way to sham reporting of the pilgrims' 'own words'. The dramatic qualities of Chaucer's pilgrimage have drawn much attention, and appropriately so, for his decision to let his characters talk for themselves was, and remains, altogether inspired. Less frequently noticed, however, is the degree to which even this grows out of a traditional understanding of *auctoritas*, and how richly Chaucer works the drama notion against it for comic effect. When, for example, his narrator begs forgiveness (I, 3167–86) for quoting the Miller verbatim, as if the Miller were an *auctor* (and 'the Reve eek and othere mo'), and his 'cherles tale' not a tipsy utterance *ex tempore* but an authoritative text, the 'mateere' of which it would be an offence to 'falsen' (a cross-over of oral and written subtly underscored by the fiction of a *reciting* narrator's admonition to us, his 'auditors', to 'Turne over the leef and chese another tale'), the humour is enhanced by a slight but unmistakable genuflection towards the *auctoritas* tradition, with its high emphasis on the near-sanctity of the authorial book, requiring our exact replication.

In earlier works incorporating visions and dreams, Chaucer found still another means to hold *auctoritas* safely at stave's length and allow his creative faculties room to breathe. Dreams and visions had the effect of liberating the medieval writer from the charge of literary weightlessness, of responsibility for merely 'making things up', thereby telling 'fables and swich wrecchednesse', as the Parson would have it (X, 34). Chaucer had good company in this, both ancient (one thinks especially, perhaps, of Boethius and Macrobius) and more modern: the great, serial collaboration of Guillaume de Lorris and Jean de Meun providing the most important example. No other single poem had such demonstrable influence on poets of the later Middle Ages as did the *Roman de la Rose*, so emphatically – and significantly – the story of what a lover encountered while asleep. At that inspiring fountain Chaucer drank deep, both directly, as a first-hand reader and thoughtful translator (a version of which may have reached Eustache Deschamps in France), and indirectly, through the help of others' transformations of the *Roman*, most notably Guillaume de Machaut's.

If we examine Chaucer's poetry chronologically (or as chronologically as we can, given that the dating of most of his work is an imprecise science at best), the course of his dependence on dream and vision is easily chartable. Excluding the shorter lyrics, everything until *Troilus and Criseyde* incorporates a dream vision, but nothing after it, save perhaps the unfinished (and undatable) *Legend of Good Women* – in many ways, including formally, an anachronistic work for Chaucer, particularly if we take on faith the usual posit that its composition spans his finishing *Troilus* and starting the *Canterbury Tales*.

It used to be fashionable to divide Chaucer's writing into three periods of influence: French, Italian and English. Subsequent scholarship has carefully refined these broad categories almost out of existence, and rightly so, for they were too broadly conceived to be truly useful. Nevertheless, the notion has some relevance to an understanding of Chaucer's ultimate accommodation of authority and originality. The early humanistic system of pedagogy that elevated *auctoritas* was designed first to teach Latin grammar and rhetoric, and then the other liberal arts, through replication of approved models. 'Authors' were read to be imitated essentially, not striven with or overcome in some literarily Oedipal fashion. Young Chaucer (like most apprentice poets, now as then) would have 'learned' poetry in just this way – by imitating the acknowledged best models. If, in the fourteenth century, one maintained the trajectory of the schools and stuck to Latin verse, the choice was essentially simple: Ovid, Statius, Virgil (if one felt especially ambitious), perhaps a little Horace. On the other hand, if one elected to write in either of the vernaculars common in the courts of Edward III and Richard II, the situation was more complicated. How to negotiate the shoals of proprietary *auctoritas*? Here, Chaucer's gravitation towards dream and vision models represents his first – French, in a sense – solution. As much excellent research has shown, Chaucer followed French examples – the *Roman de la Rose*, and various works of Froissart and Machaut – at first, establishing as his poems' frameworks dreams or extraordinary events with dream-like qualities which could be *reported* on, rather than claimed as acts of the imagination. Their protective fiction of 'real' dream was of course borrowed along with his imagery and plots from his French 'authorities' – a fact that in itself must have been reassuring to Chaucer, particularly at the beginning of his career when his concern for the 'rules' must have been greatest. During these years, in addition to short works now lost, he probably translated the *Roman de la Rose*, and wrote the *Book of the Duchess* and the *Parliament of Fowls*.

Troilus, it is believed, was begun in the early 1380's – just shortly after Chaucer returned from what could have been his second trip to Italy in 1378. Without conceding too much to the hoary periodicity theory of Chaucer's writing, it is nevertheless striking how different his new work sounds after 1378. The change has been acclaimed as his discovery of an entirely new 'Italian' voice, but it may be described just as accurately as a fresh solution to the dilemma of individuality and *auctoritas*. Not insignificantly, perhaps, Chaucer may have started work on two other poems – the *House of Fame* and 'Anelida and Arcite' – before commencing the masterpiece that is his *Troilus*, and not insignificant either is the unfinished state in which he left them. Much energy has been committed to guessing why he broke these poems off, to no universally agreed conclusion. However, observable in each is a tension between elements that makes them somewhat difficult to read, and doubtless to sustain. In both cases the conflict seems to emanate from an unsuccessful integration of disparate compositional models: that is, in the *House of Fame*, from an attempt to reconcile elements of Dante's *Commedia* with the more familiar dream-vision structure with which Chaucer had grown comfortable, and in the 'Anelida' from a similar failed yoking of French-derived love complaint with the Italo-Latin epic mechanics of Boccaccio's *Teseida*, the story of Theseus.

A simpler way to put this, perhaps, is that Chaucer returned from Italy with new definitions of *auctor* and authority. Not that he gave up the bedrock concept of *imitatio* altogether, but now he had different models, both physically – bound between the covers of the copies of Boccaccio's *Teseida*, *Filocolo* (a romance of Floris and Blanchefleur) and *Filostrato* (and probably the *Decameron*, although Chaucer's direct knowledge of that remains in dispute) which he must have brought back – and intellectually, inspired by the individualist solutions managed by the Italians right under the nose, so to speak, of an *auctoritas* ever looming, even there. What the *Troilus* represents, in contrast to the *House of Fame* and the 'Anelida', is thus less a shift from French to Italian 'periods' (keeping firmly in mind that Chaucer wrote in English exclusively) than a fresh imagining of what had been done, and *could* be done, with authorities, brought this time to exemplary fullness.

Chaucer's new approach to *auctoritas*, like that of the Italians, was at once to honour it while simultaneously asserting a claim upon it, not as an acolyte to an incomparable master but rather as a rightful heir acknowledges a benefactor. The change can be quickly illustrated by comparing how Ovid's tale of Ceyx and Alcyone is handled in the *Book of the Duchess* with the conclusion of *Troilus and Criseyde*. In the former, Chaucer describes his source as a 'romaunce' found in a book of 'fables' and 'many other thinges smale' that 'clerkes had in olde tyme, / And other poetes, put in rime' (48, 59, 52–4). Neither Ovid himself nor the *Metamorphoses* (the story appears at XI, 410–749) is named in the passage, perhaps because Chaucer apparently turned to the original only incidentally, instead working primarily from Machaut's dream poem, the *Dit de la fonteinne amoreuse [The Fountain of Love]* and the French allegorical version of Ovid's *Metamorphoses*, the *Ovide moralisé*. All sorts of reasons can be offered for this, from Chaucer's greater facility with French than Latin to a question of available source texts. (We cannot assume, after all, that Chaucer had an original Ovid at hand as he wrote.) Still, Chaucer clearly would have known the ultimate source for the tale, and might have presented otherwise the book that set him dreaming. He could, for instance, have asserted Ovid as his *auctor* true or not, rather than suggesting that he had a French intermediary, as he does with his use of 'romaunce'. But – all questions of Chaucer's private honesty aside – to do that may have been to reach higher than his self-esteem would allow at that time. To emulate 'publicly' a vernacular writer and a near contemporary, albeit a famous one, was perhaps enough in 1369 or thereabouts; certainly as a theory it fits the self-effacing language of the *Book of the Duchess*, and particularly this passage, with its diminutive 'fables' and its 'other thinges smale'.

At the end of *Troilus*, diminuendo is voiced again, but it is crucial to observe how differently, and to what a different purpose. To see it properly, the two familiar stanzas must be viewed in full:

Go, litel bok, go, litel myn tragedye,
Ther* God thi makere yet, er that he dye,   *May
So sende myght to make* in some comedye!   *compose
But litel book, no makyng thow n'envie*,   *don't vie with
But subgit be to alle poesye;
And kis the steppes where as thow seest pace
Virgile, Ovide, Omer, Lucan, and Stace.

And for there is so gret diversite
In Englissh and in writyng of oure tonge,
So prey I God that non miswrite the,
Ne the mysmetre for defaute of tonge;
And red wherso thow be, or elles songe,
That thow be understonde, God I biseche!
                              (V, 1786–98)

Here again, the vernacular work, this time Chaucer's own rather than a source, is described as 'litel' – three times, lest we miss the point. Moreover, the poem is personified and charged with three commissions: first, to intercede with God to inspire the narrator/Chaucer to write a kind of complement to the 'litel bok' itself, a 'comedeye', apparently to balance the 'tragedeye' just completed; second, to envy 'no makyng' but to be 'subgit' ('subject') 'to alle poeseye'; and third, to 'kis the steppes where as thow seest pace / Virgile, Ovide, Omer, Lucan and Stace'. Clearly, Chaucer is working the 'humility *topos*' for all it is worth. But it is important to note what else he is up to here, with the careful vocabulary in which he chooses to couch these three requests.

First: tragedy and comedy are genres of *auctoritas*, and those who write them, at least by strong implication if not completely by definition, *auctores*. The very existence of (even) a 'litel' book, a 'tragedeye' sufficiently worthy to badger God for a matching comedy, is thus presented as a kind of claim of achieved authority by Chaucer. It is understated, but it is there: the little book has authority written all over it. Second: the apparently innocent pairing of 'makyng' and 'poeseye' in the next two lines is more complex than it initially seems. As suggested earlier, these words belong to near-contradictory literary terminologies, the one invoking the production of minstrels, the other of divinely inspired *auctores*. What does it mean to say – to a *tragedy* – to envy no 'makyng' but to be 'subject' to poesy instead? Two things, perhaps. If 'makyng' and 'poeseye' are taken as doublets, then Chaucer's intent was to humble his work, and relegate it to an appropriate spot in the background (that is, the usual reading of this passage); but if, as might very well have been the case here, 'makyng' would have stood out immediately as a synonym for 'minstrelsy' to schools-educated readers like himself, then a contrast is created with 'poeseye', a genre of authoritative pedigree equivalent to 'tragedye' – even so 'litel' a one as this *Troilus* the reader holds in his hand.

Third, and perhaps most important: only tragedy, not mere 'makyng', deserves to reach the company of 'Virgile, Ovide, Omer, Lucan and Stace', whether or not, once there, it kisses the ground – a vexed enough gesture in itself, simultaneously both honorific and possessively claimant. (Some at least among Chaucer's schools-trained readers would have detected an echo of a common foundational story from the *auctores*, that of how Lucius Junius Brutus established his right to Rome by pressing his lips to his 'mother', his native soil.) To the hypercritical reviewer's objection that such close parsing demands extraordinary linguistic awareness, Chaucer might have directed attention to the very next stanza, where (as we see above) he warns pointedly against 'miswriting', 'mismetering' and careless reading, all of which lead to misunderstanding of a very subtle text.

When Chaucer came back from Italy in 1378, then, he carried with him a fresh sense of literary purpose that transformed his writing. From the struggles and experiments with and against the antique world of books and *auctoritas* of Dante, Petrarch and especially Boccaccio (the only one of the three with whose work he never acknowledges an acquaintance, but upon whom he relied the most), Chaucer gleaned both new ambition and ways to realize it for himself. One such, immediately, was to attribute the original authorship of *Troilus*, his next poem and a reworking of the *Filostrato*, to one 'Lollius' (I, 394), a fictitious, implicitly Roman *auctor* mentioned first in the *House of Fame* (1468) alongside the chroniclers of the Trojan war, 'Dares' (Phrygius), 'Tytus' (Dictys Cretensis) 'And Guido eke de Columpnis' (Guido delle Colonne). Quite likely Chaucer borrowed the trick of inventing an *auctor* from Boccaccio's early *Filocolo*. But just as Boccaccio (and Dante and Petrarch before him) subsequently moved away from manipulating the mere surface of authoritative convention to engage tradition more deeply in his mature work, so Chaucer did as well, and to precisely the same purpose. As the concluding lines of *Troilus* illustrate, Chaucer's enterprise transformed itself; he sought to earn inclusion in – as he put it some time after 1385 in one of the two *Prologues to the Legend of Good Women* (G 308) – 'the world of autours'.

While the importance of this transformation cannot be overemphasized – had Chaucer left his sights unraised and his poetic reach unextended he would not also have remade English poetry – it must nonetheless be seen for what it is, a direct beneficiary, in its way, of contemporary ideas of literary authority. By maintaining the *auctores* atop their pedestals (the way the dreamer 'Geffrey' finds them in the *House of Fame* [1419–1519]), medieval reverence for authoritative books and *auctoritas* achieved two obvious ends: holding out, with one hand, clear evidence of a kind of individual immortality letters alone might bring and, with the other, apparently denying its attainability to all but the privileged (perhaps even the supernaturally empowered) few. Yet because the world of *auctoritas* was past and gone it had the advantage of being, by definition, *whole*. It could therefore be apprehended as a completed entity and safely utilized, part by part, according to need. As we have seen above, standard educational practice in Chaucer's day encouraged precisely this; so too did the proliferation of *florilegia* that supplied sermon-writers with authority on demand, *sans* context.

It was this precedent, this malleability of the past, that the Italians perceived first among Chaucer's contemporaries and exploited, just as – from Dante on – they fostered literary expression in the vernacular. The traditions of *auctoritas* had kept a goal alive for the Middle Ages, a laurel to be yearned for all the more keenly because it seemed, first entirely, later relatively, unattainable. But as is often the case, the very constraints of *auctoritas* in the end were energizing, demanding that the essence of authority be understood, disassembled and rebuilt according to the individual vision. After his return from Italy it is this energy, born there of dissatisfaction with and rejection of a convention simultaneously limiting and, if properly comprehended, ultimately liberating, that Chaucer adapted to propel the work of his maturity.

See also chapter 1, POLITICS AND LONDON LIFE; chapter 2, MANUSCRIPTS AND AUDIENCE; chapter 8, TRAGEDY AND ROMANCE IN CHAUCER'S 'LITEL BOK' OF TROILUS AND CRISEYDE; chapter 13, READING CHAUCER ALOUD.

References and Further Reading

Astell, Ann W. (1996). *Chaucer and the Universe of Learning*. Ithaca, NY: Cornell University Press.

Backus, Irena (1996). *The Reception of the Church Fathers in the West*. Leiden: Brill.

Baswell, Christopher (1995). *Virgil in Medieval England: Figuring the Aeneid from the Twelfth Century to Chaucer*. Cambridge: Cambridge University Press.

Boitani, P. (ed.) (1983). *Chaucer and the Italian Trecento*. Cambridge: Cambridge University Press.

Burrow, J. A. (1982). *Medieval Writers and Their Work: Middle English Literature and its Background 1100–1500*. Oxford: Oxford University Press.

Coleman, Janet (1981). *Medieval Readers and Writers, 1350–1400*. New York: Columbia University Press.

Coleman, Joyce (1996). *Public Reading and the Reading Public in Late Medieval England and France*. Cambridge: Cambridge University Press.

Curtius, Ernest Robert (1953). *European Literature and the Latin Middle Ages*, trans. W. R. Trask. New York: Bollingen Foundation. [First published in German in 1948.]

Edwards, Robert R. (2002). *Chaucer and Boccaccio: Antiquity and Modernity*. Basingstoke: Palgrave.

Fleming, John V. (1990). *Classical Imitation and Interpretation in Chaucer's* Troilus. Lincoln: University of Nebraska Press.

Gellrich, Jesse M. (1985). *The Idea of the Book in the Middle Ages*. Ithaca, NY: Cornell University Press.

Green, Richard Firth (1980). *Poets and Princepleasers: Literature and the English Court in the Late Middle Ages*. Toronto: University of Toronto Press.

Havely, N. R. (1980). *Boccaccio: Sources for Troilus and the Knight's and Franklin's Tales; Translations from the Filostrato, Teseida and Filocolo*. Cambridge: D. S. Brewer.

Jeffrey, David Lyle (1984). *Chaucer and Scriptural Tradition*. Ottawa: University of Ottawa Press.

Justice, Stephen (1994). *Writing and Rebellion: England in 1381*. Berkeley: University of California Press.

Lerer, Seth (1993). *Chaucer and His Readers: Imagining the Author in Late Medieval England*. Princeton, NJ: Princeton University Press.

Markus, Robert (1990). *The End of Christian Antiquity*. Cambridge: Cambridge University Press.

Minnis, A. J. (1982). *Chaucer and Pagan Antiquity*. Cambridge: D. S. Brewer.

Minnis, A. J. (1984). *Medieval Theory of Authorship: Scholastic Literary Attitudes in the Later Middle Ages*. London: Scolar Press.

Muscatine, Charles (1957). *Chaucer and the French Tradition: A Study in Style and Meaning*. Berkeley: University of California Press.

Neuse, Richard (1991). *Chaucer's Dante: Allegory and Epic Theater in the* Canterbury Tales. Berkeley: University of California Press.

Nolan, Barbara (1992). *Chaucer and the Tradition of the Roman Antique*. Cambridge: Cambridge University Press.

Orme, Nicholas (2001). *Medieval Children*. New Haven and London: Yale University Press.

Palmer, R. B. (ed.) (1999). *Chaucer's French Contemporaries: The Poetry/Poetics of Self and Tradition*. New York: AMS Press.

Pearsall, Derek (1992). *The Life of Geoffrey Chaucer: A Critical Biography*. Oxford: Blackwell.

Wallace, David (1985). *Chaucer and the Early Writings of Boccaccio*. Woodbridge, Suffolk: Boydell and Brewer.

Wallace, David (1997). *Chaucerian Polity: Absolutist Lineages and Associational Forms in England and Italy*. Stanford, Calif.: Stanford University Press.

Wetherbee, Winthrop W. (1989). *Geoffrey Chaucer:* The Canterbury Tales. Cambridge: Cambridge University Press.

Wimsatt, James I. (1968). *Chaucer and the French Love Poets: The Literary Background of the* Book of the Duchess. Chapel Hill: University of North Carolina Press.

Wimsatt, James I. (1991). *Chaucer and His French Contemporaries: Natural Music in the Fourteenth Century*. Toronto: University of Toronto Press.

Windeatt, B. A. (ed.) (1980). *Chaucer's Dream Poetry: Sources and Analogues*. Cambridge: D. S. Brewer.

Part Two

Dream Visions

The Court of Mirth, in a late fifteenth-century manuscript of the *Roman de la Rose* produced by Robinet Testard (Bodleian Library MS Douce 195, fol. 7 recto).

Chapter Four

Dreaming

Steven F. Kruger

Dreams are everywhere in Chaucer's work, from the translation of the *Roman de la Rose* that stands near the beginning of Chaucer's poetic career to the long poems of Chaucer's maturity, *Troilus and Criseyde*, the *Legend of Good Women*, and the *Canterbury Tales*. (Dreams figure in 'The Nun's Priest's Tale', of course, but also in 'The Knight's Tale' [I, 1384–98], 'The Miller's Tale' [I, 3681–6], 'The Man of Law's Tale' [II, 803–5], 'The Wife of Bath's Prologue' [III, 576–84], 'The Summoner's Prologue and Tale' [III, 1675–1706, 1854–68], 'The Squire's Tale' [V, 347–72], 'The Tale of Sir Thopas' [VII, 787–89], 'The Monk's Tale' [VII, 2154–8, 2740–60], 'The Second Nun's Tale' [VIII, 260–4] and 'The Parson's Tale' [X, 605, 912–14].) Four of Chaucer's major poetic works – the *Book of the Duchess*, the *House of Fame*, the *Parliament of Fowls* and the *Prologue to the Legend of Good Women* – are in fact 'dream visions', a popular and widespread medieval genre in which the main action occurs in a dream-state. In most twentieth- or twenty-first-century writers, such a repeated return to the material of dreaming would no doubt signify a deep interest in human psychology, in the unconscious to which dreams, following Freud, have been closely connected. Chaucerian dreams might also sometimes reveal psychology: Criseyde dreams of exchanging her heart for that of a noble eagle – a clear love allegory – at the very moment when she has become more susceptible to loving Troilus (*TC* II, 899–903, 925–31). The dream's violence, with the eagle tearing out Criseyde's heart and placing his own heart in 'hire brest', suggests Criseyde's strong reluctance to give in to love, but at the same time the violence occurs without causing fear or pain: 'Of which she nought agroos*, ne nothyng smerte' (*was frightened: II, 930). The dream thus shows Criseyde ready to love, even as it acknowledges that she may not be wholly in control of her own involvement in love.

As we will see, however, the psychological is not the only, or even the predominant, way of approaching dreams in the Middle Ages. Medieval theories of dreaming acknowledge a psychological component to dream experience but also see the dream as intimately connected to both the physiological and the metaphysical. Dreams might be purely a reflex of the body, the result of overeating or an imbalance of the four humours, thought (in classical, medieval and early modern medicine) to shape the body's health; but they might also arise from outside the body (and the mind) of the individual, reflecting cosmic influences, or the activity of malign (demonic) or benign (angelic or divine) forces. Chaucer is clearly aware of this complex range of possibilities for the dream: he explicitly evokes dream theory several times in his writing, and he implicitly exploits dream experience's complex possibilities wherever he represents dreams and especially within his fullest explorations of the dream-state, the four dream-vision poems.

Chaucerian Dream Theory

Repeatedly reproduced and evoked in the Middle Ages was the discussion of dreaming found in Macrobius' late antique *Commentary on the Dream of Scipio*, a wide-ranging discussion of geographical, astronomical, mathematical, metaphysical, political and other questions presented as a detailed commentary on Cicero's 'Dream of Scipio', a Latin dream vision originally part of *De Republica* (a work of political philosophy lost, except for the 'Dream', until its rediscovery in the nineteenth century). For Macrobius, dreams belong either to 'the gate of ivory', 'the composition of which is so dense that no matter how thin a layer of it may be, it remains opaque', or to 'the gate of horn', 'the nature of which is such that, when thinned, it becomes transparent' (I.iii.20); that is, dreams are either true or false, reliable and prophetic or not. But Macrobius does not describe dreams by means of a simple binarism: instead, he suggests that all dreams fall into five categories, two false and three true. The *insomnium* is a psychologically or physiologically determined dream, arising 'from some condition or circumstance that irritates a man during the day and consequently disturbs him

when he falls asleep' (I.iii.5). It is this kind of dream, with 'no prophetic significance' (I.iii.3), that Chaucer evokes in the *Parliament of
Fowls* when his dreamer-narrator, having read 'Tullyus [Cicero] of the
Drem of Scipioun' (31), falls asleep and dreams of 'Affrican', the adop-
tive grandfather who appears to Scipio in Cicero's 'Dream':

> The wery huntere, slepynge in his bed,
> To wode ayeyn his mynde goth anon;
> The juge dremeth how his plees been sped;
> The cartere dremeth how his cart is gon;
> The riche, of gold; the knyght fyght with his fon;
> The syke met* he drynketh of the tonne*;   *dreams; *barrel
> The lovere met he hath his lady wonne.
> (99–105)

Though the narrator comments, agnostically, 'Can I not seyn if that
the cause were / For I hadde red of Affrican byforn, / That made me
to mete that he stod there' (106–8), his evocation here of dreams that,
like the Macrobian *insomnium*, arise from daily concerns, at least raises
the possibility that we should interpret the *Parliament* as a dream
'caused by mental or physical distress, or anxiety about the future'
(Macrobius I.iii.4). The second type of unreliable dream in Macrobius
is the *visum*, which occurs 'in the moment between wakefulness and
slumber': 'the dreamer thinks he is still fully asleep and imagines he
sees spectres rushing at him or wandering vaguely about' (I.iii.7).

Opposed to the untrue *insomnium* and *visum* are three types of
dream with truth value. In the *oraculum*, 'A parent, or a pious or
revered man, or a priest, or even a god clearly reveals what will or
will not transpire, and what action to take or to avoid' (I.iii.8). (If we
think again of Chaucer's *Parliament of Fowls*, we might argue that the
dignified figure of Affrican, certainly a 'revered man', is as appropriate
to an *oraculum* as he is to an *insomnium*.) The *visio* is a dream that
'actually comes true', as when 'a man dreams of the return of a friend
who has been staying in a foreign land' and 'presently meets his friend'
(I.iii.9). Finally, the *somnium*, while it contains truth, 'conceals' and
'veils' this 'with strange shapes and . . . ambiguity', 'requir[ing] an
interpretation for its understanding' (I.iii.10). In its five-fold classification of dreaming, Macrobius' *Commentary* presents a continuous
hierarchy: on the one hand stand completely false dreams, on the
other obviously true ones. But in the centre, bridging the true and the
false, stands the *somnium*, a sort of dream that, while ultimately true,

operates through fiction. Unlike the *oraculum* and *visio*, which present the truth directly, but also unlike the unreliable *insomnium* and *visum*, the *somnium* brings together truth and falsehood, demanding, like allegorical fiction, a proper interpretation.

Similarly complex understanding of dreams characterizes other late antique writers known in the Middle Ages such as Calcidius, author of the *Commentary on Plato's Timaeus*; Christian writers of the same period likewise emphasize the dream's potential for conveying both truth and falsehood and the possibility that dreams, like Macrobius' *somnium*, might convey truth in veiled, oblique, fictional ways. In his most extensive discussion of dreaming, in Book XII of his literal commentary on Genesis, St Augustine emphasizes that all dreams belong to a kind of vision that is neither 'corporeal' on the one hand nor 'intellectual' on the other, but instead 'spiritual'; this is an intermediate sort of vision, associated with the imagination, standing between body and abstraction, materiality and transcendent truth. Dreams for Augustine, moreover, are 'sometimes false and sometimes true', and true dreams are of several different types: 'sometimes quite similar to future events' (like Macrobius' *visio*), or 'even clear forecasts [*aperte dicta*]' (like *visio* or *oraculum*), or 'predictions given with dark meanings, and, as it were, in figurative expressions' (like Macrobius' *somnium*) (XII.18.39). Somewhat later, St Gregory the Great developed a schema of dream types that, reiterated in both his *Morals on the Book of Job* (VIII.24.42–3) and his *Dialogues* (IV.50–1), again emphasizes both true and false dreams and dreams that mix true 'predictions' with less reliable material. For Gregory, dreams might be wholly internal and physical, arising 'either by a full stomach, or by an empty one'. They might, on the other hand, arise wholly from outside the dreamer, either by demonic 'illusion' or by divine or angelic 'revelation'. In addition, according to Gregory, dreams might reflect a mixture of external and internal activity, arising from 'our thoughts combined with illusions' or 'our thoughts combined with revelations'. The classification of dreams in Gregory is thus particularly complex. Dreaming might be either a phenomenon of the individual or of cosmic (demonic and angelic) forces, or a mixture of these. It might also benignantly reveal truth or be empty of meaning (as with dreams of the 'stomach') or actively and malignantly deceive; further, benignant/true and malignant/false dreams might each be complicated by the dreamer's own psychology ('thoughts').

Schemata such as Gregory's, Augustine's and Macrobius' were well-known throughout the Middle Ages – copied, commented upon and revised, but consistently understood as emphasizing the *complexity* of dream experience. In the later Middle Ages, with the (re)introduction into Western Europe both of Aristotelian ideas deeply sceptical of the dream's meaningfulness and of medical lore concerned with the dream's purely somatic connections, we find writers emphasizing more strongly the 'lower', unreliable end of dream experience. It becomes a commonplace, for instance, to associate dreams with humoral imbalance, as in the twelfth-century *De spiritu et anima*: 'The sanguine and the choleric see red and mottled dreams, while phlegmatics and melancholics dream in shades of black and white' (chapter 25, 221). But even in the work of writers most interested in the bodily causes and consequences of dreams, the possibility that dreams might not be *simply* corporeal – that they might in fact give access to some kind of truth – is almost always acknowledged. Dreaming remains, even for late medieval thinkers and writers, a realm touching both truth and falsehood, the transcendent and the mundane.

The consistently acknowledged complexity of dream experience gives rise to two interrelated and difficult questions. First, given any specific dream, how can one decide whether it is true or false, empty of meaning or reliably predictable, demonic in origin or angelic? As Gregory the Great notes, one must be 'very reluctant to put one's faith in' dreams, 'since it is hard to tell from what source they come' (*Dialogues* IV.50.6). Second, even if one could be assured that a particular dream contained some important truth, *how* would one go about discovering that truth? If the dream were a Macrobian *visio* or *oraculum* (but how can we know for sure before the advent of its predicted outcome?) its import should appear directly, but if it were a *somnium*, its meaning would need to be excavated by means of an exegetical process not itself dictated by the dream's content. (Thus, in 'The Miller's Tale', Absolon interprets having dreamt 'Al nyght' that he 'was at a feeste' [I, 3684], along with the fact that his 'mouth hath icched al this longe day' [I, 3682], as 'a signe of kissyng atte leeste' [I, 3683]; as we discover, however, the dream portends not the kind of kiss Absolon expects but instead his encounter with Alison's 'naked ers', which he kisses 'Ful savourly' [I, 3734–5]. The dream reliably, if comically, predicts a future action, but Absolon does not have the key to reading it properly.)

The individual dreamer concerned to determine whether a particular dream might be meaningful, and if so how, is thus faced with a vexing uncertainty. But such uncertainty presents writers (rather than real-life dreamers) with rich possibilities: the dream hovers between body and intellect, earth and heaven, truth and falsehood, meaning and nonsense, and hence it provides the imaginative artist with a unique ground upon which to explore the complex relations between such opposed, but not easily separable, entities. Given, too, that dream experience as understood in the Middle Ages so easily leads into questions of interpretation, it also provides medieval writers with an opportunity for metafiction, for self-conscious exploration of the interpretive problems that might be presented when, in the words of the *House of Fame*, we find 'fals and soth compouned', entering the world 'Togeder' as 'oo tydynge' (2108–9).

Chaucer repeatedly exploits the complexities, ambiguities, and uncertainties of dreams, their causes and their interpretation, and in ways that make clear his firm and detailed knowledge of medieval theories of dreaming. (Pratt [1977] suggests persuasively that one source of the dream theory Chaucer incorporates into his work was the Latin writing of the English thinker Robert Holkot.) Thus, in 'The Nun's Priest's Tale', a tale that foregrounds problems of interpretation in multiple ways, Chaucer puts the dream experienced by the cock Chauntecleer at the centre of the action:

> Me mette how that I romed up and doun
> Withinne our yeerd, wheer as I saugh a beest
> Was lyk an hound, and wolde han maad areest*   *seized
> Upon my body, and wolde han had me deed.
> His colour was bitwixe yelow and reed,
> And tipped was his tayl and bothe his eeris
> With blak, unlyk the remenant of his heeris;
> His snowte smal, with glowynge eyen tweye.
> Yet of his look for feere almost I deye.
>
> (VII, 2898–2906)

Almost half the tale consists of a debate between Chauntecleer and his mate Pertelote over this dream's potential meaningfulness and specifically its predictive qualities. Pertelote takes an up-to-date (late medieval) medical approach to Chauntecleer's dream, declaring that 'Nothyng, God woot, but vanitee in sweven is' (VII, 2922) and reading the dream as a clear expression of Chauntecleer's excess of red and black choler, which explains why he dreams of a red and black beast:

> Swevenes* engendren of repleccions*,   *dreams; *overeating
> And ofte of fume* and of complecciouns*,   *stomach vapour;
>   *bodily humours

Whan humours been to habundant in a wight.
Certes this dreem, which ye han met to-nyght,
Cometh of the greete superfluytee
Of youre rede colera, pardee,
Which causeth folk to dreden in hir dremes
Of arwes*, and of fyr with rede lemes*,   *arrows; *flames
Of rede beestes, that they wol hem byte,
Of contek*, and of whelpes*, grete and lyte;   *strife; *dogs
Right as the humour of malencolie,
Causeth ful many a man in sleep to crie
For feere of blake beres, or boles* blake,   *bulls
Or elles blake develes wole hem take.
(VII, 2923–36)

The dream's consequences are, for Pertelote, purely physical ones, demanding a prescription of 'digestyves' and 'laxatyves' (VII, 2961–2) intended to rebalance the humours. Chauntecleer argues, to the contrary, that dreams are, at least sometimes, meaningful and predictive, 'significaciouns / As wel of joye as of tribulaciouns / That folk enduren in this lif present' (VII, 2979–81). He presents *exempla* from 'Oon of the gretteste auctour that men rede' (VII, 2984; probably Cicero or Valerius Maximus) of dreams that were reliably predictive. (Another such *exemplum* is presented, in the tale that precedes the Nun's Priest's, in the Monk's 'tragic' story of Croesus [VII, 2740–60].) The ensuing action of 'The Nun's Priest's Tale', in which Chauntecleer is captured and almost killed by a fox, would seem, on the face of it, to confirm Chauntecleer's more credulous approach to dreams. Indeed, the tale's narrator makes clear his sense that the cock's dream was accurately predictive: 'Thou were ful wel ywarned by thy dremes / That thilke day was perilous to thee' (VII, 3232–3). It is, however, also true that, if the dream predicts Chauntecleer's demise, Chauntecleer – through his own wit and action – avoids that fate, escaping the fox's clutches. And though the dream may be read as predictive, Chauntecleer nonetheless bears responsibility for endangering himself: if he hadn't allowed himself to be 'ravysshed' by the fox's 'flaterie' (VII, 3324), he could easily have avoided danger. Must we see the dream, then, as truly and straightforwardly predictive or (alternatively, and closer to Pertelote's view) revelatory only of something in Chauntecleer, his characterological (even humoral) make-up, something that makes him susceptible to the fox's successful exploitation of his pride?

The culminating book of *Troilus and Criseyde* is similarly structured around the problem of dream interpretation, though here the action is less light-hearted than in Chaucer's comic beast epic-fable. Separated from Criseyde, desperately awaiting her return from the Greek camp, the lover Troilus dreams 'the dredefulleste thynges / That myghte ben; as mete he were allone / In place horrible making ay his mone, / Or meten that he was amonges alle / His enemys, and in hire hondes falle' (V, 248–52). Confronted with a despairing Troilus, Pandarus reviews the various theories about dreams and their meaningfulness; his discussion closely resembles that of Gregory the Great (though imaginatively transposed into the pagan terms of Chaucer's Troy), noting that 'prestes of the temple tellen . . . / That dremes ben the revelaciouns / Of goddes, and . . . / That they ben infernals illusiouns; / And leches seyn that of complexiouns / Proceden they, or fast, or glotonye' (V, 365–70). He also notes dreams that, like Macrobius' *insomnium* as well as the dreams in Gregory that involve 'thought', arise 'thorugh impressiouns, / As if a wight hath faste a thyng in mynde' (V, 372–3). But Pandarus, like Pertelote, is deeply sceptical of the dream's potential meaningfulness, and he reads Troilus' disturbed dreams as proceeding 'of thi malencolie' (V, 360) – 'I counte hem nought a bene!' (V, 363).

Later, Troilus dreams a more specific, viscerally disturbing dream:

> So on a day he leyde hym doun to slepe,
> And so byfel that yn his slep hym thoughte
> That in a forest faste he welk to wepe
> For love of here that hym these peynes wroughte;
> And up and doun as he the forest soughte,
> He mette he saugh a bor with tuskes grete,
> That slepte ayeyn the bryghte sonnes hete.
>
> And by this bor, faste in his armes folde,
> Lay, kyssyng ay, his lady bryght, Criseyde.
> For sorwe of which, whan he it gan byholde,
> And for despit*, out of his slep he breyde.   *chagrin
>   (V, 1233–43)

Troilus himself reads the dream as sent by the 'blysful goddes' (V, 1250) and as revealing a clear truth: 'My lady bryght, Criseyde, hath me bytrayed' (V, 1247; the reader of *Troilus and Criseyde* is liable to adopt this view too, knowing in a way Troilus himself does not that Criseyde has already 'falsed Troilus' [V, 1053]). Pandarus tries again to comfort Troilus by now insisting not that dreams are trivial or meaningless but that they are easily subject to misinterpretation: 'Have I nat seyd er this, / That dremes many a maner man bigile? / And whi? For folk expounden hem amys' (V, 1276–8). Pandarus indeed presents an alternative reading of the dream, proposing that it is about Criseyde's reunion with her father and not about any new romantic entanglement (V, 1282–8). But Troilus cannot put his disquiet about the dream out of his mind (V, 1443–4) and, to confirm his suspicions, he takes his dream to his sister, the prophetess Cassandra, who reads the dream as indeed revealing Criseyde's untruth: 'This ilke boor bitokneth Diomede . . . And thy lady, wherso she be, ywis, / This Diomede hire herte hath, and she his. / Wep if thow wolt, or lef*, for out of doute, / This Diomede is inne, and thow art oute' (*leave it: V, 1513, 1516–19). Cassandra's reading is proved right by the action of the poem. Still, Pandarus' insistence on the difficulty of dream interpretation, the possibility that even a true dream might be read in two or more very different, even contradictory, ways, is not to be simply dismissed. (Book V of *Troilus and Criseyde* emphasizes, in various ways, problems of interpretation, and the depiction of dreaming certainly contributes to this emphasis.) It is also not wrong to see Troilus' dreams (as does Pandarus early on) as reflecting Troilus' strongly disturbed psychological state. Can dreams belong simultaneously to the Macrobian categories of *insomnium* and *somnium*; can they be both reflections of personal anxiety and allegorically true and predictive? The dreams of *Troilus and Criseyde* certainly suggest that they can.

Chaucer's Dream Visions

One of Chaucer's fullest engagements with the details of medieval dream theory occurs in the *House of Fame*, which begins with a lengthy consideration of the causes of dreams. The narrator here notes that some dreams are reliably predictive, others not: 'th'effect folweth of somme, / And of somme hit shal never come' (5–6). He focuses extensive attention on dreams that are somatically or psychologically produced:

> As yf folkys complexions
> Make hem dreme of reflexions*,   *reflections (of waking events
> Or ellys thus, as other sayn,   or of humoral complexions)
> For to gret feblenesse of her brayn,
> By abstinence or by seknesse,
> Prison-stewe* or gret distresse,   *prison-cell

Or ellys by disordynaunce*   *disordering
Of naturel acustumaunce*,   *custom
That som man is to curious
In studye, or melancolyous,
Or thus so inly ful of drede
That no man may hym bote bede*;   *offer a remedy
Or elles that devocion
Of somme, and contemplacion
Causeth suche dremes ofte;
Or that the cruel lyf unsofte
Which these ilke lovers leden
That hopen over-muche or dreden,
That purely her impressions*   *sensations, emotions
Causeth hem avisions.
                                        (21–40)

But he also suggests that dreams might come from beyond the self: 'Or yf that spirites have the myght / To make folk to dreme a-nyght' (41–2), a statement that leaves open the possibility of evil as well as good spirits influencing the dream. The narrator suggests that the 'parfit' nature of the human 'soule' might make it susceptible to fore-knowledge (43–8), but he also notes that predictive dreams may operate indirectly, 'be figures' (48), and that the body might interfere with the soul's ability to see clearly what is being revealed: 'But that oure flessh ne hath no myght / To understonde hyt aryght, / For hyt is warned to derkly' (49–51). The narrator's discussion uses various Middle English terms to refer, it seems, to different types of dream – 'avision', 'revelacion', 'drem', 'sweven', 'fantome', 'oracles' (7–11) – and critics have tried to line Chaucer's different terms up with, for instance, Macrobius' dream schema. Notably, however, Chaucer presents this list of dream terms without definitions, separate from the more detailed cataloguing of the different sorts of dream that follow; in that more detailed discussion too, he uses a term like 'avision' to refer to dreams that seem to correspond to *both* the Macrobian *insomnium* (40) and the *visio* or *somnium* (depending upon how we read 'avisions' and 'figures' in 48 – as parallel terms, or as contrasting ones). Rather than present a systematizing treatment of dreaming parallel to Macrobius or Gregory or Augustine, then, Chaucer in the *House of Fame* evokes the complexity of medieval dream theory but in an unsystematic, indeed perhaps deliberately confusing, manner. The dreamer-narrator of the *House*, faced by the myriad possibilities about dreams, their causes and their meaning, in fact throws up his hands in dismay, beginning and ending his discussion of dreaming with a prayer: 'God turne us every drem to goode!' (1); 'But oonly that the holy roode, / Turne us every drem to goode!' (57–8). Faced by the difficulty of deciding what kind of dream he himself has experienced, or what precisely that dream might mean, if anything, the dreamer turns to God to ask that the dream at least have a good outcome. (This kind of gesture is one we also find elsewhere in Chaucer's writing: in 'The Nun's Priest's Tale', for instance, Chauntecleer prays, 'Now God . . . my swevene recche* aright*' [*interpret favourably: VII, 2896].)

Given Chaucer's demonstrable knowledge of dream theory, one strong critical impulse has been to assign his dream visions to one definite category or another (Macrobian *insomnium* or *oraculum* or *somnium*). The tendency in the twentieth century has been especially to privilege psychological readings: after all, the dream visions are first-person narratives, and hence susceptible to autobiographical interpretation. In their frames, the dream poems often focus attention on the dreamer and a certain psychological disturbance he experiences: in the *Book of the Duchess*, his sleeplessness; in the *House of Fame*, his 'wonder' (2) at the dream he has experienced; in the *Parliament of Fowls*, his 'astonyed' 'felynge' about love (4–5) and his enigmatic statement, 'For bothe I hadde thyng which that I nolde, / And ek I ne hadde that thyng that I wolde' (90–1); in the *Prologue to the Legend of Good Women*, his devotion to books and, in springtime, to his beloved daisy. But the dream visions are also susceptible to readings that would see the dream taking the dreamer outside himself, to a realm that transcends his individual worries or obsessions: the *Book of the Duchess* leads the dreamer into an encounter with a social superior whom he engages in philosophical discussion; in the *House of Fame*, the dreamer is carried into the heavens by a talkative and knowledgeable eagle and brought to the house of the goddess Fame; in the *Parliament of Fowls* he is, as we have seen, guided at first by the oracular figure of the 'Dream of Scipio', Affrican, and he gains a vision of the goddess Nature; in the *Prologue to the Legend of Good Women*, he also encounters a god (here, the god of Love) and his court. In each case, we can see the poems taking up not just personal or psychological concerns but also more philosophical, even theological, questions. (For one recent, extended reading of Chaucer's dream visions as serious philosophical texts, see Lynch 2000.)

As we see in the treatment of dream theory at the opening of the *House of Fame*, however, Chaucer works to confound the easy or simple

81

identification of his dream poems with a single kind of dream. Here he learns from earlier poems in the dream-vision genre, especially Guillaume de Lorris' and Jean de Meun's immensely popular, thirteenth-century *Romance of the Rose*. That poem opens (to cite the Middle English translation that may be Chaucer's own) by evoking the duality of false and true dreams:

> Many men sayn that in sweveninges
> Ther nys but fables and lesynges*;   *lies
> But men may some sweven[es] sen
> Which hardely that false ne ben,
> But afterward ben apparaunt*.   *come to pass
>
> (1–5)

It goes on to pursue, in allegorical detail, a dream that shows how a lover identified with the poem's first-person narrator falls in love and pursues his beloved (the rose). In this it seems especially concerned with the psychological and embodied individual. But much other, more philosophical, even metaphysical material reflecting on human life and the nature of the cosmos is incorporated into the poem, especially in the part composed by Jean de Meun, where such personifications as Nature and Reason present lengthy, learned discourses.

In the tradition of the *Romance of the Rose*, Chaucer tends to use the dream-vision form to open up multiple possibilities rather than to focus our attention on a single unified action. Each of the dream poems is formally complex, incorporating varied elements that critics have often struggled to see as unified. And perhaps, after all, diversity rather than unity is the main structural principle of the Chaucerian dream vision. The *Book of the Duchess* composes a triptych, focused first on the narrator's sleeplessness (1–44), then on the reading he undertakes of the Ovidian story of Seys and Alcyone, which enables him to fall asleep and dream (45–290), and finally – and most extensively – on the dream proper. That dream is itself various: the dreamer awakes into his dream in a richly decorated bedchamber (291–343), joins the hunt for a hart (344–86), follows a whelp into a wondrous wood (387–444), discovers a Man in Black lamenting (444–513) and engages in a dialogue with that man, in which the course of the man's love affair with the Lady White is elaborated and explored (514–1310). The poem ends by circling back briefly to its earlier concerns. When the conversation between the dreamer and the Man in Black ends, we are reminded of the hunt, which is described only now as concluding (1311–23; these lines provide the basis for the widely credited idea that the poem is, at least seen from one angle, an elegy for Blanche, the Duchess of Lancaster); the poem also invokes again the narrator's sleeplessness and the reading that allowed him to fall asleep (1324–9). Having awakened, the dreamer-narrator promises to 'put this sweven in ryme' (1332).

The *House of Fame* is even more structurally elaborate, typically divided by editors into three books, each with its own 'proem' or 'invocation' (1–110, 509–28, 1091–1109). Book I, after focusing our attention, as we have seen, on dream theory and then invoking the 'god of slep' (69), concerns a 'temple ymad of glas' (120) that belongs to Venus (130) and that depicts on its walls the story of Eneas and Dido (140–467). When the narrator leaves the temple, he finds himself in 'a large feld' (482) 'of sond' (486) and then sees an enormous eagle approaching. In Book II that eagle picks up the terrified dreamer and carries him into the heavens, telling him he is being carried to a place, the 'Hous of Fame' (663), where he can gather 'tydynges' (644) to use in his writing. Along the way, the eagle instructs the dreamer on the nature of sound, the stuff that makes up the realm of fame (706–883); he also shows him the earth above which they soar (888–924) and the heavens into which they ascend (925–1017). Book III has the dreamer inspecting the palace of the goddess Fame from the outside (1110–1340) and inside (1341–1519). He then observes the goddess handing down decisions to petitioners, granting or denying fame in a wholly capricious manner (1520–1867). Dissatisfied with what he witnesses, the dreamer then enters another house, this one less grand than Fame's palace; 'ful of tydynges' (1957), and often referred to by critics as the House of Rumour, this is where the raw material of fame takes shape. Apparently incomplete, the poem ends abruptly with the vision, never developed, of 'a man', who 'semed for to be / A man of gret auctorite' (2155–8).

Next to the sprawling structure of the *House of Fame*, the *Parliament of Fowls*, composed in rhyme royal stanzas, seems positively lapidary. But, again, its material is varied and not necessarily unified. The dream is framed by a reflection on love (1–14) and then a focusing on the narrator's reading, particularly of the 'Dream of Scipio' (15–84). The narrator falls asleep in anxious thought and dreams of Affrican, who promises him a reward for the 'labour' (112) of reading 'Macrobye' (111). Affrican brings him to a garden of love (its Dantean gates suggest an ambivalent realm of 'hertes hele and dedly woundes cure' [128] on the one hand and 'mortal strokes of the speer' [135] on the other), telling the dreamer that he will here 'se' love even if he cannot participate in it (163). On entering, the dreamer encounters first a fertile garden (169–210), in which Cupid and such love personifications as 'Lust', 'Beute', 'Delyt' and 'Meede' stand (211–29). He then encounters a 'temple of bras' (231) that, like the temple of glass in the *House of Fame*, foregrounds Venus and love (230–94). Returning to the garden landscape, the dreamer finally finds the 'noble goddesse Nature' (303) presiding over a parliament of birds intended to provide each bird the opportunity to find his or her mate but stalled by the contest among three noble 'tersel egles' (393) for the hand of a 'formel egle' (373). The debate that ensues, involving not just the eagles themselves but representatives of all the social 'classes' of birds, ends in a stalemate when the 'formel' insists on a year's respite before she chooses a lover. As they go off to mate, the birds sing a Valentine's Day song that awakens the narrator; he ends the poem determined to read 'othere bokes' (695), hoping that these will stimulate further dreams that will enable him 'to fare / The bet' (698–9).

The latest of the dream visions, the *Prologue to the Legend of Good Women*, which exists in two authorial versions (F and G; here I will treat only the earlier version, F) is the simplest structurally, focused more fully on a single scene – the dreamer-narrator's encounter with the god of Love and his 'queen' Alceste. Still, the poem is various in its themes: the dream narrative is framed by the narrator's reflections on how we human beings might know things – like 'hevene' or 'helle' (2) – inaccessible to our experience, and he concludes that one way is through 'olde bokes' (25), which provide 'of remembraunce the keye' (26). The narrator confesses his own love of books, but also his 'affeccioun' (44) for the daisy, which is depicted, in a comic but also persuasively romantic paean, as the narrator's beloved – 'She is the clernesse and the verray lyght / That in this derke world me wynt* and ledeth' (*directs: 84–5). Out in the fields, in devotion to his lady-flower, the narrator describes the earth's transformation by spring. Going to bed outside, 'in a litel herber that I have' (203), the narrator falls asleep and dreams that he sees 'The god of Love, and in his hand a quene' (213) who seems a human representation of the daisy, and is later identified with the mythological wife, Alceste (511, 518). The narrator observes the court of Love celebrating and honouring 'the dayesie' (293), but when he moves to join in that celebration, the god of love confronts him, identifying him as a traitor to love, an author who has – in 'the Romaunce of the Rose' (329) and his poem 'of Creseyde' (332) – attacked Love and his 'folk' (322). Alceste defends him, but when the dreamer himself tries to refute the god of Love's interpretation of his poetry, she rebukes him for contradicting Love (475–7). Alceste assigns the dreamer-narrator a poetic penance: he must write 'a glorious legende / Of goode wymmen' (483–4) to make up for his earlier writing. That 'legende' is, of course, the *Legend of Good Women* itself. The last action of the *Prologue* focuses on the identity of Alceste (498–551). Without marking an end to the dream, the narrator concludes the *Prologue* by moving on to the 'making' of his 'Legende' (579).

Such complex poems admit complex and even contradictory readings, and the centrality of dream experience in each enables their exploration of the full range of experience to which dreams might be connected, from the somatic and psychological to the transcendent, even the divine. Thus, one strand in the *Book of the Duchess* emphasizes somatic phenomena: sleeplessness and melancholia in the dreamer; Alcyone's disturbed physical and psychological state; the physiological state of the Man in Black when the dreamer first comes upon him. All of this might suggest that the dream Chaucer here presents indicates humoral imbalance – excess melancholy facilitating, after all, dreams 'in shades of black' – and readings that emphasize embodiment, and in recent criticism especially questions about gender and sexuality, are enabled by conceiving the dream in this way. The somatic is clearly connected intimately to the psychological, melancholy being simultaneously physiological and psychological, and that the dream explores the psychology of love becomes explicit in the dialogue between the dreamer and the Man in Black. The hart-hunting, more implicitly, evokes love allegory: the *Book of the Duchess* exploits puns on 'hart' and 'heart', with the heart itself standing ambiguously for the beloved lady and for the wounded heart of the lover (see the medicalized description of the Man in Black, especially 491). But the *Book of the Duchess* and its dream also address more profound philosophical questions about the nature and value of life, and the relation between life (and love) and death. Indeed, one common line of critical reading emphasizes the poem's evocation of Boethius' *Consolation of Philosophy*, a serious (and deeply influential) late antique argument for how human beings must ultimately detach themselves from the uncertain things of the world, those things governed by Fortune.

The *House of Fame* also leaves itself open to such a wide range of reading. It is, of course, a dream of ascent into the heavens, and it explicitly evokes Boethius (972), as well as biblical (588) and classical (589, 915–24) stories of revelation; as they fly to the house of Fame,

85

the eagle offers the dreamer a cosmic education like that Scipio receives from Affrican. But the eagle is a comic figure, and the *House of Fame* – for all its echoes of such serious philosophical and theological texts as Dante's *Divine Comedy* – never moves wholly into the realm of the divine. In addition, even as the dreamer is carried into the sky, the poem emphasizes not spirit or soul but embodiment; as the eagle notes, the dreamer is himself 'noyous for to carye' (574). And the dreamer turns away from the heavens just at the point when he is promised the fullest vision of its secrets (1011–17). While the realm of fame has certain transcendent qualities and a goddess of its own, it is a place that serves to explain not some divine, unchangeable quality of the cosmos but instead the functioning of a human realm of unpredictability. The tidings with which the Chaucerian narrator is confronted at the end of the poem are themselves embodied figures rather than abstract claims; these tidings are moreover both true and false, and they enter the world in such a way that it is not easy – and perhaps even impossible – to disentangle their truth from their falsehood.

The *Parliament of Fowls* is clearly a dream poem concerned with love and, as we have seen, it presents at least the strong suggestion that its dream is psychologically determined. But it is also a dream presided over (at least at first) by the serious figure of Affrican, the figure who also presides over Scipio's serious political and cosmic vision. If we move here through a temple and a garden strongly evocative of love allegory, we end up in a political parliament. Though the explicit subject of the parliamentary debate is still love – which of the 'tersel' eagles deserves the love of the 'formel' – the parliament also introduces into the poem a different set of problems: the question of different estates or classes in society, how they might best be ruled, how various political voices might be heard without society devolving into chaos. (As Marion Turner notes, several critics have suggested that this avian parliament echoes and comments upon actual English parliaments such as the 'Good Parliament' of 1376.) And the parliament is presided over by Nature, which suggests that these specifically human, political problems are intertwined, in some significant way, with questions about cosmic governance: Nature is, in a continuous poetic and philosophical tradition going back to the twelfth century (and specifically to the writer Alain de Lille), the vicar of God's rule, a figure of cosmic order. If love in the *Parliament* sometimes clearly refers to a specific romantic relationship between two human beings, it also evokes a force of cohesion that binds together both human social orders and a divinely ordained cosmos.

Finally, the *Prologue to the Legend of Good Women* presents an encounter with a god, but of course this is the god of Love, the god of an embodied, psychological realm. The poem seems most concerned with whether the narrator, a figure of Chaucer the poet who has translated the *Romance of the Rose* and written *Troilus and Criseyde* – here understood (by the god of Love) as works that attack women, and hence love – is a faithful servant of love, and, if he is not, what his proper punishment or penance might be. The poem opens, however, with a reflection on how *any* truth beyond direct human corporeal experience might be known, and one might see the specific question at its centre, of whether 'Chaucer' has been a faithful poet of love, as entailing a series of more abstract, serious, philosophical questions (and even eventually theological questions, in so far as the poem's opening suggests that the question of human knowledge extends to realms beyond living experience like 'hevene' and 'helle').

Any given reading of Chaucer's dream poems is likely to emphasize one theme or concern over another, to argue that the poems are about embodied experience, gender and sexuality, 'courtly' love, human politics, specific incidents in late fourteenth-century England, philosophical consolation or an orderly cosmos. But what seems to hold all the dream visions together is their mixing, their easy movement back and forth between the individual human body and the cosmos, philosophy and physiology, 'courtly' and divine love. All are hence susceptible to a wide range of – more or less embodied, more or less transcendental – readings. Like the medieval dream itself, Chaucer's dream visions – in their variety, their indeterminate status as true or false, as somatic, psychological or externally motivated, as directly revelatory or 'darkly' figural – focus attention on *problems* of interpretation and multiple interpretive possibilities. Indeed, we might read each of the dream visions as an *ars poetica*, an attempt to work out, beginning early in Chaucer's career, problems concerning what it means to be a poet, negotiating the presentation of certain truths via fictionality. And the dream visions also call our attention to what it means to be a reader, how one might approach something like a poem (or, in fact, a dream) that is neither absolutely true nor necessarily false, that might be read in several (contradictory or complementary) ways. Wherever we settle in our readings of Chaucer's dream poems, difficult questions remain. The poems insist on unsettling our interpretations, on opening up new questions, new possible spaces for reading. As at the end of the *Parliament of Fowls*, they return us to the problems of interpretation and the process of reading itself:

> And with the shoutyng, whan the song was do
> That foules maden at here flyght awey,
> I wok, and othere bokes tok me to,
> To reede upon, and yit I rede alwey.
> I hope, ywis, to rede so som day
> That I shal mete som thing for to fare
> The bet, and thus to rede I nyl nat spare.
>
> (693–9)

See also chapter 3, BOOKS AND AUTHORITY; chapter 5, COURTLY WRITING.

References and Further Reading

Alain de Lille (1980). *The Plaint of Nature*, trans. James J. Sheridan. Toronto: Pontifical Institute of Mediaeval Studies.

Augustine (1982). *The Literal Meaning of Genesis* [*De Genesi ad litteram*], trans. John Hammond Taylor. 2 vols. New York and Ramsey, NJ: Newman Press.

Boitani, Piero (1984). *Chaucer and the Imaginary World of Fame*. Cambridge: D. S. Brewer.

Brown, Peter (ed.) (1999). *Reading Dreams: The Interpretation of Dreams from Chaucer to Shakespeare*. Oxford: Oxford University Press.

De spiritu et anima. Treatise on the Spirit and the Soul (1977), trans. Erasmo Leiva and Benedicta Ward. In Bernard McGinn (ed.). *Three Treatises on Man: A Cistercian Anthropology*. Kalamazoo, Mich.: Cistercian Publications, pp. 179–288.

Delany, Sheila (1994 [1972]). *Chaucer's House of Fame: The Poetics of Skeptical Fideism*. Gainesville: University Press of Florida.

Edwards, Robert R. (1989). *The Dream of Chaucer: Representation and Reflection in the Early Narratives*. Durham, NC: Duke University Press.

Fradenburg, L. O. Aranye (2002). *Sacrifice Your Love: Psychoanalysis, Historicism, Chaucer*. Minnesota and London: University of Minnesota Press.

Freud, Sigmund (1965). *The Interpretation of Dreams*, trans. and ed. James Strachey. New York: Avon Books.

Gregory the Great (1959). *Dialogues*, trans. Odo John Zimmerman. New York: Fathers of the Church.

Gregory the Great (1844–50). *Morals on the Book of Job*. 3 vols. Oxford: John Henry Parker; and London: F. and J. Rivington.

Guillaume de Lorris and Jean de Meun (1971). *The Romance of the Rose*, trans. Charles Dahlberg. Princeton, NJ: Princeton University Press.

Kiser, Lisa J. (1983). *Telling Classical Tales: Chaucer and the Legend of Good Women*. Ithaca, NY: Cornell University Press.

Kruger, Steven F. (1992). *Dreaming in the Middle Ages*. Cambridge: Cambridge University Press.

Lynch, Kathryn L. (2000). *Chaucer's Philosophical Visions*. Woodbridge, Suffolk: D. S. Brewer.

Lynch, Kathryn L. (1988). *The High Medieval Dream Vision: Poetry, Philosophy, and Literary Form*. Stanford, Calif.: Stanford University Press.

Macrobius (1952). *Commentary on the Dream of Scipio*, trans. William Harris Stahl. New York: Columbia University Press.

Minnis, A. J., with V. J. Scattergood and J. J. Smith (1995). *Oxford Guides to Chaucer: The Shorter Poems*. Oxford and New York: Oxford University Press.

Percival, Florence (1998). *Chaucer's Legendary Good Women*. Cambridge and New York: Cambridge University Press.

Pratt, Robert A. (1977). 'Some Latin Sources of the Nonnes Preest on Dreams'. *Speculum* 52, 538–70.

Quinn, William A. (ed.) (1998). *Chaucer's Dream Visions and Shorter Poems*. New York: Garland.

Russell, J. Stephen (1988). *The English Dream Vision: Anatomy of a Form*. Columbus: Ohio State University Press.

Schibanoff, Susan (forthcoming). *Chaucer's Queer Poetics: Rereading the Dream Trio*. Toronto: University of Toronto Press.

Spearing, A. C. (1976). *Medieval Dream-Poetry*. Cambridge: Cambridge University Press.

Chapter Five

Courtly Writing

Barry Windeatt

I had lain in bed . . . thinking that the birds were singing Greek choruses and that King Edward [VII] was using the foulest possible language among Ozzie Dickinson's azaleas . . .

Virginia Woolf, 'Old Bloomsbury'

'The fine Courtier wil talke nothyng but Chaucer,' grumbles Thomas Wilson as late as 1553 in his *Arte of Rhetorique*, reflecting how the style, diction and themes of Chaucer's poems had long been accepted as quintessential models and exemplars of courtly writing in English, so educating the taste by which they were read. Fifteenth-century lovers – in literature and even in life – echoed the speeches, letters and complaints of lovers in Chaucer's poems and expressed themselves in a sub-Chaucerian idiom. By tradition, Chaucer's poems have been read as the courtly products of a courtly culture, not least because Chaucer's own association with the English royal court is suggested by extant documents. As the son of a well-to-do vintner with court connections, Chaucer spent his youth as a page in the household of the Countess of Ulster, wife of Edward III's son Lionel. His adult career was passed in what might now be called civil service posts but which were still salaried through the extended royal household as the seat of governance. His wife's sister was the long-term mistress and eventually the third wife of Edward III's powerful fourth son, John of Gaunt, whose son Henry Bolingbroke – by his first wife Blanche, Duchess of

Lancaster – usurped the throne in 1399. In 1395/6 Henry presented Chaucer with a scarlet gown with fur trimmings, and Chaucer's last known work is a little begging poem, 'The Complaint to his Purse', asking the new King Henry for money. Unlike the Prioress in the 'General Prologue' Chaucer evidently had no need 'to countrefete cheere / Of court' (I, 139–40), yet there may be a trace of Chaucer's sense of his place in society when the Middle English *Romaunt of the Rose* translates a line from the *Roman de la Rose* ('And whoso wole have freendis heere, / He may not holde his tresour deere', 1179–80), but omits the immediately following French line ('But acquire friends by making handsome gifts'), for in the surviving records Chaucer throughout his life is the recipient of gifts from those in a position to bestow them. When 'The Knight's Tale' bothers to note that Arcite, while living as a squire at Theseus' court, also secretly draws his own inherited income from home (I, 1442–3), this quietly insists that, despite appearances, the knightly hero is not actually a court functionary dependent on the Duke's gold. Continually in debt as records show Chaucer was throughout life, his poems are alert to the dependent and petitionary circumstances of many within courts and of courtly writers.

In 'The Knight's Tale' cameo of how Arcite gets on in life at court Chaucer was perhaps – however indirectly – writing of himself, for Arcite's courtly career parallels something of Chaucer's recorded early career and subsequent promotions on merit within the royal household. Chaucer writes more inwardly of the hierarchical structure of office and advancement at court than his source in Boccaccio's *Teseida* (4, 59) where Arcita, returning incognito from banishment, serves Teseo so assiduously as to become his most cherished servant. Instead, Chaucer's Arcite is first employed by one of Emelye's household servants ('He fil in office with a chamberleyn,' 1418) and for one or two years 'he was in this servyse, / Page of the chambre of Emelye the brighte' (1426–7). From this position he is promoted by the Duke, 'That of his chambre he made hym a squier' (1440), because, despite Arcite's uncertain origins, his qualities win recognition 'thurghout al the court', including those who recommend his advancement to the Duke (1431–2). Chaucer might have been writing of himself when Theseus' courtiers feel it would be a kindness in the head of the court to promote Arcite and 'enhauncen his degree, / And putten hym in worshipful servyse, / Ther as he myghte his vertu excercise' (1434–6).

Yet although Chaucer's career saw promotion 'Ther as he myghte his vertu excercise', there remains scant internal evidence from his work as to how far Chaucer was ever a court poet, in the sense of writing at the behest of courtly patrons to fulfil commissions or to seek favour. Apart from his short poem 'Lak of Stedfastness' and his 'Tale of Melibee', he writes little in the tradition of offering advice to princes. Nor is Chaucer a court poet who directly addresses the perilous politics of the court as a career, summed up by Arcite: 'And therfore, at the kynges court, my brother, / Ech man for hymself, ther is noon oother' (1181–2). Chaucer's discretion implies a certain artistic independence from the courtly world even as it exemplifies one aspect of the courtly values that many of his poems explore. Chaucer's poems contain no prefaces presenting his works to grand patrons; manuscripts of his poems contain no pictures recording such presentations. An early fifteenth-century frontispiece in a manuscript of *Troilus and Criseyde* (see p. 12) – much reproduced and once confidently captioned 'Chaucer reading to the Court of Richard II' – is currently taken instead to visualize the refined courtly audience that the poem implies as its ideal readership, and this points a helpful way forward in understanding the imaginative fiction-alization of courtliness in Chaucer's poems more largely. For although how far the historical Chaucer was in or of the royal court can now be little more than inference, his poems bespeak a courtly civilization of the heart – even as they may deploy its idiolect to critique it.

Possibly reflecting his oblique relationship to the courts of his day, Chaucer's poems tend not to locate their narratives at the heart of courts, even though the poems address the ethos and practice of courtly conduct. In *Troilus* the action takes place in a city which is the seat of a royal court and involves people who move in that court, as when Chaucer's Pandarus (but not Boccaccio's) can prompt his friend Prince Deiphebus to host a dinner party, where Criseyde mixes easily with at least two princes of the blood and the consort of another. The charac-ters' emotional challenges are those of courtly people, but the narrative proceeds on the sidelines of the court and off-stage to it: Chaucer's Pandarus is reported (as if it is routine) to have had to spend a day with the King (5, 284–6; not in *Filostrato*), but this is to explain his enforced temporary absence from where the poem's real action is. This sense of a courtly centre and fount of values at a certain remove is a recurrent feature of the four courtly dream visions that Chaucer wrote in every decade of his creative life: the *Book of the Duchess* (after 1368), the *House of Fame* (later 1370s), the *Parliament of Fowls* (early 1380s) and the *Prologue to the Legend of Good Women* (later 1380s; revised 1390s).

In 'The Squire's Tale' is one of Chaucer's few extended depictions of the rituals of court life: the king crowned and enthroned in state, sumptuous feasting and ceremonious etiquette, along with marvellous minstrelsy and fashionable dancing in tapestried chambers. But here too are 'subtil lookyng and dissymulynges* / For drede of jalouse mennes aperceyvynges*' (*dissimulations, *perceptions: V, 285–6). Here is drunken courtiers' over-indulgence that produces meaningless dreams not worth relating (357–9). However, the gift of the mirror inspires a prophetic dream in the virtuous heroine Canacee, 'in hire sleep, right for impressioun / Of hire mirour, she hadde a visioun' (371–2), and awakening for an early-morning walk in a park, she overhears a female falcon's eloquent complaint recollecting her court-ship and betrayal by her faithless lover. When Canacee makes a sym-bolically ornamented pen for the bird, covered with blue velvet ('In signe of trouthe that is in wommen sene', 645), it is painted on the outside with various faithless male birds to represent how the uncourtly is literally turned out, just as more largely form, space and decoration encode significant arguments within courtly writing. Linked here with life at court are key motifs to which Chaucer's dream poems recur: the dreamer, set apart by a reflective autonomy, experiences strange encounters in exclusive enclosures, often on the sidelines of the courtly world but commenting upon it. One signal difference, however, is that in the Squire's romance Canacee's magic ring allows her to understand bird language, and so she can experience waking what others might dream. In Chaucer's dream visions the enabling magic is the dream (of undoubted significance but doubtful interpretation), which trans-ports us to where birds speak English, the poet eavesdrops on cele-brities and – through dreaming and the subsequent poem that inscribes it – reflects on his own creative process as an author in imaginative interaction with his sources and traditions.

The distinctive identity of the dream poems as courtly writing derives in part from their bold negotiations with their sources in continental courtly texts, and these lie behind their innovative struc-tures and experimental narrative technique. It is as courtly vision that Chaucer is much influenced by the *Roman de la Rose*, the seminal medi-eval European dream vision which the *Legend* Prologue records him as having translated into English, probably early in his career since Chaucer's sense of the *Roman* is so pervasively absorbed into his work. The *Roman* is a courtly vision in which the centre is uniquely else-where: the dream vision of a young man's love where the lady does not appear as such. Instead, she is experienced allegorically by the Lover through her aspects: her Fair Welcome, her 'Daunger' or disdainful reserve, her barely ambiguous Rose, eventually possessed by the Lover, all within the allegorical setting of a paradisal garden where courtly figures engage in an elegant 'carole' or round dance with singing, an apt emblem of participation in love. Here is a dream fantasy not unlike some Salvador Dali painting, where the poet dreamer lives his courtly love life and experiences his girlfriend only surreally disassembled into fetishized parts. All that is courtly inhabits the privileged interiority of the enclosed garden, the 'locus amoenus' (delightful place) of tradition, with its temperate climate of perpetual spring, its lush verdure, trees and flowers, sparkling streams and rapturous birdsong. Depicted on the garden's outside wall, turned out from courtly experience, are Hatred, Villainy, Avarice, Envy, Sorrow, Old Age, Poverty and what Chaucer translates as 'Pope-Holy', meaning sanctimonious hypocrisy and religiosity. Precisely because Chaucer honours the *Roman* with his close English verse translation (probably only the surviving Fragment A is his) tiny divergences intrigue more: the *Romaunt* adds that Love's bow is 'diapred' (934), which can aptly emblematize the decorated surfaces, the repeat patterns of figures and geometrical designs of Chaucer's dream poems. In translating, Chaucer also emphasizes the agency of seeing in the dream narrator, so as to consolidate the dreaming I/eye as a kind of moving camera, in a way that looks forward to his own dream visions.

These four poems set themselves apart in Chaucer's writings as first-person narratives: the reported dream experience of a fictionalized persona of the poet constitutes the story. This foregrounds a kind of narrative continuum distinct from Chaucer's works where his imagination responds to a source text or a remembered analogue. Instead of Chaucer's plots and denouements about heroines and heroes, these fictions centred on versions of his dreaming self offer something open-ended: a process, an exploration. Although Chaucer knew a rich tradition of earlier dream visions, his dream poems never follow a single such source but are reconfigured selectively from a range of sources. As forms and fictions of self, these poems hence express distinctive concerns, and as the supposed reports of visionary experience they accord a role exceptional in Chaucer's writings to the implications of visualized setting. Chaucer emulates the dreamer persona in many earlier dream visions, yet he still makes something uniquely – learnedly, expressively, comically – his own, as befits poems so focused on inward experience and so defined by negotiations between the authority of tradition and the claims of individual imagination.

Chaucer's chief narrative models were the 'dits amoureux' of such fourteenth-century French poets as Guillaume de Machaut and Jean

Froissart. Highly sophisticated and poised, these are courtly narrative poems deploying framing devices, inset lyrics and a poet persona, in subtle explorations of the solaces and disquietudes of love for noble minds. Machaut's diffident poet persona makes a play of not always being in control of events – in his *Dit de la Fonteinne amoureuse* he declares himself more cowardly than a hare, and in his *Jugement dou Roy de Navarre* represents himself as comically distracted while engrossed in hunting hares – and this offered a flexible model for Chaucer's persona, whom Harry Bailey later twits, 'Thou lookest as thow woldest fynde an hare, / For evere upon the ground I se thee stare' (*Canterbury Tales* VII, 696–7). Professed modesty can be an enabling stratagem, deployed by both Machaut and Chaucer within a manifest technical accomplishment that belies any need for such modesty, as they both well knew. The writerly persona of the poet in Machaut and other French courtly writing lent Chaucer a model for his dreamer's tentative stance and subordinate station. For in poems often focused on judgement the author presents himself as unjudging: a more prestigious and decisive figure than the writer is cast as judge, and the poet is presented as a bookish character, deferential and unassertive. In his *Remede de Fortune* Machaut expressly pronounces 'He who does not compose from out of his own feelings ['de sentement'] counterfeits his work and his song' (407–8), and 'The Squire's Tale' declares 'He moste han knowen love and his servyse / And been a feestlych* man' in order to recount the life of love and courtliness which 'a dul man' cannot describe (*con-vivial: V, 278–87). Yet the poet of Chaucer's dream visions writes more as an introvert than a 'feestlych' man, and as a professed outsider to love who is dismissed for his dullness within his own fictions ('although that thow be dul', *Parliament of Fowls* 162). Chaucer's self-caricature in the *House of Fame* as an office-worker with no social life, who goes home from his 'rekenynges' (presumably his job as a Customs official from 1374) to evenings spent hunched over a book (647–60), is calculatedly not the image of a court poet on the inside of things. In the *Book of the Duchess* the dreamer seems to miss the point (unless it is the uncourtly modern reader who misreads the dreamer's courtliness); in the *House of Fame* he seems bewildered by disjunctions and turns of events; in the *Parliament of Fowls* he cannot follow thematic connections; and in the *Prologue to the Legend of Good Women*, ostensibly patronized and humiliated, he has to be excused as one who may not have understood the implications of his own writings, yet his position recalls the *Navarre* where Machaut, although reproached for earlier work, declines to withdraw anything he has written.

The poem that the *Canterbury Tales* 'Retraction' entitles 'the book of the Duchesse' (X, 1086) is listed in both *Legend* Prologues as 'the Deth of Blaunche the Duchesse' (G 406), while the Man of Law's Introduction recalls that 'In youthe he made of Ceys and Alcione' (II, 57). This dream poem in which the narrator reads Ovid's tale of Ceyx and Alcyone and then dreams he meets a black-dressed nobleman mourning his lost lady, fair 'White' – and which in concluding puns on the titles of John of Gaunt, Duke of Lancaster and Earl of Richmond – was apparently written sometime after the death of the Duke's wife Blanche in 1368, possibly for an annual commemoration of her death and perhaps before John's remarriage in 1371. The poem's structure derives from the way Chaucer's imagination seizes on expressive episodes from at least four French *dits amoureux*. The opening with the narrator's insomnia is from Froissart's *Paradys d'Amours*; the story of Ceyx and Alcyone, although ultimately from Ovid's *Metamorphoses* (11, 410–749), has been prompted by its occurrence in Machaut's *Fonteinne amoureuse*; the dreamer's overhearing a lover's lamentation is also from the *Fonteinne*; the dreamer's listening to a grieving lover's retrospect on a past courtship and on the beloved's excellent qualities rewrites both text and context from Machaut's *Jugement dou Roy de Behaingne*; the Man in Black's reproaches of Fortune echo some phraseology from Machaut's *Remede de Fortune*.

Yet even to list the component parts from which Chaucer has assembled the *Book* is to be reminded how boldly he reconfigures these borrowed fragments into his own design to make them new. Chaucer retains only the narrator's insomnia from the opening of Froissart's *Paradys*, but replaces its attribution to love with a more mysterious bafflement ('For sorwful ymagynacioun / Ys alway hooly in my mynde', 14–15) and a conviction that excessive sorrow goes against nature. In the *Fonteinne* the lover (a projection of Machaut's patron, the Duke of Berry) thinks he must induce Morpheus to send a semblance of him to his lady – just as Ceyx was sent to Alcyone – so that he may declare his love to her. But in the *Book* it is the dreamer who picks up as bedtime reading this tale about coming to acknowledge a spouse's death, and Chaucer leaves any parallels with Ovid's story to emerge only when his whole poem can be seen complete. In the *Fonteinne* the poet persona overhears (and simultaneously transcribes) the princely lover lamenting his imminent separation from his lady. Later, the poet can produce this version instantly with a flourish when the prince commissions him to pen a 'lay or complaint' for him, while praise for its marvellous rhyme scheme complements both himself as poet and the prince who supposedly voiced it. Intriguing parallels suggest themselves in the *Book* with the dreamer's unseen overhearing of the Man in Black who 'made of rym ten vers or twelve / Of a compleynte to hymselve – . . . / He sayd a lay, a maner song' (463–72) and with the care with which this music-less lyric is then inset into the poem's text ('for ful wel I kan / Reherse hyt', 473–4). Yet in the *Book* the overhearing of the unidentified man's lyric of complaint is both brief and remains opaque, whereas in *Fonteinne* the princely lover's identity is revealed from the start, so that the circumstances of his overheard complaint are clear. Also overheard by the poet, in *Behaingne*, is a most courtly disputation as to whose suffering is greater: a lady whose lover has died or a knight who has been jilted. Numerous phrases from the French knight's recollections of the lady he courted and lost find an echo in the Man in Black's recollection of his lady, which thus fuses the rhetoric of courtly praise and of idealized memories of courtship with an elegiac retrospect, explicit in Machaut but mysteriously implicit in the *Book*.

In the manner of a film editor, Chaucer shapes what each reader experiences of these often diffuse sources in the mind's eye, determining pace, emphasis and connectivity by means of cuts, joins and splicings, effecting transitions and juxtapositions, and interplay between narrative and visualization through various modes of shot. Thus, Chaucer deploys the Ceyx and Alcyone episode prominently as a thematic prelude, making it more instrumental than in *Fonteinne* and rewriting its implication from Ovid. The drowned king's ghostly injunction to his widow in the *Book* to cease from irremediable sorrow is not in *Fonteinne* and positively reverses Ovid's version, where the husband enjoins his wife not to let him go unlamented (11, 669–70). Only in the *Book* does Ceyx request his wife 'that ye / Bury my body' (206–7), which both squares with Chaucer's suppression of Ovid's metamorphosis of Ceyx and Alcyone into birds and prepares a parallel with the Man in Black's commemoration of White. It is in Chaucer's rewriting that the dead husband takes an affectionate farewell, praying that his wife's sorrow be alleviated and remarking on the brevity of happiness (209–11). Although his Alcyone soon dies of grief, Chaucer's emphasis on how she dreams her dead husband wishes her to move beyond mourning foreshadows the poem's implicit later counsel that the Man in Black should also transcend his own mourning. Only Chaucer's Alcyone explicitly prays Juno for a revelatory dream about her husband's fate, and the length of Chaucer's account of the visit to the cave of Morpheus (135–91), within his much shorter version of Ovid's narrative, foregrounds a curiosity with the process and mechanism of how what is seen in the unconscious comes about, even if all is presented with comic lightness. Two details of Chaucer's French courtly reading – the dreamer's prayer in *Paradys* to Morpheus and Juno for a cure for his insomnia, and the lover's plan in *Fonteinne* to bribe Morpheus with a feather bed – are fused so as to highlight the comic transitional moment when Chaucer's insomniac dreamer 'in my game' promises Morpheus not only a feather bed and pillows with fine bedclothes but also a hall painted in gold and hung with fine tapestries – and promptly falls asleep (238–75). There is a comparable coalescence of scattered sources in the *Book* when a puppy draws the dreamer after him through a forest to where the Man in Black sits. To effect this transition Chaucer superimposes two or three episodes from his sources: in *Behaingne* the lady's yapping little dog gives away the poet's hiding place although this allows him to introduce himself, but Chaucer's 'whelp' behaves more like the courtly lion in Machaut's *Dit dou Lyon* (325–31) who similarly 'joyned hys eres' (393) and guides the poet about, while in leading the poet to a significant setting the puppy assumes the role of the bird followed by the poet at the start of *Behaingne*. Both these moments represent key transitions in a narrative that develops its thematic unity through the implications of juxtaposition and association. From a chamber luxuriously storiated with stained glass on Trojan themes and wall-paintings from the *Roman de la Rose*, to the hunting party with 'th'emperour Octovyen', which he follows and falls behind, to the delightful forest where the Man in Black sits beneath a great oak, the narrator's dream-like progress conjoins in sequence a montage of archetypally courtly settings and pastimes which lead dreamer and reader to the poem's centre in the Man's long monologue.

In order to explain to the dreamer what he has lost, the Man in Black, with courtly indirection, narrates how he won his lady's love. His speech therefore assembles all the courtly rhetoric of courtship in idealizing feminine beauty and womanly virtue of character. In keeping with medieval tradition, his lady is recalled not through individualizing idiosyncrasy, for she excels in so far as she conforms to an archetypal ideal of loveliness and virtue – although the emphasis on moral character, even if conventional in its terms, reads like some more personal tribute to an individual's goodness, 'mesure' and spirit. The idiom used is much indebted to, and often translates, French courtly poetry, but probably not in the sense that Chaucer needed his Machaut open beside him as he wrote (even though nearly three-quarters of the poem's lines have some French parallel). The Man in Black draws from a shared idiolect of courtly discourse in which Chaucer had been schooled by French poetic models that he might remember intimately and often by heart. His courtly audiences were likely both to perceive his poem's homage to *Behaingne* and to realize how Chaucer's merging into one mourner of Machaut's two courtly competitors in sorrow leaves the Man in Black's grief uniquely uncontested. If his speech ignores his nine-year married life, this is because the courtship narrative and idiom can emblematize all their mutual love and understanding, just as the lover in *Fonteinne* wants his lady to know of his undeclared love even though the Duke of Berry was recently wedded to his love when the poem was written. But the Man in Black and his White in the poem both are and are not the historical John of Gaunt and Duchess Blanche. This poem does not serve as an obituary or funeral eulogy; it aims neither at biographical record nor religious consolation. With its graceful indirection and startling flippancy ('Of quenes lives, and of kinges, / And many other thinges smale', 58–9), the poem's courtly focus offers a more oblique commemoration and no 'Pope-Holy' consolations. The sheer uncertainty over whether or how the lady is 'lost' remains unresolved during the Man in Black's speech and so deepens the poignancy of the praise that makes her live again. But if an offer of condolence is to say much more than 'Be God, hyt ys routhe!' (1310) and venture some praise of the dead, one awkwardness can be that the person condoled with, almost by definition, will possess a greater knowledge of what is to be praised in the dead. This poem's courtly masterstroke of tact is to offer to someone bereaved a dream poem where a figure of himself utters the praise of his dead wife that only the bereaved man knows 'of sentement' and can voice so as to bring all the idiom of courtly idealization alive again with the urgent authority of a passionate sincerity.

Differently but no less reflective of the ambivalent position of the author, now somewhere between the court and a public servant's career, the *House of Fame* foregrounds poetry's interrelation with its sources of inspiration, juxtaposing within its series of books a striking montage of materials. Although some lines of *Fame* correspond closely to lines in other texts, most of its narrative derives from a bold reconfiguring of its sources of inspiration, recontextualizing key images and motifs within new structures, and so exemplifies the poem's preoccupation with how all and any transmission – describing, reporting – will necessarily interpose interpretation and hence distortion. A narrative in pursuit of 'tydynges' – a studiedly modest and secular form of revelation – *Fame* explores how nothing may be known independently of how it is reported.

In opening by linking the difficulties of interpreting dreams with the ambiguities of their nomenclature and categorization, the first proem presents a bewildering array of possibilities within a kind of anxious exuberance that aptly prefigures the flamboyant style and structural method of the poem to come. When the narrator then dreams he is 'withyn a temple ymad of glas', its busy Gothic surface (120–7), encrusted with pinnacled niches and ledges for figures and images (and hence, by implication, storiated with characters linked with love), is typical of *Fame*'s recurrent preoccupation with the plasticity of how memory formulates itself. In Book I the dreamer's description of the *Aeneid* as of a mural painted on the walls of Venus' temple includes matters that could scarcely be painted, because it models how the mind processes and recalls a narrative text through a fusion of reading, remembering and picturing in the mind's eye. The mismatch with the *Aeneid* in *Fame*'s hurried résumé of the whole compared with its disproportionate emphasis on the story of Dido, destroyed by shame and fame – an editing together of Virgil's and Ovid's contradictory accounts, in some modification of each – represents through its own form how in memory the original structure of a text is reconfigured in proportion to the interest some sections may provoke. Here, *Fame*'s Dido-centred account of the *Aeneid*, as modified by recollection of Ovid's *Heroides*, VII, suggests how a poet's remembering and rewriting is inseparable from the reshaping that constitutes a reinterpretation. Not that *Fame*'s narrator can ever stand back enough to understand what he observes. Leaving his solitary inspection of the temple of Venus, anxious at knowing neither who created it nor where he is, he craves some human companion and guide but finds himself only in a featureless sandy waste, representing the imaginative aridity of lacking anything to see or describe. From this, his ascent into the heavens in Book II, gripped in the talons of a garrulously didactic eagle, enacts Philosophy's notion that thought flies winged with her feathers (*Boece*, 4.m.1), in a burlesque reversal into some wordy science teacher of Dante's eagle of divine revelation from *Purgatorio* (IX, 28–30). Here is a mock apotheosis in which the apprehensive dreamer timidly declines the opportunity to verify through experience what books report of the heavens (which he is content to take on trust). Here is a sky journey like that of Troilus' soul, but experienced by an overweight mortal as in an in-flight lecture on the physics of sound waves, which demotes all communication to 'eyr ybroken' (765) – implicitly, just flatulence and gas. What will bring a closural perspective to *Troilus* serves here only as a transition, bringing the dreamer not to a cosmic overview but to the ambivalent houses of Fame and Rumour.

Near the close of Book II the eagle's account of how speeches assume the forms of their speakers when they ascend to the house of Fame – which seems a spoof on the general resurrection of the dead at Judgement Day – presages how Book III explores questions about media, report and representation through a startlingly plasticizing imagining of forms, shapes, structures and settings. Fame herself is a creature all ears, eyes and tongues, constantly morphing between smallness and skyscraping height: she sits enthroned in a palace with walls of beryl which 'made wel more than hit was / To semen every thing, ywis' (1290–1). Her castle is another Gothic structure, bristling with gargoyles and pinnacled niches filled not with sacred images but with minstrels and storytellers. Her court is crowded with signifiers and signified: harpists and other entertainers, conjurers and illusionists, as well as heralds bearing coats of arms from three continents. All this sits cheek by jowl in Fame's court with high culture: the nine Muses (first invoked in English in *Fame*) sing around her throne; her hall has caryatid pillars where the figures of poets – such as Statius, Virgil, Ovid, Lucan and Claudian – literally bear the various literary historical traditions (although the Trojan pillar includes a dispute about Homer's prejudice). Entertainment culture and high art share one space under Fame's roof: both deal in representation and report, and in Homer's alleged lies learned tradition is no less open to interpretation and distortion. Fame's cruelly arbitrary allocation and broadcasting of good or bad name reads like a burlesque of the Last Judgement and ends with the antics of a company of court fools with cap and bells, one of whom (sadly familiar to today's world) has sought infamy by destroying a landmark building (1839–45).

Juxtaposed with the architectural form and masonry of Fame's court, the dreamer – his search for 'tydynges' still unfulfilled – finds the labyrinthine house of Daedalus, itself an echo of Ovid's version of Fame's dwelling (*Metamorphoses*, 12, 39–63). A vast, interwoven network, full of creaks and whisperings, and constantly spinning round, it generates a hubbub that reverberates across Europe, from northern France to Rome (1927–30). Of no strength in itself, the structure is built to last as long as events drive news (1980–5). A humming factory of news as comment and hearsay, it is shaped less by its contents than its porousness: a network of openings for leaks. Here all report is compromised with misinformation in every act of transmission. In Rumour's spinning house there is a spin to all news. It is as if Chaucer's dreamer has had a prophetic dream of cyberspace and the information explosion: the aptly named worldwide web or internet, or 24-hour global news media that can ignore the Cave of Sleep (1956–7). Yet Rumour's emissions have to be named and their duration determined by Fame (2111–17), which implies the permeable interrelation of high and low media in all communication. Indeed, near the end of what Chaucer has written his dreamer is still searching 'Ther men of love-tydynges tolde' (2143) and it is during an undignified jostling for these that someone who 'semed for to be / A man of gret auctorite' appears, yet no more is written. A sense that the poem's montage might extend further, freed from imposing artificial conclusiveness by an unending search for tidings, challenges readers' attempts to perceive patterns of thematic or formal unity.

In dividing his *Fame* into books with proems Chaucer pioneers an unprecedented dignity for English vernacular writing, but although his *Parliament of Fowls* also has a tripartite structure and culminates in an assembly scene, its transitions and juxtapositions make their thematic effect without formal demarcation. By Chaucer's day it was traditional to liken the different estates of society to different species of birds: groupings of birds offered parallels with human groups and assemblies. The courtship displays and performances of birds, and therein the role of song, prompted many traditional analogies in courtly writing with mankind's devotion to love and love poetry. In the *Book*, the dream opens with the dreamer marvelling at how, in a chorus of birdsong, harmony derives from such diverse voices in unison (291–320). In the *Legend* Prologue, the dreamer sees birds singing 'layes of love' in honour of their mates, hailing Saint Valentine (in May) as they choose their partners, and then making love (F 130–52). To be alive to greet summer – to have survived winter and escaped the fowler's net – is cause for joy and song. In a passage removed in revision, unfaithful birds 'songen hire repentynge', but eventually win compassion 'Thurgh innocence and ruled Curtesye', abandoning all vice and malice in their resolve to love (153–70), unlike the faithless falcon lover in the 'Squire's Tale'. In that birds' lives might be construed as constituted entirely of loving and of singing for love, a bird debate offers apt closure in the *Parliament* to a poem that also equates human life with love and its art. Chaucer would know many courtly models for such assemblies – such as Jean de Condé's *Messe des Oisiaus* [*Mass of the Birds*] or Oton de Grandson's *Songe Saint Valentin* [*Dream of Saint Valentine*] – together with poems posing questions of love and debating choices of lover.

Chaucer's originality of design is the dreamer's progress en route to the Valentine's Day parliament, and its culminative thematic implications. His opening wonderment at love's paradoxes – key to what ensues – and his reading of the *Dream of Scipio,* which condemns this world but commends a love of the public good, are followed by his own dream (derived from Palamoun's prayer to Venus in Boccaccio's *Teseida*) of exploring a quasi-paradisal garden of love that includes a temple inhabited by Venus. Set between love as civic duty in the dreamer's tattered old book and the pairings in love presided over by Nature that eventuate in procreation, this central garden scene is profoundly ambivalent in itself and in its juxtaposition with what precedes and follows. Compared with Boccaccio's, Chaucer's garden is more lushly verdant, colourful and sparkling, in a plenitude unaffected by time or change where none grow sick nor old (207). Yet if Chaucer removes *Teseida*'s figure of Procuring or Pimping from the group of Cupid's companions, he also stresses that Cupid's arrows kill as well as wound (217). In rituals and petitions, women dance round Venus' temple in a continual observance, while inside men assiduously garland Priapus, and two young supplicants are seen frozen on their knees in perpetual petition to Venus (278–9); the goddess lies on a golden bed 'naked from the brest unto the hed'(269), while the rest of the temple is decorated with a fuller list than in *Teseida* of those undone by passion. In retrospect from the airy sweetness of Nature's glade, Venus' garden and the love within appears as double as the gate to it that Chaucer transplants from Dante's entrance to hell. Chaucer rewrites *Inferno*'s uniformly despairing inscription ('Abandon every hope . . .', 3, 1–9) so as to baffle the dreamer with simultaneous (inextricable?) promises of both a healing 'welle of grace / There grene and lusty May shal evere endure' and a fruitless, sterile entrapment for the slighted heart (123–40). Unlike *Teseida*'s observer, Chaucer's dreamer is unaccompanied and has no message to deliver to Venus, adding to the impression of a disengaged, even uncomprehending, witness. The reader is left to improve if he can on such a culminative understanding of love presented through equilibrium and juxtaposition over the poem as a sequence. The bookworm narrator turns back to his books, oblivious of the enlightenment available in the dream prompted by his earlier reading.

In Arcite's courtly career in 'The Knight's Tale' he is promoted because of his reputation not only for his actions but for his way with words ('his name is spronge, / Bothe of his dedes and his goode tonge,' 1437–8). Chaucer's courtly writings – like courts themselves – are sites for displaying and exercising the powers of courtly language in its functions of praise, plaint, petition and persuasion. Although modern interest in dream and the subconscious has fostered invaluable recent interpretations of Chaucer's dream visions, current lack of inwardness with courtly culture means less attention is paid to how all four poems culminate in episodes which crucially turn on the art of courtly speaking. Through praise or detraction courtly careers can be made or undone, and warnings against flatterers' influence at courts are an ancient topos ('The Nun's Priest's Tale', VII, 3325–6), which Alceste in the *Legend* Prologue pairs with a warning to Love against tattling slanderers 'in youre court' (G 328–9). For Dante (*Inferno*, 13, 64–5) Envy was court whore, but for Alceste (G 333–6) Envy is court laundress, when even dirty washing may bear witness. At court, where the lord's perception of truth may be obscured by flatterers 'That plesen yow wel moore, by my feith, / Than he that soothfastnesse* unto yow seith' (*truthfulness: 'The Nun's Priest's Tale', 3327–8), the role of right speaking is all the greater. Indeed, the English *Romaunt* claims, unlike the *Roman*, that flatterers at Wealth's court actually cause the deaths of many worthy men (1062–3). In 'The Merchant's Tale' Placebo – who has been 'a court-man al my lyf' (IV, 1492) – has never contradicted any lord he advised ('With that he seith, I holde it ferme and stable; / I seye the same, or elles thyng semblable*,' *similar: IV, 1499–1500); he represents the corruption by such flattering yes-men of courts as sites for the dispensation of justice. For it is by constituting themselves as a law court, with Queen Guinevere as chief justice, that the ladies of Arthur's court in the 'Wife of Bath's Tale' adjudicate the knight's success in his quest to resolve their testing question (resembling a *demande d'amour* or love puzzle) of what it is that women most desire. Here Guinevere's court is also the fount of justice to which the Loathly Lady resorts for enforcement of her just claim that the knight keep his word (III, 1048–9). As the supreme judge of all, Christ may be likened to a lord whose courtesy is his mercifulness ('The Parson's Tale', X, 245), and courts in this world should emulate Christ's example. In the *Romaunt* Dame Fraunchise fears to be over-severe (1228–9; not in French), and in his 'Tale of Melibee', one of Chaucer's infrequent additions to his French source serves to underline that a lord's courtesy, manifested through compassionate judgements, wins obedience as its reward:

> And therfore, if ye wole that men do yow obeisance*, ye moste deemen
> moore curteisly; / *this is to seyn, ye moste yeven* moore esy sentences and*

juggementz. / For it is writen that 'he that moost curteisly comandeth, to hym men moost obeyen'. (*obedience, *give; Chaucer's addition in italics: VII, 1855–7)

Key sequences in Chaucer's courtly dream visions are structured around scenes of petition, arraignment and arbitration, in which courtly speech is deployed in supplication to those possessed of power. Appraisal of presented arguments, and fine discriminations between described states of feeling and experiences, are often at the heart of the French poems of debate and judgement, where a certain formality and balance – in style and in set-pieces of procedure – lend authority and privilege the role of composition. In Froissart's *Paradys* the lover is advised by the figure of Plaisance to put what he has to say into a lay, to which Love will listen and respond 'according to the counsel and appeals' of those around him. Yet while comparison with Chaucer's French courtly reading only underlines how much vigour and movement animate his poems that draw on these traditions of formal plaint, debate and judgement (as in the assemblies presided over by Nature and Fame), the comparison also shows how Chaucer has sustained in his own work – for all its animation – some of that underlying formality, that sense of procedure and grouping of figures found in his courtly reading. The *Parliament*, after the dream vision of the garden and temple of Venus, focuses on the petitions for favour by the three suitor falcons – a kind of verbal tournament in courtly speech-making – where courtly discourse distinguishes itself by contrast with the comments of more vulgar birds. Comparably in *Fame*, after the visionary sequences of Venus' temple and the dreamer's spoof apotheosis, a substantial sequence in the third book is devoted to the presentations of their petitions by seven groups, and the capriciously favourable or disobliging reactions of the enthroned Fame to these kneeling supplicants (the sixth and seventh companies seeking undeserved fame as lovers; 1734–5). In the *Book* the Man in Black's discourse also conforms to this pattern by rehearsing his courtship of his lady and hence his role as courtly petitioner for her mercy upon him.

Such patterns of structure, observance and ceremony provide some context for Chaucer's last experiment with dream-poem form in his *Legend* Prologue, whose survival in two versions – from the 1380s (F), and revised after 1394 (G) – implies that this remained a project in progress that drew Chaucer back to its themes. As the prologue to a larger work, this dream poem aims less at a free-standing thematic and formal autonomy than at a meditative and associative sequence, self-reflexive of the artist's concerns with authority and interpretation. What 'happens' in the narrative is shaped around archetypal courtly ritual. When the poet pays honour to May, this conforms to a pattern of courtly observance added to Chaucer's sources across his writings, which includes Arcite's resolve 'to doon his observaunce to May' by making a garland (I, 1500), Pandarus' wish to honour May with dancing (II, 111–12), or the timing of Aurelius' declaration to Dorigen in a May garden (V, 906–12). The poet's devotion to the daisy belongs within a courtly French tradition of marguerite poems, and Chaucer also alludes to some contemporary rivalry between courtiers who took as their emblem the flower or the leaf, perhaps advocates of transient pleasure or more perdurable, virtuous love. Chaucer's exquisite *balade* 'Hyd, Absalon' (G 203–23) is performed as a dance-song by a company of ladies who then seat themselves round about 'As they were of degre, ful curteysly' (G 231). Witnessed by this elegant circle occurs the poet's arraignment before a god of Love offended by his *Romaunt* translation and *Troilus*, where the listing of the poet's writings reads like an inversion of a manuscript presentation picture depicting the patron receiving the poet's work. Here is the extended sequence – as only in a dream – where a queen and heroine of classical myth takes it upon herself to intercede for the poet in an eloquently courtly petition, enjoining Love 'ryght of youre curteysye' to be both 'ryghtful, and ek mercyable' (318–23), as a lord should listen to his people's 'compleyntes and petyciouns' (363).

Alceste's arguments for compassion and judgement in the powerful may connect with contemporary unease at Richard II's autocratic tendencies, but do Chaucer's courtly writings define themselves as courtly more largely because at some level – as in the *Book* – they address historical figures and concerns at the English court in his time? The *Parliament* has been read as rehearsing (and differentiating by courtly criteria) the competing claims for the hand of Anne of Bohemia of her three suitors, of whom the first is Richard II. It is especially tempting to read a link between Richard II and Queen Anne and the imperious god of Love and his peace-making queen in the *Legend* Prologue, because the poet imagines himself instructed to present his poem to 'the quene' at the palaces of Eltham or Sheen (F 496–7; omitted in G, presumably after Anne's death in 1394). In *Behaingne*, when the jilted knight and the bereaved lady cannot agree, they take their cases for arbitration to the elegant court of a historical figure, Machaut's patron the King of Bohemia, at his castle of Durbuy. This king's decision in favour of the knight is reversed – and the poet critiqued and set to write subsequent poems as a penance – in a subsequent work featuring another royal patron, Machaut's *Jugement du Roy de Navarre*, which was evidently a model for the *Legend* Prologue. Indeed, comparison with how Machaut's patrons make celebrity guest appearances with walk-on roles in his poems only highlights how much more tangentially related are Chaucer's poems to any courtly occasion to which they may once have belonged. By keeping their distance from historical courts, personages and circumstances, Chaucer's dream visions maintain their liberty to examine all the more clearsightedly the checks and balances of power in courtly life, and women's role within it. Through a dream-like coalescence of attributes and powers in his Alceste, Chaucer fuses the cult of the daisy in French marguerite poetry – its white purity and golden dignity, its identification with light, its unchangingness – with his invented myth of Alcestis' stellification, her Marian assumption and intercessory role. The Alcestis ready to die in her husband's place is here reinvented through dream as a woman whose nature, both virtuous and merciful, is a guide that bridges the 'fyn lovynge' of courtly love and 'of wifhod the lyvynge, / And all the boundes* that she oughte kepe' (*restraints; G 535–6). Since Alceste points out that Love can never be argued with (G 465–7), and yet she carries her point about the dreamer, her successful advocacy can symbolize fulfilment of a humble devotion pursued for love's sake – like the poet's for his daisy – and also its inscription in art.

In their endings, the seeming absence, or avoidance, of conclusive resolution has been significant for recent appreciation of these four poems as dream-like in form and mode (especially their life-like endings in the interruption of waking up, or their film-like fade-outs). Moreover, Chaucer has so extended and deepened beyond his models the moral and philosophical implications that his dream poems may contain – and has so developed the experimental potential of the dream form to explore and reflect on the dynamic between tradition and individual talent – that the very possibility of settled resolutions at the poems' close is belied by what has been broached before. Yet how Chaucer has these poems end also reflects their function within a courtly culture where the puzzles and choices highlighted in such imaginative fictions served as cues for discussion amongst a courtly audience after the book has been read: Which suitor best deserves his lady and upon what grounds? How long should one mourn a lost lover and how best is such hurt assuaged? How soon might one relinquish an unreciprocated love? Can faithfulness in love be strengthened by stories of infidelity, and without traducing women? May 'fyn lovynge' and 'wifhod' really be at one? Through such implied debates the philosophical and the bookish can find a context in courtliness, and it is from such an intertextuality that Chaucer fashions a courtly style in English such that, for some generations to come, courtly writing 'wil talke nothyng but Chaucer'.

See also chapter 2, MANUSCRIPTS AND AUDIENCE; chapter 3, BOOKS AND AUTHORITY; chapter 4, DREAMING.

References and Further Reading

NB: Works suggested as further reading in the preceding essay by Steven F. Kruger are not repeated here.

Burnley, David (1998). *Courtliness and Literature in Medieval England*. Harlow: Longman.

Chaucer, Geoffrey (1997). *Chaucer's Dream Poetry*, ed. Helen Phillips and Nick Havely. Harlow: Longman.

Condé, Jean de (1982). *La Messe des Oisiaus*. In Windeatt (ed.), *Chaucer's Dream Poetry*, pp. 104–19.

Froissart, Jean (1982). *Le Paradys d'Amours*. In Windeatt (ed.), *Chaucer's Dream Poetry*, pp. 41–57, and also in *Jean Froissart: An Anthology of Narrative and Lyric Poetry*, ed. and trans. Kristen M. Figg with R. Barton Palmer. London: Routledge, 2001, pp. 35–101.

Given-Wilson, Chris (1986). *The Royal Household and the King's Affinity: Service, Politcs and Finance in England, 1360–1413*. New Haven: Yale University Press.

Grandson, Oton de (1982). *Le Songe Saint Valentin*. In Windeatt (ed.), *Chaucer's Dream Poetry*, pp. 120–4.

Green, Richard Firth (1980). *Poets and Princepleasers: Literature and the English Court in the Late Middle Ages*. Toronto: University of Toronto Press.

Hanly, Michael (1997). 'Courtiers and Poets: An International Network of Literary Exchange in Late Fourteenth-century Italy, France and England'. *Viator*, 28, 305–32.

Kelly, H. A. (1986). *Chaucer and the Cult of St Valentine*. Leiden: Davis Medieval Texts.

Lorris, Guillaume de and Meun, Jean de (1994). *Le Roman de la Rose*, trans. Frances Horgan. Oxford: Oxford University Press.

Machaut, Guillaume de (1988). *Le Jugement dou Roy de Behaingne; and Remede de Fortune*, ed. and trans. James I. Wimsatt and William W. Kibler. Athens, Ga.: Chaucer Library.

Machaut, Guillaume de (1988). *Le Jugement dou Roy de Navarre*, ed. and trans. R. Barton Palmer. New York: Garland.

Mathew, Gervase (1968). *The Court of Richard II*. London: John Murray.

Saul, Nigel (1997). *Richard II*. New Haven: Yale University Press.

Scattergood, V. J. and J. W. Sherborne (eds) (1983), *English Court Culture in the Later Middle Ages*. London: Duckworth.

Vale, Juliet (1982). *Edward III and Chivalry: Chivalric Society and its Context, 1270–1350*. Woodbridge: Boydell and Brewer.

Vale, Malcolm (2001). *The Princely Court: Medieval Courts and Culture in North-West Europe*. Oxford: Oxford University Press.

Wilson, Thomas. *Art of Rhetorique*, cited from Derek Brewer (ed.) (1978). *Chaucer: The Critical Heritage, I, 1385–1837*. London: Routledge, p. 103.

Wimsatt, James I. (1970). *The Marguerite Poetry of Guillaume de Machaut*. Chapel Hill: University of North Carolina Press.

Wimsatt, James I. (1991). *Chaucer and His French Contemporaries: Natural Music in the Fourteenth Century*. Toronto: Toronto University Press.

Windeatt, B. A. (ed. and trans.) (1982). *Chaucer's Dream Poetry: Sources and Analogues*. Cambridge: D. S. Brewer.

Woolf, Virginia (1978). 'Old Bloomsbury'. In *Virginia Woolf: Moments of Being. Unpublished Autobiographical Writings*, ed. Jeanne Schulkind. London: Hogarth Press, p. 162.

Part Three

Troilus and Criseyde

Pandarus talking to Criseyde in the *Roman de Troie*, a late fifteenth-century French translation of Boccaccio's *Il Filostrato* (Bodleian Library MS Douce 331, fol. 431).

Chapter Six

Love in Wartime: *Troilus and Criseyde* as Trojan History

Andrew Lynch

Medieval readers beginning *Troilus and Criseyde* must have been surprised to find the Fury Tisiphone begged to assist in the writing of a pathetic love story. The appeal to Tisiphone, the 'cruwel Furie, sorwynge evere in peyne' (I, 9) possibly recalls Boethius' *Consolation of Philosophy*, where the Furies 'wepyn teeris for pite' at Orpheus' music (*Boece*: iii, m.12); it also recalls Oedipus' horrific invocation of her malice against Thebes in Statius' *Thebaid* (Statius 1992: I, 103–9). Such an unlikely invocation at the outset indicates the unstable subjectivity of the narrator (Wetherbee 1998: 249). It also draws attention to the uneasy mixtures – love and war, romance and history, pathos and horror – which made up the later medieval tradition of Troy. Troy was a notorious battleground of authorities and interpreters in both classical and medieval times, with the effect that, as Barry Windeatt writes, '*Troilus* is constantly being set in relation to other writing ... with acknowledgement that it is one interpretation of a story which exists in a number of sources' (Windeatt 1992: 41).

So much European history was traced back to Troy in the Middle Ages that it was considered the narrative from which all the other narratives came. Thomas Gray's *Scalacronica*, commenced in 1355, saw all historiography as supported on two bases, the Bible and the Troy story (Gray 1836: 2). Troy was the most famous secular narrative because it was seen not only as a disastrous end, but also as a fertile beginning of other nations and histories. In Joseph of Exeter's phrase, 'Troy, with its rich loss, filled realms with nations and cities with people' (Joseph 1970: 8). Britain itself was supposedly named after a descendant of Trojan refugees, Brutus, and Chaucer's London was occasionally styled 'New Troy', apparently a controversial matter, since it became an accusation to use against political enemies, including Richard II (Windeatt 1992: 7–8). Recent scholarship debates the existence of a split between the 'Virgilian' 'propagandistic' and 'imperialistic' Troys stemming from Geoffrey of Monmouth's *Historia Regum Brittaniae [History of the Kings of Britain]* (*c.*1135), and the 'anti-imperialist' emphasis on violence and destruction of versions stemming from Guido delle Colonne's *Historia Destructionis Troiae [History of the Fall of Troy]* (1287) (Federico 2003: xvi). Yet in any version, medieval Trojan history could always function as a commentary on the present time. As Sylvia Federico writes, 'medieval claimants to Trojanness invent not just Troy but also themselves in the process of imagining the ancient city' (Federico 2003: xii).

Chaucer's invocation of Tisiphone reminds readers that the Trojan war was only one in a long line of ancient disasters, such as the preceding war of Thebes. (Even Thebes had not always been there, but was founded by exiles from Tyre, as Ovid's *Metamorphoses*, the most popular classical text of the Middle Ages, attested [Ovid 1986: III, 541ff.]). Thebes looms grimly behind the action of *Troilus*, sustained by two strategic references given with increasing detail. On the May morning that Pandarus visits Criseyde to win her love for Troilus, he finds her with others listening to a maiden reciting 'the geste / Of the siege of Thebes', apparently just at the section describing the death of Amphiaraus (II, 100–5). We may take Criseyde's text to be a romance, like the well-known medieval *Roman de Thèbes*, since she refers to events present in it but not in Statius' *Thebaid*. Pandarus' dismissive comment, that he already knows about Thebes in 'bookes twelve' (II, 108), points to Statius' work as the more canonical, masculine version. In the *Thebaid*, by comparison to the *Roman*, where it features in shortened form as a marvel, Amphiaraus' death is a central instance of the waste and horror of war that characterizes his whole poem. As a modern commentator has expressed it, in Statius' narrative ' "[f]renzy and bloodshed" . . . hold sway; and blind "fortune" . . . drives reason, virtue, faith, and pity from the darkened, blood-soaked world' (Statius 1992: xxiii). The priest Amphiaraus is easily the best of the forces besieging Thebes, a major character. He strongly opposes the war and, like Helenus in the Troy story, is attacked as a coward for it, with an argument – 'It's fear that first / Created gods' – that Criseyde says she will use herself on Calchas (IV, 1408). At Thebes, knowing he is fated to die, Amphiaraus wins a 'futile glory' committing slaughter in the field before he hands his wreath of bays back to Apollo and descends to the Underworld (Statius 1992: VII, 690–823). Later in *Troilus*, when the war has ceded Criseyde to the Greeks, Cassandra interprets Troilus' dream to him through an account of Diomede's ancestry, with substantial reference to the Theban horrors – slaughter, siege, Furies, burning, drowning, thunderbolt, 'how Amphiorax fil thorugh the grounde', fratricide, the grief of widows and the eventual destruction of the whole city (V, 1485–1512). Manuscripts of *Troilus* usually introduced a Latin summary of Statius' plot at this point. Through his evocations of the *Thebaid*, Chaucer points to the grim nature of siege warfare, which remains a more distant impression in *Troilus*. The memory of Thebes should be a mirror for Trojans (and by extension for the New Trojans of 1380s London), but Pandarus interrupts the story, and Cassandra, as ever, is not heeded.

If Troy had an important contemporary resonance in Chaucer's time, it was not least because medieval history was predominantly the record of that continuing human instability of which Troy was the emblem. Another later fourteenth-century English poem, *Sir Gawain and the Green Knight*, takes the burning of Troy as a frame to set off its theme of earthly transience, and to initiate its view of British history as the alternation of 'blisse and blunder' – the happiness of peace and the disaster of war. Trojan inheritance is seen behind both the 'wynne' ('joy') in which Brutus founds his new nation and the 'tene' ('harm') which soon arises from 'baret' ('strife') amongst its aristocracy (*Sir Gawain and the Green Knight* 1967: 1–22). Chaucer seems to have treated the 'fame' of Troy as hybrid and protean, subject to the bias of writers. He had already illustrated its flexible scope by varied references in earlier allegorical poems. In the *Book of the Duchess*, a unified version of the whole story, from Laomedon and the Argonauts onward, is represented in the glass windows of the dream bedchamber, giving a much wider sweep of events than we find in *Troilus* itself (326–31). Then in the *House of Fame*, Chaucer points to 'Omer' (known only in a Latin account at this time), but also to the anti-Homeric line of Dares the Phrygian (see Frazer 1966), Benoît de Sainte-Maure's *Roman de Troie [Romance of Troy]* (*c.*1160) and Guido, as well as the *Historia* of 'Englyssh Gaufride', Geoffrey of Monmouth (1465–80). In the *Parliament of Fowls*, where the poem's 'matere' is more clearly to do with forms of love, the figures of Helen, Troilus, Paris and Achilles, briefly seen amongst the wrecked lovers of the temple of Venus, are the only references to the Trojan war (290–1). By contrast, *Troilus and Criseyde* is a self-consciously 'historical' work, which depicts life in the last years of the city of Troy, understood both as a place vulnerable to the forces of historical change, and as the focus of a long and contested historiographical tradition.

The knowledge of generic and historiographical variety shown in his earlier Trojan references carries over into Chaucer's free treatment of his sources for *Troilus and Criseyde*, a feature which was also tacitly traditional. Just as Chaucer never mentions that Boccaccio is his main source, Boccaccio himself falsely claimed to be following ancient legends; Guido delle Colonne says his *Historia* is based on the (supposed) eyewitness accounts of Dares the Phrygian and Dictys the Cretan, and never admits its real main source – Benoît's *Roman*. But it might have been apparent to Chaucer that Guido was so in debt to Benoît, with the consequent revelation that Latin prose writers did not necessarily have any better claim to historical truth than vernacular poets, and that there could be no clear distinguishing in this case between history and invention. In any case, Chaucer must have realized he was favouring the less trusted and often reviled poetic accounts over the 'truth-telling' prose historians (Nolan 1992: 203). One of *Troilus and Criseyde*'s most perceptive early readers, Robert Henryson, noted the uncertain relation of 'authorised' truth and 'newly feigned' poetic fiction in the poem (Henryson 1981, *Troilus and Cresseid*: 64–70).

Chaucer's break with mainstream Trojan historiography in *Troilus and Criseyde* comes substantially from his following Boccaccio's *Il Filostrato* (*c*.1340). It has been said that there is 'a compositional imbalance between the *Filostrato* and the medieval Trojan stories', because the author is 'indifferent to the vicissitudes essential to an historical development' of the narrative in the traditional terms (Gozzi, in Boccaccio 1986: xvii), and much the same can be said of Chaucer in *Troilus*. Boccaccio is not interested in giving a connected, explicit account of the macro-political action, so that he is not really an historical source per se for *Troilus*, but a major influence on its oblique method of delineating the historical events. Chaucer lets us find out a great deal about the manners and mentality of the Trojans, but he gives us relatively few connected material facts about the history of the war, or even about the public lives of the main agents. Pandarus' exact social status and civic position remain unclear, for instance. The formal descriptions of Diomede, Troilus and Criseyde, usually thought to be drawn from Joseph of Exeter, come so late in Chaucer's narrative (V, 799–840) that they question the information value of such rhetorical devices more than they direct our knowledge of the characters (Patterson 1991:

150). In a text where so much is dramatically presented through intense personal negotiation and direct speech – Pandarus' detailed interactions with both Troilus and Criseyde in Books I and II are good examples – the function of traditional historical fact and explicit commentary is less secure than in, say, Guido's work. Instead of a truth-voice which marshals divergent facts into a single narrative, we often have the impression in Chaucer's text of various commentators and discourses hovering around the action, with competing claims. Criseyde's change of heart, for instance, is reacted to in very differing ways by the narrator (pity), Troilus (anguish) and Pandarus (righteous anger), and (indescribably) by Criseyde herself, together with her premonition of anti-feminist treatment which women will be encouraged to internalize: 'O. rolled shal I ben on many a tonge! / Throughout the world my belle shal be ronge! / And wommen moost wol haten me of alle.' (V, 1061–3). Chaucer knew this anti-feminist tradition. Benoît de Sainte-Maure, despite all his psychological subtlety, which influenced Chaucer, still depicts a furious Troilus shouting insults about Criseyde in public hearing (Benoît 1904–12: 20079–103), and makes misogynist comments himself (Benoît 1904–12: 13425–94). But readers of Chaucer's poem do not necessarily reach any firm conclusion on his Criseyde. She retains the opacity of a complex character acting in difficult circumstances, and resists the breakdown of her specificity into exemplary applications. As with Chaucer's attitude to the whole Troy story, her common 'fame' is not what he was mainly interested in. He gives us her private thoughts, dreams and fears – material that no eyewitness could have observed and only a poet could have invented.

Together with its notable originality and relativity of viewpoint, the most striking feature of Chaucer's treatment of the Troy story is its comparative selectivity in both incidents and narrative emphases. Most medieval writers wanted to tell the whole story or a great deal of it, and to amplify it by additional incidents, characters and descriptions. Chaucer's limited historical and thematic focus, an aspect of his complex debt to Boccaccio (see Wallace 1985), makes *Troilus and Criseyde* radically different from wide-ranging texts like those of Dares and Dictys, Benoît or Guido. The entire rationale of these predecessors is different. Benoît, for instance, says in his Prologue that he is obliged to pass on to others his knowledge of what really happened, and gives a very detailed summary of the whole poem. He follows through the ten-year course of the war on both sides, structuring the narrative by battles interspersed with truces and council scenes. He has not one, but four doomed love stories. Guido takes this material and dignifies it with moral and philosophical commentary, named authorities, and a narrative preoccupation with historical truth (Guido 1974: xv–xvi). Chaucer, by contrast, confines himself to a few historical events and a much narrower chronological range, gives us little of the Greek side, concentrates on one love relationship, is vague about authorities, and apparently surrenders the conduct of the poem to a very subjective narrator whose highest aim is to help Love's servants. The blank prolepsis at the end of the introduction to Book I (I, 55–6) tells us not that Troy will fall, but that Troilus will suffer twice for love and that Criseyde will forsake him before *she* (not he) dies. That is to say, the actions of lovers take precedence as a theme over the death of the warrior whose name traditionally implied his whole city.

The emphasis on love defines Chaucer's text, which succeeds, on one plane, in making readers forget for long periods the fateful context in which the lovers exist. The obvious 'dramatic irony' of the Trojan lovers' position causes no lack of sympathy for them. The sad ending to the love-story, with the gradual revelation of human inconsistency and fallibility, does not devalue though its ironies the importance of the characters' own history, as experienced by readers, or of their choices. The politics of the war are acknowledged to have great power over the narrative outcome, but the conduct and feelings of individual Trojans remain its central concern; compared to Statius or Guido, Chaucer places more emphasis on free will than on sheer fate. He attempts to render with sympathy a credibly ancient Troy and a Trojan mind-set, 'how they thought and behaved in their historical time and place' (Minnis 1982: 6). But he also largely avoids long-range historical moralizing, preferring instead, through his too deeply engaged narrator, to concentrate on the unfolding present action. When there is moralizing it is mainly of a different kind, especially in the first three books of the poem. We hear a lot of sententious utterance, for example, about how Cupid takes down Troilus for his flippant attitude to love, but nothing about the futility of the Trojans' prayers to the Palladium (the image of Pallas Athene, the goddess of wisdom and war: I, 148–68), in the face of the prophecy that 'Troye sholde / Destroyed ben, ye, wolde whoso nolde' (I, 77–8), and the medieval audience's knowledge of what will happen after the Palladium is stolen by Diomede. When overt historical moralizing about Trojans does arise, it is through the narrator's outrage at their betrayal of Criseyde (IV, 197–210). It is always possible, though hardly necessary, to take Chaucer's relatively light use of long-range perspectives as an invitation to supply our own moral on the blindness of pagans and the futility of trusting to this world, as the narrative finally does (V, 1828–53). Yet in terms of sheer narrative attention, the effect of closeness to the lovers makes for an insider's 'Trojan' view of the action, though not for a partisan justification of Troy. The Trojan share of responsibility for the war, especially through the ravishing of Helen, is acknowledged at the outset and tellingly reprised (I, 62–3; IV, 547–8, 608–9; V, 890–6). Pandarus' careless reference to ravishment as a red-blooded Trojan characteristic is especially jarring:

> 'Artow in Troie, and hast no hardyment*   *daring
> To take a womman which that loveth the
> And wolde hireselven ben of thyn assent?
> Now is this nat a nyce vanitee?
> Rise up anon, and lat this wepyng be,
> And kith* thou art a man.'   *make known
> (IV, 533–8)

The comment shows that Troilus offers a different example of masculinity from Paris or Pandarus, but also that he cannot escape the situation which attitudes like theirs have brought about.

A major difference between Chaucer's treatment of the story and the historical sources is that 'the Greeks' in his poem are largely a faceless and distanced military force. Before Criseyde is sent from Troy, only one scene is set amongst them – Calchas' plea to exchange her for Antenor (IV, 29–133). Detailed involvement of Greeks with the narrative arises only through Criseyde's exchange, and we view her still for some time as a Trojan, 'with wommen fewe, among the Grekis stronge' (V, 688). Once she has left Troy in spirit as well as body, her life with the Greeks fades from direct view and is accessible only through dream (V, 1233–52), by letter (V, 1590–1631), and by the brooch found on Diomede's captured coat-armour (V, 1646–66). The Greeks themselves, much as before the exchange, are seen only in the field of battle from that point onwards. The poem's evocation of the Greek menace, so important in the delineation of Criseyde's frightened behaviour, is linked to the narrative distancing of them as unknown aggressors. They receive little credit for chivalry, and we see little sign of their having other interests beyond absolute revenge on Troy. There is nothing of the rivalry, betrayal, mixed motives and love intrigue that characterize the invading force in other versions. This means that 'sodeyn' ('sudden') Diomede, when we come to meet him, can stand for all the Greeks in a way that Chaucer's Troilus never really stands for Troy, differentiated as he is from a dozen other Trojans, and viewed within more varied life contexts, like some other contemporary medieval heroes, Gawain in *Sir Gawain and the Green Knight* or Theseus in Chaucer's 'Knight's Tale'. By contrast, the keynote of Chaucer's Greeks is their obsessive military implacability, which Diomede makes very clear to Criseyde (V, 883–917). After this brutal ploy, it is impossible to give credence to Diomede as a man truly in love, such as he is in Benoît's account. He seems as much a predator on Criseyde as he is on Troy, and his blushes and shaking voice look like a cheap version of Troilus' earlier behaviour. It is hard to remember that Troilus, the true lover, is at least as fierce and lethal a warrior as Diomede, though readers are eventually forced to acknowledge it, after he is changed by the loss of Criseyde.

A very distinctive feature of Chaucer's poem as a Troy story, especially an English one, is the relative lack of interest in the battles. From the outset, the poem apparently attempts to bracket off the war narrative as something already 'wel wist' (I, 57). It is even implied that the great fame of the fighting, traditionally the main reason for writing about Troy at all (*Laud Troy Book* 1902: 65–86), is the poet's justification for choosing a different 'matere' (I, 144). Reference to combat is distant and impersonal – 'The thinges fellen, as they don of werre' (I, 134), one war seeming like any other – and we are tersely directed to Latin texts, 'Omer', Dares and Dictys, for what happened: 'Whoso that kan may rede hem as they write' (I, 147). A clear and original break with Trojan historiographical precedent, especially the Dares/Dictys line, is signified. Benoît had attempted to write equally about both love and war, with fierce characters such as Diomede and Achilles truly suffering the pangs of love sickness, and copious detail about Troilus as a fighter. Guido delle Colonne reduces the colourfulness of Benoît's battles to some extent (Guido 1974: xiii–xiv), but he still uses battle narratives, including many involving Troilus, to make some of his most serious moral points, and because he leaves out or plays down love stories (Benson 1980: 4), the importance of fighting descriptions looms even larger. The death of Troilus in Guido's narrative is a good example. Achilles manages it only after more than a thousand Myrmidons have tired out his victim, and 'he killed him more dead than alive' (Guido 1974: 281–85). The horrific scene becomes the occasion for a vaunting of Guido's higher claims to historical truth over biased poetic accounts: 'Notice, miserable Homer, that Achilles never killed any valiant man

except by treachery' (Guido 1974: 340). Yet even by this condemnation of Achilles, Guido indicates that the main currency of his text is
martial prowess and honour – who deserves most praise for which
killings – in the manner of a contemporary 'aristocratic chronicle'
(Benson 1980: 13–14). Throughout the course of Chaucer's poem,
there is virtually no such articulation of battles into their various
'strokes', with one named knight pitted against another, as we see
frequently in other medieval English Troy versions, such as the *Laud
Troy Book* (c.1400), where 'rarely is an opportunity missed to increase
the violence or call attention to the exploits of . . . [the] favourite
heroes' (Benson 1980: 71). Hector is killed in Chaucer's text by an
'unwar' stroke, of which both Achilles and he may be unaware (V,
1558–1600). As in the accounts of the laconic Dares Phrygius and of
Boccaccio, we do not even hear with what weapon Achilles kills
Troilus; narrative attention to the moment seems perfunctory and
banal, in popular style: 'But – weilawey, save only Goddes wille /
Despitously him slough the fierse Achille' (V, 1805–6). Overall, Chaucer's pointed lack of interest in nearly all the battle material he found
in earlier writers means that both his characters and the whole action
must be assessed in other ways.

Chaucer remarked again on his neglect of the subject of arms
towards the end of *Troilus and Criseyde*:

> And if I hadde ytaken for to write
> The armes of this ilke worthi man,
> Than wolde ich of his batailles endite;
> But for that I to writen first bigan
> Of his love, I have seyd as I kan –
> His worthi dedes, whoso list hem heere,
> Rede Dares, he kan telle hem alle ifeere.
>
> (V, 1765–71)

Amongst all the possible historical sources Chaucer could have cited
here, 'Dares' (if Dares Phrygius is meant) would provide the shortest,
most summary treatment of combats – 'alle ifeere' ('all together') – not
the nineteen battles of Benoît or Guido's elaborations. If by 'Dares'
Chaucer means Joseph of Exeter's *Iliad* (based on Guido), as most
scholars think (Windeatt 1992: 75), then it is still the case that Joseph
collects much of Troilus' prowess conveniently together in a few
pages of his sixth book. Joseph concentrates on battles, often in
repellent terms:

The detestable joys of Mars and his savage delights were boiling and bubbling everywhere. One had been blinded, and his eye dribbled down over his face. Another grinned hideously, his chin, his tongue and his nose hacked away. On others a lopped-off ear, or hand, or shoulder, dangled. Some pressed back their gaping innards with their hands. Others fell down, their knees hacked into, and crawled away from their enemy. (Joseph 1970: 60)

If that is what Chaucer meant by '[r]ede Dares', then he was directing his audience to one of the most violent and least chivalric of Trojan war narrative treatments. He was also implicitly indicating his own very different version of masculine evaluation, one articulated through conduct in both peace and war, love and arms. The difference is not merely that Joseph subordinates love to arms, but that he makes it very hard to imagine his Troilus type as a possible lover at all, certainly not of the kind Chaucer created: 'He was a man of violent temperament, one who thirsted after war and whose advice was always the sword' (Joseph 1970: 30). Joseph writes in the tradition that treats love as a potential distraction from arms: 'The heroes did not give their limbs to embraces, did not traffic in kisses – all these they shunned so that war might not be delayed' (Joseph 1970: 10).

In Benoît's narrative, Chaucer had found an equally war-minded Troilus, who, for instance, sways Priam's council to support Paris' abduction of Helen, accusing his brother, the priest Helenus, of cowardice for warning against it. (The irony of Troilus' earlier warmongering is made clear when he himself becomes the victim of a later council's decision.) Benoît's poem is greatly complicated by the fact that his Troilus is an equally passionate lover, so that judgement of his actions (like those of Diomede and Achilles) 'will encompass the largest questions about human conduct and ethical value', amongst them 'public honour and reputation *versus* private passionate love' (Nolan 1992: 70). Because Chaucer's Troilus, unlike Benoît's, keeps his love very secret, that conflict is played out for him (and Criseyde) as an agonizing series of personal inhibitions rather than as an open topic. Despite Chaucer's use of a debate structure between allegorical personifications – Love *versus* Reason – to decide how Troilus should act, the result in favour of public honour seems inevitable. Troilus cannot support Criseyde's cause personally '[l]est men sholde his affeccioun espye' (IV, 153). Fear of popular opinion also dissuades him from taking her away, for various reasons: he does not want to be seen to oppose 'the townes goode', and if he asks Calchas for her he could damage her reputation without getting what he wanted; (IV, 547–74); Criseyde argues that the people would say he was motivated by 'lust voluptuous and coward drede', and that her 'name' would be lost for ever (IV, 1569–82). Troilus, in effect, is ultimately permitted only one legitimate role – Trojan warrior – and always has to hide his role as lover. His situation is something like Benoît's Achilles, secretly in love with the Trojan enemy, Polixena, and it also resembles to some extent that of Lancelot, in love with a married woman and attempting to 'serve' her without compromising her. On a more mundane level, Pandarus compares the case of people who see their secret lovers married off to others by family pressure (V, 344–50). Most of the important action involving Troilus takes place in chambers, closets and other private spaces. Nearly all his conversations are held tête-à-tête. One can read that as a sign that the supposedly all-powerful agency of human love really operates within narrow and delusive limits – 'Nothing is altered by the consummation of love' (Wetherbee 1984: 107) – but perhaps it is also an acknowledgement that some of the deepest causes of history are off the public record, and must be supplied by poetic invention.

In this context of privacy, the belated reappearance of Troilus in the field in V, 1800–6 has been seen as absurd, 'underlining the arbitrariness of the rhetorical gestures' involved:

> Chaucer's evocation of Troilus's 'wrath' clearly recalls the opening of the *Iliad*, but its placement at the end of the poem rather than the beginning is faintly absurd . . . Troilus's wrath is a medieval embellishment of Dares Phrygius, as alien to Chaucer's carefully fashioned classical world as Pandarus himself. (Wetherbee 1998: 245)

And yet, however little we have seen of his actual combat, Troilus' status as fighter in the poem has been repeatedly insisted on. He is 'Ector the secounde' (II, 158), 'holdere up of Troye' (II, 645), acknowledged by the street crowd as much as he is boosted by Pandarus. And in some traditional ways, the poem's matter of love is represented as depending on and serving to underwrite Troilus' value as a knight. As the stricken but hopeful lover, he becomes a lion in battle (I, 1074). Love, which drives out all fear, propels him into the field. Criseyde's Isolde-like question, 'who yaf me drynke?' (II, 651), comes at the sight of his returning victorious through Troy from a skirmish (II, 640–51), with a hint of Geoffrey of Monmouth's benign symbiosis between chaste women and proven warriors in his Arthurian New Troy

(London), where deeds of arms in tournaments inspire love and love inspires men to arms (Geoffrey 1966: 229). Troilus' 'excellent prowesse' (II, 659) is the first of his lovable qualities Criseyde calls to mind, though not the chief. As acknowledged lover, Troilus becomes her 'wal of stiel' (III, 479–80), engaged by day with all his might 'in Martes heigh servyse', as he is by night with thoughts of love (III, 437–41). As the fulfilled true lover, he increases in bravery and strength in all the town's wartime requirements (III, 1773). Finally, as the despairing betrayed lover 'in many cruel batailles' he is even more effective in the field, the bane of 'thousands' of Greeks before he dies (V, 1751–1806).

So although Chaucer does not write about Troilus' historical battles in detail, he does give his military role strong significance within the love story. Prowess in 'arms' is made a ground, an accompaniment and a sustained correlative of Troilus' love. How love relates to arms becomes an issue, as in the *Roman de Troie*, but one raised by different narrative means. Chaucer's Troilus, unlike Benoît's, cannot ultimately sustain a strict division between the warrior gentle to his friends and fearful to his foes, which we have seen in Pandarus' first description of him to Criseyde: ' "the frendlieste man" ' (II, 190–207). The brooch Troilus gave to Criseyde that turns up on Diomede's coat-armour (V, 1646–66) precipitates the transfer of his emotional energy as lover into 'wrath', ostensibly against the Greek. But he cannot, like Pandarus, or like Benoît's Troilus, bring himself to 'hate' Criseyde and wish her death (V, 1730–43), so the persistence of love for her means that the anger which love now generates is also turned suicidally against himself (V, 1672–3): ' "Myn owen deth in armes wol I seche" ' (V, 1718).

In one obvious way Chaucer does try to maintain a structural and discursive division between the two 'materes' of arms and love. In stark contrast to other writers on Troy, who follow the military out on their deeds, he nearly always keeps the focus within the city, or later within the Greek camp, while the fighting is conducted elsewhere and viewed from the perspective of a non-combatant civilian. We are offered a rather feminized reading position, in medieval terms, perhaps a clerical one; we share our superior knowledge of the war's outcome with two priestly figures, Calchas (the coward) and Cassandra. Yet given that the initial picture (I, 148–9) is of citizens shut in and entirely surrounded by a hostile army, beleaguered Troy keeps surprisingly much of its 'old usage' (I, 150) like a peacetime place of 'lusty life' (V, 393), oddly untouched physically by the war. After many years of siege it is (remarkably, yet unremarked upon) well-fed, leisured, gracious and much preoccupied with traditional peacetime business, including love itself (Meecham-Jones 2004: 148–50).

The non-specific nature of Chaucer's war descriptions in *Troilus and Criseyde* supports the general resemblance of them to any prolonged international war, including contemporary medieval conflicts. In retrospect from the 1380s, a view of the long intermittent English hostilities with France, with their shaky causality, alternating fortunes, and involved and unsuccessful diplomacy, may well have resembled specific aspects of the Trojan–Greek conflict in the historical sources. To follow the exhortation to 'read Dares' would put the Trojan war in the similar context of a series of failed negotiations between enemies from the time of Jason and Laomedon onwards, a failure compounded by the folly of the Greeks in refusing to listen to Priam's emissary Antenor, and then by Priam's foolish revenge, intractability and unpreparedness. Certainly, Chaucer does not draw direct or obvious links between Troy and New Troy, but London life around the time of the poem, with its alternation of relative calm and periods of great fear and disruption, bore some similarity to the double wartime/peacetime Troy of *Troilus and Criseyde*. The year 1377 saw splendid pageants for Richard II's coronation, but where Chaucer lived, over the wall at Aldgate, a portcullis, barbicans and chains were added in fear of French invasion, one of many special measures taken that year (Crow and Olson 1966: 145). We find reference in *Troilus* II, 617–18 to 'the yate . . . / of Dardanus, there opyn is the cheyne'. It was through Aldgate that the peasant rebels were treacherously allowed to enter the city in 1381 (Myers 1972: 15–16). Chaucer's lease for his rooms at Aldgate stipulated that they could be requisitioned for the defence of the city when necessary (Crow and Olson 1966: 145). Alternating with or parallel to these intimations of war was a policy of truce, peace settlement and military retrenchment. Royal documents of the period referred habitually to 'the afflictions, tribulations and evils which Christian people have suffered and suffer from day to day in the wars . . . [with France], on which griefs we have the greatest pity and compassion' (Rymer 1740: III, ii, vii, 410. 12 September 1383; My translation). In 1382 'an eight- to twelve-year truce' was confidently anticipated (Palmer 1972: 45), and in 1384 the Commons (mainly worried about money) asked for peace with France as ' "the most noble and gracious aid and comfort" that could possibly be devised for them' (Palmer 1972:14). Similarly, in *Troilus and Criseyde*, the initial picture of constant siege is modified by direct and prospective references to times of peace and truce, derived from the historical sources, where the discussion of when and how long to make truces is considerable. Criseyde hopes that peace negotiations – 'Alday men trete of pees' – will make free departures and returns from Troy the normal state (IV, 1352–8). In interludes of peace, Troilus, like an English nobleman, visits his friends in the country, or goes hunting and returns to town under Criseyde's gaze (III, 1779–85), providing a further nexus between love and masculine prowess in the 'field'. Yet at other times Criseyde is afraid to death of the Greeks (II, 124), and Pandarus jokes about Troilus' becoming 'lean' as an effect of the siege (I, 553), perhaps a hint of depression, or even of threatened food supplies. Consciousness of the war dominated London life at times in the later 1370s and earlier 1380s, and the French were very much the 'visible foes' referred to in the poem's final stanza. Fear of French invasion was common. Soon after *Troilus* was finished, in the summer of 1386, the prospect of French military invasion filled the south-east with panic, and 'one writer compared . . . [the French fleet] to the fleet which destroyed Troy'. In London, measures expecting a siege were undertaken: aldermen were ordered to put their wards in array; householders were to lay in three months' provisions; special forces were stationed within a sixty-mile radius of London; people fled the city; houses near the wall were pulled down; and there was an outbreak of 'last chance' consumer spending before the French came (Palmer 1972: 74–6). Hysteria like that of 1386 was always a potential, reflecting something of a siege mentality, which had built up as the periods of war had grown longer and more intensive. Only four years in the period 1369–89 were covered by truces (Palmer 1972: 1).

It is not surprising therefore that in Chaucer's Troy, as in his London, there is an odd mixture of peacetime and wartime elements. Consciousness of war is translated into many other discourses of the fictional city. War becomes a matter of military settings out and returns, of peace embassies, parliamentary discussions, literary appreciation (as in Criseyde's reading of a *Roman de Thèbes*) and talk of strategy, rather than direct witness to combat. Pandarus, hardly a man without leisure, spends all day with Priam, presumably in a war council (V, 284), and advises on the defence of the city. But in one respect Chaucer's representation of Troy differs crucially both from the Trojan histories he knew and the experience of his contemporary Londoners. We do not mainly find in *Troilus* the normal alternation of discrete periods of peace and war typical of the Troy sources, and of English experience in the wars with France and Scotland. Neither the cycle of a time of peace following war that is invoked by Criseyde,

> And if so be that pees heere-after take,
> As alday* happeth after anger game,   *frequently
>   (IV, 1562–5)

nor the typical relief of a truce mentioned by Pandarus,

> · 'This town is ful of lordes al aboute,
>   And trewes* lasten al this mene while.'   *truce
>   (V, 400–1)

comes about. Instead we receive a version of the hero's daily life which, impossibly, includes both war and peace, anger and game. Troilus apparently goes off to the war each day and returns home at night through the city gates, like a commuter. He spends his days killing Greeks and his nights loving Criseyde, in a strangely rapid version of the traditional war/peace cycle. His agency is split into that of a secret lover visible to the reader, and a public but largely unseen fighter, whose renown the narrator 'reads' or 'finds' in his sources rather than witnesses directly (V, 1754, 1758). The only battle Chaucer narrates with an epic list of names concerns the capture of Antenor, and amongst nine knights listed, Troilus is not present (V, 36–56). A consequence of this narrative separation is that it becomes harder than usual to reconcile conceptually the hero's roles as fighter and lover.

Of course, Chaucer could not ignore the traditional chivalric notion that prowess in arms inspires love and love inspires men to arms. But that tradition arguably loses something of its hold in the Trojan context. This war is not allowed to 'prove' the value of knightly love in the normal honorific and unmotivated way, because Paris' initial love vision leading to the ravishing of Helen is such a notorious historical cause of damage. The recurrent Trojan mixture of love and war is a problem, not a resolution. Moreover, the symbiotic relation between love and arms is principally a motif of 'peace is good after war' descriptions – of court ceremonial, as in Geoffrey of Monmouth and his romance successors – rather than of siege warfare. The punitive nature of this war, which can bring about no peace and is beyond any end but victory or disaster for Troy, suggests that it is truly a 'noble *game*', an aristocratic sport, to regard the blushing Troilus, hero of some unspecified 'scarmuch' ('skirmish'), as another Mars, god of battle (II, 610–44), and it is worrying too, given Mars' 'traditional association with impetuous, angry behaviour, and even death' (McCall 1979: 23).

This passage in Book II is by far the most elaborate and embodied chivalric description of the whole poem, with its wounded horse and spectacular damage to armour focusing vision on a central named knight, with a civilian crowd bearing witness to his prowess, and the heroine looking on. Yet it occurs outside the battlefield, made strategically irrelevant in the context of a total war ruled by Fortune. Nor does it truly inspire love. Despite her role in the chivalric tableau, Criseyde later specifically distinguishes 'worthinesse . . . / In werre or tourney marcial' from the 'moral vertu, grounded upon trouthe' on which she bases her love of Troilus (IV, 1670–3). In saying so, she allows 'moral vertu' to mean far more than knightly 'doing well' before female spectators in romance combat narrative. The woman, normally the love-struck witness to masculinist forms of virtue, here claims her own power to evaluate the man. Why she loves Troilus rests with her; he is her 'pees' ('peace') and 'suffisaunce' ('sufficiency') as much as her 'knight' (III, 1309).

As Lee Patterson notes, Troilus' strenuous martial activity should protect him from criticism as a civically irresponsible casualty of Venus (Patterson 1991: 105–6), but it does not prevent him from finally becoming a casualty of Mars. Chaucer has denied the normal respectful engagement with the military action, and has distanced the 'field' so as to prevent an audience from being caught up in the fighting. His rapid alternation of quasi-peace and war, love and hate, the hero's civilian and military roles, questions the chivalric and epic narrative codes that treat killing in arms as a special moral case. Troilus' ultimate 'wrath' as warrior in Book V can therefore be seen as more troubling than merely inappropriate or 'absurd', especially coming so close to the poem's dedication to Chaucer's contemporary, 'moral Gower' (V, 1856). R. F. Yeager has pointed out that in the *Mirour de l'omme*, John Gower claims that acts are good or ill not in themselves, but according to the inner state of the warrior. In the *Vox Clamantis*, Gower treats war 'as a violation, not a state, of being' (Yeager 1987: 104). In *Confessio Amantis*, war comes under the heading of the sin of 'wrath' and its counter-virtue 'mercy' (Yeager 1987: 105–6). In Gower's view, Troilus would be fully entitled to fight in the legitimate defence of his home, but not to indulge a private anger by his killings. Gower's distinction fits well with Chaucer's careful charting of Troilus' changing motivation in warfare: first from emulation of his brothers, then to impress Criseyde, with no hate for the Greeks or civic feeling (I, 477–82), progressing todutiful actions '[i]n alle nedes for the townes werre' (III, 1772), and finally to half-suicidal, half-vengeful pursuit of Diomede (V, 1751–1806).

In the conclusion of *Troilus and Criseyde*, an implicit moral analysis of war emerges, in which cruel strokes, great words, anger and mass killings are not simply vouched for as virtue. This is partly because the methods of evaluating Troilus' actions in love and war are seen to differ so much. Given the absence or disabling of the normal practices of chivalric narrative, this poem's chosen method of battle description, with its generalizing, pluralizing tendencies, takes on a new, disturbing potential. Within the city, as lover, Troilus is specifically distinguished in kind from the false 'avauntour' or 'lyere' (III, 310) he might be, the inferior kind of lover Paris or Pandarus or Diomede is. But as fighter in the field, according to the traditional method of description which subsumes both combatants into a unitary 'they', he now becomes essentially *like* his opponents. He is Diomede's equal and other half, for instance, as they so often 'meet' in battle, each side alternately 'paying for' the other's anger. The resemblance is the more striking for coming soon after the formal character descriptions of Troilus and Diomede in very different terms. The traditional reciprocity and bilateral exchange of chivalric combat here enforce a moral equation between them, in a context where the combatants' mutual anger has ceded control to 'Fortune' (V, 1763–4), as we have been told from the outset: 'and thus Fortune on lofte / And under eft gan hem to whielen bothe / Aftir hir course, ay whil that thei were wrothe' (I, 134–40).

Such war is impersonal hazard rather than providential adventure. Its outcome will reflect the remote decision of 'heighe Jove' (V, 1543) mediated through Fortune, rather than an evident declaration of the worth of either side. Fortune, in this case, is a Boethian force empowered by the subjection of the suffering participants to its workings, rather than the exculpating 'Destiny' of Guido and the *Laud Troy Book*. Accordingly, Troilus' pursuit of Diomede presents a futile, recurrent tableau of war rather than any decisive closure:

> And, God it woot, with many a cruel hete
> Gan Troilus upon his helm to bete!
> But natheles, Fortune it naught ne wolde
> Of oothers hond that eyther deyen sholde.'
> (V, 1761–4)

Chaucer's discourse in Book V heavily emphasizes the number of the battles his text has so far excised from the record, and their generic ferocity, rather than anything which would distinguish the combatants: 'In many cruel bataille'; 'ful cruwely'; 'ofte tyme I finde that they mette / With blody strokes and with wordes grete' (V, 1751–60). Martial virtue becomes fully quantitative, as Troilus kills 'thousandes' and so proves himself again second to none but Hector (V, 1800–6). The poem's early comparisons of Troilus to Hector have also cited his ' "vertu . . . / As alle trouthe and alle gentilesse / Wisdom, honour, fredom, and worthinesse" ' (II, 159–61), and how 'he bareth hym here at hom so gentily' (II, 186). Now, for the first time the comparison of the heroes is based solely on arms and uses the body-count standard found in typical Troy accounts, for instance in the *Laud Troy Book*'s praise of Hector:

> And ther was the best bodi in dede
> That euere ȝit wered wede*,   *garment
> Sithen the worlde was made so fere,
> That was Ector, in eche a werre,
> Ne that neuere sclow so many bodies –
> Fyghtyng In feld with his enemyes –
> Off worthi men that doughti were,
> As duke Ector of Troye there;
> For ther was neuere man that myght stand
> A strong stroke of Ectores hand,
> That he ne deyed In that stounde*   *place
> With his dynt* and falle to grounde,   *blow
> But the strong Achilles,
> That was best of all that pres*   *crowd
> Off the kynde of Gregeys*.   *Greeks
> (*Laud Troy Book* 1902–3: 49–63)

Chaucer's final comparison of Troilus to Hector, so soon after Hector's death, functions mainly as a sign of the younger brother's impending end. In its impersonal style of war narrative so far, the text has largely forbidden both the martial enthusiasm of romance and the impressiveness of epic slaughter. Now these old generic traits emerge, with a sense of the Trojan historiographical tradition, like the war itself, closing in on Chaucer's independent vision. Though taken from Boccaccio, like most of the battle details in Book V, Troilus' 'wordes grete' to Diomede, so unlike his shy demeanour as hero in Book II, and unlike his courtesy in other contexts, now align the text more with Benoît's (Windeatt 1992: 40), or the *Laud Troy Book* where Troilus 'reviles' Diomede 'as he were a theff', and defies Achilles to hell (*Laud Troy Book* 1902–3: 13436–8; 14243–50). Likeness to Hector implies a further likeness to Achilles, the older brother's great rival and killer. The more Troilus excels as warrior, the more he loses his individuality, becoming simply the latest principal vessel of the ancient 'wrath' between Greeks and Trojans, in the hopeless tradition made up of innumerable battles where each insult, each death, only increases the ferocity of reciprocal action. Love cannot inflect the values of this 'field'; there is no conclusive showdown with Diomede over Criseyde, and although Chaucer well knew the Achilles–Polixena sub-plot, a potential parallel linking love and war, he leaves it out here. There is no mismatch, as in Virgil's *Aeneid*, between an unfortunate boy and a hardened warrior (Virgil 1974: I, 474–8), no distinction made, as in Guido's text, between a brave, outnumbered Trojan and a treacherous Greek. As the killer of thousands Chaucer's Troilus above all *resembles* the fierce and pitiless Achilles. Seeking his 'owen deth in armes' (V, 1718), he finds it in an image of what he has finally become, a man with nothing left to him but war.

Troilus' death in battle might be read as a more significant moral conclusion for the hero and the poem, were it not such a blind alley for most of the preceding narrative. His public death is thoroughly irrelevant as an ending to his private love story. His plan of revenge on Diomede is frustrated by Fortune; his 'summary' romance ending 'puts [him] back into the world of artifice', and the poem moves on to higher things (Wallace 1985: 140). The death might also be seen as a failure on Chaucer's part to control the traditional historical discourse of a 'matere' he has mainly chosen to ignore, but which now necessarily obtrudes. In whatever reading, the lesson of this ending is also that the prolongation of the war through Trojan and Greek inability to conclude a peace dooms Troilus as lover, as it has earlier doomed Criseyde. Peace after war, 'game' after 'anger' is the necessary condition of a benign medieval relation between lover and warrior. Without peace, 'the noble life is at odds with itself, fulfilling its deepest romantic needs in a context that dooms them to extinction' (Patterson 1991: 162). Chaucer's narrative treatment of the historical sources has emphasized that love can neither be kept separate from the war, nor made to coexist happily with it.

Troilus' death, the penultimate historical event mentioned in the text (the last is the Crucifixion), initiates a move towards the Christian eternal, away from '[T]his world that passeth soone as floures faire' (V, 1841). The poem's ending rebukes and dismisses secular history as 'by definition the realm of the imperfect' (Patterson 1991: 18). And yet, however we read the text's historicization of Troilus – as limited pagan or honorary medieval Christian – it is not possible to follow him into the post-historical state in which he laughs at the sorrow of the world. As Freud wrote, '[w]henever we make the attempt to imagine . . . [our own death] we can perceive that we really survive as spectators' (Freud 1953: 15). *Troilus and Criseyde* offers a tragic medieval version of history, leading to death, but through its poetic depiction of love in the great city of Troy it also implicates readers in the great enjoyment of being alive. And in linking the love tragedy so closely to a limitless war, it puts the whole weight of medieval historical tradition behind the necessity for peace.

See also chapter 1, POLITICS AND LONDON LIFE; chapter 7, LOVE AND THE MAKING OF THE SELF: *TROILUS AND CRISEYDE*; chapter 8, TRAGEDY AND ROMANCE IN CHAUCER'S 'LITEL BOK' OF *TROILUS AND CRISEYDE*.

References and Further Reading

Benoît de Sainte-Maure (1904–12). *Le Roman de Troie*, ed. L. Constans. 6 vols. Paris: Firmin Didot.

Benson, C. David (1980). *The History of Troy in Middle English Literature*. Woodbridge, Suffolk: D. S. Brewer.

Boccaccio, Giovanni (1986). *Il Filostrato*, ed. Vincenzo Perricone; trans. Robert P. apRoberts and Anna Bruni Seldis. New York and London: Garland.

Boitani, Piero (1989). 'Antiquity and Beyond: the Death of Troilus'. In Piero Boitani (ed.), *The European Tragedy of Troilus*. Oxford: Clarendon Press, pp. 1–19.

Crow, M. M. and Clair C. Olson (eds) (1966). *Chaucer Life-Records*. Oxford: Clarendon Press.

Federico, Sylvia (2003). *New Troy. Fantasies of Empire in the Late Middle Ages*. Medieval Cultures 36. Minneapolis and London: University of Minnesota Press.

Frazer, R. M., Jr (trans.) (1966). *The Chronicles of Dictys of Crete and Dares the Phrygian*. Bloomington: Indiana University Press.

Freud, Sigmund (1953). *Civilization, War and Death*, ed. John Rickman. London: Hogarth Press.

Geoffrey of Monmouth (1966). *History of the Kings of Britain*, trans. Lewis Stone. Harmondsworth: Penguin.

Gozzi, M. (1968). 'Sulla fonti del *Filostrato*'. *Studi sul Boccaccio* 5, 123–309.

Gray, Thomas, of Heton (1836). *Scalacronica, by Sir Thomas Gray of Heton, Knight*, ed. J. Stevenson. Edinburgh: Maitland Club.

Guido delle Colonne (1974). *Historia Destructionis Troiae*, introd. and trans. Mary Elizabeth Meek. Bloomington: Indiana University Press.

Henryson, Robert (1987). *The Poems*, ed. Denton Fox. Oxford: Clarendon Press.

Joseph of Exeter (1970). *Joseph of Exeter. The Iliad of Dares Phrygius*, trans. G. Roberts. Cape Town: A. A. Balkema.

The Laud Troy Book (1902–3), ed. J. Ernst Wülfing. 2 vols. Early English Text Society, Original Series 121–2. London: Kegan Paul.

McCall, John (1979). *Chaucer and the Pagan Gods*. Philadelphia and London: Penn State University Press.

Meecham-Jones, Simon (2004). 'The Invisible Siege – The Depiction of Warfare in the Poetry of Chaucer'. In Corinne Saunders, Françoise Le Saux and Neil Thomas (eds), *Writing War: Medieval Literary Responses to Warfare*. Cambridge: D. S. Brewer, pp. 147–77.

Minnis, A. J. (1982). *Chaucer and Pagan Antiquity*. Cambridge: D. S. Brewer.

Myers, A. R. (1972). *London in the Age of Chaucer*. The Centers of Civilization Series, 31. Norman: University of Oklahoma Press.

Nolan, Barbara (1992). *Chaucer and the Tradition of the 'Roman Antique'*. Cambridge: Cambridge University Press.

Ovid (1986). *Metamorphoses*, trans. A. D. Melville. Oxford: Oxford University Press.

Palmer, J. J. N. (1972). *England, France and Christendom, 1377–79*. London: Routledge.

Patterson, Lee (1991). *Chaucer and the Subject of History*. London: Routledge.

Rymer, T. (ed.) (1740). *Foedera*. 3rd edn. London.

Sir Gawain and the Green Knight (1967), ed. J. R. R. Tolkien and E. V. Gordon; rev. N. Davis. 2nd edn. Oxford: Oxford University Press.

Statius (1992). *Thebaid*, trans. A. D. Melville; introd. D. W. T. Vessey. Oxford: Clarendon Press.

Virgil (1974). *Aeneid*, ed. and trans. H. Rushton Fairclough. 2 vols. Rev. edn. Cambridge, Mass.: Harvard University Press.

Wallace, David (1985). *Chaucer and the Early Writings of Boccaccio*. Cambridge: D. S. Brewer.

Wetherbee, Winthrop (1984). *Chaucer and the Poets: An Essay on* Troilus and Criseyde. Ithaca, NY: Cornell University Press.

Wetherbee, Winthrop. (1998). 'Dante and the Poetics of *Troilus and Criseyde*'. In Thomas C. Stillinger (ed.), *Critical Essays on Geoffrey Chaucer*. New York: G. K. Hall, pp. 243–66.

Windeatt, Barry (1992). *Troilus and Criseyde*. Oxford Guides to Chaucer. Oxford: Clarendon Press.

Yeager, R. F. (1987). 'Pax poetica: On the Pacifism of Chaucer and Gower'. *Studies in the Age of Chaucer* 9, 97–121.

Chapter Seven

Love and the Making of the Self: *Troilus and Criseyde*

Corinne Saunders

'Thorgh me men gon into that blysful place
Of hertes hele and dedly woundes cure;
Thorgh me men gon unto the welle of grace,
There grene and lusty May shal evere endure.
This is the wey to al good aventure.
Be glad, thow redere, and thy sorwe of-caste;
Al open am I – passe in, and sped thee faste!'

'Thorgh me men gon,' than spak that other side,
'Unto the mortal strokes of the spere
Of which Disdayn and Daunger is the gyde,
Ther nevere tre shal fruyt ne leves bere.
This strem yow ledeth to the sorweful were
There as the fish in prysoun is al drye;
Th'eschewing is only the remedye!'

(Parliament of Fowls 127–40)

The Dreamer in the *Parliament of Fowls* may safely enter the gates that bear this ominous message promising both delight and dread, for, his guide tells him, it is directed only to 'Loves servaunt' (159). The scene plays on Dante's depiction of the gateway into Inferno, with its chilling message, 'Abandon hope, all ye who enter here,' but combines this with a promise of bliss: the experience of those who are lovers, the inscription suggests, will be at once paradisal and infernal. It is not coincidental that Chaucer's narrators tend to draw back from love, for

134

Chaucer repeatedly treats love as an irresistible but potentially destructive force. The stories depicted on the walls of the temple of Venus in the *Parliament of Fowls* are all tragic, and in the narrative of the parliament itself it seems that the three rivals for the formel eagle's hand are likely to re-enact this negative paradigm. Chaucer narrates at more length a sequence of tragic love stories in his *Legend of Good Women*, each legend so patterned by the experience of passion, betrayal and death that the text can seem bizarrely reductive as well as shot through with the pathos of the female lamenting voice. Critics disagree on how to treat the *Legend*'s ambiguities, but few would argue that it celebrates love, although it may illuminate female *trouthe*. In 'The Knight's Tale' too, love is accompanied by disaster, reducing Palamon and Arcite, cousins and blood-brothers, once inseparable friends, to the status of wild animals fighting to the kill in a forest glade:

> Thou myghtest wene that this Palamon
> In his fightyng were a wood leon,
> And as a crueel tigre was Arcite;
> As wilde bores gonne they to smyte,
> That frothen whit as foom for ire wood.
> Up to the ancle foghte they in hir blood.
>
> (1655–60)

Here again, the pains of love are emphasized in the images found in Venus' temple, 'The broken slepes, and the sikes* colde, / The sacred teeris, and the waymentynge*, / The firy strokes of the desirynge / That loves servauntz in this lyf enduren' (*sighs; *lamenting: 1920–3). Although Theseus defends lovers, and we hear of Emilye's eventual happiness in her marriage to Palamon, the savage force of the battle in the forest is echoed in the 'furie infernal' (2684) sent by Saturn to throw Arcite to his death. Chaucer leaves us uncertain as to the good of this heightened, inevitable and tragic love, and the tale gains much of its dramatic tension from the difficulty of reconciling the positive and negative in love, or of rewriting a destiny played out by callous gods as the enactment of the beneficent providence expressed in Theseus' image of 'the faire cheyne of love' (2991) that binds the elements and moves the spheres.

Love is repeatedly portrayed in terms of paradox, ambiguity, duality in Chaucer's writing. In the triple roundel 'Merciles Beaute' (usually ascribed by editors to Chaucer), love is characterized in terms of a more light-hearted duality:

> Your yen two wol slee me sodenly;
> I may the beautee of hem not sustene,
> So woundeth hit thourghout my herte kene.
> . . .
>
> Sin I fro Love escaped am so fat,
> I never thenk to ben in his prison lene;
> Sin I am free, I counte him not a bene.
>
> (1–3, 27–9)

The haunting sadness of the first lyric, with its easy, elegant use of the conventions of courtly artifice, particularly the images of love as wound and illness, and the lady as physician, contrasts with the comic realism of the final lyric, in which the narrator undercuts the possibility of himself as courtly lover.

Such dualities, whether bittersweet or tragicomic, are characteristic of Chaucer's polyphony, lightness of touch and unwillingness to offer closure, but they also reflect the complicated, multi-faceted quality of attitudes to love in the medieval period. The difficulty of generalizing about love in medieval writing partly underpins the critical debate that has accompanied the concept of a literary mode of *fin'amors*, refined love or 'courtly' love. The French scholar Gaston Paris (1883) first identified a distinctive medieval mode of love, which he termed *amour courtois*; the critic W. G. Dodd wrote on the English treatment of the phenomenon in his study *Courtly Love in Chaucer and Gower* (1913); and C. S. Lewis in *The Allegory of Love* took up the notion with special reference to the thirteenth-century treatise of Andreas Capellanus, *De arte amandi*, to argue compellingly that medieval literature depicted 'love of a highly specialized sort, whose characteristics may be enumerated as Humility, Courtesy, Adultery, and the Religion of Love' (1936: 2). In its ideal form, Lewis argued, this love would not be consummated, but would echo Dante's sublime love for the celestial Beatrice. For Lewis, the great medieval examples are Lancelot and Guinevere, Tristan and Isolde, Troilus and Criseyde, and the celebration of such love is always shadowed by a sense of transience and human frailty, 'never . . . more than a temporary truancy. It may be solemn, but its solemnity is only for the moment. It may be touching, but it never forgets that there are sorrows and dangers before which those of love must be ready, when the moment comes, to give way' (1936: 42–3).

The role of Lewis in illuminating the complexities and delicacies of medieval writing cannot be overestimated, but the problems of his theory are well known, in particular his insistence on adultery, which causes the many depictions of married love in medieval romance to be dismissed as poor shadows of the ideal, and his notion of love as a fixed religion, despite the fact that Andreas Capellanus' treatise, on which Lewis based his idea of a code of love, was not widely circulated beyond a clerical audience. E. Talbot Donaldson wrote sceptically, 'courtly love provides so attractive a setting from which to study an age much preoccupied with love that if it had not existed scholars would have found it convenient to construct it – which, as a matter of fact, they have, at least partially, done.' Donaldson emphasized the idiosyncrasy of Andreas Capellanus and the fact that *amour courtois* was not a current medieval term, and remarked the 'spell' that Lewis' definition cast on readers, obscuring the truth that, despite celebrated examples such as that of *Troilus and Criseyde*, 'there is very little adultery' in medieval literature (1965: 155). The term *fin'amors* has come to seem preferable to 'courtly love' in that it implies a set of courtly conventions without the fixity of Lewis' definition and with the possibility of marriage.[1] Yet even this more fluid term can seem to indicate a defined set of attitudes, conventions and rituals of love of a more fixed kind than the actuality of medieval writing may suggest, and a more sustained, idealized treatment of emotion. We need to see Chaucer's *Troilus and Criseyde* not as the paradigm, but as extraordinary.

It is to twelfth-century writers such as Marie de France and Chrétien de Troyes, as well as to the lyrics of the *troubadours* and *trouvères*, that the rarefied treatment of love may be traced – although it also finds its origins in the classical poetry so widely read in the Middle Ages, in particular that of Ovid. Love typically takes the protagonist into a world of heightened emotional experience, so intense that he may lose all control of his reason, for, as Chrétien wrote in his romance of Lancelot, *Le Chevalier de la Charrete [The Knight of the Cart]*, love and reason are always at war, 'Reason . . . does not follow Love's command' ('Reisons, qui d'Amors se part: 1972, 1, 365; trans. Kibler 1991: 212). The irrationality born of great love can inspire great deeds of prowess in war or single combat, or the single-handed undertaking of great adventure. In *Le Chevalier de la Charrete*, for instance, Chrétien recounts the emblematic episode of the Sword Bridge: urged on by love for Guinevere, Lancelot takes the most direct but also most dangerous path to rescue her from her abductor, a path that culminates in black, treacherous water traversed only by 'a sharp and gleaming sword' ('une espee forbie et blanche': 1972, 3022; trans. Kibler 1991: 244), with two lions at its end. Lancelot crosses, much wounded, but guided and healed by love, only to discover that the lions were illusory. In *Le*

Chevalier de la Charrete, love madness rather than reason underpins high chivalric achievements, and Chrétien plays with this pattern in different ways in both *Le Chevalier au Lion (Yvain)* and *Erec et Enide*, while *Cligés* offers a rather more satirical perspective. Chrétien insists repeatedly, sometimes comically, on the power of love to detach the lover from the physical world and from everyday experience. Marie de France too explores the complex balance of reason and passion in love, perhaps most strikingly in *Les Deux Amants*, where the lover refuses the assistance of a magic potion, meeting the challenge of climbing a mountain with his beloved in his arms through the strength she inspires, only to die at the summit. Marie memorably characterizes great love as lacking in moderation through its very nature, but is not unequivocal in her celebration of such emotion.

Like Chrétien and Marie, and like Ovid before them, Chaucer probes the rarefied extremes of emotion, illuminating both the inspirational and destructive qualities of love, and opening out the subject of *fin'amors* to include complex philosophical questions, while remaining aware too of the human, even humorous side of love. While the subject of love of different kinds, comic and tragic, robust and elevated, sacred and secular, forms a leitmotif across Chaucer's writing, *Troilus and Criseyde* is his great canvas, its epic narrative providing scope for exploration of the heights and depths of love. As a narrative of *fin'amors* treating a celebrated episode of epic history, and written in the elevated form of *rime royal*, *Troilus* may be classified as high romance, a work very different in kind from the popular metrical romances of the period, with their focus on quests, adventures and the marvellous. Yet despite its grandeur, the poem is full of colour and variety, of wit as well as grief, of *solas* as well as *sentence*. It presents a kind of chiaroscuro landscape: although the poem's tragic outcome is stated in its opening lines, the progression towards this is delicately accomplished, the poem's emotions shifting in light and quality.

In selecting as his subject-matter the story of Troilus and Criseyde, Chau cer was already setting himself a complex task in terms of treatment of love, for he was choosing to tell a celebrated tale of betrayal. Chaucer's primary source, Boccaccio's *Il Filostrato*, is presented as a cautionary tale of how betrayal may destroy the lover's happiness.[2] As Andrew Lynch has shown in this volume, Boccaccio detaches the tale from the larger Trojan history, adding the sequence of events leading up to the separation of the lovers (the starting-point of Benoît de Sainte-Maure's and Guido delle Colonne's much briefer accounts of the love of Troilus): the meeting in the temple, the role of go-between played by Pandaro (in Boccaccio's version, a young courtier, friend and cousin to Troilo), the sorrow of Troilo, the use of Petrarchan imagery to describe the pains of love, and much of the characterization of Criseida. Chaucer borrows all these elements, frequently translating closely, and often following Boccaccio's stanzaic pattern of narrative and dialogue (see Windeatt 1992: 50–72 and Windeatt 1990), but at the same time, Chaucer alters, omits from and adds to Boccaccio's work. Perhaps most importantly, he may be seen repeatedly 'to move away from translation in the modern sense of rendering like with like', and 'to re-express, add and replace in his re-creative and adaptive "translacioun" '(Windeatt 1992: 52). This quality of response and remaking is fundamental to the poem. The poem's shifting quality reflects too Chaucer's interweaving of *Il Filostrato* with the text that he was translating at about the same time, Boethius' *Consolation of Philosophy*. Most obviously, Chaucer incorporates sections of the *Consolation* to shape the speeches of the central characters and their differing philosophical perspectives. But the *Consolation* is also present in the recurrent emphasis on existential questions, the tension between predestination and free will, and the transience or 'brotelnesse' (V, 1832) of earthly things, alongside the potentially transcendent or sublime nature of love. As with 'The Knight's Tale', it is perhaps most of all Chaucer's engagement with Boethius that gives the poem its depth, grandeur and hauntingly elegiac tone. In attributing all this to a fictional source, Lollius, Chaucer plays a self-consciously literary game, presenting in his narrator a fiction of the author who translates and selects from his sources, and thus engaging with the ambiguities of truth, authority and interpretation. On every level, the poem seems to present us with questions rather than answers.

In a poem of enigmas, Criseyde represents the central enigma, and much critical attention has been paid to her. Yet in fact it is Troilus' experience of love that shapes and structures the narrative: his 'double sorwe' is its subject (Windeatt 1992: 275), and he becomes the voice of love, the embodiment of extreme passion.[3] As we have seen, the audience would have been familiar with the name of Troilus as a great Trojan prince and celebrated warrior, and Chaucer to some extent takes this familiarity for granted, only occasionally reminding us of Troilus' heroic participation in the war. Chaucer's first depiction of Troilus, however, is as 'this fierse and proude knyght', 'a worthy kynges sone' (I, 225, 226), and we see him proudly guiding his young knights, laughing at lovers' follies at the feast of Palladion; Criseyde first sees him riding on his bay steed, 'al armed, save his hed, ful richely' (II, 625). It is crucial to Troilus' characterization that he is a great warrior, and not just the one prostrated by love. As with the great Arthurian knights Launcelot and Tristan, the combination of extraordinary prowess with the ability to experience the extremes of love to the point of madness and malady proves chivalric excellence. The poem's message is not that Troilus is weak, but that even so great a figure is susceptible to love, to the unmaking and remaking of the self: 'with a look his herte wex a-fere*, / That he that now was moost in pride above, / Wax sodeynly moost subgit unto love' (*on fire: I, 229–31); this is the poem's example.

Love is consistently imagined as a physical illness or wound by medieval writers, and this bodily quality of desire is especially striking in Troilus' experience. On first seeing Criseyde, he is physically affected, 'Right with hire look thorugh-shoten and thorugh-darted' (I, 325). Chaucer follows the convention of using a neo-Platonic model of sight to depict how the beams of Troilus' eye, 'percede [the crowd] and so depe it wente, / Til on Crisyede it smot, and ther it stente': the image of Criseyde passes back through Troilus' eyes, the way to the heart, which is caused to 'sprede and rise', wounding and quickening his affections (I, 272–3, 278). He thus manifests the typical symptoms of the malady of love: weeping, sighing, swooning, melancholy and physical decline. Chaucer employs the conventions of Petrarchan poetry to present love as a series of paradoxes: living death, feverish cold, thirst-provoking drink. The lady is both cause and cure of the illness of love. Throughout the poem, the motifs of love and death are interwoven: love is depicted as inevitable, but also as a kind of death-wish. Troilus becomes a pale figure of death not unlike the Man in Black in Chaucer's *Book of the Duchess*, and his speeches repeatedly employ the imagery of death: he feels himself 'evere dye and nevere fulli sterve*' (*die: IV, 280); he fears he will die, 'streght unto the deth my herte sailleth' (I, 606); he is ready to commit suicide when he believes Criseyde to be dead and when he dreams of her unfaithfulness. While Chaucer uses a familiar set of images, the physicality of his descriptions is extraordinary, particularly in Books IV and V, when Troilus is literally unmade by love. His suffering is characterized by swoons, frenetic madness, nightmares, the refusal to speak, his felonous look and pitiful face, until finally he wastes away to a shadow of his former self:

> He ne et ne drank, for his malencolye,
> And ek from every compaignye he fledde:
> This was the lif that al the tyme he ledde.

He so defet* was, that no manere man   *enfeebled
Unneth* hym myghte knowen ther he wente;   *scarcely
So was he lene, and therto pale and wan,
And feble, that he walketh by potente . . . *   *crutch
(V, 1216–22)

His complaint is of grievous pain around his heart (V, 1231–2). It can seem ironic that Troilus' death comes about neither through love-malady nor suicide, although it is the result of his rash heroics in a battle in which he no longer cares for his life. His desire for revenge on Diomede in a sense remakes Troilus physically, and the final passages return to the heroic, warrior image of Troilus, 'this ilke noble knyght' (V, 1752), although Chaucer directs us to Dares should we wish to read more of 'the armes of this ilke worthi man' (V, 1766), reminding us that love is ultimately his focus.

The interplay of the ideas of illness, death and love, then, place love as in many ways a negative, certainly a tragic, force. Yet if love unmakes Troilus, it also shapes his identity, and the sufferings of love interweave in the first half of the narrative with a sense of its sublimity, its capacity to elevate the individual to new realms of being. Its power is destructive but also creative, opening onto the ineffable. The experience of extreme pain in love proves the refined, courtly intensity of the individual nature; thus Troilus' sufferings assert his greatness as a knight in the same way that the love madness of the great romance heroes, Launcelot, Yvain and Tristan, does, and love represents the fulfilment of the self. Strikingly, the experience of extreme emotion leads Troilus to create, to compose songs: he is the romantic poet, 'the lover as lyric artist' (Windeatt 1992: 168). The narrative is interspersed with his lyrics, his first song a Petrarchan sonnet on the joys and pains of love (I, 400–20: 'If no love is, O God, what fele I so?'); Chaucer's is the first translation of the sonnet into English. In Book III, even more strikingly, Chaucer gives Troilus a Boethian song, 'Benigne Love, thow holy bond of thynges' (III, 1261–74), employing the same passage as that used in the speech of Theseus at the end of the 'Knight's Tale', the vision of the fair chain of love. It is not coincidental that this song precedes the consummation itself, following the beautiful description of Troilus' sensual experience of Criseyde's body, 'Hire armes smale, hire streghte bak and softe, / Hire sydes long, flesshly, smothe, and white' (III, 1247–8). The fulfilment of desire opens Troilus' vision to divine love, and occasions a song in praise of God's marvellous harmony, the ordering of the world through love: secular and sacred, earthly and spiritual love intersect.

For Troilus, Criseyde is not simply an earthly woman, though she is that also. Her being embodies the power of love to bind up and order the universe, and her presence opens the way to the celestial: in her eyes, Paradise stands 'formed' (V, 817). Book III ends with a further song, a great celebration of love as a force in the universe, 'Love, that of erthe and se hath governaunce' (III, 1744–71). Through love, the elements 'discordable' are held in harmony; the sun and moon in peaceful rule of day and night; the sea 'that gredy is to flowen' constrained in its tides; and in the same way peoples and individuals are held in virtuous accord. Love emanates from a loving God, 'So wolde God, that auctour is of kynde*, / That with his bond Love of his vertu liste / To cerclen hertes alle and faste bynde' (*nature: III, 1765–7), and its effect is to elevate the individual in virtue. Thus Troilus himself is depicted as surpassing in moral excellence: he is without pride of rank, 'Benigne he was to ech in general', and Love leads him away from vice, 'That Pride, Envye, Ire, and Avarice / He gan to fle' (III, 1802; 1805–6).

The experience of sublime passion perhaps necessarily approaches the mystical, and hence is more contemplative than active. Thus while Troilus is in one sense the romance hero, experiencing 'the marvellous inward adventure of love' (Windeatt 1992: 145), at the same time he is characterized by an inability to act. *Fin'amors* taken to such an extreme is ravishing but also incapacitating, in something of the manner of the ravishment of the soul in extreme religious experience. Mysticism does not seem compatible with everyday life. To the modern reader particularly, Troilus can seem absurdly passive in his sufferings, his swoons, his inability to pursue the opportunities Pandarus creates for him. The story indeed gains much of its comic momentum, an important counterbalance to the tragic impetus, through the contrast between Troilus' inactivity and Pandarus' activity: throughout the first three books, Pandarus busily promotes the love affair. He is a somewhat unusual go-between, combining friendship and forcefulness, an unsuccessful lover who delights in progressing the game of love. His dubious avuncular machinations include fabricating the plots that allow the lovers to meet, but also urging Troilus to act to the extent of physically placing him in bed with Criseyde, after reviving him from his swoon. On bringing Troilus to Criseyde's bedside, Pandarus withdraws to the fire, 'and fond* his contenaunce, / As for to looke upon an old romaunce' (*set: III, 979–80): he is, as it were, writing the romance of Troilus and Criseyde, shaping their destinies. To some extent, Pandarus plays the role of Fortune in the first half of the narrative, turning Troilus' desire into reality.

Troilus' dependence on Pandarus, however, is an aspect of a more generally fatalistic attitude. Just as he does not take the initiative in love, he does not take it in opposing the decree that Criseyde be exchanged for Antenor. Lament rather than action defines his responses: 'What is lacking in Troilus is equilibrium between action and introspection' (Martin 1972: 64). Troilus' vision of himself as victim of destiny reaches its height in his extensive consideration of the problem of free will in Book IV (a speech based closely on Boethius' discussion in Book V of the *Consolation of Philosophy*). Troilus posits different meanings of 'necessity' but his conclusion, 'For all that comth, comth by necessitee: / Thus to be lorn, it is my destinee' (IV, 958–9), leaves no scope for the enactment of free will, 'We han no fre chois' (IV, 980). Troilus never discovers Boethius' answer to the problem of reconciling free will and predestination, that God, situated beyond time, sees all at once, past, present and future, even while man, within the temporal world, acts through his own free will. Troilus' earlier celebration of divine love is replaced first by this resignation to a cruel destiny, and then by a different kind of acceptance of the celestial, when at the end of the poem Troilus looks down from the eighth sphere, hearing the music of the spheres. Now, however, the vanity of 'this wrecched world' is bitterly contrasted to the 'pleyn felicite' of heaven, and passion becomes laughable (V, 1818–19) rather than the way to eternity.

The construction of Troilus' psyche, and his reflections on love and destiny, give the subject of love a profound philosophical underpinning. It is possible to see all three main characters as representative of philosophical stances, largely enacted in relation to love: Pandarus, the opportunist, into whose speeches are woven optimistic passages on fortune from the *Consolation of Philosophy*; Troilus, the fatalist, who voices the laments of the imprisoned Boethius awaiting his death; Criseyde, the rationalist, optimistic regarding her free will, but constrained by social expectations and the fear of public shame. It is essential that the plot unfold within a pagan universe, for this allows Chaucer to weave a fabric of references to astrology, Fortune, Fate and the classical gods, and thus to create a sinister aura of predestination, particularly emphasized in the grandiose, allusive proems to each book. This contrasts markedly with the apparent free will of the characters, who seem to make their own choices in the game of love, and whose emotions and decisions provide much of the suspense of the work. Chaucer does not make his figures incompatible with a Christian perspective: Boethius was viewed as a great Christian philosopher;

Troilus' speeches in particular are monotheistic; and the morals of the poem are largely those of a fourteenth-century Christian society. At the same time, the pagan world of the poem invests the images of looming tragedy and fall, the turning of Fortune's wheel, and the apparent cruelty of the gods, with immediate force, and fuels the existential crisis of Troilus, which is resolved only when he reaches the eighth sphere and recognizes the worthlessnes of temporal things. For the reader, the end is highly problematic, for the story's power comes precisely from its evocation of the passion and tragedy of the temporal world. We cannot but recall that the human passions finally dismissed as false, brittle, vain were once so sublime as to open the self to eternity, and to create that vision of the marvellous harmony of love. Through Troilus' experience, the poem raises unanswerable existential questions regarding the possibility and meaning of roman-tic love, of man's situation within an uncaring, fickle universe, the untrustworthiness of which is symbolized by Criseyde's changing nature, and the problem of belief in beneficent providence.

If Troilus expresses the physical, intellectual and spiritual power of love to make and destroy, Criseyde presents a very different perspective on love, less romantic, less extreme, more pragmatic and perhaps ultimately more tragic.[4] She is the great untrue lover. Near the end of the poem, Criseyde laments:

> 'Allas, for now is clene ago
> My name of trouthe in love, for everemo!
> . . .
>
> Allas, of me, unto the worldes ende
> Shall neyther ben ywriten nor ysonge
> No good word, for thise bokes wol me shende*.   *shame
> O, rolled shal I ben on many a tonge . . . '
> (V, 1054–61)

The words function powerfully to convey Criseyde's sorrow at her own falseness, but also draw attention to the self-consciously literary status of the text, recalling the place of Chaucer's telling in a long-standing tradition: Criseyde's name has already been 'rolled . . . on many a tonge' as one that epitomizes female unfaithfulness and betrayal in love by Benoît de Sainte-Maure, Guido delle Colonne and Boccaccio – and will continue to be so by writers as diverse as Henryson and Shakespeare. Her reputation has been shaped and reshaped by a procession of male writers, just as within the text she is passed from one man to another – from father, to uncle, to lover, to father; from Trojan to Greek. It is in light of these previous and subsequent tellings that we become most keenly aware of the extraordinary nature of Chaucer's treatment of Criseyde. Within a strongly antifeminist tradition, no writer, before or after, has allowed Criseyde so strong a voice, or presented her through the eyes of so sympathetic a narrator: 'she so sory was for hire untrouthe, / Iwis, I wolde excuse hire yet for routhe' (V, 1098–9).

Central to Chaucer's defence of Criseyde is his nuanced treatment of the psychological process of her love for Troilus from start to finish. While Boccaccio's telling emphasizes Criseida's sexuality and moves all too clearly towards her betrayal of Troilus, Chaucer leaves us finally uncertain regarding the motivation of his Criseyde; he both allows more insight into her psyche, particularly in the earlier books, and is highly selective in terms of conclusive detail. Criseyde remains enigmatic, yet is placed at the centre of a web of suggestive imagery and emotion. She is represented in terms of the idealized lady, but she is also carefully individualized. Whereas Troilus tends to express and enact conventions of love, Criseyde is depicted very differently, as making choices in love that are the result of intersecting desires, fears and social constraints. From her first appearance in the temple at the feast of the Palladium, she is characterized not by sexuality but by duality, on the one hand a vulnerable figure, dressed in black, standing alone near the door, 'ay undre shames drede', but on the other, 'debonaire of chere, / With ful assured lokyng and manere' (I, 180–2). She is assigned all the attributes of female beauty and nobility, but is also 'somdel deignous* . . . for she lat falle / Hire look a lite aside in swich manere / Ascaunces*, "What, may I nat stonden here?"' (*haughty; *as if to say: I, 290–2). Chaucer depicts a woman at once uncertain and self-possessed, who is distinguished too by a quality of game-playing – all emphases that are sustained in his treatment of Criseyde.

Chaucer's narrative of Criseyde's love is deeply complicated by Pandarus' role in promoting the affair. Whereas Troilus sees Criseyde and is immediately overcome by love, Criseyde hears through Pandarus' subtle rhetoric of persuasion that she is the object of desire: she is a pawn in his game. Her relationship with her uncle is characterized as an odd mixture of game and threat, a friendship that it is difficult to interpret. On the one hand, Pandarus amuses her with his 'japes', his 'many wordes glade and frendly tales' and 'merie chiere' (II, 148–9), and the scenes with Pandarus repeatedly emphasize laughter and 'play'. On the other, Pandarus' emotional manipulation of Criseyde towards love is disturbing: she is threatened with the suicide not only of Troilus but also of Pandarus, if she refuses to return Troilus' love (II, 446). The images of death that accompany Troilus' love occur again in relation to Criseyde, but here they characterize her fear of the consequences of love, 'Criseyde, which that wel neigh starf for feere, / So as she was the ferfulleste wight / That myghte be' (II, 449–51). Whereas Troilus suffers the pains of love, but looks out to the marvels of the universe, Criseyde looks fearfully inward, caught within her imaginings of differently constraining situations.

Fear is not Chaucer's sole emphasis, however: he is also concerned to depict Criseyde's love for Troilus in terms of animated emotion. Thus when she sees him riding by, her response is one of instinctive desire, described like Troilus' through the convention of the imprint of the eyes on the heart, and the Petrarchan image of love as drink, satiating thirst, and yet inspiring it, 'Criseÿda gan al his chere aspien, / And leet it so softe in hire herte synke, / That to hireself she seyde, "Who yaf me drynke"' (II, 650–1). This experience is swiftly followed, however, by an extended monologue, perhaps the most sustained insight we are given into Criseyde's psyche, and striking for its highly rational and pragmatic approach: it could not be more different from the voice of Troilus expressing the wound of irresistible love. Criseyde insists on her freedom to choose whether to have 'mercy and pitee' (II, 655) on Troilus, setting out the case for and against love, and her voice is memorable for its assurance and independence:

> 'I am myn owene womman, wel at ese –
> I thank it God – as after myn estat,
> Right yong, and stonde unteyd* in lusty leese*,   *untethered;
>   *pleasant pasture
>
> Withouten jalousie or swich debat:
> Shal noon housbonde seyn to me 'Chek mat!'
> For either they ben ful of jalousie,
> Or maisterfull, or loven novelrie*.   *new loves
>
> (II, 750–6)

The idea of love raises questions that recur across Chaucer's writings, of the nature of marriage and the possibility of freedom for women. Yet despite Criseyde's pragmatic, apparently proto-feminist approach to love, the monologue is also characterized by uncertainty. It progresses through the opposition of one point of view with another, positive and negative, and the image of clouds rushing across an uncertain March sky suggests Criseyde's changeable mind, the interplay of her hopes and fears with her underlying desire. She will become both a willing participant and a victim of manipulation in the game of love.

Chaucer's portrayal of Criseyde in terms of fear, both of the consequences of love and of refusing to love, is enhanced by his emphasis on her uneasy social status. While adultery is not morally condemned in the neoclassical world of the poem, we are made acutely aware of the importance of the notions of honour and reputation, and of the potential shame that discovery or, later, elopement would represent. In making Criseyde a widow, Chaucer engages with the issue of female independence, but also with the vulnerability of a woman without a protector in a chivalric world. The secrecy of the affair and the concern for honour are explicable in terms of the political impossibility of a liaison between a prince of Troy and the daughter of an arch-traitor, even one defended as firmly as Criseyde is by Helen, Deiphebus and Hector, but there is also the sense that secrecy is a dangerously definitive aspect of the game of love: *fin'amors* is contingent on it. Pandarus overtly plays on Criseyde's social predicament, inventing a lawsuit in order to effect a meeting between the lovers at Deiphebus' house. On the one hand, Criseyde is perhaps cast by Pandarus as more of a victim in social terms than she actually is; on the other, she becomes a victim of a different sort, the pawn, 'all innocent' in Pandarus' games of secret love. Yet she is by no means exclusively an innocent victim: just as she is earlier characterized as experiencing desire on seeing Troilus, so her interest is made explicit when she enters Troilus' chamber for the first time. She approaches him 'esily and ful debonairly' (III, 156), and her speech in defence of her own independence as lover is striking: 'A kynges sone although ye be, ywys, / Ye shal namore han sovereignete / Of me in love, than right in that cas is' (III, 170–2). Criseyde here chooses to commit herself to Troilus on an equal and free basis – even while she is skilfully manipulated by Pandarus into advancing the affair.

This peculiar combination of independence and victimization, desire and fear recurs in more extreme terms in Chaucer's account of Criseyde's dream in which an eagle tears out her heart, replacing it with its own (II, 925–31). She is described as feeling no pain, 'nothyng smerte' (II, 930), and yet this violent image of the tearing out of the heart is disturbing. The theme of force is reiterated through the details of the nightingale that sings as Criseyde falls asleep, recalling the classical story of Philomela, metamorphosed into a nightingale after having her tongue cut out by her rapist Tereus, and it is striking that Pandarus is earlier awakened by the 'sorrowful lay' of the swallow, Procne, which seems to recount the story of her sister Philomela to him (I, 63–9). Chaucer's reference to the nightingale's 'lay of love' sung in 'briddes wise' (II, 921–2) again evokes the idea of metamorphosis, and recalls a violent story of rape, heightening the sense of unease created by the violence of Criseyde's dream.

In the consummation scene itself, alongside Troilus' joy, Criseyde's fear again is emphasized. Chaucer carefully reshapes Boccaccio's telling to present the encounter as orchestrated not by Criseyde but by Pandarus, and we are left uncertain as to whether Criseyde suspects that Troilus will be present, 'Nought list myn auctour fully to declare / What that she thoughte' (III, 575–6). Once again Criseyde seems the victim of conflicting emotions, both attracted by and afraid of the game that she is half-coerced into playing, a figure very far removed from the bold, sensual lover of Boccaccio's consummation scene. Chaucer replaces the eagerness of Boccaccio's Criseida to cast off her garments with the disturbing image of the lark held by the sparrowhawk (III, 1191–2); the subtext of force is reiterated. It is Criseyde's timidity that is most emphasized when Troilus first embraces her, 'Criseyde, which that felte hire thus itake, / . . . Right as an aspes leef she gan to quake,' and even when her fear is replaced by joy, she is compared to the 'newe abaysed* nyghtyngale', an echo of the earlier reference (*startled: III, 1198–1200, 1233). Fear and violence are set aside for the description of the blissful night passed by the lovers, and yet perhaps they remain in the memory to shadow the confidence with which Criseyde utters her vow of faithfulness to Troilus: 'first shal Phebus fallen fro his speere, / And everich egle ben the dowves feere,* / And everich roche out of his place sterte, / Er Troilus oute of Criseydes herte' (*dove's companion: III, 1495–8).

The motif of force is also troublingly present in Pandarus' physical relations with Criseyde, alongside his emotional blackmail: he thrusts Troilus' letter into Criseyde's bosom (II, 1155), and, more surprisingly, thrusts his arm beneath the sheets on the morning after the consummation:

> With that she gan hire face for to wrye*   *hide
> With the shete, and wax for shame al reed;
> And Pandarus gan under for to prie,
> And seyde, 'Nece, if that I shal be ded,
> Have here a swerd and smyteth of myn hed!'
> With that his arm al sodeynly he thriste
> Under hire nekke, and at the laste hire kyste.
> (III, 1569–75)

While some critics have read this scene as an actual rape, emphasizing the phrase, 'Pandarus hath fully his entente' (III, 1582), such interpretations seem to ignore Chaucer's suggestive ambiguity (see Weisl 1995: 38; Chance 1995: 107–67). The poem certainly, however, raises questions about the nature of Pandarus' avuncular love, and his role in the affair as voyeur as well as friend. Criseyde is surrounded by images of fear, force and violation which counterbalance the emphasis on her own independence of mind, and thus place her as victim as well as culprit within a patriarchal world.

Once Fortune's wheel has turned and Criseyde has been offered in exchange for Antenor, Chaucer portrays Criseyde's extreme grief as written on her body: her face, once 'lik of Paradys the ymage', is now 'al ychaunged in another kynde' (IV, 864–5); her laughter is replaced by the tears that leave a purple ring around her eyes. Criseyde, however, engages much less than Troilus with the notion of herself as a victim of Fortune in love, and much more with the false nature of happiness generally; and she very swiftly returns to the realities, present and future, of her predicament, echoing the process of her response to the possibility of love in Book II. Again, however, this sense of realism is characterized by a multiplicity of possibilities and perspectives, and by the characteristic mixture of fear and confidence. Her confidence is specifically rooted in the future possibility of her return, by contrast to her fear of resisting in the present the political decree that she must be exchanged for Antenor. She believes not in the inexorability of Fortune, but rather that in the future she will be able to change Fortune; that love *will* have a transformative effect. In the present, however, an aggrandized respect for the authority of government demands silence about love and causes Criseyde to accept her departure: 'My goyng graunted is by parlement / So ferforth that it may nat be withstonde / For al this world' (IV, 1297–9). Her fear of disobeying law and contravening social dictates emerges again in her consideration of the possibility of elopement with Troilus and the potentially negative consequences of 'ravishment': betrayal of friends and city; the impossibility of returning if peace were made; loss of honour and name. Criseyde's solution, that she will orchestrate a reunion once she is in the Greek camp, is considerably more risky than elopement might be, but this danger is masked by a multiplicity of imagined possibilities: peace; persuasion; bribe. Criseyde leads in these scenes, meeting Troilus' excesses of grief and his desire to flee with an assurance that she will be able to effect her return. Fear of the present is countered by a quite unshakeable faith in her ability to act in the future.

The gap between real and imagined future, however, is poignantly evoked once Criseyde is seen within the Greek camp. Her plan to return is by no means easy to set into action: Calchas refuses to let her go, 'My fader nyl for nothing do me grace / To gon ageyn' (V, 694–5), and we are presented with a vulnerable figure, one of 'wommen fewe, among the Grekis stronge' (V, 688). She emphasizes the shame flight might bring on her: she might be held a spy or, worse, fall 'in the hondes of som wrecche' (V, 705), an image that echoes earlier references to violence and violation, but also reminds us that ravishment by Troilus would have been preferable. The narrative leaves us uncertain as to how well-founded Criseyde's fears are, but depicts very clearly her own sense of the impossibility of returning to Troy, a kind of social paralysis true to the psyche created earlier for her. And in the description of Diomede's accompanying pursuit of Criseyde, the motif of force that seems consistently to characterize Criseyde's relations with men recurs, as Diomede plots to bring her 'into his net,' to 'fisshen hire he leyde out hook and lyne' (V, 777).

It is striking that Chaucer chooses to place the celebrated portrait of Criseyde in this final book of the poem, in the context of her betrayal of Troilus, for it is memorably evocative both of her physical perfection and her sublime promise: 'Paradis stood formed in hire yën' (V, 817). The description ends, however, with the detail that she is 'Tendre-herted, slydynge of corage' (V, 825), and at this point it is indeed fear that most of all seems to characterize Crisyede. It is striking too that we are offered a formal picture, in which the voice of the narrator intrudes self-consciously, 'But trewely, I kan nat telle hire age' (V, 826). Criseyde's actions are presented more and more from an exterior viewpoint, left for the reader to assess. That she does not depart on the tenth day is not explained in terms of internal debate, but set in the context of the conversation held with Diomede as she laments her separation from Troilus (V, 864–5): evening falls, and we see her still in the Greek camp, remembering that she is 'allone and hadde nede / Of frendes help' (V, 1026–7). She is a fearful and forlornly resigned figure, who will 'shortly' (V, 1032) return the affection of Diomede and fail to keep her promise and return to Troy, although the long lament that follows this strangely brief account voices her recognition of her own frailty, and her sorrow.

Ultimately, resignation characterizes this Criseyde, who foretells her own reputation, but now sees herself as without choice, 'to late is now for me to rewe' (V, 1070); she can only be faithful to Diomede, even while her final prayers are for Troilus. Loss in love opens onto a much larger sense of loss in Criseyde's expression of profound regret and statement of the transience of all things, 'al shal passe; and thus I take my leve' (V, 1985). The last of her voice is heard at a remove, in the enigmatic letter she sends to Troilus. Its prevarications about rumour and the difficulty of returning, its discussion of her fear of writing, and its ambivalent promise of friendship are painfully evasive, yet all seem less than its poignant opening:

> 'How myght a wight in torment and in drede
> And heleles*, yow sende as yet gladnesse?   *ill
> I herteles*, I sik, I in destresse!   *disheartened
> Syn ye with me, nor I with yow, may dele,
> Yow neyther sende ich herte may nor hele.'
> (V, 1592–6)

Apart from the veiled words of her letters, however, Criseyde has faded out of the story: the narrator withholds the details of her love for Diomede, declining to take responsibility for his sources, 'the storie telleth,'; 'Men seyn – I not – that she yaf hym hire herte' (V, 1037, 1050).

While the narrator attempts to absolve Criseyde from blame, 'she so sory was for hire untrouthe, / Iwis, I wolde excuse hire yet for routhe', he concludes by fleeing from his subject-matter and from all 'payens corsed olde rites' (V, 1098–9, 1849). For the reader, aware from the start of the peculiar mixture of fear and confidence that defines Criseyde, perhaps her behaviour is more explicable than for the partisan narrator. Her individualization allows Chaucer to create a suggestive web of motivation in love and betrayal, taking her far beyond the emblem of the faithless woman. But as well, Chaucer suggests that her fault is partly rooted in a difficulty common to all mankind, the difficulty indeed that characterizes Boethius' laments and permeates the narrative of *Troilus* in different ways, of escaping the fixity of time, of seeing beyond the apparent interminability of the present. As she looks out over Troy's walls and towers, Criseyde raises the philosophical question of the situation of the individual within time, 'On tyme ypassed wel remembred me, / And present tyme ek koud ich wel ise, / But future tyme, er I was in the snare, / Koude I nat sen; that causeth now my care' (V, 746–9). This sense of being caught in the present, defined by memory, yet unable correctly to foresee the future, is crucial to Chaucer's portrayal of Criseyde. She attempts again and again to imagine a future, with and without Troilus, with a return to Troy, even with her death. The tragedy is that she believes, in an odd trick of self-confidence, that she will be able to shape her future. But in actuality, when Fortune's wheel turns she is caught by the impossibility of acting within the constraints of the present. She finds herself unable to do other than to yield to the demands of father and new lover, just as she has yielded to the demands of uncle, lover and society. In her power to love and in her failure to sustain love beyond the present, Chaucer's Criseyde is finally, fragilely, believably human.

The contrasting perspectives and complex psychological portrayals of Troilus and Criseyde, and the dynamic of their interactions with Pandarus and with each other, allow for a treatment of love that weaves together convention and originality, shaping of 'olde bokes' a new and profound matter, and moving from sorrow through the sublime and back again. Chaucer creates a poetic mode that allows him to pose, if not to answer, some of the most difficult questions of human existence – about death, free will, fate, providence, time, and most of all, of the nature of love. Love, finally, both makes and unmakes the self. The experience of love is at once the great subject and the great tragedy.

See also chapter 5, COURTLY WRITING; chapter 6, LOVE IN WARTIME: *TROILUS AND CRISEYDE* AS TROJAN HISTORY; chapter 8, TRAGEDY AND ROMANCE IN CHAUCER'S 'LITEL BOK' of *TROILUS AND CRISEYDE*.

Notes

1 For a sensitive treatment of medieval marriage, which argues against the predominant association of love with adultery in the literature of the period, see Neil Cartlidge, *Medieval Marriage: Literary Approaches, 1100–1300* (Cambridge: D. S. Brewer, 1997), in particular pp. 1–32. See also Conor McCarthy, *Marriage in Medieval England: Law, Literature and Practice* (Cambridge: Boydell Press, 2004).

2 For translations of Boccaccio's *Il Filostrato*, see Gordon 1978 (also includes extracts from Benoît's *Roman de Troie* and Henryson's *The Testament of Cresseid*) and Havely 1980 (also includes extracts from Benoît's *Roman* and Guido's *Historia Destructionis Troiae*). For a parallel text edition of Boccaccio's and Chaucer's poems, along with extensive scholarly discussion of each work and of Chaucer's process of translation, see Windeatt 1990. See also Lewis' influential essay, 'What Chaucer Really Did to *Il Filostrato*' (1932), in Benson 1991. The most comprehensive, acute and approachable discussion of the poem, to which this essay is greatly indebted, is that found in

Windeatt 1992. For a discussion of the history of criticism on *Troilus and Criseyde* and selected critical extracts, see Saunders 2001: 129–88. Influential collections of essays are found in Salu 1979, Barney 1980 and Benson 1991; Schoeck and Taylor 1960–1 and Vasta and Thundy 1979 also contain a number of influential essays on the poem. Useful introductory studies are offered by Spearing 1976, Bishop 1981 and Frantzen 1993. On love, see in particular Rowe 1976.

3   Influential essays on Troilus as chivalric warrior and as bound by his devotion to truth include Stanley 1976 and Barney 1972.

4   Criseyde has attracted a plethora of critical discussion. Influential early studies include E. Talbot Donaldson's two essays, 'Criseide and her Narrator' and 'Briseis, Briseida, Criseyde, Cresseid: Progress of a Heroine': see Donaldson 1970 and Vasta and Thundy 1979. Particularly influential more recent considerations have been those of Fries 1977, Aers 1979, Dinshaw 1989, Martin 1990 and Mann 1991.

References and Further Reading

Aers, David (1979). 'Criseyde: Woman in Medieval Society'. *Chaucer Review* 13, 177–200.

Barney, Stephen (1972). 'Troilus Bound'. *Speculum* 47, 445–58.

Barney, Stephen A. (ed.) (1980). *Chaucer's Troilus: Essays in Criticism*. London: Scolar Press.

Benson, C. David (1990). *Chaucer's* Troilus and Criseyde. London: Unwin Hyman.

Benson, C. David (ed.) (1991). *Critical Essays on Chaucer's* Troilus and Criseyde *and his Major Early Poems*. Milton Keynes: Open University Press.

Bishop, Ian (1981). *Chaucer's* Troilus and Criseyde: *A Critical Study*. Bristol: University of Bristol Press.

Cartlidge, Neil (1997). *Medieval Marriage: Literary Approaches, 1100–1300*. Cambridge: D. S. Brewer.

Chrétien de Troyes (1972). *Le Chevalier de la Charrete*, ed. Mario Roques. Les Romans de Chrétien de Troyes III. Paris: Champion.

Chrétien de Troyes (1991). *The Knight of the Cart (Lancelot)*. In *Arthurian Romances*, trans. William W. Kibler. Harmondsworth: Penguin.

Dinshaw, Carolyn (1989). *Chaucer's Sexual Poetics*. Madison: University of Wisconsin Press.

Donaldson, E. Talbot (1965). 'The Myth of Courtly Love'. Reprinted in Donaldson, *Speaking of Chaucer*. London: Athlone Press, 1970, pp. 154–63.

Donaldson, E. Talbot (1970). 'Criseide and her Narrator'. In Donaldson, *Speaking of Chaucer*. London: Athlone Press, pp. 65–83.

Donaldson, E. Talbot (1979). 'Briseis, Briseida, Criseyde, Cresseid: Progress of a Heroine'. In Vasta and Thundy (eds), *Chaucerian Problems*, pp. 3–12.

Frantzen, Allen J. (1993). Troilus and Criseyde: *The Poem and the Frame*. New York: Twayne; Toronto: Maxwell Macmillan Canada; New York: Maxwell Macmillan.

Fries, Maureen (1977). ' "Slydynge of Corage": Chaucer's Criseyde as Feminist and Victim'. In Arlyn Diamond and Lee R. Edwards (eds), *The Authority of Experience: Essays in Feminist Criticism*. Amherst: University of Massachusetts Press, pp. 45–59.

Gordon, R. K. (ed.) (1978). *The Story of Troilus*. Mediaeval Academy Reprints for Teaching 2. Toronto: University of Toronto Press, in association with the Mediaeval Academy of America.

Hansen, Elaine Tuttle (1992). *Chaucer and the Fictions of Gender*. Berkeley: University of California Press.

Havely, N. R. (1980). *Chaucer's Boccaccio: Sources for* Troilus *and the* Knight's *and* Franklin's Tales; *Translations from the* Filostrato, Teseida *and* Filocolo. Chaucer Studies 5. Woodbridge: D. S. Brewer.

Klassen, Norm (1995). *Chaucer on Love, Knowledge and Sight*. Cambridge: D. S. Brewer.

Lewis, C. S. (1932) 'What Chaucer Really Did to *Il Filostrato*'. Reprinted in C. David Benson (ed.), *Critical Essays on Chaucer's* Troilus and Criseyde (1991), pp. 8–22.

Lewis, C. S. (1936). *The Allegory of Love: A Study in Medieval Tradition*. Oxford: Oxford University Press.

Lewis, C. S. (1964). *The Discarded Image: An Introduction to Medieval and Renaissance Literature*. Cambridge: Cambridge University Press.

Mann, Jill (1991). *Geoffrey Chaucer*. Feminist Readings. Hemel Hempstead: Harvester Wheatsheaf.

Marie de France (1986). *The Lais of Marie de France*, trans. Glyn S. Burgess and Keith Busby. Penguin Classics. Harmondsworth: Penguin.

Martin, June Hall (1972). *Love's Fools: Aucassin, Troilus, Calisto and the Parody of the Courtly Lover*. Serie A – Monografias, 21. London: Tamesis.

Martin, Priscilla (1990). *Chaucer's Women: Nuns, Wives and Amazons*. Iowa City: University of Iowa Press.

McCarthy, Conor (2004). *Marriage in Medieval England: Law, Literature and Practice*. Cambridge: Boydell Press.

Mitchell, Jerome and William Provost (eds) (1973). *Chaucer the Love Poet*. Athens: University of Georgia Press.

Paxson, James J. and Cynthia A. Gravlee (eds) (1998). *Desiring Discourse: The Literature of Love, Ovid Through Chaucer*. Selinsgrove: Susquehanna University Press; London: Associated University Presses.

Rowe, Donald W. (1976). *O Love O Charite! Contraries Harmonized in Chaucer's* Troilus. Carbondale: Southern Illinois University Press; London: Feffer and Simons.

Salu, Mary (ed.) (1979). *Essays on* Troilus and Criseyde. Chaucer Studies 3. Cambridge: D. S. Brewer; Totowa, NJ: Rowman and Littlefield.

Saunders, Corinne (2001). *Rape and Ravishment in the Literature of Medieval England*. Cambridge: D. S. Brewer.

Schoeck, Richard and Jerome Taylor (eds) (1960–1). *Chaucer Criticism*. 2 vols. Notre Dame, Ind.: University of Notre Dame Press.

Spearing, A. C. (1976). *Chaucer:* Troilus and Criseyde. Studies in English Literature 62. London: Edward Arnold.

Stanley, E. G. (1976). 'About Troilus'. *Essays and Studies* ns 29, 84–106.

Vasta, Edward and Zacharias P. Thundy (eds) (1979). *Chaucerian Problems and Perspectives: Essays Presented to Paul E. Beichner C. S. C.* Notre Dame, Ind.: University of Notre Dame Press.

Wack, Mary (1990). *Lovesickness in the Middle Ages: The* Viaticum *and its Commentaries*. Philadelphia: University of Pennsylvania Press.

Weisl, Angela Jane (1995). *Conquering the Reign of Femeny: Gender and Genre in Chaucer's Romance*. Chaucer Studies 22. Cambridge: D. S. Brewer.

Windeatt, Barry (ed.) (1990). *Troilus and Criseyde: A New Edition of* The Book of Troilus. 2nd edn. London: Longman.

Windeatt, Barry (1992). *Troilus and Criseyde*. Oxford Guides to Chaucer. Oxford: Clarendon.

Windeatt, Barry (ed.) (2003). *Troilus and Criseyde*. Penguin Classics. London: Penguin.

Chapter Eight

Tragedy and Romance in Chaucer's 'Litel Bok' of *Troilus and Criseyde*

Norm Klassen

Introduction: 'Double'

Troilus and Criseyde announces its preoccupation with sadness in its opening phrase: 'The double sorwe of Troilus' (I, 1). The phrase suggests that the theme of the poem will be an intensely and unremittingly sad one, a 'double portion' of misery. Such an impression soon needs to be qualified, though not abandoned, as the audience (reader) is given a larger context in which to situate and refine their understanding of the opening claim: the sorrow in question pertains to 'lovynge' (I, 3). That information forces a shift in outlook and expectation because love is not unremittingly sad. Love means hope, if not outright gladness. The audience knows that pain accompanies love; it is part of its nature and part of the attraction. But so too is the prospect of happiness. The following line confirms the revision and clarifies the meaning of 'double' as signifying reiteration: 'Fro wo to wele, and after out of joie' (I, 4). Troilus will start in a condition of 'wo', then later be out of joy and back in a sorrowful state. The connotation of intensity persists, however, with the suggestion that the experience of woe a second time is surely worse than the first and, furthermore, that the second woe is all the sharper because of its contrast with intervening gladness: 'out of joie' gets its texture from both the initial 'wo' and from 'wele'. If this be tragedy, Chaucer's approach suggests that for him it has a twofold structure and an inbuilt elusive quality. One does not speak of sorrow *simpliciter*.

Paradoxically, Chaucer illustrates the elusiveness of sorrow by making it seem straightforward. The initial 'wo' threatens to escape scrutiny. It seems to be an uncomplicated originary point of reference for the poem. Yet when Chaucer first introduces Troilus, the audience does not find him sad. The contrast with Criseyde on this point is striking. Her situation is such that it could serve as an originary point of reference, one in which woe gets its definition from public loss and shame. But unlike Criseyde, who begins the poem in a state of double sorrow, both mourning her husband and enduring her father's treachery, first impressions of Troilus constellate around his smug self-satisfaction (I, 183–205). The reader meets him holding court, smiling, casting ironic judgement, looking 'ascaunces' (I, 205). Chaucer gives every indication that Troilus' behaviour on this occasion typifies his deportment: 'as he was wont' (I, 183). The woe comes later, with the god of love's angry response and a fateful glance.

When it does appear, the first condition of woe, far from being a self-contained point of reference, takes its definition from the experience of love at first sight. In the case of 'the double sorrow of Troilus', woe is intricated with love. Intrication (that is, complication) indicates pre-existing involvement, mutuality, relationality. Sorrow is elusive because it does not exist on its own. This understanding of sorrow as structurally binary is paradigmatic for Chaucer's approach to genre. Just as sorrow turns out to be difficult to pin down, so too does the poem's genre. However readily we may accept Chaucer's designation of the work as tragedy (V, 1786), discussion of its qualities as romance persists. The collocation of the two generic terms derives from Troilus' experience of sorrow. To put the case baldly, it would appear that 'sorwe' indicates the genre of tragedy and 'lovynge' that of romance, and that Chaucer both works with such a division and at the same time insists upon their mutual interdependence.

The ending of the opening sentence establishes, as a context for the questions regarding sorrow and loving already raised, the author's purpose. To tell of Troilus' double sorrow, 'My purpos is, er that I parte fro ye' (I, 5). In typical Chaucerian fashion, the author draws attention to himself as part of his work. This gesture heightens the awareness of a distinction between author and narrator, another doubling. Chaucer will shortly elaborate on the role of the narrator and raise questions about his experience, credentials and trustworthiness, similar to reservations we have about Pandarus; as many readers have noticed, Pandarus and the narrator have similar roles. Chaucer's most important purpose in self-reflexivity is to draw attention to the limitations of an audience's or a reader's ability fully to appreciate the perspective of anyone who initiates communication, including the author, and the need for circumspection in exercising trust. From the outset of the poem through to its end, he speaks as a creation, that is, with a sense of separation from himself. Chaucer anticipates by some 600 years recent sensitivity to the free play of the signifier. Chaucerian reflexivity gets at the very root of our limited ability to know the perspective of another person and the limitations of our own point of view, including our own knowledge of ourselves.

This orientation has implications for the argument and critical strategy that Chaucer speaks through the narrator for much of the time and *in propria persona* at other times. One critic exploits this distinction to suggest that the mistaken narrator, not the knowing author, calls *Troilus and Criseyde* a tragedy (McAlpine 1978). That reading strategy requires that the interpreter have a mechanism or a reasonable sense of when Chaucer makes the switch; it also reifies the idea of an author whose 'real' voice we hear at last, and so actually militates against the understanding of reflexivity proffered above. I think that the notions of such a mechanism and a final unveiling sit uneasily with Chaucer's sensibility as we glean it from his works as a whole. That sensibility puts the emphasis on limitation.

Chaucer's sensitivity to limitations of perspective translates into an attitude of humble, prudential engagement. He evinces just such an interest in issues of relationship and limitation in his handling of genre. Genre indicates an awareness of limitation. It suggests the contours of a worldview. As Helen Cooper has written, 'Different genres give different readings of the world: the fabliau scarcely notices the operations of God, the saint's life focuses on those at the expense of physical reality, tracts and sermons insist on prudential or orthodox morality, romances privilege human emotion. Each genre defines its own vocabulary and imagery, its own area of experience, and its way of signifying that experience' (1989: 19). In the *Canterbury Tales,* the different genres of the tales contribute significantly to the impression of individuals in community with their competing and overlapping perspectives. In *Troilus,* the question of genre similarly contributes suggestively to the impression of a narrator with a specific perspective and, behind him, the poet's larger yet still limited commitments informing the project. Both narrator and author contribute to a concern with worldview and therefore with a significant dimension of genre.

Genre, as several theorists have observed, amounts to a contract between writer and reader (audience). In the absence of the face-to-face situation governing everyday speech, genre helps to supply 'other types of directions, if the text in question is not to be abandoned to a drifting multiplicity of uses (or *meanings*, as the latter used to be termed)' (Jameson 1975: 135). There is tension but no contradiction between Chaucer's reflexive sensibility (the acknowledgement of limited control) and an interest in genre so as not to abandon his texts to 'a drifting multiplicity of uses' (that is, the desire to control reception). Awareness and handling of this tension contribute to Chaucer's prudential engagement.

The problem of absence looms over the poem from the first stanza onward: 'er that I parte fro ye'. The context is the promise of disclosure, yet at the same time it declares the impending separation of author and audience. Inevitably, a parting will come, and with it the need for generic guidance. That guidance comes as the moment of parting nears. Chaucer announces the generic category of the poem to be that of tragedy:

> Go, litel bok, go, litel myn tragedye,
> Ther God thi makere yet, er that he dye,
> So sende myght to make in some comedye!
> (V, 1786–8)

The poem's opening urges caution regarding such straightforward statements, though not necessarily distrust of the narrator. The pattern of the opening stanza does not suggest that Chaucer negates straightforward statements; rather, as in the case of 'wo', he suggests that concepts do not resolve into singularities. He discloses additional possibilities, deepens the sense of a range of meanings and brings them into proximity with one another. The desire to provide guidance confronts and perhaps sublimates the reality of doubling, of intrication.

The centrality of doubling in *Troilus and Criseyde* suggests that the question of ultimate outlook may be undecidable. Several critics have confronted this dilemma directly. All must negotiate it in trying to make sense of the ending. For my part, I wish to suggest that Chaucer's understanding of perspective, limitation and worldview also includes a sense of compressed spatiality. In contemporary usage, notions like perspective and worldview are generally taken to mean discrete points in a boundless universe. Where the ending of *Troilus* is concerned, discussions usually invoke the ending as palinode, in which the outlooks associated with tragedy and romance represent opposite nodes in a linear schema, with a huge space (potentially an infinitely huge

159

space) between them. Chaucer thinks of genre differently, in terms of compression and immanence, in terms not of vast and potentially infinite spaces but of little ones. Among the concepts that disclose hidden riches when viewed in a twofold way, the word 'litel', which appears twice in the generic labelling of the poem, indicates both diminution and a compressed range of possibilities. Differences remain real and genuinely problematic, but the sense of paradox and intrication is palpably stronger than we typically imagine.

'Tragedye'

If tragedy and romance indicate sorrow and love respectively, both concern states of privacy and interiority. That would mean a change, for tragedy in the fourteenth century is most ready associated with public life, with the fall of a great man from prosperity into misery. Chaucer refers to tragedy in two of his works, in *Troilus* and in 'The Monk's Prologue and Tale'. A comparison and contrast of these usages and contexts reveals differences in public/private orientation and in the degree of narratorial involvement.

Chaucer explicitly defines tragedy in the *Canterbury Tales*. The Monk, in the Prologue to his tale, offers the following definition:

> Tragedie is to seyn a certeyn storie,
> As olde bookes maken us memorie,
> Of hym that stood in greet prosperitee,
> And is yfallen out of heigh degree
> Into myserie, and endeth wrecchedly.
> (VII, 1973–7)

The misery in this definition belongs to 'hym that stood in greet prosperitee'. Another description of tragedy, recorded in the *Letter to Can Grande* ascribed to Dante, simply associates it with an unhappy ending. Chaucer's English contemporary, Thomas of Walsingham, notes both mournful endings and 'the old deeds and crimes of wicked kings and tyrants' (quoted in Kelly 1997: 48). The definition in 'The Monk's Tale' combines a public emphasis with ending in misery but does not specify crimes, wickedness and tyranny.

'The Monk's Tale' exemplifies a *de casibus* tradition of stories of fall from prosperity into misery. Chaucer had it modelled for him in Giovanni Boccaccio's *De casibus virorum illustrium [Of the Falls of Illustrious Men]* (1360) and *De claribus mulieribus [Of Celebrated Women]* (1362);

his own experiment in 'The Monk's Tale' provides a vital link between tragedy and the *de casibus* tradition in fifteenth-century works such as Lydgate's *Fall of Princes* (1431–8) and the very successful sixteenth-century collection of such stories, *The Mirror for Magistrates* (1559 onward). Chaucer specifies what 'tragedy' means both at the outset and at the end of the Monk's telling of the story of Croesus (VII, 2761–6). In the *de casibus* tradition, the plot is historical, the style elevated (but narrative, not dramatic), the philosophy stoical in the vein of *contemptus mundi*, and the characters of high rank. The focus in *de casibus* works is public and political, the fall of great individuals from prosperity into misery. *Troilus and Criseyde* does not relate such a public fall but rather a fall in loving. While the definition from 'The Monk's Tale' provides a useful point of reference, it does not fully account for Chaucer's use of the term in the *Troilus*.

A second distinction between 'The Monk's Prologue and Tale' and the *Troilus* concerns the narrator's attitude towards his audience and tragic material. The Monk's attitude towards his audience would not appear to emphasize their ability to empathize with those in tragic circumstances. The prosperous serve as illustrations, as memorials to tragedy. For the Monk, they teach folk not to trust prosperity: 'Lat no man truste on blynd prosperitee / Be war by thise ensamples trewe and olde' (VII, 1997–8). This advice, along with the introduction to tragedy in the Prologue, is measured and moralizingly objective.

While the Monk offers a dispassionate introduction, he adopts a performative mode in the telling of the tales: 'I wol biwaille in manere of tragedie' (VII, 1991). This enactment tends to take the form of apostrophe ('O Lucifer' (2004)), pathetic introduction ('Loo Adam' (2007)) and lament ('Allas Fortune!' (2367)). The Monk reinforces this performative aspect of tragedy, perhaps a vestige of drama, at the end of the story of Croesus:

> Tragedies noon oother maner thyng
> Ne kan in syngynge crie ne biwaille
> But that Fortune alwey wole assaille
> With unwar* strook the regnes that been proude.   *unexpected
> For whan men trusteth hire, thanne wol she faille,
> And covere hire brighte face with a clowde.
> (VII, 2761–6)

'The Monk's Prologue and Tale' suggest a bifurcated handling of tragedy, on the one hand detached and moralizing, on the other performatively involved.

For the Monk, tragedies can instruct; for Boethius, the main source for a definition of tragedy behind the Monk, that is doubtful. The label of tragedy Chaucer adds to *de casibus* he takes from Boethius, who serves as the most reliable guide to a working definition of the genre in England in the fourteenth century. The *Consolation of Philosophy* supplies a definition very close to the one Chaucer gives in the Prologue to 'The Monk's Tale' and even more tightly linked with the reference to tragedy at the close of the tale of Croesus. Boethius, together with a fourteenth-century commentator, also suggests a link between tragedy and interiority not readily apparent from the *Consolation's* emphasis on detached acceptance of Fortune's turning wheel.

Imagining a speech by Fortune making a defence of her fickle ways, Lady Philosophy says this:

> 'What other thynge bywaylen the cryinges of tragedyes but oonly the dedes of Fortune, that with an unwar strook overturneth the realmes of greet nobleye?' (II, pr. 2)

This definition emphasizes the work of Fortune in overturning the realms of the great, a focus entirely oriented towards the public rather than the individual or his interiority. That the speech is meant to represent Fortune's perspective lends to the quotation an ironic quality. While it sounds as though Lady Philosophy is inviting the reader to take a detached view of changes in fortune, it is actually Fortune herself who is scorning tragedy as an art form dominated by 'cryinges' and bewailing. This twofold disdain hyperbolizes the nature of tragedy, and next to it Nicholas Trevet's gloss on the term, which Chaucer includes in his translation of Boece, represents objectivity itself: 'Glose. Tragedye is to seyn a dite of a prosperite for a tyme, that endeth in wrecchidnesse' (II, pr. 2). The gloss offers the Monkish suggestion that one might be able to learn from tragedies; it inflects tragedy as a technical term, which Trevet snatches from the mouth of Fortune, and which Chaucer then gives to an English literary readership in what one medievalist misleadingly calls a 'superficial literary definition' (Robertson 1952: 2), *together with* the attitude of crying and bewailing which Fortune mocks and which the *Consolation* applies to the condition of the prisoner at the start of the book. Both matter to Chaucer. The definition puts the 'literary', including ascriptions of genre, into the camp of the detached, while tragedy itself embodies passionate involvement.

From Lady Philosophy's point of view, crying betrays one's allegiance to Fortune, one's forgetfulness of one's place in the cosmos. In the Boethian formulation, one forgets that what appears to happen by chance actually is part of a larger design. The muses, far from offering instruction, are to blame. The *Consolation* opens with the imprisoned narrator weeping and promising poetry of sorrowful matter:

> Allas! I wepynge, am constreyned to bygynnen vers of sorwful matere, that whilom in florysschyng studie made delitable ditees*. For lo, rendynge* muses of poetes enditen* to me thynges to ben writen, and drery vers of wretchidnesse weten my face with verray teres. (*poems; *tearing; *dictate: I, m. 1)

The language strikingly resembles the opening stanza of *Troilus and Criseyde*, with a similar emphasis on sorrow, on sad verse and on a weeping narrator. In the opening *prosa* which follows, Lady Philosophy appears and banishes the muses. They do not relieve suffering but rather nourish it:

> And whan she saughe thise poetical muses aprochen aboute my bed and enditynge wordes to my wepynges, sche was a litil amoeved . . . [Thise comune strompettis] nat oonly ne asswagen noght his sorwes with none remedies, but thei wolden fedyn and noryssen hym with sweete venym. (I, pr. 1)

The muses encourage a vicious circle. The 'endited' words are sweet venom, and they feed tears; such words belong to tragedy as described by Fortune. Thus begins the prisoner's instruction and eventual recovery.

Tragedy in Boethius, then, is a work that embodies the attitude of having forgotten providence and bewailing changing Fortune. By implication, it can also apply to the attitude itself (bewailing, crying), either of the person confronting Fortune or even the response of the person reading about the workings of Fortune. By contrast, in the commentary tradition that reaches Chaucer, one can approach tragedy in an attitude of artistic detachment and perhaps even learn from it. Ironically, what one learns from it is a Boethian lesson. From the point of view of the observer trained in the school of Lady Philosophy, the genre refers to a story that illustrates the fall of a great man but that does not necessarily throw the reader into emotional turmoil.

Chaucer is, arguably, picking up on a distinction latent in the Boethian text, one which the commentary tradition brings to light with the gloss on 'tragedy'. This distinction accentuates differences in point of view. The twofold possibilities for working with the term allow Chaucer, probably fresh from having translated Boece, to explore the implications of perspective, to elevate it as a governing principle in his aesthetic. Boethius privileges stability and a detached, cosmic perspective, yet Chaucer may have found something within Boethius that allowed him fully and faithfully to engage Boethian philosophy and at the same time to move well beyond Boethian concerns to meditations that could look like contrasting and competing commitments: appeal to the muses and, more importantly, a powerful willingness to be involved. In the *Troilus*, even more so than in 'The Monk's Prologue and Tale', Chaucer understates but performatively experiments with detachment and involvement as parallel tragic tracks. Chaucer exploits this potential for bifurcation in the contrast between the detachment of the Monk (and Pandarus) and the emotional involvement of the narrator and Troilus.

The first stanza of *Troilus and Criseyde* indicates an orientation certainly different from the detachment of the Monk. The narrator is desperately involved: 'Thesiphone, thow help me for t'endite / Thise woful vers, that wepen as I write' (I, 6–7). The narrator invokes the aid of a Fury to help him tell the story because he, the narrator, is weeping. Chaucer's storyteller, quite unlike the Monk, is moved to tears by this tragedy. While the Monk wants his audience to listen to the stories objectively and to learn, Chaucer's narrator is passionately involved. He wants to represent lovers like Troilus, to stand in solidarity with them: 'Help me, that am the sorwful instrument, / That helpeth loveres, as I kan, to pleyne' (I, 10–11). He serves the god of love's servants, standing in a position relative to the tragic figures quite different from that of the dispassionate Monk with his chance collection.

The invocation of the muse contains an ambiguity that reinforces the theme of involvement. The 'that' clause ('that wepen as I write') is unclearly connected to an antecedent. Though I presumed initially that the narrator is weeping while he writes, the clause could as easily refer to Thesiphone, whom we learn in the next stanza is 'sorwynge evere in peyne' (I, 9). As goddess of torment, the Fury stands in circular relation to all who are in the state Chaucer ascribes to Troilus. She both causes the torment and sorrows in pain. Greek conceptuality invites the paradoxical construal of her both lashing out at others because of her own pain and sorrowing in the meting out of pain, which feeds back into lashing out because of her own pain, and so on. The 'that' clause could also refer to the lines of poetry themselves, in keeping with a worldview that countenanced animation and enchantment, a very rich form of personification. All three possibilities for the ambiguous 'that' clause underscore involvement rather than detachment. There may be lessons to be learned from this tragedy, but the poem's beginning puts the narrator's attitude towards tragedy on a different footing from 'The Monk's Tale'. This difference also calls into question the applicability of the model of tragedy described in the 'Prologue to the Monk's Tale'.

Ovidian material also influences *Troilus* as tragedy. It helps to cement the involvement of the emotions, notably love, which puts pressure on the strict association of tragedy and tale with public fall. In the course of his elaborate self-defence in the *Tristia*, Ovid claimed that the theme of love regularly appears as part of the matter of tragedy. This observation augments the emphasis in Boethius and the *de casibus* tradition. Indeed, it is difficult to tell whether, in general, the emphasis for Ovid is on stories that end badly or on the vagaries of love. One quite plausible line of argument has it that interest in formal tragedy was stimulated by tales of ill-fated love inspired by Ovid, and that Chaucer played a role in a transition from tales of tragic love to the reinvention of dramatic tragedy (Clough 1982: 212; Dalrymple 2002: 159–60). Ill-fated love did not become associated with formal tragedy until much later; in the Middle Ages such sadness (as in the case of *Tristan and Isolde*) fell under the rubric of romance, a capacious term to which we must shortly turn our attention. *Troilus and Criseyde* supplies a similar focus on interiority and emotional fall into sorrow, but explicitly under the rubric of tragedy.

The Ovidian notion of 'tragic love' suggests a degree of intrication that may have contributed to Chaucer's doubling of romance and tragedy. The story of Procne and Philomela, to which Chaucer alludes at the beginning of Book II, accentuates doubling in a tale that appears to hold the promise of accord between love of kin (father for daughter, sister for sister) and marital love, but descends into violence and chaos. For Ovid, Tereus' violence complicates the sisters' relationship, lending to it a tragic dimension, especially from Philomela's perspective:

> 'O wicked deed! O cruel monster,
> Barbarian, savage! Were my father's orders
> Nothing to you, his tears, my sister's love,
> My own virginity, the bonds of marriage?
> Now it is all confused, mixed up; I am
> My sister's rival, a second-class wife, and you,

> For better and worse, the husband of two women,
> Procne my enemy now; at least she should be.'
>
> (6, 533–8)

The tragic dimension entails both a downward turn and paradoxical confusion. The sudden rivalry between the sisters underscores the theme of doubling. Ovid pursues this idea throughout the story, notably with reference to Tereus, driven by 'a double fire . . . his own passion and his nation's' (6, 460) and responding to Philomela's lament with 'The double drive of fear and anger' (6, 549–50). Ovid presses doubles to emphasize sorrowful fate. Where Tereus is concerned, doubles suggest intensity of passion and reaction; Philomela's speech gestures towards bifurcation and paradox, eliciting the story's intrication of love and tragedy. The twofold use of the double motif recalls the opening of *Troilus*.

Ovidian material – the recognition of the common appearance of love in tragedy, tales of ill-fated love, and the accent on doubles in his tale of Procne and Philomela – helps account for a pressing together of tragedy and romance motifs. Both Boethius and Ovid contribute to a twofold understanding of tragedy and, in their own ways, to involvement and interiority.

'Romaunce'

While the spectre of tragedy falls over *Troilus and Criseyde* with the announcement of double sorrow and with a narrator in darkness, far from the help of the god of love (I, 18), Chaucer quickly affirms some level of positive experience in love. It is mooted in the phrase, 'how his aventures fellen / Fro wo to wele' and made explicit with the identification of happy lovers 'that bathen in gladnesse' (I, 22). Chaucer moves the poem out of unremitting 'derknesse' or a realm of 'sorwynge evere in peyne'.

These happy lovers provide an invaluable point of reference for the poem, a *telos* that does not privilege Boethian abandonment of the vicissitudes of this life. They have endured 'hevynesse' and now need only to persevere and to pray for others less fortunate than themselves. It would appear that the narrator is addressing primarily men: they need 'myght hire ladies so to please / That it to love be worship and plesaunce' (I, 45–6). Troilus is their point of comparison. Though the prevailing tenor is male-oriented, the narrator does include both sexes in the falsely slandered for whom the fortunate are to pray. In this way, happy lovers provide a universal point of reference for those who are in Troilus' unfortunate situation or endure something like his 'unsely* aventure' (*unhappy: I, 35). They provide the explanation as to why one would not simply abandon the enterprise of loving, as Chaucer instructs young folk to do at the end of the poem.

Such optimistic zeal suggests the world of romance: the focus is now on 'lovynge', on those lovers who bathe in gladness, and on a narrator entirely devoted to faithful service, a romance motif familiar through 'courtly love'. The ethos suggests characters who are high-born, and the poem will bear out this hint. If romance means loving, it also connotes happiness, especially the happy ending of comedy. The vast majority of romances end happily, and while some of the most famous ones do not (for example, the stories of Lancelot and Guinevere, Tristan and Isolde), they include happiness in love as the apex of the lovers' experience and a defining feature of the romance. In a story like that of *Tristan and Isolde*, the tragic double death nonetheless betokens a bittersweet union and triumph of an ideal love. Chaucer flirts with this motif in Book IV when Troilus thinks Criseyde has died and plans to join her, and Criseyde vows that she would have killed herself had she recovered from her swoon to find Troilus dead (IV, 1156–1241). Such bittersweet triumph contributes to the difficulty of assigning some of Ovid's tales of ill-fated love, and Chaucer's *Troilus* as well, to tragedy or romance.

Critics agree that a precise definition of romance as a medieval genre is impossible to generate. This difficulty may in fact indicate an anticipation of recent interest in the dynamic nature of genre and textuality. The term can refer to a wide range of thematic, rhetorical and stylistic details, not least in its source in Old French (Field 1999: 152; Copeland 1991: 219; Strohm 1971: 354). If 'romance' is so capacious a term as to resist definition, one wonders whether it can serve as a generic category, for genre implies such specifics as contract and worldview. Yet people proceed as if they knew roughly what romance entails. Thus Fredric Jameson can write confidently of 'the constitutive raw materials of magic and otherness which medieval romance found ready to hand in its socioeconomic environment' (1975: 142) and Lee Patterson of how, in *Troilus*, 'the private stands wholly apart from and seeks to efface the public, just as, at the level of genre, romance, a story focused on the fate of a single individual, seeks to preempt tragedy' (1991:107). Romance both has recognizable features as a genre and resists definition.

167

Romance resists becoming outdated because of a built-in archaism. Numerous critics have analysed this archaizing attitude, noting that a view of the past that presents it as uniform and unchanging has historically contingent uses. Cooper observes in *The Cambridge History of Medieval English Literature* that romance after 1400 conjures stability in a time of increasingly fractious political and theological debate (Cooper 1999: 690; see also Field 1999: 175; Copeland 1991: 220). If romance endures as an archaizing attitude, it also loses some of its distinctiveness as a historically contingent social agreement. Jameson accounts for the durability of the genre by arguing that romance has a heightened ability to draw attention to the worldviewishness of presenting a world:

> Romance as a literary form is that event in which *world* in the technical sense of the transcendental horizon of my experience becomes precisely visible as something like an innerworldly object in its own right, taking on the shape of *world* in the popular sense of nature, landscape, and so forth. (Jameson 1975: 142)

The form itself suggests medieval sensitivity to genre as worldview.

Romance as a genre that does not easily admit of generic definition accords with recent genre theory. Medieval usage of romance may have anticipated current sensitivities. The view that genre is simply a classificatory system has contributed to static and dichotomizing tendencies in English studies, such as a separation between form and content, and the notion that forms constrain the individual, entrenching a dichotomy of individual and society (Devitt 1993: 573–4; Cohen 1986:204). Recent theory has focused on genre as a 'dynamic patterning of human experience' (Devitt 1993: 573) and genres as 'open systems' in which 'each genre is related to and defined by others to which it is related' (Cohen 1986: 210). Furthermore, changes in genre can be a social act and can reveal social changes (Cohen 1986: 216; Jameson 1975).

Discussion of *Troilus and Criseyde* in generic terms is susceptible to dichotomous thinking, as discussion easily gravitates towards the poem's ending (as the site where the downward or upward direction of the action contributes significantly to the assignment of genre, even without Chaucer's explicit labelling) and interpretation of its 'palinode'. To think of tragedy and romance together in terms of an 'open system' of 'dynamic patterning' may help reduce the pressure to choose sides and to carve up the poem as a testimony to one impulse or its opposite, though assuredly debates of genre will not simply evaporate. Writing in the last quarter of the fourteenth century, Chaucer benefits from a long view of categories for story, especially those that cluster around related features we tend to call, however provisionally, romance. He would have no illusions of its having a narrowly set form, and could certainly see how such a cluster of defining features changed over time.

Critics also widely recognize that Chaucer exemplifies a time period of profound innovation, albeit one with diachronic connections. Whereas in other contexts writers evidently invoked romance as a stabilizing fantasy, Chaucer may have exploited just that heterogeneity of romance materials to suggest an open system. For Chaucer to have thought seriously about genre in general, and to have participated in a 'radical rethinking of romance' in the time of Richard II in particular (Cooper 1999: 693), contributing to the dynamism of genre, would support Claudia Rattazzi Papka's view that Chaucer repeatedly defers ending in *Troilus* and thereby 'annihilates dualism' through 'the magic of textuality' (1998: 277). The non-closure that numerous critics have recently highlighted makes it difficult to organize a discussion of the poem's genre, at least as indicating a set category, primarily around how it ends.

Whether or not the poem is ultimately comic, its opening declares the promise of several features of romance which can be charted all the way through the poem, notably a concentration on love and on privacy. It takes the audience into the personal realm of the narrator's plans, ambitions and personal involvement with tragic material (making it difficult to sustain a sharp binary of romance as private and tragedy as public), and shortly afterwards into Troilus' inner transformation and meditations as well as the private exchanges between the different pairings among the three principal characters, culminating in the beautiful intimacy and eroticism of Book III.

Chaucer uses the term 'romaunce' in the poem only in a very general sense, one which reminds us of a pedestrian function that extends the range of meaning for the term beyond comedy, love, privacy, or other suggestions of generic delimitation and balances emotional involvement with detachment. Chaucer's two references conform to the innocuous use of the term to describe a book written in the vernacular. Both instances associate romance with emotional detachment. At the start of Book II, Pandarus finds his niece with two other ladies listening to a story. Pandarus wonders if it is about love, and Criseyde's response makes them both laugh. Laughter and idle speculation about love provide the context for Criseyde to disclose that ' "This romaunce is of Thebes that we rede" ' (II, 100). The context in the story suggests tragedy in the sense of a sad story and in the sense of movement from prosperity to misery: they had just heard about Laius, Oedipus and 'al that dede' (II, 102), up to the point where 'the bisshop, as the book kan telle, / Amphiorax, fil thorugh the ground to helle' (II, 103–4). In this context, the term 'romaunce' hardly connotes the opposite of tragedy in any sense of the word, and yet the laughter, talk of love and suggestion to 'don to May som observaunce' (II, 112) do. At the very least, they suggest emotional distance from the matter of Thebes, an attitude of detachment.

The second reference is only marginally more helpful. In the central bedroom scene, once Pandarus has brought Troilus to Criseyde's bedside, he withdraws to the fire and makes a face 'As for to looke upon an olde romaunce' (III, 980). The narrator does not say whether he has a book in hand, but in the context romance is supposed to mean something other than love, in effect a focus for Pandarus other than the love affair being conducted right before his eyes. Like the term 'tragedie', the term 'romaunce' can be used to signify distance and objectivity. In this case, it means Pandarus' supposed non-involvement in the scene of happy love before him. In the first example, it means a neutral story safe to tell a woman in mourning. Like tragedy, romance can connote emotional detachment, a safe world of books.

'Litel'

Chaucer's experimental and complex emphasis on doubles and tight entwining of tragedy and romance cause vexation when he apparently comes clean to describe his work as a tragedy. While the passage has received extensive consideration, the word 'litel' has never stimulated much reflection. Though not a key to the passage, it does suggest a context and orientation. Clearly, the passage belongs to an ancient humility topos, a point which has been observed. H. Marshall Leicester has the word 'litel' in mind and plays with the humility topos when he refers to not just this but any text as 'a kind of orphan', the reception of which an author cannot be sure (1987: 18). Leicester's deconstructive remarks remind us of one of the tasks of genre, to attempt to assure the proper response, but they do not particularly encourage contemplation of the relationship between 'litel' and the nature of the genre of this poem. The humility topos gives Chaucer the opportunity to echo (twice in the line, once more in the stanza) a word that he uses repeatedly throughout the poem. While he often employs 'little' to signify diminution or, through litotes, its opposite, he also uses the term to suggest compression and immanence, an environment charged with possibilities that are discrete yet close together. To understand Chaucer's repeated reference to 'little' in this stanza in this twofold way fits the pattern of his interest in doubles. In the latter sense of compression, 'little' points to the intrication of tragedy and romance and suggests an aspect of a worldview that allows such discrete possibilities to stand pressed together.

As a book on a sad theme, the poem works at close quarters with seemingly large oppositions, such as that between fate and free will, pagan and Christian, tragedy and romance. I have suggested that the earliest and perhaps best example of this compactness is the interrelatedness of sadness and love in the opening stanza of the poem. Love, in the context of this work, is constitutive of tragedy. Similarly, a few lines later, for a few lucky lovers 'passed hevynesse' is very much a part of present gladness. Chaucer's little tragedy then plays itself out in little spaces that similarly compress it with romance. In the temple Criseyde stands unassumingly in her black weeds behind others, in a little space: 'And yet she stood ful lowe and stille alone, / Byhynden other folk, in litel brede' (I, 178–9). She does not occupy much space. Her woeful circumstances press upon her and the gay throngs celebrating the festival of Palladium dwarf her. Yet from this space the dynamic and concentrated power of the poem is released by the power of Criseyde's gaze. This little space compresses Troilus' destiny, as well as her own. After love converts him, he acts as love dictates; simultaneously, her woe is transmuted into his woe.

Subsequent dialogue and action occur principally in Troilus' chamber, the enclosed bed in Pandarus' 'litel closet' (III, 663), in Criseyde's bed, where they reach the fateful decision for her to go to her father for a little time, and in an unidentified tent in the Greek camp. The focal point of the poem as romance is Pandarus' 'litel closet'. Patterson has alerted us to the spatiality of this scene and has argued that enclosed spaces, little spaces, indicate the privacy and transcendence of romance (1991: 108). (Transferred to the context of the generic designation, such an association of 'litel' with romance would only make the phrase 'litel myn tragedye' all the more jarring.) He observes that history is always at hand despite the romance, re-entering through the back door, through reminders of the social and military context, representing the triumph of history and of tragedy

(Patterson 1991: 109). Yet for others, the eroticism of Book III suggests an enduring affirmation of human love. Commenting on Troilus' swoon in this little space, Jill Mann suggests a compression of possibilities when she writes, 'taken together with its causes and its consequences, it demonstrates the rich multiplicity of potential relationships in the love which here reaches its consummation' (1980: 332).

The little spaces of love compress romance and tragedy. 'Little' contributes to the sense that they are two sides of the same coin. Chaucer had experimented with such proximity earlier, with the gate to the park in the *Parliament of Fowls*, over which words 'of ful gret difference' (125), of encouragement and doom, appear side by side. For him, quite different experiences and the worldviews they engender lie inexplicably close to one another. Chaucer keeps tragedy and romance together, intricated with one another. History may triumph, but not triumphalistically. Conversely, the recurring suggestion that 'Christian triumphalism' contributes to 'competing and largely irreconcilable alternatives when interpreting how the ending of Chaucer's work relates to its antecedent narrative' (Pearcy 2002: 280–1) encourages a sense of spatiality that the poem qualifies. Distinctions and alternative visions do exist; however, they occupy a compressed space, fostering an outlook on life that recognizes intrication and the proximity of paradox.

Medieval literature contains striking examples of something small used in this sense. Julian of Norwich deploys the beautiful image of the world as a hazelnut in the palm of her hand:

> And in this he shewed a little thing, the quantitie of an haselnott, lying in the palme of my hand, as me semide, and it was as rounde as a balle. I looked theran with the eye of my understanding, and thought: What may this be? And it was answered generaelly thus: It is all that is made. I marvayled how it might laste, for me thought it might sodenly haue fallen to nawght for littlenes. And I was answered in my understanding: It lasteth and ever shall, for god loueth it; and so hath all thing being by the loue of god. (V, 9–16)

In the context, this image is world-affirming. It betokens Julian's incarnational outlook, a theological orientation in which she turns to the world as the theatre of God's activity. It evokes the loving relationship between creator and creation, with tenderness and involvement symbolized by the open hand. The world may be little, but one need not fear its disappearance. It contains all the possibilities of creation compressed into a small sphere.

William Langland's image of the half-acre similarly compresses a world of possibilities in an image of something relatively small. He transforms the pilgrimage motif from a linear, stretched-out activity to a localized, paradoxically stay-at-home one. He does not merely internalize pilgrimage; rather, he promotes one's local environment as a place – the only realistic and relevant place – for the working out of justice and a this-worldly spirituality. Chaucer himself adopts an image of compactness in 'The Second Nun's Prologue' (VIII, 43–9). Borrowing from Dante, Chaucer invokes the Virgin Mary as the paradoxically small, enclosed space of limitless love and peace. Her womb contains and compresses an expansive range of possibilities.

I would suggest that such an outlook feeds into the humility topos, which is after all more than a well-worn literary device. Real literary greatness often shines through in an artist's ability to recognize, engage and convey his or her inability to understand the immanence of suffering and joy, tragedy and romance. In its political structures and theological trajectories, the late fourteenth century may have been delicately poised in ways that the fantasies of romance and the sureties of *de casibus* tragedy after 1400 could not imagine. Like sayings that become clichés, truths that become truisms, the humility topos can become a mere reflexive rhetorical device. There is probably always something slightly disingenuous about a humility topos, although I think we tend to assume rather too readily that self-promotion motivates such self-effacing gestures. Even the close of the stanza, in which Chaucer envisages his poem sharing space with great poets, retains an aspect of genuine humility.

Yet we should note two ways in which the phrase 'litel bok' cannot simply be taken at face value. Both teasingly suggest aspects of romance. For one, at over 8000 lines, the poem is hardly little in terms of length; it has the size typically associated with romance, quite different from the length of the tragic tales told by the Monk. That Chaucer claims for his work the status of a book also suggests the backhand of the humility topos and connects the work with the world of romance. The term 'romance' implies a vernacular textual tradition at pains to distinguish between oral and textual culture. Vernacular literature aspires to the durability and cultural authority of writing and of Latinity, an aspiration which finds early expression in the works of Chrétien de Troyes. The term 'romance' links the idea of the book and themes of love and interiority (Copeland 1991: 218–19). Chaucer is making a claim in calling his poem a 'litel book', and at the same time drawing it closer to the world of romance, broadly understood, even while, in the next breath, he will call it a 'litel tragedy'.

The use of the word 'litel' to suggest compressed possibilities stands in tension with the use of the word to express diminution. In a poem structured around doubles, one would not expect otherwise. It is tempting to give the word its coloration from its usage subsequent to the stanza about genre:

> And down from thennes faste he gan avyse* *look at
> This litel spot of erthe that with the se
> Embraced is, and fully gan despise
> This wrecched world, and held al vanite.
> (V, 1814–17)

'Litel', in this its final appearance in the poem, clearly carries with it connotations of denigration and unworthiness. It can signify lack or, in a negative construction, excess. As a quantifier, it isolates one quality, a singularity, rather than suggesting a compact area when contrasting possibilities meet and take their meaning from one another. Troilus does not know what he has let himself in for by taking a proud attitude towards the ways of love: 'This Troilus is clomben on the staire, / And litel weneth that he moot descenden' (I, 215–16). 'Litel', here figured as a lack of understanding, will render his climb-down all the more humiliating. Chaucer also uses 'little' as a quantifier near the beginning of his translation of Boece. When Lady Philosophy first appears, she is 'nat a litel wroth' with the prisoner. The phrase focuses attention on the unsatisfactory condition of his soul, on the specific problem the *Consolation* will address, and points towards Boethian detachment.

'Litel', then, carries a twofold valency. As a quantifier, it draws attention to diminution or fosters the impression of a singularity; on the other hand, as a spatial descriptor it can draw attention to a zone of possibilities, the compression but not the cancellation of differences. In an age of sensationalism, identity politics and polarized debate, it can be difficult for us to appreciate an intellectual environment in which differences could be held together without diminishing in their significance. In the second half of the fourteenth century, perhaps scholasticism appeared to be degenerating into similar polarizations. Chaucer's response, like Julian's and Langland's, was to recall an intellectual ideal that kept in view the whole as part of the enigma of what it means to be human. Seeing the whole constitutes an important part of how an ancient tradition, one shared by classical and Christian sources, defines what it means to be human.

It has been said that Thomas Hobbes taught philosophy to speak English, and to do so with a particular tone of voice: 'the tone is very much that of the sane and moderate *savant* beset on all sides by fanaticism and stupidity' (Skinner 1996: 436). Chaucer taught philosophy to speak English much earlier, a poetic English that strove to hold things together. He taught it the tone of subtlety without pedantry, understatement without indifference. Under the pressure of an increasingly fractious religious and sociopolitical environment in the fifteenth century, writers invoked romance for more politicized ends. In response to Chaucer, it becomes harder to envisage compactness. Robert Henryson takes Criseyde out onto the open road. Troy and the Greek camp become polarities, and the road between them an expanse where Henryson can dramatize Criseyde's perfidy and the clarity of the options. There is no question that her life ends in misery. In the short term, Chaucer's lessons were difficult to sustain; in the long run, they were perhaps relearned under a different guiding rubric.

See also chapter 6, Love in Wartime: *Troilus and Criseyde* as Trojan History; chapter 7, Love and the Making of the Self: *Troilus and Criseyde*; chapter 9, Genre in and of the *Canterbury Tales*.

References and Further Reading

Brewer, Derek (1989). 'Comedy and Tragedy in *Troilus and Criseyde*'. In Piero Boitani (ed.), *The European Tragedy of Troilus*. Oxford: Clarendon Press, pp. 95–109.

Clough, Andrea (1982). 'Medieval Tragedy and the Genre of *Troilus and Criseyde*'. *Medievalia et Humanistica* 11, 211–27.

Cohen, Ralph (1986). 'History and Genre'. *New Literary History* 17, 203–18.

Cooper, Helen (1989). *Oxford Guides to Chaucer: The Canterbury Tales*. Oxford: Oxford University Press.

Cooper, Helen (1999). 'Romance after 1400'. In David Wallace (ed.), *The Cambridge History of Medieval English Literature*. Cambridge: Cambridge University Press, pp. 690–719.

Copeland, Rita (1991). 'Between Romans and Romantics'. *Texas Studies in Literature and Language* 33, 215–24.

Dalrymple, Roger (2002). '*Amoryus and Cleopes*: John Metham's Metamorphosis of Chaucer and Ovid'. In Phillipa Hardman (ed.), *The Matter of Identity in Medieval Romance*. Cambridge: D. S. Brewer, pp. 149–62.

175

Devitt, Amy J. (1993). 'Generalizing about Genre: New Conceptions of an Old Concept'. *College Composition and Communication* 44, 573–86.

Field, Rosalind (1999). 'Romance in England, 1066–1400'. In David Wallace (ed.), *The Cambridge History of Medieval English Literature*. Cambridge: Cambridge University Press, pp. 152–76.

Jameson, Fredric (1975). 'Magical Narratives: Romance as Genre'. *New Literary History* 7, 135–63.

Julian of Norwich (1978). *A Book of Showings*, ed. Edmund Colledge and James Walsh. Toronto: Pontifical Institute of Medieval Studies.

Kelly, Henry Ansgar (1997). *Chaucerian Tragedy*. Cambridge: D. S. Brewer.

Leicester, H. Marshall, Jr. (1987). ' "Oure tonges difference": Textuality and Deconstruction in Chaucer'. In Laurie Fink and Martin Shichtman (eds), *Medieval Texts and Contemporary Readers*. Ithaca, NY: Cornell University Press, pp. 15–26.

Mann, Jill (1980). 'Troilus' Swoon'. *Chaucer Review* 14, 319–35.

McAlpine, Monica E. (1978). *The Genre of* Troilus and Criseyde. Ithaca, NY, and London: Cornell University Press.

Ovid (1955). *Metamorphoses*, trans. Rolfe Humphries. Bloomington: Indiana University Press.

Papka, Claudia Rattazzi (1998). 'Transgression, the End of Troilus, and the Ending of Chaucer's *Troilus and Criseyde*'. *Medium Ævum* 32, 267–81.

Patterson, Lee (1991). *Chaucer and the Subject of History*. Madison: University of Wisconsin Press, chapter 2.

Pearcy, Roy (2002). ' "And Nysus doughter song with fressh entente": Tragedy and Romance in *Troilus and Criseyde*'. *Studies in the Age of Chaucer* 24, 269–97.

Robertson, D. W. (1952). 'Chaucerian Tragedy'. *ELH* 19, 1–37.

Skinner, Quentin (1996). *Reason and Rhetoric in the Philosophy of Hobbes*. Cambridge: Cambridge University Press.

Strohm, Paul (1971). '*Storie, spelle, geste, romaunce, tragedie*: Generic Distinctions in the Middle English Troy Narratives'. *Speculum* 46, 348–59.

Windeatt, Barry (1998). 'Introduction'. In Geoffrey Chaucer. *Troilus and Criseyde*, trans. Barry Windeatt. Oxford: Oxford University Press.

Part Four

The Canterbury Tales

The opening of 'The Knight's Tale', from the Ellesmere manuscript of the *Canterbury Tales*, produced *c.*1400 (Huntington Library MS EL 26 C 9 fol. 72/Bridgeman Art Library, London).

Chapter Nine

Genre in and of the *Canterbury Tales*

Judith Ferster

The opening of the 'General Prologue' of the *Canterbury Tales*, some of the most famous lines of English poetry, suffers from a genre problem. The expansive spring opening leading from new growth in the natural world to the heavenly rotation of the constellations seems to promise a dream vision, an allegorical poem in which a dreamer wakes up in an allegorical garden – usually in spring – and discovers something about love (Cunningham). The liveliest line offers us a sly explanation for the birds' amorous activities: '(So priketh hem nature in hir corages*)' (*hearts, spirits: I: 11). The sexual connotations of 'priketh' and 'corages' might lead us readers to recite them with an insinuating air. But the very next line rhymes 'corages' with 'pilgrimages', which might produce a let-down that takes us from the quickening nature to the world of dutiful piety. So what kind of work are we in, readers might ask. The question is relevant to many of the *Canterbury Tales* because some of the energy of the work comes from Chaucer's active vigorous interrogations stretching the generic envelopes.

My title is double because the *Canterbury Tales* is itself a collection of many differing stories. The genre *of* the work is a compendium or *compilatio*, but what is collected *in* the work are stories of various genres. This distinguishes it from collections that include only one type of story – saints' lives, for instance, or beast fables. Chaucer, author of the *Legend of Good Women*, clearly knew of this kind of collection and the Canterbury book is capacious enough to include one in the form of 'The Monk's Tale', a collection of tragedies, but Chaucer's collection

179

is a cornucopia of kinds. In this essay I will discuss the concept of genre, some of the genres that Chaucer used in the 'General Prologue', a few tales, and the narrators that influence and animate them. Although an essay of this length cannot survey all the tales, I hope I can suggest some of the ways that Chaucer invokes and rejects some of the requirements of genre. His playfulness invites us to take genre of and in the *Canterbury Tales* seriously.

The Concept of Genre

According to idealist Italian philosopher Benedetto Croce, since all works of art are unique, generic categories that divide them into kinds are meaningless (cited in Chandler). Each work is a rule unto itself. But according to Jacques Derrida, we can no more write without genre than without language: 'A text cannot belong to no genre, it cannot be without . . . a genre. Every text participates in one or several genres' (1981: 61). We write, and indeed understand our lives, in accordance with familiar generic patterns.

Yet genres are peculiar entities because while members of a culture have a sense of them, they don't exist anywhere. One common procedure for a definition argument is to list the characteristics of a class, list the characteristics of an item that needs classification, and then compare lists to see whether the homeless item shares enough qualities with the class to be included in it. But there is nowhere to go for a definitive set of criteria for a genre. The national departments of official standards have no specifications for the quintessential epic or the prototypical romance. Definitions involve us in the hermeneutical circle because we define the category according to its members and label its members according to their category.

Definitions of genres may be fluid and subject to continual revision, but names for kinds of music are abundant and well policed. Associate a heavy metal band with grunge or punk and you are likely to be corrected by aficionados. Most of us can distinguish between rap and blues. Even without theories of genre, most people have a sense of genres, their integrity, and the intriguing possibilities of crossover forms. In film, we can distinguish between westerns, romantic comedies, science fiction and fantasy. In literature, most visitors to bookshops can navigate the categories of the sections of shelving like fiction, nonfiction, mystery, poetry and self-help.

The same was probably true in the Middle Ages, when there was a rich lexicon of generic terms. Among those that Chaucer uses, some refer to a form (rondel, virelai, ballade, play), some to a narrative pattern (comedy, tragedy) and some to content (saint's life, miracle, complaint). These three kinds – form, narrative and content – can be thought of as a poetical triangle. As each corner is tugged, the elements at the other corners change too. In addition, each work can slide up and down on the scale of tone and style so that epic can shade into mock epic and 'To Rosemounde', labelled 'A Balade', can shade into parody or burlesque when its speaker claims that 'Nas never pyk walwed in galauntyne* / As I in love am walwed and ywounde*' and hyperbolically calls himself 'trewe Tristam the secounde' (*steeped in galantine; *wound up: 17–18, 20). The mismatch between a lover and cooked fish and the lack of proportion between the fishy speaker and Tristan push the ballad out of its generic niche. Should we call it a mock ballad? As the *Canterbury Tales* also demonstrates, Chaucer not only knows a myriad genres and subgenres but is also a master of generic combination and variation.

The Genres of the *Canterbury Tales* and the 'General Prologue'

Several kinds of categories are relevant to the 'General Prologue' of the *Canterbury Tales*. It is not enough to say that the work collects stories of varying genres, because the 'General Prologue' and the links between the tales tell the story of how the stories are collected. That creates what Derek Pearsall calls an 'organic' frame tale in which the relations among the tellers enliven the tales (1985: 33, 39), making them currency in the exchanges between the tellers. Since the work collects stories from a variety of genres rather than just a single kind of tale, it must also collect a variety of tellers.

There are many medieval analogues for framed collections, among them Arabic ones like the *Panchatantra* and the *Thousand and One Nights* (Gittes 2002: 153, 161). An important analogue is Boccaccio's *Decameron*, in which a group of tellers displaced from home amuse themselves by telling stories, but the tellers are all of the same age and social status so the contrast and conflicts among them are not as sharp. There is still no consensus on Chaucer's relationship to the *Decameron* (Bryan and Dempster 1941: 14–20). Robin Kirkpatrick says that the evidence cannot prove that he used it. Helen Cooper thinks he might have known about it, which might account for the large percentage of stories that have analogues in the *Decameron* (1989: 8–9). David Wallace argues that while we do not know whether he owned a copy, 'there is little doubt that Chaucer was profoundly inspired by the *Decameron*' (2000: 221).

Whatever Chaucer's direct and indirect sources for the framed collection of stories, the idea of a collection of tales seems to have provided Chaucer with his understanding of his role as narrator. He treats the entries with the same respect that scholarly compilers accorded to their learned sources, with the understanding that, as we have seen, what he is collecting is not books but people. He claims that he must take down their words verbatim, leaving no room for his own creativity or initiative:

> Whoso shal telle a tale after a man
> He moot reherce* as ny* as evere he kan   *repeat; *close
> Everich a word, if it be in his charge,
> Al speke he never so rudeliche* and large*,   *ignorantly; *freely
> Or ellis he moot telle his tale untrewe,
> Or feyne thyng*, or fynde wordes newe.   *make things up
> (I, 731–6)

The narrator presents himself as a mere copyist, avoiding the sins of inaccuracy and invention. He deferentially attributes the qualities of the tale to its pilgrim teller, thus avoiding any personal responsibility for the tales' content, style or genre. The responsibility is the pilgrim's, and perhaps, because the narrator has described the pilgrims so thoroughly, the reader's (Minnis 1984: 190–210). The Miller 'is a cherl' and so tells a 'cherles tale' (I, 3182, 3169), the narrator reminds us. We should be warned and if we are worried in advance that we will be offended, we should 'Turne over the leef and chese another tale . . . Blameth nat me if that ye chese amys' (I, 1377, 1381).

For this kind of dodge to work, there must be a credible teller with enough believable qualities to be credibly blamed for the tale. The 'man' (that is, person) 'after' whom the author tells a tale has to appear to be responsible for the qualities of 'his' product. When he is made a partner in responsibility with the reader and the writer (once you know that 'The Miller is a cherl', you'd better choose your reading matter carefully or 'Blameth nat me'), the illusory rhetorical triangle gives the character a reality equal to our own.

That Chaucer gives the pilgrims the kind of *gravitas* required for his modesty trope is attested to by the staying power of the dramatic hypothesis about the *Canterbury Tales*, the approach that emphasizes the relationships among the pilgrims and treats the tales as expressions of their personalities and interests (Kittredge 1915; Lumianksy 1955). According to this approach, the Miller tells a tale about a cuckolded carpenter because he saw the adultery of the wife of the Reeve, who is a carpenter. The clues are in the name of the carpenter's servant Robin in the tale and his talent for bursting through doors (I, 3466). This makes him the twin of the Miller on the pilgrimage (I, 3129, 550), implying that Robin the Miller was an eyewitness to the Reeve's domestic troubles. His tale then seems to be a tabloid-worthy revelation and the Reeve's tale about a cuckolded Miller who cheats his customers looks like revenge. Similarly, the Friar and Summoner tell mutually accusatory tales out of occupational rivalry and the Nun's Priest tells a tale about an anti-feminist cock to subtly criticize his own boss. The story collection then becomes a play in which the tales are weapons wielded by the pilgrims as they act out their struggles and rivalries.

The dramatic hypothesis also charts the ways in which the energy and authority of the pilgrims shape the work: the Miller has enough heft to stage a rebellion against the Host's notions of orderly procession of tellers by rank (Patterson 1991: chapter 5), several pilgrims have enough to interrupt others, and the Canon and Canon's Yeoman have enough to impose themselves on the pilgrimage mid-course. The pilgrims have to have enough weight to sustain their formation of a community of travellers who, under the leadership of the Host, form a quasi-government in which there are agreed-upon rules of behaviour and punishments for disobedience (Wallace 1992: chapters 2 and 3; Ferster 1985: chapter 7). Through their interruptions and responses and their use of tales as weapons in their rivalries and debates, they help to shape the form of the poem.

One of the obstacles to the dramatic hypothesis is that in many ways the pilgrims are not consistent characters who imitate the conditions of real people. Even if the Miller's low status could explain the lewdness of his tale, as C. David Benson points out (1986: 65), it could not explain the delicacy of its style. It could also not explain the subtle humor with which it plays against the tradition of vernacular lyric (Donaldson 1970: 13–29), or how the Miller could accomplish these literary feats while so inebriated he can hardly ride (I, 3121). In Benson's view, the pilgrims 'are not so much characters in a drama as signals of artistic individuality' (1986: 31). The drama, as his title claims, is one of style not personality (see also Jordan 1987: chapter 6). He is right that the dramatic approach is limited by the lack of detailed characterizations for a number of the pilgrims who tell tales (e.g., the Nun's Priest, the Second Nun) and all of those who don't (e.g., the five aldermen).

The lack of consistency in the characters is in some ways a problem of genre. Jill Mann has shown that Chaucer's generic model for a collection of varying tellers is the estates satire, usually a series of portraits of people representing the different ranks of society and describing the shortcomings of each. Although including occasional pictures of ideal exemplars, this genre of social commentary specializes in pointing out how people fall short of the roles they are supposed to fulfil and thus explains why society doesn't function the way it should. Mann (1973) carefully maps the relations of the 'General Prologue' with the estates satires from which Chaucer draws, including his friend John Gower's *Vox Clamantis* and *Mirour de l'omme,* and less well-known works in Latin and several vernaculars.

The problem that this analysis of the work's genre produces is that estates satires gather caricatures that cannot pull their weight in the modesty trope that Chaucer calls upon to deflect the blame for the crude language and content of some of the tales. To respond to the problem created by the fact that estates satires are repositories of stereotypes, Mann attempts to explain how Chaucer fashioned this material into a gathering of pilgrims who seem so realistically lively that scholars have been tempted to search for their real-life models. Though we might expect Chaucer to add surprising concrete details to the portraits to individualize the pilgrims, instead Mann finds that even when he invents details, they fall comfortably within the stereotypes of social satire.

Mann discovers that Chaucer has a number of other techniques for encouraging his audience to see the pilgrims as individuals who transcend stereotype:

> Chaucer calls forth contradictory responses – a positive emotional or sensuous response, conflicting with an expectation that moral disapproval is called for – in order to make us feel the complexity of his characters. He makes us uncertain of the 'facts' that lie behind their social or professional façades. He uses a sense of past experiences, discernible from present appearance, personality or behaviour, to give us the conviction that his characters are not eternal abstractions but are affected by time. And he incorporates an awareness of their point of view – their reactions to the traditional attitudes to their existence, their terminology and standards of judgement – which also gives us a strong sense of their independent life. Chaucer forces us to feel that we are dealing with real

people because we cannot apply to them the absolute responses appropriate to the abstractions of moralistic satire. (1973: 189)

Through Mann's careful work we can see Chaucer turning the caricatures of the estates satires into characters.

One of the most powerful of these techniques is the fourth, allowing the pilgrims to express their own points of view. Many estates satires chastise religious figures for caring more for hunting than for their religious duties. But Chaucer makes the moral error perfectly clear, 'while circumventing the moral judgements it aimed to elicit' (Mann 1973: 27), by handing the estates material to the Monk himself. The rule of cloistered life against which he must be measured and found wanting is subjected to his disapproval because it is 'old and somdel streit*' (*strict: I, 174). He therefore becomes its explicator and critic ('But thilke text heeld he nat worth an oystre'), and claims flouting it as his proud personal philosophy (I, 174–82). If the audience is tempted to think that 'disapproval is called for', we are at least given pause when the narrator seems to affirm the Monk's stance ('And I seyde his opinion was good' [I, 183]) and to restate it in his own words [I, 184–7]), so that finally pilgrim and narrator seem to be speaking in concert ('Lat Austyn have his swynk to him reserved' 188 ['If Augustine is so enthusiastic about work for religious orders, let him do it']).

Thus, one of the ways that Chaucer circumvents the disapproval called for by estates satire is through the narrator, who is, in other cases besides the Monk's, recruited to the pilgrim's point of view. We are led to 'feel that we are dealing with real people' by the intercession of the first-person narrator (e.g., I, 20, 31, 34). As later painters and poets discovered, objects seen through other eyes take on an extra aura of actuality and are seen with extra sympathy. But a Chaucer gullible enough to concur with the Monk's misplaced obsession with hunting, the Friar's extraction of money from destitute widows, or the Prioress' dietary indulgence of the dogs she is not supposed to keep is troubling. How heartfelt is his praise of the Friar as 'the beste beggere in his hous' (I, 252), of the Shipman as a 'good felawe' (I, 395) when he navigates well but throws his enemies overboard (I, 400–4), of the Doctor as 'a verray parfit praktisour' (I, 422) when he takes kickbacks from apothecaries (I, 427) and profits from the plague (I, 441–4), of the heavily armed Miller as a 'stout carl* for the nones*' (*fellow; *indeed: I, 545) when one of the qualities that makes him admirable is how 'wel' he steals corn from his customers (I, 562), or of the Summoner as a 'gentil harlot and a kynde' (I, 647) when he is a lecher who can be bribed into neglecting his official duties (I, 626, 649–51)?

Mann's reading of the 'General Prologue' depends on a special understanding of the narrator's place in the poem. In his essay 'Chaucer the Pilgrim' (1954), E. Talbot Donaldson divides Chaucer into three figures or functions, Chaucer the pilgrim, Chaucer the poet and Chaucer the man. The pilgrim, who joins the gathering at the Tabard Inn and talks to everyone the night before the pilgrimage departs, is agreeable in the way a contemporary talk-show host is genial to guests. He may be naïve or friendly as a tactic for getting along with the pilgrims and learning about them. But we should not take his comments as the judgements of either Chaucer the writer or Chaucer the man we know as a civil servant and diplomat. As H. Marshall Leicester points out, the past tense of the verb in his report ('And I seyde his opinion was good') may hint that what he said then was not what he thought or thinks at the time of writing (1990: 388). The notion of the possible distance between these figures frees critics to speculate about the amount of calculation we should find in the dramatized narrator's comments about the pilgrims. Donaldson's division of Chaucer's roles in the 'General Prologue' allows readers to interrogate his seeming approval of many of them as being the best of their kind.

This openness of the moral categories of the 'General Prologue' has allowed debates to simmer about the moral appraisal of several pilgrims. For instance, the judgement of the Prioress changes according to how the portrait is read against literary and historical contexts. Nuns should ideally be called to a life of service or prayer and guided by their vows of celibacy, poverty and chastity. The Prioress on the pilgrimage, with her jewellery (I, 158–62), her concern for table manners and other courtly behaviour (I, 127–41) and her interest in the welfare of small animals to the exclusion of human sufferers (I, 142–5), might be seen as insufficiently spiritual. The mention of her 'conscience' and 'charitable' impulses leads to what must be the disappointing revelation that they are expended on mice. Most readers agree that although the pilgrim narrator seems taken with her (as Donaldson points out, he qualifies her attributes with superlatives more than seven times; 1970: 3), the poet means to criticize her to some degree. The question 'to *what* degree?' is hard to answer because so many of the clues are ambiguous.

One of the most famous readings of her portrait is by J. L. Lowes, who traces many of the aspects of the description to their origins (1919: 60–7). Her facial features, including eyes, forehead and nose, come from the descriptions of courtly ladies in French poetry, the motto on the brooch hanging from her rosary comes from Virgil, her table manners come from the *Romance of the Rose*. Chaucer transfers and transforms the idioms and conventions of these other works (which inhabit, we might note, other genres) to reveal 'the engagingly imperfect submergence of the feminine in the ecclesiastical' (Lowes 1919: 60). The reader is charmed; the satire is gentle.

Chauncey Wood replies that she is rather 'a completely failed ecclesiast' (1981: 100). He rereads her brooch harshly. She should not own gold jewellery and its motto, though it can be interpreted *in bono* or *in malo* (as leading towards good or evil, salvation or sin), weighs more heavily on the carnal side. In Virgil's eclogue, 'Amor vincit omnia' (I, 162) refers to secular love, and although it had long before been recruited for religious duty, referring to the love of God, Wood believes that 'the Virgilian sense was almost certainly stronger, since it [the eclogue] was undoubtedly a school text' (1981: 98). Dante, Jean de Meun and Gower use the phrase carnally, and its inscription on proscribed gold jewellery (the *Ancrene Riwle* advises nuns to avoid it) means that 'its supposed spiritual significance is undercut' (99). According to D. W. Robertson, all the symbols make her 'a particularly striking exemplar of false courtesy' (1962: 246).

Jill Mann measures the satire as gentle because she contextualizes the portrait using anti-feminist satire. That genre takes for granted Lowes's opposition between the feminine and spiritual vocation. The faults of women religious are therefore the faults of women, who are seen as 'sensual, quarrelsome or recalcitrant, deceitful, fond of luxury, unable to keep a secret, lacrimose, and hungry for praise' (1973: 129; I quote her without the footnotes that reference each accusation). In contrast to the monsters created by anti-feminist satire, the Prioress' sins are more venal than mortal. Furthermore, Chaucer's 'gentle treatment' of the Prioress also comes from the sense that her failings are allowable. Even if it is better for 'conscience' to lead one to ponder moral questions of right and wrong, concern for small animals is 'less elevated (but not *im*moral)'. The Prioress may be a 'worldly nun' (130), but not, as Wood claims, a completely failed one.

The other mitigating factor in our judgement of the Prioress should be the compatibility between courtesy and spirituality. In the fourteenth century, the Virgin Mary is spoken of as the 'Quen of cortaysye' and nuns are advised to receive Christ as their heavenly Bridegroom, who is discussed in terms appropriate to a courtly lover. Courtly concerns for cleanliness, purity and even elegance are thus given spiritual readings appropriate to female religious (I, 133–5).

But even if we thought the Prioress' version of courtly elegance to be more worldly than spiritual, there is another way of understanding her as a successful nun. Susan Hagen contextualizes the portrait historically, saying that her position as head of a nunnery forces her to have working relationships with visiting nobility and local gentry in order to care for and educate their daughters, take in their widows and play her role in the social and economic affairs of the local community. A prioress would not have been able to be strictly cloistered and would have had to be conversant with the 'cheere / Of court'.

The Prioress' moral status remains debatable. Both possibilities reveal the 'General Prologue' escaping from the usually strict moral binary of most estates satire portraits, which are either all positive or all negative. Chaucer's portraits seem carefully crafted to avoid such simple choices. In different literary and historical contexts, the Knight's battles and the Prioress' courtliness look very different. In this way, Chaucer escapes the bonds of the usual conventions of estates satire that govern so much of the 'General Prologue'.

While it is tempting to think of Jill Mann's analysis of the 'General Prologue' as a neat solution to the problem of the lack of realistic, individualized characters in estates satires, in a sense we do not have to choose between style and character. As Larry Benson and Theodore Anderson say in their study of *The Literary Context of Chaucer's Fabliaux* (1971), the differences between Chaucer's poems and his sources and analogues produce subtler characterization and therefore greater psychological believability (4, 85–86). Style enables character.

Furthermore, while making his case against the dramatic approach to the *Canterbury Tales*, C. David Benson analyses narrative voice (e.g., 1986: 72–5, 94–6). He is not looking for consistent characters but rather characterizing poetic techniques. Nevertheless, the two concerns come together when we consider how language conjures up speakers to voice it. In this way, Benson's anti-dramatic approach melds with the approach of H. Marshall Leicester, who, in *The Disenchanted Self*, takes an extreme version of the dramatic approach in the sense that he wants to give the pilgrims responsibility for all the tonal and stylistic effects of their tales. He wants to delay turning to 'Chaucer the poet' until after making as full a case as possible for the pilgrims as the speakers of their tales. The approach meets Benson by taking the dramatic approach so far that it reverses its priorities: 'It is the tale that specifies the portrait, not the other way around' (Leicester 1990: 12). As this discussion shows, analysis of the play of style and characterization cannot be confined to the 'General Prologue'. It demands the addition of the pilgrims' tales.

The Genres in the Canterbury Tales

When the narrator acknowledges that some of his readers are afraid of the Miller's 'cherles tale' (I, 3169) and shifts the responsibility for a comfortable reading experience to them, he offers a quick overview of the genres available in the *Canterbury Tales*:

> For he shal fynde ynowe, grete and smale,
> Of storial thyng that toucheth gentillesse,
> And eek moralitee and hoolynesse.
> Blameth nat me if that ye chese amys.
> The Millere is a cherl; ye knowe wel this.
> So was the Reve eek and othere mo,
> And harlotrie they tolden bothe two.
> Avyseth* yow, and put me out of blame;   *consider
> And eek men shal nat maken ernest of game.
>   (I, 3178–86)

Lydgate agrees that the three major categories are 'knyghthode loue and gentillesse', 'parfit holynesse', and 'ribaudye' (quoted in C. David Benson, 1986: 4). Derek Pearsall concurs enough to use them to organize his book, *The Canterbury Tales* (1985: chapters 4–6 are called 'Romances'; 'Comic Tales and Fables'; 'Religious Tales'). But, of course, it is not always obvious which tale goes into which category. Pearsall counts four romances, 'The Knight's, Squire's, and Franklin's Tales', along with 'Sir Thopas'. Helen Cooper, in *The Oxford Guides to Chaucer: The Canterbury Tales* (1989), counts five since she includes 'The Wife of Bath's Tale'. Pearsall lists four fabliau, the Miller's, Reeve's, Merchant's, and Shipman's tales. Cooper counts five because she includes 'The Cook's Tale'. She does not include 'The Merchant's Tale', which she calls romance with elements of debate (1989: 203), but does include 'The Summoner's Tale', which Pearsall excludes because he considers sex to be a requirement for fabliau. For him, both the Summoner and the Friar tell 'satirical anecdotes' (1985: 166).

One reason the counts vary is that there are so many tales that are not 'pure' examples of a genre. There may be no such thing as a pure example because, as I said earlier, there is no standard definition to which a work can conform. The poem includes a dizzying array of subgenres, generic variation and genre mixing. If 'The Wife of Bath's Tale' is a romance, it also has elements of folk tale and fairy tale. 'The Cook's Tale' may be a fabliau, but it also parodies one. 'The Clerk's

Tale' is religious, following in some ways the model of a saint's life, but it also has elements of a folk tale, romance, exemplum and debate (Cooper 1989: 187). 'The Man of Law's Tale' also partakes of both saint's life and romance (Cooper 1989: 126).

Maybe what we are seeing is not only that there are no standard recipes for genres but also that Chaucer, in so far as he has recipes, does not follows them slavishly. He is too free and creative a cook. In a number of places, he announces a rubric and then provides samples that don't fit the rubrics. The generalizations don't succeed in managing the particulars. This is a miniature version of the genre problem – examples that always seem to elude the categories that try to contain them.

An example is found in Dorigen's soliloquy in 'The Franklin's Tale' as she despairingly reviews her choice between breaking her promise to sleep with Aurelius if he makes the rocks of the coast of Brittany disappear or breaking her marital vow to Arveragus. Finding the choice impossible, she offers a list of women who committed suicide rather than betray their husbands or their virtue. Their 'stories beren witnesse' that death is preferable to dishonour (V, 1367). In the event, she tells tales of these female martyrs at such length that Arveragus comes home, interrupting the recitation. The narrator assures us that she meant them as suicide inspiration:

> Thus pleyned Dorigen a day or tweye,
> Purposynge evere that she wolde deye.
> But nathelees, upon the thridde nyght,
> Hoom cam Arveragus, this worthy knyght,
> And asked hire why that she weep so soore.
> (V, 1457–61)

The casual counting of days in line 1457, their stretching into a third night, and the exception, 'nathelees' (V, 1459), all make us doubt the steadfastness of Dorigen's purpose. But part of the joke undermining her histrionics is her padding the list with Penelope, Rodogone and Valeria, who proved their virtue with methods less lethal than suicide. The 'genre' of martyrs for virtue gets stretched in the service of delay.

Individual tales have similar problems of generic wobble. 'The Monk's Tale' is an especially interesting example because, as I noted earlier, it is a miniature version of the *Canterbury Tales* embedded in the *Canterbury Tales*. It is true enough to its parent genre to begin with, its narrator apologizing for his inability to tell things in the proper order (VII, 1984–90) and discussing literary theory. In the Monk's case, the literary theory is about genre. He defines tragedy in both the prologue and the tale proper:

> Tragedie is to seyn a certeyn storie,
> As olde bookes maden us memorie,
> Of hym that stood in greet prosperitee,
> And is yfallen out of heigh degree
> Into myserie, and endeth wrecchedly.
>   (VII, 1973–7)

> I wol biwaille in manere of tragedie
> The harm of hem that stoode in heigh degree,
> And fillen so that ther nas no remedie
> To brynge hem out of hir adversitee.
> For certein, whan that Fortune list to flee,
> Ther may no man the cours of hire withholde.
> Lat no man truste on blynd prosperitee;
> Be war by thise ensamples trewe and olde.
>   (VII, 1991–8)

There is also a generic definition in the Latin title that begins the poem: *De Casibus Virorum Illustrium [Of the Falls of Illustrious Men]*. What all three agree on is that the protagonist of the case starts in high estate.

The 'hym' and 'Virorum' seem to be general references to human beings since both Chaucer and Boccaccio, whose work is the source of the Latin title, include the cases of women who fell from 'heigh degree'. Boccaccio has it both ways, since he also wrote *De Claris Mulieribus [Of Celebrated Women]*, as if women needed their own category. A number of the men in the Monk's collection fall through the influence of women (Samson, Hercules, Holofernes), but one woman is the subject of her own tragedy. Zenobia, queen of the Syrian city of Palmyra, rules because of her noble blood reinforced by her skills 'in armes', in which no creature surpasses her (VII, 2249–50) and in wrestling, in which she specifically defeats men (VII, 2266–7). In hunting, she tears wild animals apart 'in hir armes' (VII, 2262), which means either with weapons or bare-handed. In any case, her success results from her rejection of 'Offices of wommen' (VII, 2256). She accedes to marriage, and then to sex with her husband only as much as it takes to conceive children, believing that any other sex is 'to wyves lecherie and shame' (VII, 2293), and her calculations about how to have the minimum amount of intercourse are laid out with precision (2279–94). Then her empire is conquered by the Romans, and to the usual humiliations of a triumphal parade of captive rulers is added demotion to female attire and occupation:

And she that helmed* was in starke stoures	*wore a helmet; violent battles
And wan by force townes stronge and toures	
Shal on hir heed now were a vitremyte*;	*woman's headdress
And she that bar the ceptre ful of floures	
Shal bere a distaf, hire cost for to quyte*.	*to pay for her keep

(VII, 2370–4)

The fall of one illustrious woman thus includes a fall into femininity.

A difference between the two verse definitions of tragedy is that one includes the agency of Fortune, a figure derived from Boethius' *Consolation of Philosophy* (Book II pr. 2, 68–72) and the *Roman de la Rose* (5403–5560). Often pictured as a female figure who turns a wheel determining the success or failure of human ventures, she represents chance or accident, whatever forces prevent humans from realizing their intentions. According to Boethius, there is no such thing as chance, but causation looks random to us because we cannot see the true order of the world (Book IV pr. 6, 168–223). Chance is a cognitive mistake. In a Christian world, Fortune stands between the human world and divine providence, blocking human knowledge of God's plan.

But if Fortune is a generic requirement, the very first case, Lucifer, violates the rule, because 'Fortune may noon angel dere*' (*harm: VII, 2001). Lucifer falls 'for his synne / Doun into helle' (VII, 2002–3; the line break cleverly emphasizes Lucifer's descending trajectory), setting the pattern for a number of cases that do not seem to be caused by the operation of accident at all but are rather punishments for wrongdoing. Sometimes the Monk's heroes are blameless, even where their sources think them guilty (e.g., Hugelino of Pisa, Holofernes), but often the wrong-doing, appropriately for men of high degree, is tyranny. The moral that the audience might learn from these examples is not to 'be war' of 'blynd prosperitee' but to 'be war' of playing the tyrant.

The proud Nero, for instance, killed senators, slept with his sister, killed his brother, dissected his mother, burned Rome (VII, 2479–86) and murdered Seneca (VII, 2503–10). This prideful tyranny at last rouses Fortune, who has a conversation with herself in which she resolves to be harder on him ('I am to nyce' [VII, 2522]), swearing twice

'By God' (VII, 2522, 2525) and invoking His moral standards against someone so viciously abusing the power of his 'heigh degree'.

If Fortune becomes an agent of God in the story of Nero, she is discarded in favour of direct divine intervention in the cases of Nebuchadnezzar and his son Balshazzar. Despite the interpretive help of the prophet Daniel, Balshazzar ignores the writing on the wall, persists in his prideful idolatry and is destroyed. The Monk insists that we should learn from his story that lordship is no protection from Fortune (VII, 2239–46), but his interpretation seems ineffectual because, with the intervention of God, the story has pretty clearly slipped the leash of the genre as the Monk defined it.

Nebuchadnezzar's tale is an even clearer violation of the terms of the genre the Monk sets out. As he sees it, each hero 'endeth wrecchedly' (VII, 1977), but Nebuchadnezzar goes through an ordeal (being turned into an animal [VII, 2170–76]) that, even without a helpful prophet, he correctly interprets as a sign of God's displeasure at his prideful defiance. Through the direct intervention of God, morality is enforced and the hero is restored to his wits and mends his ways (VII, 2177–82). The Monk does not even try to recover this story for his generic category. Perhaps it is too clearly a comedy rather than a tragedy. One of the lessons of this story collection within a story collection is that even when the author intends to provide no variety among the kinds of stories collected, the examples escape the category.

But the Monk, by returning to his pattern of reporting the falls of great men for various moral or fortuitous causes, refuses to leave his audience laughing. His tale had threatened to be even longer (VII, 1972), but it is called to a halt. The Knight interrupts the Monk (with another clever line break) on the grounds that 'litel hevynesse / Is right enough' (VII, 2769–70). Then in lines 2771–3 he describes the Monk's genre in terms that precisely fit one episode of his own tale: the Theban queens are cast down from their high estates by the tyrant Creon, a turn of Fortune's wheel that Theseus, to the best of his ability, reverses by attacking and defeating Creon. The Knight thus invites us to look back to consider the genre of his own tale. The Host's further complaint of the Monk's 'hevynesse' (VII, 2787) and demand that the Nun's Priest 'Telle us swich thyng as may oure hertes glade' (VII, 2811) invite us to look ahead to the genre of 'The Nun's Priest's Tale'. I will briefly look both ways in order to suggest the kinds of generic play in which individual tales can engage.

'The Knight's Tale' is a romance marked by its epic forebears, Statius' *Thebiad* and Boccaccio's *Teseida* (accounts in elevated language about the clash of armies led by heroes), as well as Boethius' *Consolation of Philosophy* (the account of an allegorical figure named Philosophy advising a man that he will be happier if he can remain detached from worldly events). 'The Knight's Tale' is a chivalric and a philosophical romance dealing with noble lovers, the clash of states and the cause of events in the sublunary world. It contains well-described battles, an idealized lady and ardent aristocratic lovers.

But it also contains within it critiques of both epic and romance. Its opening battle transforms warrior Amazons into ladies and their queen into a wife (the Monk's Zenobia rehearses this pattern); its second deposes a tyrant and destroys his city. By the end of the tale, another political marriage makes another Amazon a wife and produces peace between Athens and Thebes. Is Theseus a bringer of peace, justice and natural order, doing just what noble leaders should do? Since regime change was all that was really required to right the wrong that Creon has visited upon the Theban queens, Theseus' thorough-going destruction of Thebes and repeated attempts to impose his will have lead some critics to see him as tyrannical in his own right (Rigby 1996 summarizes the argument well in his second chapter).

The tale itself overturns Theseus' dictatorial impulses. Almost every one of his final decisions – to keep Palamon and Arcite in prison forever (I, 1023–4), to kill them when he finds them fighting in the grove (I, 1747), and to give Emily as a wife to the winner of the tournament he plans (I, 1860–1) – is contravened. For all his ability to set himself up as a 'god in trone' (I, 2529) presiding over the theatrical lists he has constructed, he cannot rule events as he plans. In order to convince the reluctant Emily to marry, and marry the wrong man at that, he invokes a benevolent order in the universe (I, 2987–3089) that presides over the progression of generations in 'the faire cheyne of love' (I, 2988). Yet his own creation, the lists for the tournament, contains in its symmetrical temples to Mars, Venus and Diana images that belie the fairness of the world's order. All of the temples are decorated with scenes that depict the chaotic and violent forces that rule over (and within) human lives. To the gods of the characters, the Knight then adds Saturn, the true bringer of order to the world the Knight depicts. H. Marshall Leicester rightly says that the tale is 'an act of rereading the generic discourse of chivalry' (1990: 225).

Love also comes in for critique. The lovers themselves see the indignity of their behaviour (Arcite characterizes the pair quarrelling over the unknowing Emily as dogs fighting fruitlessly over a bone: I, 1177–8); the Knight paints their pining misery so lavishly that the exaggeration becomes comic, and at times seems to dismiss the lovers, as when he says that their moods swing 'Now up, now doun, as boket in a welle' (I, 1533).

Most readers understand 'The Miller's Tale' as a parody of the Knight's: it transfers its love triangle to a lower estate, makes it quadrangular by giving the object of desire a husband, turns the elaborate lists with their three symmetrical temples into three tubs hanging from the roof of a barn, demotes the gods depicted to an astrologer's tricks, and becomes explicit about the sexual desires – or lack thereof – exhibited by the lovers. But in many ways, the ridicule is redundant because 'The Knight's Tale' contains its own parody (Leicester 1990: 238).

When the Knight calls a halt to 'The Monk's Tale', he may be recalling the Theban queens of his own tale, who invoke Fortune (I, 915), or the victorious Arcite, who dies before he can claim his bride. They might be seen as victims of Fortune. But his tale is clear about the causes of both falls. Creon defeats the queens' warrior husbands and forbids the burying of their bodies; once Arcite has made himself vulnerable by taking off his helmet and looking at his lady rather than at the ground in front of him, Saturn sends a spirit to startle Arcite's horse. Thus, by the time the Monk tells his tale, Fortune has already been unmasked.

'The Nun's Priest Tale' continues the examination of causation in the guise of a beast fable stuffed with pieces of other genres – a treatise on dreams complete with exemplary narratives, a pillow-lecture delivered (in the barnyard) by a pecking hen-wife, an epic description of a heroic rooster and, in the analysis of Peter Travis, commentary on medieval epistemology. It claims to be a tragedy by blaming Chauntileer's fall on destiny and the powerlessness of Venus, but then rejects tragedy by reversing the direction of Fortune's wheel (VII, 3403). In fact, it comments on the whole genre of narratives of Fortune by showing quite clearly that Fortune's wheel has spun a comedy because of Chauntecleer's resourcefulness and the fox's inability to resist prideful display. The attributes of the actors in the tale seem quite enough to account for the events of the plot. The tale's mixture of different genres and the resulting jangle of tones and styles, as well as its treatment of character, keep it from settling neatly under the rubric of tragedy.

Conclusion

Although I have not surveyed all the *Canterbury Tales* for their play with the requirements and permutations of genre, I hope I have looked at enough to show that some of the interest of the work is watching Chaucer meet and evade the requirements of genre. On the one hand, given the unstable nature of genre, how could it be any other way? On the other, Chaucer makes the mutations both humorous and substantive; they bear on the most amusing and most serious questions explored by the *Canterbury Tales*.

See also chapter 4, DREAMING; chapter 5, COURTLY WRITING; chapter 8, TRAGEDY AND ROMANCE IN CHAUCER'S 'LITEL BOK' OF *TROILUS AND CRISEYDE*.

References and Further Reading

Benson, C. David (1986). *Chaucer's Drama of Style: Poetic Variety and Contrast in the* Canterbury Tales. Chapel Hill: University of North Carolina Press.

Benson, Larry D. and Theodore Anderson (1971). *The Literary Context of Chaucer's Fabliau*. Indianapolis and New York: Bobbs-Merrill.

Bryan, W. F. and Germaine Dempster (eds). (1941). *Sources and Analogues of Chaucer's* Canterbury Tales. Chicago: University of Chicago Press.

Chandler, Daniel (2000). 'An Introduction to Genre Theory'. (University of Wales, Aberystwyth, July 2000). http://www.aber.ac.uk/media/Documents/intgenre/intgenre1.html Accessed 8/1/04.

Cooper, Helen (1989). *Oxford Guides to Chaucer: The Canterbury Tales*. Oxford: Oxford University Press.

Cunningham, J. V. (1951–2). 'The Literary Form of the Prologue to the *Canterbury Tales*'. *Modern Philology* 49, 172–81.

Derrida, Jacques (1981). 'The Law of Genre'. In W. J. T. Mitchell (ed.), *On Narrative*. Chicago: University of Chicago Press, pp. 51–77.

Donaldson, E. Talbot (1951). 'Idiom of Popular Poetry in the Miller's Tale'. In A. S. Downer (ed.), *English Institute Essays* 1950. New York: Columbia University Press, pp. 115–40. Reprinted in Donaldson (1970), *Speaking of Chaucer*. New York: W. W. Norton, pp. 13–29.

Donaldson, E. Talbot (1954). 'Chaucer the Pilgrim'. *Publications of the Modern Language Association of America* 69, 928–52. Reprinted in Donaldson (1970), *Speaking of Chaucer*. New York: W. W. Norton, pp. 1–12

Ferster, Judith (1985). *Chaucer on Interpretation*. New York: Cambridge University Press.

Fowler, Alistair (1982). *Kinds of Literature: An Introduction to the Theory of Genres and Modes*. Cambridge, Mass.: Harvard University Press.

Gittes, Katherine Slater (1883). 'The *Canterbury Tales* and the Arabic Frame Tradition'. *PMLA* 98, 237–51. Reprinted in Kathryn L. Lynch (ed.), *Chaucer's Cultural Geography*. New York and London: Routledge, 2002, pp. 152–73.

Hagen, Susan (1990). 'The Prioress, the Church, and the Critics: Gender Bias Then and Now'. [An unpublished paper presented at the South Atlantic Modern Language Convention in Atlanta, Georgia.]

Jones, Terry (1980). *Chaucer's Knight: The Portrait of a Medieval Mercenary*. New York: Methuen.

Jones, Terry (2001). 'The Image of Chaucer's Knight'. In Robert F. Yeager and Charlotte C. Morse (eds), *Speaking Images: Essays in Honor of V. A. Kolve*. Asheville, NC: Pegasus Press, pp. 205–36.

Jordan, Robert M. (1987). *Chaucer's Poetics and the Modern Reader*. Berkeley: University of California Press.

Kirkpatrick, Robin (1983). 'The Wake of the *Commedia*: Chaucer's *Canterbury Tales* and Boccaccio's *Decameron*'. In Piero Boitani (ed.), *Chaucer and the Italian Trecento*. Cambridge: Cambridge University Press, pp. 201–30.

Kittredge, George Lyman (1915). *Chaucer and his Poetry*. Cambridge, Mass.: Harvard University Press.

Leicester, H. Marshall, Jr (1990). *The Disenchanted Self: Representing the Subject in the* Canterbury Tales. Berkeley: University of California Press.

Lowes, John Livingston (1919). *Convention and Revolt in Poetry*. Boston: Houghton Mifflin.

Lumiansky, R. M. (Robert Mayer) (1955). *Of Sondry Folk: The Dramatic Principle in the* Canterbury Tales. Austin: University of Texas Press.

Mann, Jill (1973) *Chaucer and Medieval Estates Satire: The Literature of Social Classes and the* General Prologue *to the* Canterbury Tales. Cambridge: Cambridge University Press.

Minnis, A. J. (1984). *Medieval Theory of Authorship: Scholastic Literary Attitudes in the Later Middle Ages*. London: Scolar Press.

Muscatine, Charles (1957). *Chaucer and the French Tradition*. Berkeley: University of California Press.

Patterson, Lee (1991). *Chaucer and the Subject of History*. Madison and London: University of Wisconsin Press and Routledge.

Pearsall, Derek (1985). *The Canterbury Tales*. London: George Allen and Unwin.

Rigby, R. H. (1996). *Chaucer in Context*. Manchester: University of Manchester Press.

Robertson, D. W. (1962). *A Preface to Chaucer: Studies in Medieval Perspectives*. Princeton, NJ: Princeton University Press.

Ruggiers, Paul G. (ed.) (1977), *Versions of Medieval Comedy*. Norman: University of Oklahoma Press.

Travis, Peter (1986). 'Learning to Behold the Fox: Poetics and Epistemology in Chaucer's Nun's Priest Tale'. In Roland Hagenbuchle and Laura Skandera (eds), *Poetry and Epistemology: Turninng Points in the History of Poetic Knowledge*. Papers from the International Poetry Symposium Eichstätt. Regensburg: Verlag Friedrich Pustet, pp. 30–45.

Wallace, David (1997). *Chaucerian Polity*. Stanford, Calif.: Stanford University Press.

Judith Ferster

Wallace, David (2000). 'Italy'. In Peter Brown (ed.), _A Companion to Chaucer_. Oxford: Blackwell, pp. 218–34.

Wood, Chauncey (1981). 'Chaucer's Use of Signs in his Portrait of the Prioress'. In John P. Hermann and John J. Burke, Jr (eds), _Signs and Symbols in Chaucer's Poetry_. Tuscaloosa: University of Alabama Press, pp. 81–101.

Chapter Ten

Morality and Immorality

Richard Firth Green

According to the *Middle English Dictionary*, the word *morality* first appeared in English in Chaucer's lifetime – indeed, Christopher Cannon (1998: 333) attributes to Chaucer himself the first recorded use of the noun, although the actual credit may be due to Walter Hilton. In the case of the adjective *moral*, only a single citation, in Richard Rolle, certainly predates Chaucer's earliest use of it in *Troilus and Criseyde*. Far more important than the matter of priority, however, is the meaning of these words in Middle English. Derived from the Latin *mos/moris*, 'a custom, usage, or fashion', *moral* and *moralite* retain a flavour of public probity, as opposed to private piety, throughout the period. This is particularly true of the phrase *moral virtue*, a phrase frequently used by Chaucer, Gower, Lydgate and other medieval authors. A simple Anglicization of the Latin *virtus moralis* – itself a calque on Aristotle's term *ethike arete*, 'excellence of character' – *moral virtue* stands in opposition not only to intellectual qualities but also theological ones. Thus, we might usefully gloss Criseyde's admission that she first loved Troilus for his 'moral vertu, grounded upon trouthe' (IV, 1672) in light of the fifteenth-century religious instructor Reginald Pecock's definition of *moral good* as 'þilk good . . . which longiþ to goode maners or for which a man is preiseable' ('the kind of good . . . which relates to good manners or for which a man is praiseworthy': Peacock 1927: 232). Given the ideological power of Christianity in the Middle Ages, it was inevitable that *morality* should acquire overtones of Christian virtue (as opposed to simply civic responsibility) – Pecock himself gives as examples of *moral yuel,* 'pride, coueitise, glotonye, wraþþe, and oþere' ('pride, covetousness, gluttony, wrath, and others' – but nevertheless, Chaucer's 'moral vertu' still inhabits a realm conceptually distinct from those modes of behaviour indisputably subject to Church discipline. I shall return to this distinction later in this chapter, but for now I want to discuss Chaucerian morality and immorality in the terms that have been conventionally used to categorize them in the Middle Ages.

In an article written in *PMLA* in 1914 Frederick Tupper claimed to have detected what he called an 'organic' or 'architectonic' principle underlying the *Canterbury Tales*: that of the seven deadly sins. Arguing that this principle 'came to Chaucer late', he located its particular influence in Fragments II, III, VI, VIII, IX – 'The Man of Law's Tale' (Envy), 'The Wife of Bath's Tale' (Pride), 'The Friar's Tale' and 'The Summoner's Tale' (Wrath), 'The Physician's Tale' (Lechery), 'The Pardoner's Tale' (Avarice and Gluttony), 'The Second Nun's Tale' (Idleness), 'The Manciple's Tale' (Wrath) – and, of course, in Fragment X, 'The Parson's Tale' (which treats all seven). Tupper's claims have a superficial plausibility to them. After all, Chaucer's friend John Gower uses the sins as an 'architectonic' principle in two of his works, *The Mirour de l'omme* and the *Confessio Amantis*, and William Langland puts them to vivid, if local, use at several points in *Piers Plowman*. At the time it must have seemed as if Tupper was restoring a measure of high seriousness to a poet whose reputation had suffered somewhat in previous decades (it is notable that his thesis sets aside almost all the fabliaux), but this beguiling structure was fated to survive only a very short time. Barely a year later, with a speed and thoroughness that attest to its author's formidable scholarship, a massive (134-page) article by John Livingston Lowes, again published in *PMLA*, reduced it to rubble. There is no need to reproduce Lowes' arguments in detail here: broadly, he showed that in the late Middle Ages, the seven deadly sins were not the conventionally fixed and universally agreed structure assumed by Tupper, but a rambling, baggy monster, whose complex ramifications might be enlisted in just about any cause – particularly when, as with Tupper's account of 'The Physician's Tale' or 'The Second Nun's Tale', a given vice might be represented by its corresponding virtue or, as in 'The Manciple's Tale', by one of its minor branches. 'Out of the maze of categories, with their nebulous dividing lines, their innumerable overlappings and interlacings, one may choose at will, ignore or combine at will. By such a method anything whatsoever may be proved' (Lowes 1915: 358).

I have spent time on this dusty old debate, not because it has spawned any kind of viable tradition of Chaucer criticism – Allen and Moritz's

1981 study, *A Distinction of Stories*, is rather unusual in invoking moral action as an organizing principle in at least some of the *Canterbury Tales* – but because it seems to me to raise important questions about the interpretative function of morality in medieval narrative. Most obviously and uncontroversially, both Tupper and Lowes readily acknowledge the historically contingent nature of morality – *O tempora, O mores*! Both agree in aligning the moral horizon of the *Canterbury Tales* with that of England in the late Middle Ages, not with Woodrow Wilson's America. Furthermore, they are both keen to stress the pervasive influence of catalogues of the vices in Chaucer, and their close association with his exemplary mode – what Lowes calls 'the unique place of the *exemplum* in Chaucer's art' (1915: 369). *Exempla* were vivid stories used widely, but not exclusively, by preachers to drive home their moral lessons, and (due in large part to the proselytizing efforts of the friars, particularly the Dominicans) the form became enormously popular throughout medieval Europe from the thirteenth century onward (see Bloomfield 1952: 128–32; Rigg 1992: 255–7). A good idea of the typical medieval *exemplum* can be gained from the tale of the two travellers (ostensibly illustrating the moral that 'mordre wol out', 'murder will be revealed') embedded in 'The Nun's Priest's Tale' (VII, 2984–3062). The number of Chaucer's tales (the fabliaux not excepted) that end with an explicit moral – however ironic or farfetched it may sometimes appear – reminds us that we can find a distant ancestor of the *Canterbury Tales* as a whole in such popular *exemplum* collections as the *Gesta Romanorum* ('Deeds of the Romans') and the *Alphabetum Narrationum* ('Alphabet of Tales'). Of course, there is little in such collections to match the complex ironies of 'The Pardoner's Tale' or 'The Nun's Priest's Tale', but as Larry Scanlon has recently reminded us, their shared heritage in the *exemplum* tradition set up important generic expectations for Chaucer's readers. Tupper, then, is hardly to be faulted for directing our attention to Chaucer's references to the vices or to his frequent use of the exemplary mode; what is less helpful, however, is the reductive and mechanical use to which he puts these observations.

Unfortunately, there is a tendency towards the reductive about much moral or ethical criticism, and Tupper is certainly no worse in this regard than the critical school that dominated Chaucer studies in the 1960s and 1970s – that of 'patristic exegesis'. Associated primarily with the Princeton scholar D. W. Robertson (1962), adherents of this school sought to interpret all medieval secular authors according to the fourfold method of allegoresis developed by the Church Fathers, particularly Augustine, to reconcile discrepancies between the Old and New Testaments. By this method all Chaucer's works could be reduced to allegorical treatises composed in the service of the so-called doctrine of charity. The Harvard scholar Morton W. Bloomfield, who, for all that he wrote the standard English account of the seven deadly sins (1952), was anything but a reductive reader himself, put his finger on just this weakness in the exegetical approach: 'literature has ends of its own, and even if in a Christian society these are fundamentally Christian, they are not exclusively so' (1958: 80). As is all too common among critics bent on privileging a part over the whole, however, the Robertsonians exhibited an irritating tendency to claim an inherent superiority for their method and to insist that it opened a new 'road to the riddle which [had] baffled centuries of the blind' (Utley 1965: 257). Interestingly, Bloomfield's detailed rebuttal of Robertson is very reminiscent of J. L. Lowes' assault on Tupper over forty years earlier: 'the multilevelled system of symbolism provides no criterion of corrigibility . . . There is no way, seeing the wide variety of symbolic interpretations of the same thing, to correct any particular interpretation' (1958: 80).

It is perhaps understandable to assume that in an exemplary tradition every *narracio* is potentially reducible to its own *moralitas*, but such an assumption is not always safe even with the most straightforward examples of the genre. For instance, Robert Mannyng of Brunne, the author of the early fourteenth-century *exemplum* collection, *Handlyng Synne*, gives us a particularly lively version of the tale of the cursed dancers of Colbek, in which a group of careless young people, caught merrymaking in the churchyard on Christmas Eve by the village priest, are condemned to dance away a whole year as a result of his curse. We might suppose that the obvious *moralitas* of such a *narracio* is that we should show due reverence to sacred places and that God will be swift to punish any such sacrilegious lapses in his servants – and so, of course, in part it is. This in fact is just how the tale begins:

Karolles*, wrastlynges, or somer* games,	*dance-songs; *summer
Who so eure haunteþ any swyche shames,*	*whoever engages in such shameful activities
In cherche oþer* yn cherche ȝerd,	*or
Of sacrylage he may be aferd*.	*he should beware

(8991–4)

By the end, however, a quite different moral has intruded itself – the dangers of harsh and ill-advised cursing:

A tale hyt ys of feyr shewyng,*   *This tale offers a good illustration:
Ensample & drede aȝens cursyng.*   *an exemplum to warn against
        (9252–3)

In the same way, while the moral logic of the Nun's Priest's story of the two travellers seems to lead inexorably to the conclusion that 'mordre wol out' (VII, 3052), this is not in fact the use that Chauntecleer himself puts it to: 'Heere may men seen that dremes been to drede' ('This shows that dreams should be taken seriously': VII, 3063). Probably no story, no matter how simple, can be safely relied upon to entail its own moralization, but as soon as its narrative discourse or its narrator's point of view attains any level of complexity its *moralitates* will inevitably tend to multiply and compete with one another.

In many ways 'The Pardoner's Tale', a simple story of three literal-minded young thugs who set out in search of death, is a classic medieval *exemplum*. Though their headlong rush into oblivion is related with a chilling economy of detail, it remains pregnant with moral significance. But where precisely does its moral reside? Is it in the tavern from which they set out, with its drinking and whoring, its gambling and swearing? Is it buried under the earth on which the restless old man knocks so hopelessly? Is it hidden in the bushels of fine round florins scattered beneath the oak tree? Or is it decanted in the wine, laced with its strong and violent poison, that the youngest brings back from the nearby town? If we choose to privilege any one of these details, however, we are in serious danger of weakening the overall effect of the narrative; in Jill Mann's words, 'the story is not a mere piece of machinery which provides examples of actions suitable for moral judgment; its procedures and features are a subject of interest in their own right' (1980: 61).

If the moral of 'The Pardoner's Tale' cannot be accurately restricted to the details of the narrative, perhaps it resides rather in the homiletic framework in which the narrative is embedded? The problem here is that we are given so many explicit morals to choose from. This is one:

But shortly myn entente I wol devyse:*   *briefly to express my motive

I preche of no thyng but for coveityse.*   *I preach only about (out of?) covetousness

Therfore my theme is yet*, and evere was,   *still
Radix malorum est Cupiditas*.   *[Cupidity is the root
of all Evil]

(VI, 423–6)

And another:

O glotonye, ful of cursednesse!
O cause first of oure confusioun*!   *perdition
O original of oure dampnacioun.
(VI, 498–500)

Here is a third:

Hasard* is verray mooder* of lesynges*,   *gambling;
    *mother; *lies

And of deceite, and cursed forswerynges*,   *perjury
Blaspheme of Crist, manslaughtre, and wast also
Of catel* and of tyme.   *goods
(VI, 591–4)

And a fourth:

Gret sweryng is a thyng abhominable,
And fals sweryng is yet moore reprevable.
The heighe God forbad sweryng at al,
Witnesse on Mathew.
(VI, 631–4)

And finally:

Thus ended been thise homycides* two,   *murderers
And eek the false empoysonere* also.   *poisoner
O cursed synne of alle cursednesse!
O traytours* homycide, O wikkednesse!   *treacherous
(VI, 893–6)

This surfeit of exemplarity is reminiscent of the flurry of competing morals with which 'The Nun's Priest's Tale' concludes:

'For he that wynketh*, whan he sholde see,   *keeps his
eyes closed

Al wilfully*, God lat him nevere thee*!'   *by choice;
*prosper

'Nay,' quod the fox, 'but God yeve hym meschaunce*,   *give him
                                                        bad luck
That is so undiscreet of governaunce*   *who is so
                                                        lacking in
                                                        self-control
That jangleth* whan he sholde holde his pees.'   *chatters
Lo, swich it is for to be recchelees*   *careless
And necligent, and truste on flaterye.

(VII, 3431–7)

In both cases, it is tempting to suspect that Chaucer has his tongue firmly in his cheek. 'What emerges,' concluded A. C. Spearing from a study of 'The Friar's Tale', 'The Pardoner's Tale', 'The Nun's Priest's Tale' and 'The Manciple's Tale' (all important elements in Frederick Tupper's original paradigm), 'may be a growing scepticism on Chaucer's part about the link his age expected between narrative and moral wisdom' (2003: 197). Such linkage is not always secure even in Gower's *Confessio Amantis* (see Runacres 1983), which Tupper had evoked as a parallel collection of *exempla*, and the conspicuous disjunction between *narracio* and *moralitas* that marks Robert Henryson's *Morall Fabillis* – for Denton Fox, a deliberate 'reflection of the gap between the actual and the ideal' (1962: 356) – is arguably something that Henryson learnt from his master, Chaucer. In other words, in the Chaucerian tradition it is never safe to take even something as utilitarian as a *moralitas* at face value.

Finally, then, we might search for Chaucer's moral significance, if not explicitly in the stories he tells, then implicitly in the storytellers he creates; thus, Tupper pointed to a number of pilgrims, including the Pardoner, who dramatically embodied the very vices against which they were inveighing. As Lowes remarked, however, this 'struggle to wrest a . . . complex masterpiece of ironical characterization . . . into conformity with a schematic type' (1915: 276) is similarly reductive. In fact, the whole process looks destined for failure, for it seems certain that the more complex the narrative voice, the more slippery and elusive will be the moral message. It is hardly accidental that the three tales whose narrators' personae are most fully developed (those of the Wife of Bath, the Pardoner and the Canon's Yeoman) are among the most difficult to reduce to a simple moralization, nor that those whose moral stance seems particularly ironic or cynical ('The Merchant's Tale' or 'The Nun's Priest's Tale' are obvious examples) sent an earlier generation of critics hurrying to flesh out their narrators' personal histories and expand their roles in the roadside drama. Lee Patterson has even supplied us with a way of explaining this phenomenon: he shows us how the emergence of the historical subject in Chaucer runs counter to an older idealizing model of history, making it inevitable that 'The Pardoner's Tale', for instance, should be 'transformed by the context of its telling from an exemplum about avarice into a psychological allegory that reveals the Pardoner's despair' (1991: 391).

Morton Bloomfield was quick to remind us that it is easy to overestimate the importance of the seven deadly sins (even in the field of literature, where admittedly they bulk far larger than in scholastic theology): 'medieval writers did not have the cardinal sins in mind every time they referred to sin, and to believe so does violence to a proper appreciation of medieval thought' (1952: 107). Among several other possible literary models for the treatment of vice in the Middle Ages might be mentioned venality satire (Yunck) and the complaint tradition (Peter), but by far the most important, from a Chaucerian perspective, is what Jill Mann in a major study (1973) called estates satire. Medieval political theory had traditionally divided society into three principal 'estates' – the Church, the nobility and the commons – but by the late Middle Ages the inadequacy of such a division was clearly being felt; we have only to think of the possible meanings attached to the word *yeoman* in the late Middle Ages – a landholder below the rank of squire, a youth, a household attendant, a subordinate officer in military or domestic service, a labourer – to realize the truth of this. Among several other possible types of categorization, estates satire recognizes gender (monks and nuns), status (knights and squires), vocation (lawyers and merchants) and voluntary affiliation (friars and guildsmen), each subject to its own prevailing vices. Of course, there was considerable discursive overlap between the seven sins and the estates, and even the most conventional pastoral manual would often illustrate a particular sin by reference to some occupation that was especially prone to it. By the late fourteenth century, however, their association has become almost commonplace. Thus, approximately 60 per cent of Gower's 30,000-line poem, *The Mirour de l'omme*, is taken up with the seven sins (together with their corresponding virtues), while most of the remaining 40 per cent is occupied with the various occupations (estates) that embody them; and in Passus V of the B-text of *Piers Plowman* Langland vividly personifies the vices through representatives of those callings that most commonly fall prey to them. There is, however, a clear distinction to be drawn between the two kinds of discourse: as a set, the seven sins generally appear in the context of confession and penance (as in Chaucer's 'Parson's Tale', for instance, or in Langland's description of Hawkin's soiled coat in Passus XIV of *Piers Plowman*), portrayed as stumbling-blocks along the road to personal salvation; the vices evoked in estates satire, on the other hand, are far more likely to exemplify the corruption and decline of society as a whole. Thus, it is not surprising to find one of the most methodical pairings of the two discourses in a treatise on the seven sins written by a Wycliffite, a member of the late fourteenth-century movement committed to social and religious reform (so named after the proto-Protestant John Wycliffe); this treatise divides each of the sins into three sections (according to each of the three principal estates) and concentrates many of these sections on one particularly characteristic sinner – a bloodthirsty knight representing Wrath among the nobility, for instance (Wycliffite treatise 1871: 139).

Though, as Jill Mann shows, Chaucer's 'General Prologue' is deeply indebted to a tradition of estates satire, his own use of the model is anything but traditional. Unlike standard estates satire, where 'the estates are not described in order to inform us about their work, but in order to present moral criticism' (Mann 1973: 198), Chaucer encourages us 'to see the behaviour of the pilgrims from their own viewpoints' (190). In describing the Sergeant of Law or the Doctor of Physic, for instance, he studiously omits any mention of the victims of their dubious practices (86–103); elsewhere he substitutes social or emotional sympathy for firm moral judgement, as when he calls the Shipman a 'good felawe' (I, 395) or sees the Prioress' treatment of her dogs as a mark of her 'conscience and tendre herte' (I, 150); or he deliberately leaves unexamined actions, such as the Franklin's lavish feasting, that are open to a variety of moral interpretations. The effect of such things, finally, is a moral stance diametrically opposed to that of the estates satirists; in Jill Mann's words, 'all these ambiguities, together with the 'omission of the victim' and the confusion of moral and emotional reactions, add up to Chaucer's *consistent removal of the possibility of moral judgement*' (1973: 197). For Mann, as for many other readers, Chaucer's urbane acceptance of disparate moral standards arises in part from an awareness of the slipperiness and volatility of language:

Ye knowe ek* that in forme of speche is chaunge	*also
Withinne a thousand yeer, and wordes tho*	*then
That hadden pris*, now wonder nyce and straunge*	*prestige; *silly and odd

Us thenketh hem.*   *they seem to
                                                       us
(*Troilus and Criseyde* II, 22–5)

As Mann notes, 'the shifting semantic values we give to words reveals in us relative, not absolute, standards for judging people' (1973: 196). The obverse of this is, after all, easy enough to recognize in our own day: unwavering moral convictions, as some current fundamentalist sects remind us, often go hand-in-hand with a relentless literal-mindedness.

If Chaucer's moral horizons are inadequately represented by such official taxonomies as the seven deadly sins or the estates, and if neither allegoresis nor exemplarity offer reliable instruments for determining them, we may perhaps do better with linguistic analysis. The very first portrait in the 'General Prologue', that of the Knight, begins with a list of five qualities:

> A knyght ther was, and that a worthy man,
> That fro the tyme that he first bigan
> To riden out, he loved chivalrie,
> Trouthe and honour, fredom and curteisie.
>   (I, 43–6)

Not only are all these qualities *moral*, in Pecock's sense of virtues 'which longiþ to goode maners or for which a man is preiseable' ('the kind of good . . . which relates to good manners and for which a man is praiseworthy'), but they are also semantically ambiguous. *Chivalry* and *courtesy*, as embodying the exemplary characteristics of two social types, the knight (the *chevalier*) and the courtier, exist very much in the eye of the beholder; we might ask ourselves, for instance, whether the Knight understands *courtesy* in just the same way as his son, the Squire ('Curteis he was' [I, 99]), or as the Prioress ('In curteisie was set ful muchel hir *lest' [*pleasure: I, 132]). From this perspective, *curtesie*, as Mann points out, 'is not an absolute, but an ideal that each pilgrim defines for himself' (1973: 137). Similarly, the Knight's *honour* is not necessarily the same quality that the Manciple is eager to provide for his employer ('To make hym lyve by his *propre good/In honour dettelees' [*on his own wealth: I, 581–2]) – nor does his brand of *fredom* ('generosity'? 'nobility'?) quite match the virtue that is lauded in 'The Franklin's Tale'. The most semantically unstable word of all, however, is the one that Chaucer throws into particular metrical prominence with a trochee at the beginning of the fourth line – *trouthe*. This was arguably the most important word in the moral vocabulary of Chaucer and his contemporaries, and it was undergoing rapid and significant semantic developments in the late fourteenth century. Contemplating its various meanings must have forcibly brought home to Chaucer how profoundly 'in forme of speche is chaunge'.

Though the moral significance of the word *trouthe* is evident at many points in the *Canterbury Tales*, its paramount importance is nowhere more obvious than in 'The Franklin's Tale' where Arveragus sends Dorigen off to fulfil her ill-advised promise to Aurelius with a lecture on *trouthe*:

Ye shul youre *trouthe* holden, by my fay*!	*by my faith
For God so wisly* have mercy upon me,	*certainly
I hadde wel levere ystiked for to be*	*I would rather be
	stabbed to death
For verray* love which that I to yow have,	*true
But if* ye sholde youre *trouthe* kepe and save.	*unless
Trouthe is the hyeste thyng that man may kepe.	
(1474–9)	

This final injunction sounds very like a proverb – indeed, the lines 'Do thou wele and drede no man, / For trewthe to kepe is best thou can' appears among a fifteenth-century collection of proverbs (Whiting 1968: D277) – but its general sentiment is encountered throughout the fourteenth century, from Robert Mannyng at the beginning, 'For ʒe wete weyl* & haue hyt herd / þat trowþe ys more þan al þe werld' (*well know: *Handlyng Synne*, 2764–5), to John Gower at the end, 'Among the vertus on is chief, / And that is trouthe, which is *lief / To god and ek to man also' (*dear: *Confessio Amantis*, 7, 1723–5). The importance of the word *trouthe* for Chaucer himself has been well discussed by George Kane (1980), but Chaucer is certainly not the only Ricardian poet for whom *trouthe* is a pivotal concept. William Langland begins *Piers Plowman* with a sermon on the theme, 'Whan alle tresors arn tried*, Truthe is the beste' (*tested: 1, 135), sets its main action afoot with Reason's commission, 'Seketh Seynt Truthe, for he may save yow alle' (5, 57), and concludes it with the arrival of Antichrist: 'In ech a contree* ther he cam he kutte awey truthe' (*in all regions where: 20, 56). Similarly, the hero of *Sir Gawain and the Green Knight* rides bravely out of Camelot with a pentangle emblazoned on his shield 'in bytoknyng* of trawþe' (*as a symbol of: 626), only to return a chastened man – 'Now am I fawty and falce, and ferde haf ben euer* / Of trecherye and vntrawþe' (*have always been wary: 2382–3) – with the ignominious green belt tied about him as a token of this very 'vntrawþe' (2509).

The word *trouthe* was evidently something of a keyword (in Raymond Williams' sense of the term) in the second half of the fourteenth century – that is to say, it had clearly become a prominent element in 'the vocabulary of a crucial area of social and cultural discussion' (1976: 21) and as such had generated a number of competing and sometimes contradictory meanings. The oldest senses of the word seem to have been those of a 'covenant, contract, or bargain', a sense preserved in the modern archaism *troth* – originally merely a variant form of the word *truth* itself); this is a sense that we find in 'The Pardoner's Tale':

> Togidres han thise thre hir *trouthes* plight
> To lyve and dyen ech of hem* for oother,   *each of them
> As though he were his owene ybore* brother.   *natural
> (VI, 702–4)

However, very early on more abstract senses developed from this, expressing the moral qualities that enabled a person to have confidence in someone they had made a contract with – that is to say, such senses as 'reliability, good faith, integrity'. This is how one of the rioters in 'The Pardoner's Tale' uses the word when he seeks to assure his fellow that he can trust him in their plot against the third:

> 'I graunte*,' quod that oother, 'out of doute*,   *affirm; *for certain
> That, by my *trouthe*, I wol thee nat biwreye*.'   *betray
> (VI, 822–3)

A later development of the word (one that was still comparatively new at the end of the fourteenth century) associated this quality with God (the ultimate guarantor of all morality) and by extension with the Christian faith; Valerian uses the word in such a sense when he seeks to convert his brother Tiburce in 'The Second Nun's Tale':

> 'The aungel of God hath me the *trouthe* ytaught
> Which thou shalt seen, if that thou wolt reneye*   *will renounce

The ydoles and be clene*, and elles naught*.'   *pure; *other-
                                                       wise not

(VIII, 267–9)

Chaucer's contemporary, William Langland, shows particular skill in exploiting such theological associations of the word *trouthe*. Finally, a set of new senses of the word had begun to appear by the late fourteenth century – ones that, while they are perfectly unexceptional now, must have seemed striking at the time: these are the senses that are concerned with 'verbal accuracy' or 'conformity to fact'. Chaucer, in fact, nowhere uses the word *trouthe* unambiguously in any such sense (though some of his uses of the adjective *trewe* approach it), but he could certainly have heard it in the London English of his own day. Here for instance is the confessor Genius, in John Gower's *Confessio Amantis*, examining the lover:

If thou hast stolen eny cuss*   *kiss
Or other thing which therto longeth*,   *which goes with it
For noman suche thieves hongeth,*   *since no one is hanged for
                                             such a theft
Tell on forthi* and sei the *trouthe*.   *therefore speak out

(5, 6558–61)

I have myself argued at length (Green 1998) that the emergence of these new senses of the word *trouthe* in the late fourteenth century are to be associated with the rapid spread of a literate consciousness of the late Middle Ages – something that Chaucer as a prominent royal bureaucrat was intimately involved with – and that the conflicting meanings of the word reflect a perceived moral crisis in Ricardian England. Many people seem to have believed that they were witnessing a falling off from the moral standards of an earlier age (a feeling that Chaucer captures perfectly in his short poems 'The Former Age' and 'Lak of Stedfastnesse'), and that the narrow legalism of a society dominated by writs and charters was a poor substitute for an earlier world in which the plighted word could still be taken at face value. It is in these terms that *trouthe* holds the key to many of the ethical complexities of Chaucer's *Canterbury Tales*, and perhaps to its artistic complexities as well.

Trouthe as the paramount moral virtue of the age enjoyed a complicated relationship with the moral regime of the seven deadly sins with which we began. It was not a precise antonym for any of them, nor in sets of specific *remedia* against the sins (a fairly unstable collection, but typically made up of qualities such as humility, chastity, love, patience, almsgiving, abstinence, watchfulness and so on) was there any obvious place to include it. The classic set of the seven cardinal virtues (fortitude, prudence, temperance, justice, faith, hope and charity) is far more fixed, and two of its members – justice and faith – touch on aspects of Middle English *trouthe*, but this list had origins quite independent of the seven deadly sins themselves and the two rarely impinged upon one another (Bloomfield 1955: 66–7 and n. 196). Nonetheless, at a local level the discourse of *trouthe* frequently penetrated that of the seven sins. In 'The Parson's Tale', for instance, both Pride and Envy are said to be at war with *trouthe*: 'inpacient is he that wol nat been ytaught ne undernome* of his vice, and by strif werreieth trouthe wityngly*, and deffendeth his folye' (*corrected; *deliberately: 401–2), and 'that other spece of malice is whan a man werreyeth trouthe, whan he woot* that it is trouthe' (*knows: 487); Ire, too, strives against *trouthe*: 'it bynymeth* eek goddes due lordshipe, and that is mannes soule, and the love of his neighebores. It stryveth agayn alday* agayn trouthe' (*deprives: *daily: 562). Finally, *trouthe* enables the chaste Joseph to resist the advances of Potiphar's lecherous wife in the section on Lechery: 'Allas! Al to litel* is swich trouthe now yfounde' (*too rarely: 883).

Despite this overlap, for many people *trouthe* remained less a theological quality than a moral virtue, in the Aristotelian sense with which we began – indeed, as I have been arguing, the pre-eminent such virtue for the period. Reginald Pecock, in a treatise called *The Donet* (*c.* 1445), devotes considerable space to defining moral virtue. Having divided it into those qualities which he regards as an end in themselves and those that are a means to an end, he subdivides the latter into qualities that pertain first to God, then to oneself, and finally to one's neighbour – interestingly, *trouthe* features in all three of these (though where it is a moral virtue for oneself, it is treated as an aspect of *honeste*). Under the third category (moral virtue in its social or neighbourly guise), *trouthe* is defined as being necessary 'as ofte as we wolen, or schulen, to oure nei3boris afferme or denye, bi worde, or bi signe . . . þat þe mater so affirmed or denyed bi treuþe, namelich as we trowen' ('whenever we wish to, or must, affirm or deny to our neighbour by word or sign . . . that the matter so affirmed or denied is *trouthe* – in other words, something we believe') (65). However, at least three of the remaining seven other qualities are aspects of something most people in the late Middle Ages would have called *trouthe*: one kind of *ri3twisnes*, for instance, is whenever 'we wolen, or schulen, to oure nei3boris maken couenaunt or boond or biheest . . . bi cause þat bi þilk boonde þere growiþ to oure nei3bore a ri3t of claym' ('whenever we wish to, or must, make a covenant, bond, or pact with our neighbour . . . because from such a bond arises our neighbour's right to make a claim'); and both *attendaunce* (by which Pecock means a proper respect for the social hierarchy) and *accordaunce* (which implies a commitment to the common profit) are similarly facets of *trouthe* in one or other of its Middle English meanings.

One possible way of thinking about the two contrasting moral registers in the *Canterbury Tales* – the discourse of the seven deadly sins and the discourse of *trouthe* – is through the Italian Marxist Antonio Gramsci's concept of hegemony, particularly as he opposes this to the notion of official ideology. Clearly the seven deadly sins were part of the official ideological apparatus of the ruling class. When John Gower described the iniquities of the peasants in the Great Revolt of 1381 in his *Vox Clamantis*, for instance, he found a ready model in the sins, and if we are tempted to draw a distinction between religion and politics here, we should recall that the Church maintained a complex judicial system (one in which Chaucer's Summoner was a minor official) solely to enforce its hamartiological discipline. 'The Friar's Tale' tells us something we might otherwise easily have guessed, that such discipline was widely resented and (particularly in the matter of sexual regulation) widely resisted. Among the *Harley Lyrics*, from the first half of the fourteenth century, for instance, there is a brilliant little satire on 'The Ecclesiastical Court' (Turville-Petre 1989: 28–31), written from the point of view of a man who is being forced to marry his former mistress, and who takes it very badly. There is even a petition in the *Parliament Rolls* for 1413 attempting to limit the 'pecuniary penalties on those who are found to be guilty [in ecclesiastical courts] of the great sin of adultery, or of lechery . . . with the result that your lieges of your same kingdom are greatly impoverished' (1 Henry V, 24). Similarly, there was clearly widespread scepticism about the dire threats the Church made against sinners, at least as defined by its own rules. This magnificent outburst from the thirteenth-century French romance *Aucassin and Nicolete* is unusual only for its fervour, not its general import (which is echoed in later texts):

> What do I care about Paradise? The only thing that would tempt me there would be the chance of finding my lovely sweetheart Nicolete. But I'll tell you the kind of people who end up in Paradise. Doddering clergymen, old cripples without arms and legs, forever grovelling in churches and crumbling crypts . . . These are the kind of people you'll

find in Paradise, and you can keep them! But on the other hand, I would really like to go to Hell. Down there you'll find all the fashionable men of letters, handsome knights killed in tournaments and famous battles, hearty men-at-arms and men you can trust. That's the company I want to keep. Down there are all those lovely fashionable ladies who've got two or three lovers over and above their husbands . . . that's where I would like to be. (30)

Thus, Robert Mannyng of Brunne at the beginning of the fourteenth century reports:

> Lechery ys but a lyght synne –
> He [God] wyle haue mercy of all þer ynne*.   *who commit it
> þus seye þey þat kan no gode*.   *those who don't know what's right
>
> (593–5)

And a hundred years later a character in a religious manual called *Dives and Pauper* makes the same point: 'þat simple fornicacion atwoxsyn* sengle man and sengel woman schulde* ben dedly synne Y may nout assentyn þerto*, and comoun opynyon it is þat it is non dedly synne' (*between; *must; *I cannot agree with that: 2, 76).

Unlike the ideological discourse of the seven deadly sins, however, the hegemonic discourse of truth provoked no overt resistance in the Middle Ages; in Gramsci's rather eccentric use of the term, it was part of the people's 'common sense' (a term he defines at one point as 'philosophical folklore'). Of course, no less than the sins was the idea of truth interwoven into political consciousness (in a feudal society bound together by oaths of allegiance, *trouthe* in its earliest senses was a foundational concept – as its common Middle English antonym *treason* makes abundantly clear), but no one seems to have recognized its effects as repressive in a political sense. Indeed, resistance to political oppression was itself often explicitly framed in terms of an abuse of truth, as in the following lines from a fifteenth-century complaint poem:

> A man þat xuld of trewþe telle,*   *a man who is forced to speak trouthe
>
> With grete lordys he may not dwelle;*   *is not welcome among great lords

In trewe story, as klerkes* telle,   *the learned
trewþe is put In low degre*.   *is despised
refrain: God be with trewþe, qwer he be*.   *wherever he is
I wolde* he were in þis cuntre!   *wish
(Robbins 1959: 146)

Even more strikingly, John Ball, one of the leaders of the Great Revolt in 1381, is reported to have exhorted his followers to 'stand manlike together in truth, & helpe truth, and truth shall helpe you' (Robbins 1959: 54). There could hardly be a better example of the way the concept of Truth was pivotal to the hegemonic apparatus of Chaucer's day, fully and uncritically accepted, even by those who were most open to exploitation in its name.

Chaucer himself was no revolutionary, but as a late fourteenth-century Englishman he could hardly have been unaware of the contested ethical meanings of the noun *trouthe*, and as a poet he must surely have pondered its newly emerging senses of 'veracity' and 'conformity to fact':

Whoso shal telle a tale after a man,
He moot reherce as ny as* evere he kan   *he must repeat as
                                        closely as

Everich a word, if it be in his charge,*   *each single word, if
                                        that's within his
                                        power

Al speke he never so rudeliche and large,*   *however vulgar and
                                        bawdy his speech

Or ellis he moot telle his tale untrewe.
(I, 731–5)

When the language of which Chaucer was so skilful an exponent confronted him with an inescapable opposition between *trouthe* as an ethical imperative and *trouthe* as an epistemological ideal, he must have been forced to acknowledge a rupture in the absolute morality of his own age. Out of this opposition, out of the shifting and evolving meanings of the word *trouthe*, it might be argued, emerged one of the greatest achievements of the *Canterbury Tales*, a point of view that seeks to reconcile both senses of the word in a moral universe that is pluralistic, tolerant and inclusive. It is surely this, rather than any timebound ideology of the virtues and vices, that gives his work its lasting appeal.

Richard Firth Green

See also chapter 9, GENRE IN AND OF THE *CANTERBURY TALES*; chapter 11, MARRIAGE, SEXUALITY AND THE FAMILY; chapter 12, CHRISTIANITY AND THE CHURCH.

References and Further Reading

Primary sources

[*Aucassin et Nicolete*] Trans. in Roger Pensom (1999). *Aucassin et Nicolete: The Poetry of Gender and Growing up in the French Middle Ages*. New York: Peter Lang.

Dives and Pauper, Part 2 (1980), ed. Priscilla Heath Barnum. London: Early English Text Society 280.

Gower, John (1900–1). *English Works*, ed. G. C. Macaulay. London: Early English Text Society, Extra Series 81 and 82.

Langland, William (1995). *The Vision of Piers Plowman: A Critical Edition of the B-Text*, ed. A. V. C. Schmidt. 2nd edn. London: J. M. Dent.

Mannyng, Robert, of Brunne (1983). *Handlyng Synne*, ed. Idelle Sullens. Binghamton: State University of New York.

Pecock, Reginald (1921). *The Donet*, ed. Elsie Vaughan Hitchcock. London: Early English Text Society 156.

Pecock, Reginald (1927). *The Reule of Crysten Religioun*, ed. William Cabell Greet. London: Early English Text Society 171.

Robbins, Rossell Hope (ed.) (1959). *Historical Poems of the XIVth and XVth Centuries*. New York: Columbia University Press.

Parliament Rolls of Medieval England (2005), ed. C. Given-Wilson et al. CD-ROM. Leicester: Scholarly Digital Editions.

Sir Gawain and the Green Knight (1967), ed. J. R. R. Tolkien and E. V. Gordon. 2nd edn, rev. Norman Davis. Oxford: Clarendon Press.

Turville-Petre, Thorlac (ed.) (1989). *Alliterative Poetry of the Later Middle Ages: An Anthology*. London: Routledge.

[Wycliffite treatise on the seven deadly sins (1871)]. In *Select English Works of John Wycliff*, vol. 3, ed. Thomas Arnold. Oxford: Clarendon Press, pp. 119–67.

Secondary sources

Allen, Judson Boyce, and Theresa Anne Moritz (1981). *A Distinction of Stories: The Medieval Unity of Chaucer's Fair Chain of Narratives for Canterbury*. Columbus: Ohio State University Press.

Bloomfield, Morton W. (1952). *The Seven Deadly Sins: An Introduction to the History of a Religious Concept, with Special Reference to Medieval English Literature*. East Lansing: Michigan State College Press.

Bloomfield, Morton W. (1958). 'Symbolism in Medieval Literature'. *Studies in Philology* 56, 73–81.

216

Cannon, Christopher (1998). *The Making of Chaucer's English: A Study of Words.* Cambridge: Cambridge University Press.

Fox, Denton (1962). 'Henryson's *Fables*'. *ELH* 29, 337–56.

Green, Richard Firth (1998). *A Crisis of Truth: Literature and Law in Ricardian England.* Philadelphia: University of Pennsylvania Press.

Kane, George (1980). *The Liberating Truth: The Concept of Integrity in Chaucer's Writings.* The John Coffin Memorial Lecture, 1979. London: Athlone Press.

Lowes, John Livingston (1915). 'Chaucer and the Seven Deadly Sins'. *PMLA* 30, 237–371.

Mann, Jill (1973). *Chaucer and Medieval Estates Satire: The Literature of Social Classes and the General Prologue to the* Canterbury Tales. Cambridge: Cambridge University Press.

Mann, Jill (1980). 'Now read on'. *Encounter* 55:1, 60–4.

Newhauser, Richard (1993). *The Treatise on Vices and Virtues in Latin and the Vernacular.* Typologie des sources du moyen âge occidental 68. Turnhout, Belgium: Brepols.

Patterson, Lee (1991). *Chaucer and the Subject of History.* London: Routledge.

Peter, John Desmond (1956). *Complaint and Satire in Early English Literature.* Oxford: Clarendon Press.

Rigg, A. G. (1992). *A History of Anglo-Latin Literature 1066–1422.* Cambridge: Cambridge University Press.

Robertson, D. W. (1962). *A Preface to Chaucer: Studies in Medieval Perspectives.* Princeton, NJ: Princeton University Press.

Runacres, Charles (1983). 'Art and Ethics in the *Exempla* of the *Confessio Amantis*'. In A. J. Minnis (ed.), *Gower's* Confessio Amantis: *Responses and Reassessments.* Woodbridge, Suffolk: D. S. Brewer, pp. 106–34.

Scanlon, Larry (1994). *Narrative, Authority, and Power: The Medieval Exemplum and the Chaucerian Tradition.* Cambridge: Cambridge University Press.

Spearing, A. C. (2003). 'The 'Canterbury Tales' IV: Exemplum and Fable'. In Piero Boitani and Jill Mann (eds), *The Cambridge Companion to Chaucer.* 2nd edn. Cambridge: Cambridge University Press, pp. 195–213.

Tupper, Frederick (1914). 'Chaucer and the Seven Deadly Sins'. *PMLA* 29, 93–128.

Utley, Francis Lee (1965). 'Robertsonianism redivivus'. *Romance Philology* 19, 250–60.

Whiting, Bartlett Jere (1968). *Proverbs, Sentences, and Proverbial Phrases from English Writings Mainly Before 1500.* Cambridge, Mass.: Harvard University Press.

Williams, Raymond (1976). *Keywords: A Vocabulary of Culture and Society.* London: Fontana/Croom Helm.

Yunck, John A. (1963). *The Lineage of Lady Meed, the Development of Mediaeval Venality Satire.* Notre Dame, Ind.: University of Notre Dame Press.

Chapter Eleven

Marriage, Sexuality and the Family

Neil Cartlidge

By the time that Chaucer was writing the *Canterbury Tales*, exclusive rights of jurisdiction over marriage, sexuality and the family had for several centuries been claimed – and in practice gained – by the Church. What churchmen generally taught was that these three fields of experience should overlap as completely as possible, making a kind of social continuum in which none of them, ideally, could exist in isolation from the others. More specifically, they insisted that marriage was holy in itself, one of the seven sacraments of the Church, and, as such, a ritual requiring the full participation of both the parties involved – both in heart and in mind. Consequently, the mutual consent of the partners was a necessary condition for valid marriage: indeed, strictly speaking, it was the *only* necessary condition, although ecclesiastical authorities had long encouraged people to publicize their consent by means of the formal announcement of banns, followed by a service at the church door. Sexuality, on the other hand, was a dangerous and disruptive force, but it *could* be contained successfully in marriage – or so churchmen argued. Indeed, they explicitly defined marriage as the only context in which sexual activity could ever take place legitimately or without sin, but only when its primary purpose was the establishment of a family. Ecclesiastical authorities did not permit husbands or wives to withdraw unilaterally from sexual relations with their partners, despite the Christian imperative towards chastity; nor did they regard a union as in any way devalued or invalidated if it remained childless, as long as it had been consummated in the first place and as long as it was dignified by at least the intention to bring children into the world. The family was generally regarded by churchmen as a good in itself, a microcosm of the community of Christian believers and the medium of its perpetuation into the future.

These were the principles on which the Church sought to manage the relationship between marriage, sexuality and the family. Chaucer is not, of course, a professionally 'religious' writer; and he has no demonstrable investment in either attacking or defending these principles. While it is important to recognize the role of churchmen in shaping and institutionalizing late medieval society's model of 'family values', it is equally important to recognize that Chaucer's writing accommodates a wide range of sometimes complex responses and challenges to that model. Conversely, it would be misleading to suggest that the views of the Church's clerks were categorically alien to those of secular 'clerks' like Chaucer – or to the aristocratic and mercantile identities that he also represents. In its respect for the continuities created by marriage and family and its suspicion of unregulated sexuality, the Church's priorities largely coincided with those of the laity. The tensions that did exist between ideology and reality can usually be explained in terms of the difficulty of reconciling theory with practice. So, for example, much of the business of the courts of canon law (the Church's own legal system) was created by the difficulties of applying sometimes idealistic principles to the messy realities of particular domestic situations. When the *Canterbury Tales* deal with marriage, sexuality or the family, they tend to register a similar contradiction between theory and practice – and, correspondingly, between ideal and reality, authority and experience. They also tend to exploit the intrinsic irony of the Church's involvement in social/sexual policy – that an organization spiritually dedicated to another world should so deeply concern itself with the physical intimacies of this one. As a result of this, the right to determine the nature of the responsibilities created by marriage, sexuality and the family had become the prerogative of a class of men who were in most cases professionally celibate – and so, by definition, remote from all such concerns. It is a sense of the incongruity of this situation that justifies the Wife of Bath's claim to 'speke of wo that is in mariage' (III, 3) – much more obviously than any incipient leanings towards a heretical belief in the rights of women to teach. She is not directly challenging churchmen's 'auctoritee' so much as observing their lack of 'experience' in the field in which that 'auctoritee' is exerted.

In what follows, I have deliberately avoided making a case for the interest or originality of Chaucer's views on marriage, sexuality and the family simply by contrasting the *Canterbury Tales'* impulse towards dramatic complexity with the idealistic certitude more characteristic of ecclesiastic writers on these subjects. Instead, I have tried to address the question of what basic perspectives on marriage, sexuality and the family might be deduced from a reading of the *Tales* – which means recognizing from the outset that Chaucer's purposes, as a writer, are different from those of the churchmen whose views constitute the primary evidence for any 'historical' account of attitudes towards such concepts; that he was thus capable of working both with and against the moral framework represented by the Church's ideology, on occasion taking a distinctively Chaucerian approach to these themes. I have also tried to avoid what seems to me a typically modern (and so, in this context, anachronistic) tendency towards treating marriage, sexuality and the family primarily as instruments of identity. Rather, I have focused on two alternative ways of realizing their significance. One of these I have already suggested, the difficulty of relating practice to theory – of defining the specific behaviours and responsibilities that these three fields of experience imply – since this seems to me a recurrent issue in the way that Chaucer dramatizes the relationships between them. The other key issue is discursive propriety – the extent to which what he or his characters say about the privacies and responsibilities of marriage, sexuality and the family is marked as being deliberately indecorous, shameful or offensive, and thus as a source of friction and frisson in the telling of the *Tales*.

Marriage

The most 'authoritative' account of marriage in the *Canterbury Tales* is the 'tale' told by the parish priest, the Parson. This is not a fictional work like most of the other pilgrims' offerings, despite the Parson's own description of it as 'a myrie tale in prose' (X, 46): it is a didactic text specifically intended to communicate 'moralitee and vertuous mateere' (X, 38) in the shape of a treatise on penitence, the seven deadly sins and the 'remedies' corresponding to each sin. Such treatises had become common since the Fourth Lateran Council of 1215, which had made a priority of educating the laity: although these texts usually served as manuals for the use of parish priests and were initially in Latin, they were increasingly often adapted for the use of lay readership and consequently vernacularized into Anglo-Norman or Middle English. Marriage enters the Parson's version of this kind of manual both as an argument against the sin of lust (X, 881–9) and as one of the remedies for it (X, 916–43). According to the Parson, the effect of this particular remedy is that it 'clenseth fornicacioun and replenysseth hooly chirche of good lynage, for that is the ende of mariage' (X, 919). That is, he states the orthodox view of the Church that marriage can be regarded as a mechanism for the redemption of sexuality, but only when its purpose is identified with parenthood. As a justification of marriage, this formulation might seem grudgingly back-handed, but it reflects the similarly negative arguments of authorities like St Paul – who said that, for those incapable of celibacy, 'it is better to marry than burn' (I Corinthians 7: 9; cf. the Wife of Bath's Prologue, III, 52) – and St Augustine – who suggested that procreative, marital sexuality should be seen as a means of making something good out of the 'evil' of carnal lust (*De bono conjugali [Concerning Conjugal Good]*). The Parson casts particular stress on marriage's role as an instrument of social stability: for him, a world without marriage could only present a horrifying prospect of chaos, in which 'no man ne sholde knowe his owene engendrure, ne who sholde have his heritage' (X, 923; cf. X, 883). This harmonizes comfortably with the characteristic preoccupations of secular society in this period, since this was an age in which lineage and legitimacy were crucial to the determination of social status and the inheritance of property. Moreover, according to the Parson, marriage also serves as an antidote to the 'desray' or disorder consequent on women's 'maistrie' or dominance, since it requires that 'a womman sholde be subget to hire housbonde' (X, 929). This is no invitation to engage in the gender politics that Chaucer enjoys so often elsewhere, since 'woman hardly exists in the *Parson's Tale* except as a wife, dutiful or otherwise' (Patterson 1978: 364). All of this is as conspicuously orthodox as it is socially conservative. If there is anything at all of the religious radical about the Parson – of the 'Lollere' smelt by the Host in the epilogue to 'The Man of Law's Tale' (II, 1172–7) – then there is certainly little trace of it in his ideology of marriage, which is both theologically unremarkable and strikingly free of the kind of anxieties and ambivalences that characterize Chaucer's treatment of marriage elsewhere in the *Canterbury Tales*.

It is dramatically appropriate that Chaucer should depict the Parson as an agent of moral and social conformity, since parsons were generally responsible not only for advising and instructing their parishioners about sexual behaviour, but also for officiating at marriages and baptisms; and his representation of marriage primarily as a mechanism for regulating sexuality, inheritance and the roles appropriate to gender may reflect the pragmatic purposes of the pastoral manual as a genre. Elsewhere in the *Canterbury Tales*, Chaucer demonstrates the dangers of justifying marriage in terms too narrowly focused on its moral and social expediency. So, for example, both the Wife of Bath and January, the protagonist of 'The Merchant's Tale', cheerfully accept the notion that marriage is essentially a concession to human frailty – what the Wife calls 'leve / Of indulgence' (III, 83–4). Yet, since neither of them really share St Paul's or St Augustine's sense of the urgency of repentance even for such sins of weakness, they effectively choose to interpret marriage not as a limited dispensation from the moral consequences of sexual desire, but as an unlimited licence to satisfy it just as they please. The Wife explains her failure even to aspire to chastity by expressing the (false) belief that Christ addressed his message only 'to hem that wolde lyve parfitly' – and to this she adds complacently, 'And lordynges, by youre leve, that am nat I' (III, 111–12). January, similarly, acknowledges the possibility that even some married couples might choose to 'lyve in chastitee ful holily', but then distinguishes himself from them by using exactly the same formula, 'sires, by youre leve, that am nat I' (IV, 1455–6). Both, in effect, cheerfully partake of the 'remedy' while denying that they have the 'disease'. Similarly, the Wife of Bath echoes the Parson's argument but not his intention, when she uses 'engendrure' (the engendering of children) as a key term in her defence of marital sexuality. She does so, as it turns out, only as a means of defending the *use* of the 'membres . . . of generacion' (III, 115–34), and not as a means of asserting the value or importance of their biological *product* (that is, children) as the Parson intends. In much the same way January seems to express something like the Parson's anxiety about 'heritage' when he states that he had 'levere houndes had me eten / Than that myn heritage sholde falle / In straunge hand' (IV, 1438–40). His proposed remedy for this anxiety – that he should 'Take hym a wyf with greet devocioun, / By cause of leveful procreacioun / Of children to th'onour of God above' (IV, 1447–9) – is, on the face of it, a correct reading of the Parson's own interpretation of the 'trewe effect of mariage'. Unfortunately, January's employment of this 'remedy' turns out to be all too opportunistic – what drives him to marry, as quickly emerges, is not so much his sense of a duty to engender an heir as his desire for what he perceives to be the pleasures of doing so. Indeed, he even suggests (in a spectacular perversion of the Parson's logic) that, instead of 'cleansing fornication', a marriage without the 'plesaunce' of the kind he seeks would actually cause him to commit adultery – and thus take him 'streight to the devel whan I dye' (IV, 1436). As Chaucer shows here, the Church's tendency to justify marriage in terms of a rhetorical emphasis on its social and moral utility risked the appearance of endorsing personal convenience as a motive for marrying.

Yet this pragmatic side of the Church's teaching on such matters represents only one aspect of its ideology. Neither St Paul nor St Augustine would have chosen to defend marriage solely in terms of its social function – solely as a means of regulating sexuality or of stabilizing families; nor, in fact, does the Parson, despite his primary concern with sin and social disorder. Marriage, as churchmen in this period were generally at pains to emphasize, was also a holy sacrament, an institution established by God in Paradise (cf. X, 917), a union of the will and heart of two individuals (cf. X, 936–7) – and, as such, an image of the ideal state of harmony between God and the community of Christians on earth. More specifically, theologians such as Peter Lombard and canon lawyers such as Gratian had long ago established the principle that Christian marriages were made by the mutual consent of the partners and sustained by their 'marital affection'. The Parson is optimistic enough about the power of love in marriage to suggest that a man's love for his wife should equate with Christ's love for humankind even to the point of sharing in the dignity of Christ's self-sacrifice on the Cross – or, as he puts it, 'man sholde bere hym to his wyf in feith, in trouthe, and in love, as seith Seint Paul, that a man sholde loven his wyf as Crist loved hooly chirche, that loved it so wel that he deyde for it. So sholde a man for his wyf, if it were nede' (X, 928). This certainly makes it clear that marriage is something more than a 'remedy' for the sins of sexuality or a convenient means of regulating family ties – a bond fundamentally sacred in itself. Yet the Parson evokes this ideal of marital harmony only as a means of asserting the duty of husbands to exert authority over their wives. In effect he uses the principle that husbands and wives share equally in the affective and sacramental dimensions of marriage as a justification for the view that they do not share equally in authority. This could perhaps be taken as a demonstration of the extent to which his belief in the intrinsic dignity of marriage is subordinated to – and to some extent distorted by – a sense of his responsibility, as a figure of authority in his community, to uphold the status quo. He also tells us that 'aboven all worldly thyng [a wife] sholde loven hire housbonde with al hire herte, and to hym be trewe of hir body,' and then adds, seemingly as an afterthought, 'so sholde an housbonde eek be to his wyf' – a formulation that states the necessity of reciprocity in marital relations only to deny it in the uneven way that that necessity is expressed. Yet, even if the Parson's advocacy of marriage remains enclosed in the pragmatic and socially conservative emphases of his treatise as a whole, he does acknowledge the importance of love in marriage; and to that extent it can be said that he does make due allowance for the feelings and intentions of the married couple, as well as for the physical and social aspects of their union. Even so, it is only elsewhere in the *Canterbury Tales* that the idealistic, affective and meta-physical dimensions of marriage are celebrated with anything like the persuasiveness of sincere conviction.

It is in 'The Franklin's Tale' that Chaucer provides his most em-phatically optimistic vision of marriage, presenting in the relationship between Arveragus and his wife Dorigen a model of a relationship founded on mutual trust and generosity. At the beginning of the tale, Dorigen is said to agree to take Arveragus 'for hir housbonde and hir lord / Of swich lordshipe as men han over hir wyves' (V, 742–3), but he promptly renounces any such 'maistrie' (V, 747). Instead he asserts his willingness to obey her and 'folwe hir wyl in al / As any lovere to his lady shal / Save that the name of soveraynetee, / That wolde he have for shame of his degree' (V, 749–52). In effect, the Franklin sug-gests that this marriage is an exceptionally good one, precisely because the partners agree to act as if it were not a marriage at all – as if they remained lovers and therefore in no way constrained by any obliga-tions beyond those of mutual respect. The notion that a husband should have 'soveraynetee' over his wife is one that Arveragus recog-nizes, and he feels the need to be seen to adhere to it, but he is never-theless content to treat it as a fiction. Such an idealization of marital relations seems entirely compatible with the emphasis on free consent in the Church's theological and legal definitions of marriage, but it also represents a challenge to, or even a contradiction of, the Parson's emphasis on the tangible benefits of marriage as a social institution. If marriage is defined in terms of a husband's right to rule his wife ('swich lordshipe as men han over hir wyves': V, 743), while at the same time love is fundamentally incompatible with any such 'lordshipe' ('love wol nat been constreyned by maistrye': V, 764), then loving marriage, in the Franklin's analysis, becomes too contradictory to be realized at all, except as a fundamentally paradoxical relationship. This is, of course, precisely how the Franklin does attempt to realize it:

> Heere may men seen an humble, wys accord;
> Thus hath she take hir servant and hir lord –

Servant in love, and lord in mariage.
Thanne was he bothe in lordshipe and servage.
Servage? Nay, but in lordshipe above,
Sith he hath bothe his lady and his love;
His lady, certes, and his wyf also,
The which that lawe of love acordeth to.

(V, 791–8)

Chaucerian critics have long tended to accept G. L. Kittredge's opinion (1912) that this passage provides a satisfyingly effective solution to the problem of marriage as it is debated in several of the preceding *Tales*; but, like most paradoxes, this one is satisfying precisely because it cannot be so easily resolved. The Franklin's ideal of marriage is limited by its very idealism, since it demands mutual forbearance – which he defines as 'pacience' (V, 771–90) – to a degree that only the most exceptional individuals will ever achieve. Moreover, since the marriage between Arveragus and Dorigen is ennobled only by their pretence that it is not a marriage at all – that they remain 'freendes' and lovers even after they have wedded – it perhaps serves to collapse rather than confirm the status of marriage in society. Even if the Franklin's account of their relationship is read as an affirmation of the principle that 'marriage is made by consent,' the tale he goes on to tell only problematizes the very notion of defining social obligations solely in terms of intention and consent.

Sexuality

Marital sexuality

Chaucer suggests on a couple of occasions that the spiritual and psychological burden of marital sexuality falls more heavily on wives than on their husbands – as long as the wives in question are fittingly virtuous ('The Parson's Tale', X, 940; 'The Man of Law's Tale', II, 708–14). As he puts it, such women must 'leye a lite hir hoolynesse aside' in order to fulfil their sexual obligations to their husbands. It is something like such holiness that the old lecher January salaciously imagines he might 'offende' (IV, 1829) when he first embraces his young bride on their wedding night – although, as it turns out, May is not as holy as he would like to believe. Indeed, when it comes to the discomforts of what churchmen called 'the conjugal debt' – the obligation of married partners to satisfy their partner's sexual needs – men could suffer too, as the Wife of Bath gleefully points out: 'As help me God, I laughe whan I thynke / How pitously a-nyght I made hem swynke!' (III, 201–2). Yet the doctrine of conjugal debt hardly justifies the Wife's opinion that any husband of hers is 'bothe my dettour and my thral' (III, 155) or that it is her responsibility to exact 'tribulacion . . . / Upon his flessh' (III, 156–7). Both the Wife and January clearly believe that the conjugal debt gives them the right to take sexual possession of the body of their spouse, but this is only a mockery of the Church's teaching on the subject, which in fact emphasizes, not possession, but reciprocal submission. The Wife's assertion:

> I have the power durynge al my lyf
> Upon his propre body, and noght he.
> Right thus the Apostol tolde it unto me.
> (III, 158–60)

is a conspicuously one-sided rendition of what the Apostle (St Paul) actually says: 'The wife hath not power of her own body, but the husband. And in like manner the husband also hath not power of his own body, but the wife' (I Corinthians 7: 4). What St Paul emphasizes is not only the absoluteness of the physical connection created by marriage, but also that it bears equally ('in like manner') on both parties to a marriage. It has been argued that the Wife's misappropriation of the idea of the conjugal debt only exposes the limitations of such thinking, showing how readily the contractual metaphor justified seeing sex as a kind of transaction; but there is nothing intrinsically wrong with the principle that partners should reciprocally defer to each other's sexual needs, nor is the word 'debt' (Latin *debitum*) necessarily mercantile in its connotations. The point of the Church's teaching on the conjugal debt is that 'paying' a moral debt of this kind is specifically *not* like paying a sum of money: since both partners are perpetually indebted to the other, neither can ever legitimately profit from their relationship. The Wife of Bath noisily advertises her willingness to 'use myn instrument' in wifehood 'as frely as my Makere hath it sent' (III, 149–50), but she also admits to setting conditions on her husband's access to her 'instrument' – in such a way as to make his sexuality, in effect, a weakness that she can exploit to her own advantage. As she herself says:

> I wolde no lenger in the bed abyde,
> If that I felte his arm over my syde,

Til he had maad his raunson unto me;
Thanne wolde I suffre hym do his nycetee*.   *pleasure
(III. 409–12)

She makes it perfectly clear that she is obstructive – or 'daungerous', as she puts it (III. 151) – not because of any chaste reluctance, but because of a desire for profit. By holding her husband to 'raunson' in this way, the Wife makes a transaction of marital sexuality much more literally than the Church's teaching on the conjugal debt ever does. Her tactics, in short, are not an illustration, but an evasion, of the consequences of the conjugal debt. They are also fundamentally destructive of anything like trust or love in marriage; and in that sense, they represent a philosophy of marriage that is wholly sterile.

The Wife of Bath's marriages also seem to have been literally sterile, for there is no mention anywhere in her Prologue of the difficulties or rewards of bringing up children. Chaucer provides no evidence that this is the result of deliberate contraception, but her indifference to the biological consequences of sex is nevertheless striking – and all the more so in contrast with the Parson's justification of marriage in terms of the replenishing 'of good lynage' (X, 919) and the 'engendrure of children to the service of God' (X, 938). Indeed the logic of the Wife's comparison of her 'queynte' with the flame of a lantern (III, 331–6) is that her vagina is an inexhaustible and invariable resource of sexual pleasure. Something similar is suggested in 'The Shipman's Tale', where the merchant's wife punningly refers to her vagina as a 'taille' (VII, 416) or tally – as if it were a kind of credit facility. Yet these assumptions are only true as long as sex can be practised without any physical effects. Medieval methods of contraception and abortion were more reliable than is often assumed, but it is still only a minority of women of child-bearing age who could ever have entered a sexual relationship with quite the insouciance displayed by the Wife of the Bath and the merchant's wife. Indeed, it is striking that none of the married couples whose sexual relationship Chaucer discusses in any detail at all are ever said to produce any children. The one possible exception is 'The Merchant's Tale', which concludes with a vignette of January covetously stroking his young wife's stomach in a way that might be taken to imply that she is pregnant (IV, 2414) – although we are perhaps encouraged to think that the father in this case is less likely to be her husband than her young lover. Not all of the marital relationships depicted in the *Canterbury Tales* are so markedly infertile. 'The Clerk's Tale', for example, notes that it was in itself a source of general satisfaction that Griselda 'nys nat bareyne' (IV, 448) – even when her first child happens to have been a daughter, rather than a son capable of succeeding his father. But productive unions of this kind are distinguished precisely by the veil of obscurity cast over them: how Walter and Griselda manage their sexual relationship is simply not discussed. In narrative terms, it is enough that time passes – Griselda gives birth to her daughter 'Nat longe tyme after' their marriage (IV, 442) and to their son after 'ther passed been foure yeer' (IV, 610). The implication is presumably that relationships healthy enough to result in children do not need to be discussed; and conversely, that dysfunctional relationships are marked both by the scandal of their exposure and by their sterility.

Non-marital sexuality

Most of the sexual activity explicitly depicted in the *Canterbury Tales* is furtive, unloving and illicit. Indeed Chaucer's explicitness itself tends to serve as a means of highlighting or even, at a narrative level, re-enacting the illicitness of these particular sexual encounters. So, for example, in 'The Merchant's Tale', the adulterous affair between Damyan and May is consummated with the words, 'sodeynly anon this Damyan / Gan pullen up the smok, and in he throng' (IV, 2352–3). This deliberately brusque description, with its almost violent emphasis on penetration, serves, on the one hand, to emphasize Damyan's energy and resolution (which contrasts sharply with the limp and querulous sexuality of May's elderly husband, January) and, on the other, to suggest that his conquest of May is in essence a form of invasive trespass – and, as such, an attack on the sanctioned privacy of married intimacy. At the same time, the absence of anything like tenderness or affection in this coupling is mirrored by the brutal unsentimentality with which Chaucer describes it. He even draws attention to his own failure (or, more precisely, his Merchant narrator's failure) to 'gloss' or euphemize the scene, pretending to entreat the ladies in his audience not to be angry with him for being too 'rude' a man to do so. Yet the apology hardly suggests any real contrition, only the narrator's complacent satisfaction in his own 'rudeness'. The phrase he chooses ('in he throng') turns out to be so spectacularly 'unglossed' – so pointedly uneuphemized – that no plea of mere 'rudeness' could possibly account for it. Indeed, the narrator's apparent apology effectively only expresses his determination to describe the adulterous act in words that are as unvarnished as possible. This in turn suggests that – at least for the embittered narrator of the tale – there is a certain satisfaction to be found in deliberately *not* casting any decorous veil over May's sexual infidelity. From this perspective, the aggressively explicit way in which he describes her penetration might be seen as the narrator's attempt to identify with Damyan in the very act of defiling the institution of marriage. Moreover, the subsequent events of the tale are clearly intended to imply that it is only by means of a tenacious grasp on the plain and obvious truth – without any gloss or euphemism – that husbands have any chance of avoiding being deceived by their wives, for when January suddenly rediscovers his sight, and with it a view of his wife's disloyalty, he also uses terms that are markedly uncensored: 'He swyved thee; I saugh it with myne yen / And elles be I hanged by the hals*!' (*neck: IV, 2378–9). Yet a few lines later he is apologizing to his wife, not for seeing wrongly, but for *saying* wrongly: 'if I have myssayd / God helpe me so' (IV, 2391–2). By contrast, the Merchant narrator's refusal to accept responsibility for what he 'mis-says' in describing May's infidelity quite as bluntly as he does might be read as his way of demonstrating that he himself is too worldly-wise to fall for such wordy wiles. In effect, he attempts to make plain-speaking into a talisman against the deceitfulness of women, enlisting sex itself, or at least being 'rudely' explicit about sex, into the armoury of misogyny.

Something of the same wilful transgressiveness also governs the description of sexual activity in 'The Reeve's Tale'. Here, the student Aleyn decides that Symkyn the miller owes him some sort of reparation for stealing their corn – or, as he puts it himself, the right to 'esement'. This is a technical term denoting legal access to somebody else's property, but, in this case, the means of 'access' to the property in question is the Miller's daughter. Aleyn's metaphor effectively makes her an extension of the Miller's own possessions, dehumanizing her in a way that is both manifestly unfair (in the simple sense that she is a third party, and not just part of her father's property) and palpably misogynistic in its implication that, as a woman, she is a sexual object with no individuality worth respecting. Here again, plain-speaking apparently serves as a metonym for sexual aggression: 'Yon wenche wil I swyve,' Aleyn declares (I, 4178). The deictic 'yon' is rudely abrupt, the verbal equivalent of a pointing finger; the obvious lower-class connotations of 'wenche' make it an insulting term; and the verb 'swyve' (literally, 'to work, labour away at') is a deliberately inelegant means of describing sexual intercourse – Chaucer uses it elsewhere (in 'The Cook's Tale', I, 4422) to suggest prostitution. No violence is done to marriage by Aleyn's invasion of the young woman's bed (since she is not married), but his incursion is nevertheless described in such a way as to make perfectly clear that for Aleyn her consent is immaterial, so that the attitude he takes could reasonably be described as that of a rapist, even if – as it later turns out – the girl herself is misguided enough to misinterpret his rough handling as the attentions of a genuine lover. The narrator's remark that she had no time to cry out for help before 'they were aton' (I, 4196–7) could perhaps be viewed as a tacit admission that Aleyn's behaviour should really be seen as a form of sexual assault. Meanwhile, the other student's conquest of the Miller's wife might owe something to her arrival (by accident) in his bed, but the use he makes of this opportunity again suggests both a lack of interest in the woman's consent and an interpretation of masculine sexuality only in terms of aggression – an aggression that, as the Reeve implies, borders on insanity:

> 'Withinne a while this John the clerk up leep,
> And on this goode wyf he leith on soore.
> So myrie a fit ne hadde she nat ful yore;
> He priketh harde and depe as he were mad.'
> (I, 4228–31)

The narrator of the tale tells us that this aggression is appreciated by the Miller's wife as a stirring form of forcefulness, an expression of sexual energy sadly lacking from her relationship with her husband. There is perhaps a deliberate echo here of the Wife of Bath's use of the term 'a myrie fit' (III, 42) to express her own robust appreciation of a vigorous sexual performance. Yet she can hardly be said to under-write the Reeve's optimism about the Miller's wife's enjoyment of her rough handling by the student, since the sexual performances that she alludes to are those of the biblical King Solomon – and as she wryly observes, he was blessed with a 'yifte of God' that no man alive now possesses (III, 39–40). In any case, as the Reeve makes perfectly clear, the sexual subjection of the two women in his tale is only a means of expressing his own textual aggression towards the Miller: 'His wyf is swyved, and his doghter als [. . .] Thus have I quyt the Millere in my tale' (I, 4317, 4324).

Chaucer's depictions of sexual activity are not always so joyless: the adulterous relationship between Alison and Nicholas in 'The Miller's Tale' could hardly be described as a loving one, but it clearly provides a certain amount of mutual satisfaction. Even here, though, the function served by sex in the narrative is a pointedly subversive one, since Chaucer chooses to employ the bells and choral harmony of the local friars' religious observance as an implied euphemism for sexual climax.

'In bisynesse of myrthe and of solas,
Til that the belle of laudes gan to rynge,
And freres in the chauncel gonne synge.'
(I, 3654–6)

It is debatable whether this analogy is meant to be mischievously dis-respectful of the friars, or a means of underlining the unholiness of this adulterous encounter: it could perhaps be argued that Chaucer manages to support both perspectives simultaneously. Indeed, the general effect of Chaucer's association of the explicit with the illicit is, on the one hand, to align himself with what might be seen as a con-servative social ideology, according to which extramarital sexuality is made to look distasteful by the calculated tastelessness with which he describes it; and, on the other, to cast a self-consciously subversive emphasis on the offensive potential of the tales that he tells. These contradictory effects suggest that Chaucer was more interested in the dramatic and thematic potential of narrating sexual activity than he was in analysing its moral and social consequences. Non-marital sex in the *Canterbury Tales* is apparently no more procreative than the married version – though again with the possible exception of the pregnancy hinted at in the final lines of 'The Merchant's Tale'. From this point of view, the gap between Chaucer's treatment of sex in mar-riage and his treatment of sex outside it is not quite as great as one might expect. This is not to say that he denied the possibility of a morally and socially fruitful use of marital sexuality (as in the 'procre-ative' ideology of marriage outlined by the Parson): only that, in his writing, the 'good' uses of sexuality are marked precisely by his silence about them. If sexuality enters into the realm of tale-telling at all, and specifically of *Canterbury Tale*-telling, then it is implicitly discredited to begin with, implicitly an example of the 'bad' uses of sexuality. For Chaucer, talking in any detail about sex is nearly always a means of suggesting moral and social sterility. In that sense it might be described as a rhetoric of moral distaste – no matter how comic the purposes and effects with which it tends to coexist.

'Deviant' sexuality

Sexualities that are 'deviant' (from either modern or medieval ideas of what is normal) exist in the *Canterbury Tales* – if at all – only at the level of implication, not of practice. The narrator of the 'General Pro-logue' goes out of his way to suggest that there is something queer

231

about the Pardoner, drawing attention to his long, lank, wax-yellow hair (I, 675–9), his 'smal' goat-like voice (I, 688) and his apparently permanent hairlessness (I, 689–90). Physical characteristics such as these might be taken to indicate effeminacy; and the narrator is certainly keen to suggest that the Pardoner is in some way fundamentally unmanly, for he adds, 'I trowe he were a geldyng or a mare' (I, 691). What this means, specifically, is that the Chaucerian narrator says he believes that the Pardoner does not possess a full set of male genitalia – implying that this would be the logical explanation for his lack of the secondary sexual characteristics of a male. There is no particular reason for thinking that anatomical incompleteness of the kind hinted at here indicates homosexuality (Benson 1982: 339) – and there is nothing 'presumptively heterosexual' about pointing that out (*pace* Burger 2003: 247, n. 40). Indeed it is regrettable that so many readers of the 'General Prologue' have been so ready to assume that the kind of 'non-man' that the Pardoner is said to be naturally equates with a gay man. Admittedly, the Chaucerian narrator's speculation about the inadequacy or inappropriateness of the Pardoner's sexual equipment might be taken to suggest that he is incapable of taking the 'active' masculine role in sexual intercourse and that he is therefore constrained to the part of a 'passive' homosexual. This was a role that medieval communities tended to regard as a particularly dishonourable one for a male adult to play; and it is not inconceivable that hostility towards habitually passive homosexuals is what the Chaucerian narrator is trying to excite here, although it has to be said that specifically English evidence for such attitudes is in fact rather thin. Yet homosexuality is certainly not the only possible explanation for the Pardoner's sexual characteristics. A good case has been made that what the Pardoner's effeminacy implies is an ill-disciplined heterosexual libido (Benson 1982: 345; Green 1982 and 1983). This is demonstrably how he was interpreted by the fifteenth-century author of the Prologue to the *Tale of Beryn*, who makes him an eager, though incompetent, womanizer (Bowers 1992: 60–79).

In any case, Chaucerian critics have often been generally too willing to jump from the Pardoner's portrait in the 'General Prologue' to his own sense of 'identity', and from his physical peculiarities to his sexual practice. The Chaucerian narrator has nothing to say about the Pardoner's desires: it is only his body that is presented as 'queer', not his mind. The Pardoner himself – far from expressing 'sexual dissidence' (Burger 2003: 141) – professes to have 'a joly wenche in every toun' (VI, 453) and declares himself 'aboute to wedde a wyf' ('The Wife of

Bath's Prologue', III, 166). This raises the question of why Chaucer chooses to give so much attention to the Pardoner's body in the first place; and the simplest answer is that it is part of a reductive strategy designed to discredit the Pardoner as a human being. It is no accident that the animal with which Chaucer chooses to illustrate the Pardoner's sexual status is a horse, which was traditionally a type of pride, folly and subjection, as in *Troilus and Criseyde* (I, 218–24). Elsewhere in the *Canterbury Tales*, in 'The Reeve's Tale' (I, 4064–6), it can apparently be taken as a given that horses are indiscriminately libidinous. From this point of view, the use of terms like 'geldyng' and 'mare' to illustrate the Pardoner's sexual status can hardly be seen as just a 'homely metaphor' (McAlpine 1980: 10): indeed, the effect of the comparison is to put the Pardoner's genitalia prominently on display in a way that is thoroughly demeaning. As a result, we need to be wary of taking too charitable a view of the Chaucerian narrator's attempt to 'queer' the Pardoner. It might seem like a positive move to try to 'claim the Pardoner' (Kruger 1994) – to use him as a means of admitting alternative sexualities into the social panorama of the pilgrimage; but this only reverses the direction of Chaucer's rhetoric, which makes the Pardoner's dubious sexuality a function of his dubious morality, not a clue to a particular kind of identity that is open to revaluation in its own right. The Pardoner's distortion of the categories of sexual identity is presented as an aspect of the Pardoner's wickedness in general: he is a sexual fake and a 'pretend man' (or so the narrator suggests) in just the same way that the relics he sells are fake and his flattery is 'feyned' (I, 705). In other words, it is not that Chaucer recognizes the Pardoner's sexual 'deviance' in order to facilitate a reading of the *Tales* in terms of 'deviance'; but rather, he exploits 'deviance' as a means of asserting the Pardoner's moral distance from the community of readers invoked in the 'General Prologue'.

What needs to be recognized here is the insidiousness of such rhetoric, which coerces the reader into making a connection between sexual difference and immorality. Neither genital deformity nor sexual deviance are necessarily symptoms of spiritual degeneration, but that is precisely the assumption that the Chaucerian narrator makes – and seems to expect his readers to make too. The logic of the 'General Prologue' is that because the Pardoner is an immoral man and a fake, therefore he is sexually 'different', since sexual difference is in itself a marker of immorality. Such logic can only be contested as a whole – to accept even a part of it risks a reinscription of the assumptions on which it depends. So, for example, to attempt to rehabilitate the

Pardoner even *because of* (rather than despite) his supposed deformity or deviance is to accept the Chaucerian narrator at his word that the Pardoner is, in some sexual sense, queer – and this in turn is to admit the validity of the association between sexual difference and moral duplicity. Rather than attempting to read the Chaucerian narrator's aspersions against the Pardoner's masculinity as a clue to his identity, it would make much more sense to accept that they constitute a deliberate slander against him – and on that basis try to analyse what part medieval models of sexuality have to play in the period's economy of slander. Far from opening any doors to the Pardoner's consciousness, Chaucer goes out of his way to stress how external his perspective is. 'I trowe he were a geldyng or a mare' is explicitly presented as a personal opinion – as gossip – and in such a way as to draw attention to the role of the narrator in directing our interpretation of the 'facts' of the Pardoner's appearance. Gossip often works in this way, disclaiming objectivity only as means of evading the responsibility for substantiating a damaging allegation. Chaucer's portrait of the Pardoner should be seen as an object-lesson in skilful defamation, not as an acknowledgement of the place of sexual 'deviance' in medieval society – and certainly not as the point at which queerness enters the *Canterbury Tales* as a creative principle.

Family

It is generally true to say that 'family' was more broadly defined in the age of Chaucer than it usually is today. Families were extended not just by a much wider definition of blood kinship, in which ties between cousins (like Palamon and Arcite in 'The Knight's Tale', I, 1019) carry much greater weight than we might expect, but also by kinships of community, trade and friendship. For example, the monk and the merchant in 'The Shipman's Tale' treat each other as honorary cousins because they were 'both two yborn in o village' (VII, 35). In 'The Friar's Tale' the Summoner and the fiend agree to unite themselves in brotherhood ('of bretherhede'), on the grounds that they share the same profession (III, 1395–1405); and a solidarity of a similar type is expressed by the guildsmen of the 'General Prologue', 'clothed alle in o lyveree / Of a solempne and a greet fraternitee' (I, 363–4). The Parson, meanwhile, makes it clear that god-parental relationships create family ties just as binding as the ties of blood (X, 907–8). Such networks presumably provided the 'freendes' who seem to have supplemented parents in the duties of guardianship, particularly in the case of young girls, such as Custance in 'The Man of Law's Tale' (II, 269) or Virginia in 'The Physician's Tale' (VI, 135). More generally, it is perhaps worth recalling that the basic meaning of the Latin word *familia* is not so much 'family' in the modern sense of the term as 'household' – the whole community of people living together as a single domestic unit, not just the property-owner's immediate relatives, but also retainers, servants, labourers and/or apprentices. So, for example, all the action of 'The Summoner's Tale' takes place in the presence of one or other of two households. When the friar becomes troublesome, the 'olde cherl' Thomas has his 'meynee' within earshot to chase the troublesome friar away (III, 2156–7): and when the Friar subsequently complains to the lord of the village, his complaint is resolved not by the lord himself but by his squire (III, 2243–5), who is serving food when the Friar arrives. The unfinished 'Cook's Tale' is specifically concerned with an apprentice whose riotous behaviour leads to his ejection from his master's service; and the completed tale would presumably have illustrated the importance of order and good governance in the household.

This tendency to think of the family in relatively extended terms need not exclude an interest in more immediate family ties, such as those between parents and children. A mother's love for her child, in particular, is a theme that Chaucer addresses on several occasions, and always with an insistent, even reverential, sentimentality. In 'The Man of Law's Tale', for example, he underlines the pathos of Custance's departure into an undeserved exile by describing her delicate care for the little child lying 'wepyng in hir arm' (II, 834). She kneels over him, soothes him with the words 'Pees, litel sone, I wol do thee noon harm', lays her headscarf over 'over his litel eyen' and then rocks him ('lulleth it') tightly in her arms. This may seem too contrived or kitsch to be at all moving, but Chaucer is at pains to underline his seriousness, for Custance then goes on to claim for herself something of the tragic dignity of the Virgin Mary's motherhood. It is an uncharacteristically pugnacious speech on her part, since she appeals to Mary only in terms that are provocatively sexist: she acknowledges that it was a woman who was responsible for the fall of mankind, but points out that Mary was doomed, as a result, to see her child 'on a croys yrent' (II, 842–5): and so 'is ther no comparison bitwene / Thy wo and any wo man may sustene' (II, 846–7). In other words, no man is capable of suffering as much as women can – as Mary did and as Custance does (so she implies) at this moment in the tale. This suggestion that women are in some way better qualified for sorrow than men is hardly a liberating perspective – for either gender – and it is not directly relevant here anyway, since as Custance admits, her child is not dead (II, 849); she is not going to be separated from him; and the child's 'harde fader' is in fact (unknown to her) wholly ignorant of any malice towards them. In 'The Prioress's Tale', Chaucer presents us with a much more genuinely moving depiction of a grieving mother. The poor widow whose son has been murdered by the Jews waits the whole night through for her child's return and then at sunrise sets out to look for him 'with face pale of drede and bisy thoght' (VII, 589). The tale conveys her growing panic as she searches everywhere she can think of, going 'half out of hir mynde' with worry (VII, 594): but it is a poignant situation, since we already know that she will never see her child alive again. Here the comparison with Mary is much more obviously valid, for the poor widow's son has literally suffered martyrdom; and indeed Mary is present throughout the Prioress' contribution to the *Tales*. Her Prologue consists almost entirely of a prayer to Mary (VII, 460–87); it is a hymn to Mary ('Alma redemptoris') that the little boy is singing when he incurs the Jews' hatred (VII, 544–64); and it is Mary herself who brings about the eventual miracle of the dead boy's temporary reanimation (VII, 649–69). In 'The Clerk's Tale', meanwhile, Griselda is twice condemned to the loss of a child; and, although she bears the loss of separation with almost superhuman fortitude, it is repeatedly emphasized that she loves her children deeply (IV, 543; 690; 1079–1106). She also imagines that she is giving her children up to a kind of martyrdom – 'Thy soule, litel child, I hym bitake, / For this nyght shaltow dyen for my sake' (IV, 559–60). Meanwhile, the Host, at least, seems to have interpreted Griselda herself as a saint, since he describes the tale as a 'legende' (IV, 1212d), a term that in this period usually refers specifically to saints' legends. All in all, it is difficult to escape the impression that Chaucer is keen to draw a connection between motherhood and sanctity. Even within the relatively limited corpus of the *Canterbury Tales*, he recurs to the image of grieving motherhood so often as to suggest a particular veneration for the idea of a mother's love. It is a moot point whether this helps to explain, or is explained by, the central place occupied by the Virgin Mary in the imaginative structures of late medieval Christianity.

Much more anxious is Chaucer's depiction of fatherhood, which tends to be shaped by a profound sense of moral and social responsibility – to such an extent that the affections of fatherhood seem remarkably understated. The Franklin, for example, responds to 'The

Squire's Tale' with a curious speech in which he says that he wished his own son were 'a man of swich discrecioun / As that ye been' (V, 685–6). The terms in which he criticizes his son's behaviour certainly recall the behaviour of the 'riotous' apprentice in 'The Cook's Tale', since all he wants to do, we are told, is 'pleye at dees*, and to despende / And lese al that he hath' (*dice: V, 690–1; cf. I, 4384–8). To that extent, the Franklin's worries could be seen as the reasonable worries of a man responsible (like the apprentice's master in 'The Cook's Tale') for the order and well-being of his household. He is, of course, the pilgrim specifically described as 'An housholdere, and that a greet' in the 'General Prologue' (I, 339). Yet this speech also seems to betray both a fervent, even fawning, snobbery and a deep-seated unease about the very principle of heredity. He despises his son for preferring to talk to a mere page, rather 'than to commune with any gentil wight' (V, 692–3), but his own 'communing' with the Squire is hardly a model of conversation among equals; and he declares himself willing to give up 'twenty pound worth lond' for a worthier heir, even though it is only by acquiring rather than renouncing land, of course, that he has created the question of inheritance in the first place. It is possible that the Franklin's fatherly concerns have been artificially sharpened by his social status: what the term 'franklin' suggests is that he is a substantial enough landowner for the inheritance of his property to be a significant issue, but that he is not quite an aristocrat, and is therefore deprived of the justifications for possession that aristocracy brings. Thus he defers to aristocracy, not just as a social class, but as an ideology. The idea that 'possessioun' is validated only by virtue, which he expresses in V. 686–7, reflects the literal meaning of 'aristocracy' – the right of 'the best' or most virtuous to rule. This certainly means that he sets standards for his son that are demandingly high; and, from this point of view, it might be argued that the Franklin's anxieties about rank and property are not so much the justification for his apparent lack of paternal pride or affection as the direct cause of the problem, the son's dysfunctional behaviour simply mirroring the father's dysfunctional ideology. Prosperity, it appears, has exaggerated the Franklin's sense of his heir's duties and responsibilities to the point at which anything like a father's love vanishes from view.

Similarly anxious, and even more destructive, is the account of paternal affection provided by 'The Physician's Tale', which serves to exemplify the austere belief that a father should be prepared to kill his own child, if that is the only way of averting the child's dishonour. Father-love ('fadres pitee') is acknowledged here (VI, 218–26), but only as a factor that makes the paternal duty in this case tragically difficult, a source of pathos and melodrama, but not a principle in its own right and certainly not a challenge to the tale's puritanical sense of a father's absolute responsibility for his children's (and specifically his daughters') virtue. Virginius himself, the father in question, attempts to justify his deed in terms that are self-consciously paradoxical – 'For love, and nat for hate, thou most be deed' (VI, 225); but this only underlines how contrived, if not 'blatantly false' (Farber 2004: 159), his reading of the situation actually is. Virginius' daughter Virginia offers no challenge to this emphasis on the father's responsibility, since she herself is serenely ready to die for her own chastity: 'Yif me my deeth, er that I have a shame' (VI, 249). Her saintly chastity ought to serve as an antidote to the tale's almost neurotic concern with the parental duty to police children's morals, but it does not. If anything her death seems to support the tale's equation of a father's responsibility with a matter of life or death:

> Ye fadres and ye moodres eek also,
> Though ye han children, be it oon or mo,
> Youre is the charge of al hir surveiaunce,
> Whil that they been under youre governaunce.
> Beth war, if by ensample of your lyvynge,
> Or by youre necligence in chastisynge,
> That they ne perisse.
>
> (VI, 93–9)

The tone of moral urgency here resembles that of a sermon – and parental accountability was certainly a theme on which churchmen preached (Owst 1961: 460–8) – but it does nothing to justify Virginius' drastic response to the threat to his daughter's chastity, since Virginia's 'surveiance' is never at issue in the tale. Virginia is in her mother's company – properly governed and surveyed – when she falls under the eye of the wicked judge; and there is no suggestion that her parents' example has in any way caused the disaster that occurs. Deceptive in much the same way is the narrator's digression on the importance of the role played by 'maistresses' in charge of respectable young girls, since no such figure appears in the tale itself. In any case, as the narrator himself points out, apparently with no sense of self-contradiction, 'This mayde . . . / So kepte hirself hir neded no maistresse' (VI, 106). The function of this passage seems to be to make connections with Chaucer's dramatization of gender conflicts elsewhere in the *Tales*, and particularly with the Wife of Bath, who is similarly expert in the 'olde daunce' of love (cf. VI, 79 and 'General Prologue', I, 476): but in the context of Virginius' homicidal concern for the sexual purity of his daughter, reference to the theme of gender conflict can only seem rather disturbing. It would, to some extent, justify a reading of the tale in terms of Virginius' fear of female sexuality and of an attempt to scapegoat older women for its emergence in young girls. At the very least, the tale records anxiety about the responsibilities of paternity, if not also about paternity itself. Indeed, given that the plot against Virginia actually takes the form of a spurious allegation that she is not Virginius' daughter at all (VI, 187), it could perhaps be argued that it is this literal threat to his paternity that he seeks to avert by killing her, as much as her enslavement to the judge's desires. Even if the ultimate point of the tale is to enable us to understand how God's 'father-love' can similarly be cruel to be kind (Mann 1983: 113–14), it remains a remarkably unhappy depiction of a father's feelings for his child. In that sense, it contrasts sharply with the veneration expressed so often elsewhere in the *Canterbury Tales* for the image of the loving mother.

See also chapter 9, GENRE IN AND OF THE *CANTERBURY TALES*; chapter 10, MORALITY AND IMMORALITY; chapter 12, CHRISTIANITY AND THE CHURCH.

References and Further Reading

References

St Augustine of Hippo (2001). *De bono conjugali: De sancta virginitate*, ed. P. G. Walsh. Oxford: Clarendon Press.

Benson, C. David (1982). 'Chaucer's Pardoner: His Sexuality and Modern Critics'. *Medievalia* 8, 337–46.

Burger, Glenn (2003). *Chaucer's Queer Nation*. Minneapolis: University of Minnesota Press.

Bowers, John M. (1992). *The Canterbury Tales: Fifteenth-Century Continuations and Additions*. Kalamazoo, Mich.: TEAMS.

Dinshaw, Carolyn (1989). *Chaucer's Sexual Poetics*. Madison: University of Wisconsin Press.

Farber, Lianna (2004). 'The Creation of Consent in the *Physician's Tale*'. *Chaucer Review* 39, 151–64.

Green, Richard Firth (1982). 'The Sexual Normality of Chaucer's Pardoner'. *Medievalia* 8, 351–7.

Green, Richard Firth (1993). 'The Pardoner's Pants and How They Matter'. *Studies in the Age of Chaucer* 15, 131–45.

Mann, Jill (2002). *Feminizing Chaucer*. Cambridge: D. S. Brewer.

McAlpine, Monica E. (1980). 'The Pardoner's Homosexuality and How It Matters'. *PMLA* 95, 8–22.

Owst, G. R. (1961). *Literature and Pulpit in Medieval England: A Neglected Chapter in the History of English Letters and of the English People*. Oxford: Blackwell.

Kittredge, George Lyman (1912). 'Chaucer's Discussion of Marriage'. *Modern Philology* 9, 435–67; various reprints, including one in J. J. Anderson (ed.), *Chaucer, The Canterbury Tales: A Casebook* (1974). London: Macmillan, pp. 61–92.

Kruger, Steven (1994). 'Claiming the Pardoner: Toward a Gay Reading of Chaucer's *Pardoner's Tale*'. *Exemplaria* 6, 115–40.

Patterson, Lee (1978). 'The *Parson's Tale* and the Quitting of the *Canterbury Tales*'. *Traditio* 34, 331–80.

Further Reading

Brooke, C. N. L. (1991). *The Medieval Idea of Marriage*. Oxford: Oxford University Press.

Bullough, Vern L. and James A. Brundage (eds) (1996). *Handbook of Medieval Sexuality*. New York and London: Garland.

Cartlidge, Neil (1997). *Medieval Marriage: Literary Approaches 1100–1300*. Cambridge: D. S. Brewer.

Jacquart, Danielle and Claude Thomasset (1988). *Sexuality and Medicine in the Middle Ages*, trans. Matthew Adamson. Princeton, NJ: Princeton University Press.

Leyser, Henrietta (1996). *Medieval Women: A Social History of Women in England 450–1500*. London: Phoenix.

Mann, Jill (1983). 'Parents and Children in the *Canterbury Tales*'. In P. Boitani and A. Torti (eds), *Literature in Fourteenth-Century England*. Tübingen and Cambridge: Narr and D. S. Brewer, pp. 165–83.

Murray, Jacqueline (2001). *Love, Marriage and Family in the Middle Ages: A Reader*. Peterborough, Ontario: Broadview.

Pedersen, Frederik (2000). *Marriage Disputes in Medieval England*. London: Hambledon.

Riddle, John M. (1996). 'Contraception and Early Abortion in the Middle Ages'. In Bullough and Brundage (eds), *Handbook of Medieval Sexuality*, pp. 261–77.

Sheehan, Michael M. (1997a). *Marriage, Family, and Law in Medieval Europe: Collected Studies*. Toronto: University of Toronto Press.

Sheehan, Michael M. (1997b). 'The Wife of Bath and her Four Sisters: Reflections on a Woman's Life in the Age of Chaucer'. In Sheehan, *Marriage, Family, and Law in Medieval Europe*, pp. 177–98.

Chapter Twelve

Christianity and the Church

John C. Hirsh

The mixing of literature and religion, so easy and natural in many medieval texts, so difficult now, lies at the heart of much of Chaucer's best writing. It is a mixture that, in the *Canterbury Tales* at least, is often implicit and nuanced even when the narrative which sustains it is formal and explicit, but often too it is contested by class, by individual motive, or by convention and circumstance. Still, it is important in examining the constructions and assumptions which are present in Chaucer's religious attitudes to remember that he was not finally a churchman, and that the requirements of his art, no less than those of his faith, conditioned his texts. In the end it is only by considering him both as a poet and, as he presents himself in the *Canterbury Tales*, as a believing but not uncritical Christian, that we can finally understand the insight that drives certain of his narratives, and which both springs from and powerfully informs much of his best work.

Christianity

Although there were many representations of religiousness present in late fourteenth-century England, the *Canterbury Tales* is founded upon one of the most popular such manifestations, the late medieval pilgrimage. The practice of Christianity was never an entirely private affair in the medieval period, and by the fourteenth century in England it had acquired a broadly based cultural approbation which brought into association the otherwise very disparate persons who together made up late medieval British society. Among the public manifestations that sought to give witness to religion's finally private choices, the pilgrimage was one of the most popular. There were many of them, and the one to the shrine of St Thomas Becket, martyred in 1170 at Canterbury Cathedral, was one of these, 54 miles from London along a well-known way that was, however, not entirely free from danger. It was not one of the most arduous of pilgrimages and regularly attracted pilgrims, particularly in the spring, for reasons both devout and secular. Other pilgrimages led to the shrine of Our Lady of Walsingham, to Hailes Abbey in Gloucestershire, which preserved a relic of Christ's sacred blood, or overseas, to the shrine of the Three Kings at Cologne, to many destinations in and around Rome, or even to Jerusalem, to name only a few of the more popular ones. But the pilgrimage to Canterbury, as the *Canterbury Tales* amply demonstrates, revealed both the strengths and the limitations of the late medieval Church, and as such presented both a mirror and a commentary.[1] Pilgrimage was also a metaphor for human life. Between birth and death all human beings are en route, and so understood, the ride to Canterbury becomes symbolic of a quest for a kind of spiritual perfection which is hardly to be found in this life, but a quest which is required of every Christian.

It is partly for this reason that it is worth remembering that the period of the *Canterbury Tales* was also the high period for English mysticism. Some of these mystics, like Richard Rolle (d. 1349), Walter Hilton (d. 1396), and the great fifteenth-century mystic Julian of Norwich (d. after 1416), were well known in their day, and were frequently consulted by others. Richard's and Walter's teachings seem to have been directed in the first place to those in religious orders; Richard served as a hermit, a writer (in both Latin and English) and a chaplain; Walter, both a (probable) student of canon law and subsequently a hermit, may have written in cooperation with the anonymous author of *The Cloud of Unknowing*. Julian's ministry, on the other hand, was available to all who came to her, and her teaching that 'all shall be well, all manner of things shall be well' seems calculated to support the believing Christian, while her more theologically sophisticated teachings, like that of 'Christ as mother', could have engaged the more theologically literate. Other mystics, like the anonymous fourteenth-century author of *The Cloud of Unknowing*, with his emphasis upon God's unknowability, or the now famous Margery Kempe, more closely attached to kinds of affective meditation than to mysticism per se, were rather less well known. Taken together, these powerful and affecting figures had their teachings and their practices echoed and reflected in the popular English institution of anchorites and anchoresses, single individuals, more often (in Britain) women than men, who lived immured until death in spaces assigned to them inside churches, where they could hear mass and pray, though they often gave advice and conversed with those who came to them as well.[2] Although (and interestingly) neither mystics nor anchorites appear in Chaucer's texts, they are important figures in estimating the state of Christianity in late medieval England, and, however indirectly, their presence informs Chaucer's thought-world, particularly where Christian values appear conspicuously or even simply register. Taken together, they give witness to a broad and felt understanding of the life of the spirit, and the availability of divine participation in the lives of all humans.

This larger Christian resonance echoes throughout the *Canterbury Tales*, and while the emphasis on spiritual pilgrimage occurs most powerfully at the beginning, in the narrator's declaration of the 'ful devout corage' (I, 22) with which he means to undertake his pilgrimage, and at the end, in the Parson's explicit linking of 'this viage' with 'thilke parfit glorious pilgrymage' (X, 49–51), it deeply informed the idea of pilgrimage throughout the medieval period, and would have been assumed by perhaps the majority of Chaucer's audience.[3] Of course it is difficult to gauge, still less to measure, the depth of the religiousness present in the majority of Chaucer's audience, though there is reason to believe that it was extensive, informed and devout; recent studies have revealed and documented an extraordinary variety of such devotions (Aston 1984; Bestul 1996; Brook 1984; Finucane 1977; Hirsh 1996; Vauchez 1993); these often included an equally rich variety of religious images, which played an important role in both spreading and perpetuating devotion, and also in documenting it for modern historians (Duffy 1992; Kamerick 2002; Marks 2004). Chaucer's own language, and also his religious narratives, achieve a general, though not always a modern, interest but, untypically for their time, they are almost in-variably as alert to human emotion *in extremis* as they are to the ecclesiastical, religious or theological constructions which they reveal or encode.

In recent years, certain of Chaucer's stories have often been designated as his 'religious tales', though this is something of a misnomer, since religious themes, values, attitudes and assumptions are present throughout the *Canterbury Tales,* and it is finally a mistake to attach them only to four or six texts. But 'The Man of Law's Tale', 'The Clerk's Tale', 'The Prioress's Tale' and 'The Second Nun's Tale', are all formally and explicitly religious, as in differing ways are his two prose tales, the narrator's own 'Tale of Melibee' and 'The Parson's Tale', and all of these have been the object of critical study (Ellis 1986; Benson and Robertson 1990; Hill 1991; Raybin and Holley 2000). Certain themes run through and connect the verse tales in particular, and taken together these constitute a kind of coda for what may reasonably be taken as Chaucerian attitudes. Each of the verse tales engages, in different ways and to different degrees, three themes which identify the ways in which Chaucer constructed certain religious attitudes: the theme of travel; the theme of suffering either because of, or in the interests of, Christian faith; and finally that of reward. What connects these tales as well is the closeness with which Chaucer has followed his sources: they are 'closer [to their sources] than any other group of works in the *Canterbury Tales*', as David Benson remarks (Benson and Robertson 1990: 3). The observation is important because it indicates a certain reluctance on Chaucer's part to depart from the texts upon which he was depending, as he did often enough elsewhere. But any careful examination of these tales will show that depart he did, sometimes, as in 'The Clerk's Tale', contrasting the theological implications of his narrative with the human reality with which it is also concerned. It is interesting that in such moments he never abandons the human in favour of the theological, though neither does he marginalize the theological – or, as often, the religious – dimension of his narrative.

The theme of pilgrimage is one such religious construction, and in the period in which Chaucer wrote it was often connected to travelling; both were understood to be powerful forces, with evident theological implications, in the late medieval world (Ladner 1967, 1979). Humans are by nature travellers, and the theme of the man voyaging, *homo viator*, rooted in monastic spirituality, was intimately connected with themes of alienation and of order, and the image, in 'The Man of Law's Tale' of Constance, the tale's protagonist, being sent away first by her parents, then by her (altogether evil) mother-in-law, comes to represent the Christian traveller, who must sojourn in a finally inhospitable world in order to come to life's final reward, realized allegorically in the tale, but also actually in Rome, so that her physical salvation becomes a kind of preparation for the world which is to come (Block 1953). No less abandoned, no less a traveller, is Griselda in 'The Clerk's Tale', effectively torn from her parents, then left to the inflexible will of her husband. Here Chaucer's allegory is all but palpable, and Griselda's reaction to the apparent death of her children is emblematic of the devout Christian's to the most extreme adversity, trusting in God's final justice and mercy, whether in this world or the next. The unnamed boy in 'The Prioress's Tale' travels only through the Jewish ghetto of an unnamed city 'in Asye' (VII, 1), no great distance, and his suffering there is brief, but his reward is equally evident and assured. The same pattern, changes having been made, informs 'The Second Nun's Tale', though Cecilia rejects her pagan past in favour of her new Church, and it is her soon-to-be canonized husband whose travels lead him (and his brother) through suffering to their reward. In important ways this insight – that human life has intrinsic movement directing it towards its end, which is God – proved to be one of the most important insights of the *Canterbury Tales*, and the one which most powerfully separated them from what John M. Fyler has called 'pagan survivals', which yet remained in late medieval English thought. Although attracted, both early and late, to many aspects of pagan antiquity, including in particular those that informed his use of myth, tales like the ones cited indicate how decidedly Chaucer had moved from his earlier writing in the direction of Christian thought (Fyler 2000: 349; Minnis 1982; Nolan 1992).

Yet what further binds Chaucer's religious tales together is a sense of marginality. Their suffering protagonists are often Christian women and their children, ones whose antagonists are, usually at least, powerful and well connected men. One hallmark of these Christians is a kind of secular powerlessness, accompanied by a sense of alienation in an inhospitable world through which they can finally only pass. Even Cecilia, the most personally powerful of the protagonists, meets a martyr's end, though with it comes her reward. But it is as though Chaucer has at least allowed that Christianity can have a somewhat complicated relationship with the Church that sustains it, and draws strength from those intrinsic virtues that are rooted in its origins.

Chaucer's view of Christianity is thus attached to representations and constructions of personal faith, and though it admits of suffering and conflict, it holds out no promise of triumph, except finally. Christianity is omnipresent throughout the *Canterbury Tales*, but as part of an engaged, enquiring, even secular spirituality, though one that is capable as well of embracing the totalizing *apologia* of the 'Retraction'. But it does not operate apart from the world through which Chaucer's protagonists move, and this action, as much as any other, invites a consideration of the Church.[4]

John C. Hirsh

The Church

There were probably few periods in English history in which issues concerning the church, both nationally and internationally, mattered as much as they did in Chaucer's time. The most ubiquitous sign of the Church was its clergy, whether in the person of secular priests like Chaucer's admired Parson, or in those clerics who followed a rule (Latin *regula*) and so were designated members of the 'regular' orders. These included monks, who in Britain were usually members of the Benedictine order, which followed the monastic rule of St Benedict (*c.*480–*c.*550), or of the Cistercian order, founded by St Robert of Molesme in 1098 but named after Cîteaux, where Robert also lived for a while, or of the Gilbertine order, founded by St Gilbert of Sempringham (*c.*1083–1189), the only such order founded in England, and one that from the beginning included women as well as men. But monks were usually cloistered and so not as present to their society as members of the more recently founded fraternal (Latin *frater*, brother) orders, whose vocation directed that they should preach and minister to lay persons, so that they were much more in evidence. Most often these were Franciscans, an order founded in 1209 by St Francis of Assisi (1181–1226), or Dominicans, founded in 1220 by St Dominic (*c.*1172–1221), though there were also Augustinian and Carmelite friars (Szittya 1986; Lawrence 1994 and 2001). Chaucer's Pilgrims include both a Monk and a Friar, sometimes assumed to be a Benedictine and a Franciscan, though in fact Chaucer is careful not to specify the orders of the two men, whose failures and limitations, though conventional in the literature of the day, form an important aspect of his critique of the Church. Even more reprehensible are two minor ecclesiastical officials who are also on the Canterbury pilgrimage, a Pardoner, whose office it was to collect monies within a prescribed area for Church projects approved by a bishop or religious superior, and a Summoner, intended to call to account at a Church court those guilty of breaking ecclesiastical, not civil, laws. But the Pardoner is deeply implicated in blasphemous and cynical theft of many kinds, and the Summoner is far more sinful than those he is intended to apprehend.

Less apparent is the influence of the Pope, probably Urban VI and then Boniface IX, both of whom were involved in important and public controversies throughout the period that Chaucer was writing the *Canterbury Tales*. During much of Chaucer's early life the papacy was located not at Rome but at Avignon (1309–77), yet when Pope Urban

VI (Pope 1378–89) all but brought about the so-called 'Great Schism' (1378–1417) by a personal arrogance bordering on mental derangement, and what can most kindly be described as an extraordinary lack of diplomatic tact, the English Crown was among the European monarchies who nonetheless drew to his side, and so stood against the Avignon anti-popes Clement VII and Benedict XIII, a circumstance which is echoed directly in Chaucer's 'Second Nun's Tale' (Giffin 1956: 29–48; Hirsh 2003: 82–101).

Nationally, the great issue engaging the English Church concerned the teachings of the Oxford philosopher, theologian and reformer, John Wycliffe (*c.*1330–84), Fellow of Merton College, Master of Balliol and Warden of Canterbury Hall, whose heterodox opinions were finally and thereafter often condemned, although late in the fourteenth century they were discussed and debated. During the reign of King Henry IV (1399–1413), Wycliffe's name became identified with social instability and with heresy. Wycliffe had argued, for example, that the foundation of the religious orders (the friars in particular) was not supported in scripture, and that when the clergy was not in a state of grace it could be deprived of its endowments by civil authority. No less controversially, he argued against the traditional teaching of eucharistic transubstantiation, which he believed encouraged superstition. After his 1382 condemnation at the London 'Earthquake Synod', brought about by Archbishop William Courtney (1342–96; Archbishop of Canterbury 1381–96), Wycliffe's teaching authority declined sharply, and his name became associated with the translation of the Bible into English, which his followers, not he himself, effected. His friendships at court, particularly those with John of Gaunt (1340–99) and Edward, the Black Prince (1330–76), protected him while he was alive, though the movement to which he gave birth came under repeated attack after his death, especially in the second term as Archbishop of Canterbury of the powerful and uncompromising Thomas Arundel (1353–1414; Archbishop of Canterbury 1396–7 and 1399–1414; Chancellor 1388, 1391, 1407–9 and 1412–13), when 'Lollards' (as followers of Wycliffe were called; the origin of the word is obscure) were persecuted with little mercy. It was largely to counter Wycliffe's influence that Arundel secured the death penalty for heresy in 1401 (Aston 1967; Dahmus 1966; Hudson 1988; Shinners and Dohar 1998; Watson 2000).

These historical circumstances involved Chaucer in some of the most important controversies of his day, ones which both revealed the flawed actualities of the English Church, and which would lead, in the decades following Chaucer's death, to even more powerful (and repressive) measures. Scholarly opinion concerning the impact and implications of these eventualities has shifted over the years, though few now would insist that it was the putative corruption of the late medieval Church alone which led to the Reformation, which is today understood as having been far more of a top-down rather than a bottom-up movement and institution, though Christopher Haigh has also argued that, strictly speaking, the Reformation as such never took place in England (Haigh 1993; Duffy 1992 and 2001). The difficulty in discerning socio-religious attitudes in Chaucer's writing, however, has been to understand that there were indeed laypersons like him for whom a critique of clerical and other abuses did not constitute per se an attack on the Church itself, but rather on those of its present deformities which were amenable to correction. Even by medieval standards, in which stability was more often announced than attained, the late fourteenth century was a time of quite extraordinary social, political and religious upheaval. In the last years of that century, partly because of a perceived Lollard threat, partly because a weakened monarchy turned to senior churchmen to wield civil power, the line between civil and ecclesiastical authority, effectively between Church and State, narrowed sharply, so that what happened in Westminister resonated throughout the kingdom. Towards the end of September 1399, King Richard II, long Chaucer's rather distant patron, was forced from the throne by Henry Bolingbroke, Duke of Hereford, whose lands Richard had unwisely confiscated. Whether by opportunism or design, Henry usurped Richard's throne and took the title King Henry IV, though in his early years he faced a number of violent rebellions. In the months preceding his death in October 1400, however, Chaucer seems to have ingratiated himself with the new monarch, to whom he was already connected through the former Earl of Richmond and Duke of Lancaster, John of Gaunt, Henry's now deceased father, with whom Chaucer had in his youth served in France, and for whom he had written the first of his earlier great poems, the *Book of the Duchess*. In addition, Chaucer's by now deceased wife had been the sister of Katherine Swynford, first John of Gaunt's mistress, later his wife. With connections like these, the elderly and respectable civil servant Chaucer had become survived easily under the new monarchy, and in one of his short lyrics, 'The Complaint of Chaucer to his Purse', saluted Henry IV as 'verray kyng' ('true king'), so there would be no confusion as to where he stood, nor what was his due.

These biographical points are worth remembering because, if Paul Strohm is right, there came a point when Lollardry became identified with opposition, and finally with treason, against the new, post-

Ricardian, Lancastrian monarchy, and as such seemed almost to invite persecution (Strohm 1992: 75–94 and 1998: 59). Even if the identification was not complete, it is certainly possible that the dismissal of standing authority which the Lollards' position necessitated hardly endeared them to a king whose position was, in the early years at least, constantly under attack. Still, it is worth recalling that in the last years of Richard's reign, and in the early years of Henry's, it was still possible to articulate and even to develop a reasoned critique of certain ecclesiastical practices without becoming identified as a Lollard or an enemy of the Church or Crown. Anne Hudson has pointed out that it was not until 1407 that translating the Bible into English was finally forbidden, and until the failed rebellion of the Lollard knight Sir John Oldcastle (1414), the break with orthodoxy, in some circles at least, was perhaps not quite final. It is important to remember that in the last years of Chaucer's life, and particularly for the elite, things were not as repressive as they subsequently became (Hudson 1975).

Chaucer's critique of late medieval Church practices is thus conditioned by the larger ecclesiastical and religious assumptions of the *Canterbury Tales*, but also, it must be said, by a marked sensitivity to social class that runs throughout the *Tales*, and allows him to treat certain of the Pilgrims, particularly those associated with ecclesiastical corruption, with an almost easy intellectual contempt. Thus, although the narrator may affect to hold the Pardoner in a certain awe, and even to allow that the corrupted Summoner has his points, nothing can disguise the isolating distance at which each man is also held, and the evident deformities, both institutional and personal, which they manifest. They are set against the industrious and committed Parson, and there is no doubt that it is the forms of corruption and subversion which they represent in their persons, and not the Church which they only purport to serve, that have been weighed, measured and found wanting. Yet also pointedly, though with a degree of sympathy, Chaucer opines that their multiple failures have been institutionalized, even condoned, by a Church which stands in real need of institutional change. Still, the effect of their presentation is finally less to castigate the Church than to offer a kind of conditional if conservative support for its present reformation. And so it would have seemed to his elite contemporary readers and auditors.

It is thus probably not a good idea to read Chaucer's attitudes towards Christianity and the Church more or less exclusively in the language of the political controversies of his time, influenced by them in some ways though he clearly was, and powerful as they subsequently became. Here as elsewhere, Chaucer fought shy of directly political involvement, even as he responded to some at least of the more pressing issues of his day – unworthy (but also worthy) clerics, and the power of money, chief among them. But his response to Christianity and the Church was finally relational and contingent, not absolute, and emerges indirectly and by inference.

Christianity and the Church

I hope it is by now evident that throughout the *Canterbury Tales* Chaucer responded not only to the presence of Christianity, but also to the effect, for both good and for ill, of the Christian Church. The Parson does not explain, cancel or excuse the Pardoner and the Summoner, but he does show unmistakably the ideals from which they have fallen, and the ecclesiastical practices against which they have both turned. The *Canterbury Tales* was a work which was informed, but not circumscribed, by generally philosophical, specifically scholastic, teaching, whether theological or aesthetic, but it also reflected its maker's thinking on the role of a Christian Church, and as such echoed, sometimes with irony, several formulations that his reflection, and his era, supplied.

In the recent past, Chaucer's thinking in this area has been considered deeply informed, even conditioned, by an aesthetic attached to St Augustine (354–430), whose teachings, particularly in respect to allegory, influenced certain members of an earlier generation of Chaucer scholars, particularly in the 1960s and early 1970s. According to this largely discredited school, Chaucer's texts would almost invariably reveal, to the informed eye, their hidden but true meaning, one that involved the sort of allegorical readings commonly used by biblical exegetes in commenting on narratives in the Bible. The larger issue which informed this school concerned what was taken to be a largely dichotomous dimension to Chaucer's putatively theological thinking, one which involved the opposed theological concepts of *caritas* and *cupiditas*, spiritual love and earthly desire, the first pointing upwards to God, the other downwards to things of this world (Robertson 1951 and 1980: 21–50). This opposition was assumed to operate throughout Chaucer's canon, as it was throughout medieval (and much Renaissance) literature generally, and to be firmly rooted in Augustine, whose *De doctrina christiana* was taken as its marching orders. D. W. Robertson referred to his work as 'historical criticism', and believed himself to be opposed mainly by what was then called 'New Criticism', which concerned itself with a close reading of the text and eschewed historical interpretation in general. But in assuming that St Augustine (d. 430) voiced concerns and attitudes still explicitly present a thousand years later to Geoffrey Chaucer (d. 1400) Robertson had inadvertently brushed aside an intervening millennium of theological thought and reflection, a period which had absorbed and reformulated many Augustinian teachings, even though Augustine himself continued to be copied and read throughout the Latin Middle Ages. Many of these reformulations, like much of the new thought itself, involved social and dynamic concerns that were widely understood to represent orthodox Christian teaching, and it is to these that we must turn if we are to address adequately the concerns of this chapter.

These new concerns reflect both the teachings of the great Dominican theologian St Thomas Aquinas (1225–74) and other teachings which followed or opposed them. Scholastic influence on Chaucer's thinking, though real, was primarily indirect, but it was most present in areas that informed the interaction of Christianity and the Church, and this involved, importantly, the development of the concept of the Common Good, which directly informed the relationship throughout the medieval period (Kempshall 1999; Olson 1986; Swanson 2000). Of all the scholastic ideas that are reflected in Chaucer's attitudes and assumptions, this is one in particular that can help to illuminate his thinking on contemporary and near-contemporary theological issues, and that powerfully shows how Chaucer addressed certain Christian ethical topics.

By the fourteenth century philosophical inquiry routinely and explicitly addressed questions involving social issues that had particular relevance for a writer like Chaucer, who tended to avoid abstract philosophical argument as such, but seems still to have been engaged by certain theological problems that were around him. Primary among these was the nature of the interaction between and among human beings in a morally (and actually) contingent universe. In recent years, and thanks largely to the work of Matthew Kempshall (1999), the concept of the Common Good has emerged as central to any understanding of the interaction that took place between the expressed ideals of late medieval Christianity and the social institution the late medieval Church had become. The concept neither accounted nor apologized for specifically ecclesiastical shortcomings, still less did it excuse institutional corruption, but it did offer a way of understanding how the Christian Church could bridge the gap between earthly goods, whether real or apparent, and the requirements of its divine mission.

251

The idea of the Common Good, understood in terms both Christian and social, is first attested in the writings of St Augustine as any 'good shared in common with a number of people', and is present both in his *Rule* and elsewhere in his work, particularly in Book XIX of *The City of God*. In Augustine's writing, it is seen as rooted in scripture, in Acts 4: 32, 1 Corinthians 10: 24, 10: 33 and 13: 5, 2 Corinthians 5: 15, Philippians 2: 21, Romans 15: 3 and Psalm 21: 30, among other places. In Augustine's thought the ancient jurist and philosopher Cicero also figures prominently, even though it has been objected that Augustine excised from Cicero's definition both the sense of common justice (*consensus iuris*) and the sense of shared benefit or utility (*communio utilitatis*) that figure there. In addition, as Kempshall has pointed out, the concept is related to Augustine's changing of Cicero's definition of the *res publica* from 'an association of a multitude united by a common sense of what is right and by a community of interests' to 'an association of a multitude of rational beings united by a common agreement on the objects of their love' (Kempshall 1999: 19). Augustine's texts, informed both by Cicero and by scripture, clearly advanced the concept of the Common Good in theological discourse in the late medieval period. Still, as I have noted, Augustine's treatment of the concept was only the beginning, and what finally influenced Chaucer was not the Augustinian formulation but rather the extended development the concept underwent throughout the thirteenth century.

This development was informed by the translation into Latin of certain Aristotelian texts, most importantly in the early 1240s by the translation both of a commentary and an epitome of Aristotle's *Ethics*, which was followed in 1246–7 by the English philosopher Robert Grosseteste's translation into Latin of the ten Books of the *Ethics*, together with the comments of certain Greek annotators. The translation made available to Western thinkers a number of important Aristotelian concepts, like those of happiness and goodness, concepts that seemed to lend themselves relatively easily to orthodox Christian elaboration. Thus, when Thomas Aquinas' great teacher Albertus Magnus (d. 1280) undertook the first of his commentaries on Aristotle's *Ethics*, he identified the 'good' of an individual with that of a people, though he thought too, following what he believed to be Aristotle's intention, that one was greater (*maius*) than the other. He ignored, Kempshall perceptively points out, the presence in Aristotle's text of other adjectives, 'better' (*melius*) and 'more perfect' (*perfectius*), and was so able to represent the Common Good more or less simply as 'the aggregate total of individual goods; viewed within an indefinite period of time, it is an unending sequence of individual goods' (Kempshall 1999: 30).

By the time Albertus came to write his second commentary on the *Ethics*, however, an important event had occurred, one central to the relationship between the Christian and the Church, as Chaucer (and later medieval thinkers) came to understand it. In the early 1260s Aristotle's *Politics* had been translated into Latin, and Albertus produced a commentary on it too, some time between 1263 and 1267. Not long after this, towards the end of the 1260s, Albertus wrote a second commentary on the *Ethics* in a series of extended paraphrases, clarifying, *inter alia*, his treatment of the relationship between the individual and the Common Good. Whereas Aristotle had held that happiness was 'a good composed of all those goods which are subordinate to it', Albertus now held that it was rather 'a collection of individual goods in the sense of being a potential or virtual whole' (Kempshall 1999: 30–7).

The Common Good became, in this reading, not simply a collection of separate individual goods, but a good that exists in relation to other goods, all of which are virtually present in it. Albertus referred to the victory of an army or the sailing of a ship as examples of the more complex ways in which the Common Good is realized from subordinated individual goods, but defined by the presence of a higher, even, in medieval philosophical terms, a Supreme Good, to which the individual goods have a relationship. This is the aspect of the formulation that is echoed at the end of the *Canterbury Tales*, in the Parson's description of pilgrimage, to which I have referred above. In his offer to the other Pilgrims, 'To shewe yow the wey, in this viage, / Of thilke parfit glorious pilgrymage, / That highte Jerusalem celestial' (X, 49–51), the Parson is referring very specifically to the final good to which their individual lives and stories point. His offer is not exclusively theological, though it is that too, but it holds out the possibility that there are kinds of religiousness that are present in the pilgrimage that is life.

Even the quest for personal salvation, encoded in pilgrimage, championed by the mystic, cannot by itself supplant the Common Good, the position of which, for Chaucer, is often central to achieving salvation – it is not an optional extra. Still, in Chaucer's writing there is nothing static about the perception of that good, nor in the Supreme Good itself, which assumes involvement with others as a constituent part. Dialogue and dissent are necessary human attributes in arriving at an understanding, however circumscribed, as to what the Supreme

Good, or even the Common Good, may be, and how they should be understood. The emphasis on individual salvation, present in theological thought well before Augustine, can be seen as implicated in, but existing at a distance from, the social and ethical propositions that scholastic teaching subsequently maintained, and that, in Chaucer's work, cluster around the concept of the Common Good.

This point is important because, as I have noted, Chaucer's representation of both Christianity and the Church is still often read in largely Augustinian terms, ones that indeed privilege individual salvation – a continuing theme in Thomistic and post-Thomistic thinking too – but not ones attuned to the sense of mutual interest and investment that lie at the heart of the Common Good. In this context the Parson emerges as a particularly powerful example, though in the past he has been perceived rather as an outsider, universally praised for what has seemed his almost paradigmatic virtue, but not generally regarded as an integral part of the thought-world of the pilgrimage as a whole.

It may be because the Parson's teaching, initially at least, is represented by example, rather than by precept or doctrine, that readers of Chaucer have focused more on his example than on what he teaches. When, in the course of his tale, he turns to what may well be the closest translation in Chaucer of the phrase 'the Common Good', he notes, following his source, that 'the common profit' might not 'be kept' unless 'God hadde ordeyned that som men hadde heyer degree and some men lower' (X, 773). The phrase occurs elsewhere too: 'The Clerk's Tale' remarks that not only was Griselda a good housekeeper, but also that she could promote as well the 'commune profit' (IV, 431), suggesting that, in her new office as Walter's wife, she subordinated the requirements of her own now rich household to the needs of others. The book the narrator reads before falling asleep in the *Parliament of Fowls* tells of a vision that promises success to any person, 'lered other lewed, / That lovede commune profyt' (46–7). The phrase clearly shows a consciousness of the important concept in Chaucer's writing, though it would probably be mistaken to identify it exclusively with those places where the phrase 'common profit' itself appears, and it is evident that this phrase came to represent the way in which individual goods were subordinated to perceived and agreed upon larger social and communal requirements, variously defined, not entirely unlike the way the idea of the Common Good had been developing in philosophical and theological, not courtly, circles.

Chaucer's is above all an *urban* pilgrimage, from London to Canterbury and (in theory at least) back again, and as such responsive to social no less than personal imperatives. It is in this light that the phrase 'common profit' applies, itself a Chaucerian elaboration of the orthodox teaching concerning the Common Good, though the now familiar idiom has also been given more secular readings (Olson 1986; Robertson 2001). But the phrase, like the thinking that stands behind it, gives a reasonably clear indication of the ways in which Chaucer considered and articulated the Christian and social teachings of one of the larger religious and theological constructions of his time, and the issues that arose from the Lollard challenge to traditional Christian practice.

Inclusive as the concept of the Common Good seems to be, the presence within it of a putative 'Supreme Good' has not recommended it to modern philosophy, which has found it impossible to articulate a general social good on which all humans can or should agree. For a modern philosopher like John Rawls, the idea of a Common Good is impossible in a democratic society dedicated to liberty and toleration. And Ronald Dworkin agrees, linking the Common Good to the now dated concept of the 'good life', which can no longer reasonably inform ethical decision-making. But in the more circumscribed world of the Latin Middle Ages it was clearly a liberating concept, one that sought exactly to involve and include, not diminish, though it did so against a theological absolute, which had indeed the effect of supplying mutually agreed-upon directions. It intended to exclude none from its orbit, though the resolution that the Parson (almost aggressively) offers to the Pilgrims illustrates one way in which a Supreme Good can be understood to be imposed rather than embraced. Yet it is still somewhat disingenuous to assert that certain modern social practices, which rigorously exclude many not only from participation in a rich variety of goods but also from the means of obtaining them, are markedly more inclusive than medieval ones.

In the late medieval period the Common Good carried with it meanings that are rooted in the most fundamental aspects of Christianity and the Church. Philosophically, it negotiates the sometimes conflicted space between the requirements for the personal salvation of the individual Christian, and those respecting the doctrinal orthodoxy of the larger social group, both of which fall under the teaching of the Church. But even when that has been said, it is certainly possible to believe that Chaucer's understanding of the Common Good was defined less by a single general precept than by the continuing dialogues and exchanges that the Pilgrims practised between and among themselves, exchanges which sometimes encode the presence of an agreed upon and Common Good, whether secular or, finally at least, religious. That there was an ultimate significance in their exchanges emerges in the fact of their pilgrimage to Canterbury, and explicitly, when the Parson makes it clear to them in his 'Prologue'. In that respect, Chaucer's Common Good is unexceptional, and echoes traditional formulations. But Chaucer's thinking, though sometimes constrained by medieval convention, is never finally static or complete. The shared and social goods and goals all but stated outright in the person and the actions of the Parson, and involving a considered and reflective sense of the mutual interaction of Christianity and the Church, constitute one kind of philosophical, ethical and religious coda to the *Canterbury Tales* as a whole.

See also chapter 9, GENRE IN AND OF THE *CANTERBURY TALES*; chapter 10, MORALITY AND IMMORALITY; chapter 11, MARRIAGE, SEXUALITY AND THE FAMILY.

Notes

1 The literature on this subject is not small, but for a general study of medieval pilgrimage see Jonathan Sumption, *Pilgrimage. An Image of Medieval Religion* (Totowa, NJ: Rowman and Littlefield, 1975), and for an account of its intellectual background, see in particular Dee Dyas, *Pilgrimage in Medieval English Literature, 700–1500* (Cambridge: D. S. Brewer, 2001), and also Susan Signe Morrison, *Women Pilgrims in Late Medieval England: Private Piety as Public Performance* (London and New York: Routledge, 2000), which includes a particularly interesting treatment of the Walsingham pilgrimage, pp. 26–35. There is an account of the object of the Pilgrims' devotion: see John Butler, *The Quest for Becket's Bones: The Mystery of the Relics of St. Thomas Becket of Canterbury* (New Haven and London: Yale University Press, 1995).

2 On late medieval English mysticism see the surveys by Wolfgang Riehle, *The Middle English Mystics*, trans. Bernard Standring (London: Routledge and Kegan Paul, 1981), and Marion Glasscoe, *English Medieval Mystics: Games of Faith*, Longman Medieval and Renaissance Library (London and New York: Longman, 1993), and for important studies of individual mystics, Denise Nowakowski Baker, *Julian of Norwich's Showings: From Vision to Book* (Princeton, NJ: Princeton University Press, 1994), and Nicholas Watson, *Richard Rolle and the Invention of Authority*. Cambridge Studies in Medieval Literature 1 (Cambridge: Cambridge University Press, 1993). On anchorites see A. K. Warren, *Anchorites and their Patrons in Medieval England* (Berkeley and Los Angeles: University of California Press, 1985).

3 Treatments of late medieval Christianity in Britain are legion, but for collections of illustrative texts see now Emilie Amt (ed.), *Medieval England, 1000–1500: A Reader*, Readings in Medieval Civilizations and Cultures VI

(Peterborough, Ontario: Broadview Press, 2001); Anne Clark Bartlett and Thomas H. Bestul (eds), *Cultures of Piety: Medieval English Devotional Literature in Translation* (Ithaca, NY, and London: Cornell University Press, 1999); and R. N. Swanson (ed. and trans.), *Catholic England: Faith, Religion and Observance Before the Reformation*. Manchester Medieval Sources Series (Manchester: Manchester University Press, 1993). For more specialized studies see, among many, Caroline Walker Bynum's study of European spirituality, *Jesus as Mother: Studies in the Spirituality of the High Middle Ages*, Publications of the Center for Medieval and Renaissance Studies, UCLA (Berkeley, Los Angeles and London: University of California Press, 1982); for specifically Chaucerian and British studies, see my articles in Douglas Gray (ed.), *The Oxford Companion to Chaucer* (Oxford: Clarendon Press, 2003), *s.v.* 'piety' and 'religion'; Thomas J. Heffernan (ed.), *The Popular Religion of Medieval England* (Knoxville: University of Tennessee Press, 1985); W. A. Pantin, 'Instructions for a Devout and Literate Layman', in J. J. G. Alexander and M. T. Gibson (eds), *Medieval Literature and Learning: Essays Presented to R. W. Hunt* (Oxford: Clarendon Press, 1976), pp. 398–422. On some of the more powerful forms of late medieval English spirituality, see my *The Revelations of Margery Kempe: Paramystical Practices in Late Medieval England*, Medieval and Renaissance Authors 10 (Leiden and New York: E. J. Brill, 1989).

4   Students of British medieval Christianity should be aware too of an often gendered and new school of recent historical studies, which focuses on the physical and psychological aspects of the often marginalized and devout Christian. See Sarah Beckwith, *Christ's Body: Identity, Culture and Society in Late Medieval Writings* (London and New York: Routledge, 1993); Caroline Walker Bynum, *Fragmentation and Redemption: Essays on Gender and the Human Body in Medieval Religion* (New York: Zone Books, 1991); and C. W. Bynum's earlier *Holy Feast, Holy Fast: The Religious Significance of Food to Medieval Women*. The New Historicism: Studies in Cultural Poetics (Berkeley and Los Angeles: University of California Press, 1987); Carolyn Dinshaw and David Wallace (eds), *The Cambridge Companion to Medieval Women's Writing* (Cambridge: Cambridge University Press, 2003); Sarah Kay and Miri Rubin (eds), *Framing Medieval Bodies* (Manchester and New York: Manchester University Press, 1994); A. A. MacDonald, H. N. B. Ridderbos and R. M. Schulsemann (eds), *The Broken Body: Passion Devotion in Late-Medieval Culture* (Groningen: Egbert Forsten, 1998); and Miri Rubin, *Gentile Tales: The Narrative Assault on Late Medieval Jews* (New Haven and London: Yale University Press, 1999).

References and Further Reading

Aston, Margaret (1967). *Thomas Arundel: A Study of Church Life in the Reign of Richard II*. Oxford: Clarendon Press.

John C. Hirsh

Aston, Margaret (1984). *Lollards and Reformers: Images of Literacy in Late Medieval Religion*. London: Hambledon Press.

Benson, C. David and Elizabeth Robertson (eds) (1990). *Chaucer's Religious Tales*. Chaucer Studies 15. Cambridge: D. S. Brewer.

Bestul, Thomas H. (1996). *Texts of the Passion: Latin Devotional Literature and Medieval Society*. University of Pennsylvania Middle Ages Series. Philadelphia: University of Pennsylvania Press.

Block, Edward A. (1953). 'Originality, Controlling Purpose and Craftsmanship in Chaucer's *Man of Law's Tale*'. *PMLA* 69, 572–616.

Brook, Christopher and Rosalind Brooke (1984). *Popular Religion in the Middle Ages: Western Europe 1000–1300*. London: Thames and Hudson.

Dahmus, Joseph (1966). *William Courtenay, Archbishop of Canterbury 1381–1396*. University Park and London: Pennsylvania State University Press.

Duffy, Eamon (1992). *The Stripping of the Altars: Traditional Religion in England c.1400–1580*. New Haven and London: Yale University Press.

Duffy, Eamon (2001). *The Voices of Morebath: Reformation and Rebellion in an English Village*. New Haven and London: Yale University Press.

Ellis, Roger (1986). *Patterns of Religious Narrative in the Canterbury Tales*. London and Sydney: Croom Helm.

Finucane, Ronald C. (1977). *Miracles and Pilgrims: Popular Beliefs in Medieval England*. London: J. M. Dent.

Fyler, John M. (2000). 'Pagan Survivals'. In Peter Brown (ed.), *A Companion to Chaucer*. Oxford: Blackwell, pp. 349–59.

Giffin, Mary (1956). *Studies on Chaucer and his Audience*. Quebec: Les Editions l'Eclair.

Haigh, Christopher (1993). *English Reformations: Religion, Politics and Society under the Tudors*. Oxford: Clarendon Press.

Hill, John M. (1991). *Chaucerian Belief: The Poetics of Reverence and Delight*. New Haven and London: Yale University Press.

Hirsh, John C. (1996). *The Boundaries of Faith: The Development and Transmission of Medieval Spirituality*. Studies in the History of Christian Thought 67. Leiden and New York. E. J. Brill.

Hirsh, John C. (2003). *Chaucer and the Canterbury Tales: A Short Introduction*. Blackwell Introductions to Literature. Oxford: Blackwell.

Hudson, Anne (1975). 'The Debate on Bible Translation'. *English Historical Review* 90, 1–18.

Hudson, Anne (1988). *The Premature Reformation: Wycliffite Texts and Lollard History*. Oxford: Clarendon Press.

Kamerick, Kathleen (2002). *Popular Piety and Art in the Late Middle Ages: Image Worship and Idoltary in England, 1350–1500*. The New Middle Ages. New York and Basingstoke: Palgrave.

Kempshall, M. S. (1999). *The Common Good in Late Medieval Political Thought*. Oxford: Clarendon Press.

Ladner, Gerhard B. (1967). 'Homo viator: Medieval Ideas of Alienation and Order'. *Speculum* 42, 233–59.

Ladner, Gerhard B. (1979). 'Medieval and Modern Understanding of Symbolism: A Comparison'. *Speculum* 54, 223–56.

Lawrence, C. H. (1994). *The Friars: The Impact of the Early Mendicant Movement on Western Society*. The Medieval World. London and New York: Longman.

Lawrence, C. H. (2001). *Medieval Monasticism: Forms of Religious Life in Western Europe in the Middle Ages*. The Medieval World. 3rd edn. London and New York: Longman.

Marks, Richard (2004). *Image and Devotion in Late Medieval England*. Stroud: Sutton.

Minnis, Alastair J. (1982). *Chaucer and Pagan Antiquity*. Chaucer Studies 8. Cambridge: D. S. Brewer.

Nolan, Barbara (1992). *Chaucer and the Tradition of the 'Roman Antique'*. Cambridge Studies in Medieval Literature 15. Cambridge: Cambridge University Press.

Olson, Paul A. (1986). *The Canterbury Tales and the Good Society*. Princeton, NJ: Princeton University Press.

Pantin, W. A. (1955). *The English Church in the Fourteenth Century*. Cambridge: Cambridge University Press, and Notre Dame, Ind.: Notre Dame University Press.

Raybin, David and Linda Tarte Holley (eds) (2000). *Closure in the Canterbury Tales: The Role of the Parson's Tale*. Medieval Institute Publications, Studies in Medieval Culture 41. Kalamazoo, Mich.: Western Michigan University.

Robertson, D. W., Jr (1951). 'The Doctrine of Charity in Medieval Literary Gardens: A Topographical Approach through Symbolism and Allegory'. *Speculum* 26, 24–49.

Robertson, D. W., Jr (1980). *Essays in Medieval Culture*. Princeton, NJ: Princeton University Press.

Robertson, Kellie (2001). 'Common Language and Common Profit'. In Jeffrey Jerome Cohen (ed.), *The Postcolonial Middle Ages*. New York and Basingstoke: Palgrave, pp. 209–28.

Shinners, John and William J. Dohar (1998). *Pastors and the Care of Souls in Medieval England*. Notre Dame Texts in Medieval Culture 4. Notre Dame, Ind.: University of Notre Dame Press.

Smith, H. Maynard (1938). *Pre-Reformation England*. London and Toronto: Macmillan.

Strohm, Paul (1992). *Hochon's Arrow: The Social Imagination of Fourteenth-Century Texts*. Princeton. NJ: Princeton University Press.

Strohm, Paul (1998). *England's Empty Throne: Usurpation and the Language of Legitimization, 1399–1422*. New Haven and London: Yale University Press.

Swanson, Robert (2000). 'Social Structures'. In Peter Brown (ed.), *A Companion to Chaucer*. Oxford: Blackwell, pp. 397–413.

Szittya, Penn R. (1986). *The Antifraternal Tradition in Medieval Literature*. Princeton, NJ: Princeton University Press.

Vauchez, André (1993). *The Laity in the Middle Ages: Religious Beliefs and Devotional Practices*, trans. Daniel E. Bornstein. Notre Dame, Ind. and London: Notre Dame University Press.

Watson, Nicholas (2000). 'Christian Ideologies'. In Peter Brown (ed.), *A Companion to Chaucer*. Oxford: Blackwell, pp. 75–89.

Part Five

The Sound of Chaucer

The opening of the General Prologue to the *Canterbury Tales*, from the Kelmscott Press Chaucer (1896), designed and ornamented by William Morris, with woodcuts by Edward Burne-Jones.

Chapter Thirteen

Reading Chaucer Aloud

David Fuller

*If [people] are to read poetry at all, if they are to enjoy beautiful rhythm,
if they are to get from poetry anything but what it has in common with
prose, they must hear it spoken by men who have music in their voices
and a learned understanding of its sound. There is no poem so great that
a fine speaker cannot make it greater or that a bad ear cannot make it
nothing.*

W. B. Yeats[1]

Hearing Chaucer read aloud, and reading his poetry aloud, is one of
the best ways of beginning to enjoy his work, and continuing to enjoy
it. What this primarily requires is what all reading aloud of poetry
requires: not knowledge of the sounds of the language in the south-
east midlands of England circa 1400, but an ability to give aural shape
to the structures of verse, formal and syntactic, so as to bring out their
beauty and expressivity. This is the 'learned understanding' of which
Yeats speaks. It is the understanding required by all reading of poetry
aloud – just as imagining poetry in these terms, in the mind's ear, is
fundamental to the pleasures of silent reading. Poetry can be a private
art. Reading poetry often means, properly, a silent reader alone with
a book. A Shakespeare sonnet does not imply the same reading expectations as the *Iliad*. But what the silent reader does is imagine the
soundscapes of a poem as they would be if the poem were read aloud.
And silent reading often requires the complement of reading out loud.

David Fuller

The physical voice, like the face, is both given and developed – an aural (as the face is a visual) repository of one's emotional and intellectual identity. Reading or speaking out loud is a test of the depth and sincerity of one's engagement with any words, for a priest as for a politician, for a lover as for a liar. Poetry is a special case only because full engagement requires a practised understanding of its sounds.

Sound in poetry is intrinsic to meaning; meaning in poetry is never wholly independent of sound. It is because sound is so important in poetry that poets of very different types – poets who are stylized and musical, and poets who are colloquial and prosaic – have affirmed the importance of reading poetry aloud, from Wordsworth, to Hopkins, to W. H. Auden.

> [Wordsworth] I require nothing more than an animated or impassioned recitation, adapted to the subject. Poems, however humble in their kind, if they be good in that kind, cannot read themselves.[2]

> [Hopkins] Remember what applies to all my verse, that it is, as living art should be, made for performance, and that its performance is not reading with the eye but loud, leisurely, poetical (not rhetorical) recitation.[3]

> [Auden] Poetry must move our emotions, or excite our intellect . . . and the stimulus is the audible spoken word and cadence, to which in all its power of suggestion and incantation we must surrender . . . No poetry . . . which when mastered is not better heard than read is good poetry.[4]

Though the performance of poetry was a subject of ancient literary education and criticism,[5] modern literary education has fought shy of it. But the reader who does not understand a poem's aural shapes knows only a shadow of its living reality. An ability to perform, at least to the mind's ear, is – or should be – basic to every other kind of critical procedure. Any aspect of the sound of poetry can be expressive, including, for special effects, the music of vowel and consonant, in patterns of rhyme, assonance and alliteration. But the main musical effects of poetry do not depend on any particular system of pronunciation. If they did the music of Shakespeare's poetry would be almost as lost as the music of Virgil's. If you think, as the poet Basil Bunting did, that the music of poetry consists in 'the tone relations of vowels, the relations of consonants to one another, which are like instrumental colour in music'[6] then you cannot be confident that you are hearing the music of any poetry written much more than a century ago as the poet or the first audience heard it: such music as you find you must take as a mixture of your own creation and the gift of chance. Between cockney Keats and the mellifluous Sir John Gielgud there is a great gulf fixed; and its precise contours cannot be known. The music of poetry depends not on those aspects of the sound of language that differ from one system of pronunciation to another but on those that are broadly constant, above all on the sounds of the shapes of syntax interacting with the sounds of the shapes of form. This often means an expressive interaction of different modes or structurations of language – prose or colloquial syntax cutting across the formal shapes of verse (the line, the stanza), speech rhythms interacting with metrical patterns.

In discussing the sounds and rhythms of poetry there is no avoiding some technical detail. This need not be unmitigated dry biscuit so long as one keeps in view the aim – enjoyment of beauty. This should come as easily as it can: some ears are more readily tuned than others.

Rhythm and metrical pattern, and the delicate and variable ways in which they function, seem to be among the most difficult aspects of poetry to understand. Hearing and analysing the rhythm of a poem is an art, not a science. There is never a single right scansion. Competent readers may well disagree about the aural realization of a poem's rhythms.[7] As with other aspects of criticism, alternative interpretations are often possible, and will usually relate to other aspects of interpretation – from the primary senses or feelings of a poem to issues about audience and context. In realizing rhythms the reader is listening for and aiming to recreate a musical quality, but not one that corresponds with the regular beat of Western musical notation. The rhythms of poetry are more free and irregular. Stress is irregular in periodicity. It is also irregular in degree: stress is a relative, not an absolute quality. Words can assume a degree of stress when part of a regular metrical pattern which they would not bear in prose (where no pattern of stresses has been established). A properly rhythmical reading is something that should come naturally once the reader's ears are attuned to the basic metrical pattern. A good reading should be a negotiation between the underlying metrical structure, the natural rhythms of speech, and the requirements of meaning. A reader should not read so as slavishly to follow the metre in violation of the ordinary speech rhythms or demands of emphasis required by the sense; nor should a reader follow the demands of sense or of ordinary speech rhythm in such a way as wholly to lose track of the metrical structure. When different ways of reading a line present themselves – following the colloquial stress or the metrical accentuation – whichever you choose, you are likely retain a mental impression of the alternative possibility which influences the feeling of the line. But this cannot be made audible in aural delivery. How best to negotiate between the metrical expectation and the natural spoken emphasis where that conflicts with the metre depends on the degree of stylization of the poem and the reader's own feeling about how he or she can most expressively project its words.[8]

In some early works (the *Book of the Duchess*, the *House of Fame*) Chaucer wrote in iambic tetrameter (four-beat lines alternating unstressed and stressed syllables). In his later work (*Troilus and Criseyde*, most of the *Canterbury Tales*) he wrote in iambic pentameter (five-beat lines alternating unstressed and stressed syllables) – the metre of Shakespeare, and the dominant metre of English poetry for 500 years after Chaucer's death. If a reader's ear is attuned to anything it is attuned to this. Chaucer would also have been familiar with – though he never used – a fundamentally different kind of metrical patterning – the four-stressed alliterative line of Old English poetry as it had been developed and was still used by contemporaries such as William Langland, in which there is no regular alternation of stressed and unstressed syllables. Chaucer's ear was therefore attuned, in two ways, to a four-beat as well as a five-beat line. Iambic pentameter itself has a tendency to collapse into a four-beat structure.[9] This happens because stress is dependent both on pattern and on sense, and, unless there is a deliberate aim to make them so, these are seldom identical. While words in a metrical structure may bear some stress against the requirements of sense in order to sustain a feeling of pattern, such words will usually bear a lesser stress than sense words. 'To be, or not to be; that is the question.' The structure of iambic pentameter requires a feeling of residual stress on the second 'be', but the sense does not. A competent actor will give the line four, not five, main stresses:

/   /   /   /
To be, or not to be; that is the question.

We find this same freedom in Chaucer, perhaps the more readily because his ear was attuned to various forms of the four-beat line. Actually to scan and read his iambic pentameter as though every line contains five stresses would require emphasizing syllables that will not bear full stress without distortion. A good reading aloud will both maintain a sense of underlying pattern and recognize that the structure is not a metrical bed of Procrustes in which every consideration gives way to regular recurrence. Rhythm was evidently of the utmost importance to Chaucer. His prayer at the end of *Troilus* is threefold: that the text be copied accurately; that the language be understood; and that no reader 'the [thee: *Troilus*] mysmetre for defaute of tonge' (V, 1796). But Chaucer did not aim for the smoothness cultivated by Pope. He used in his own ways the freedoms later deployed by Shakespeare, and by other poets for whom the rhythms of poetry and the rhythms of speech interact – poets such as Donne, whom Jonson thought 'for not keeping of accent deserved hanging'.[10]

Syntax too may run – beautifully and expressively – counter to the requirements of making the simplicities of metrical pattern audible. In most poetry grammatical structure is not conterminous with the line. Often some of the energy of a poem comes from an interplay between syntax and lineation, so it is important not to lose the feeling of either. The reader has to guide the listener's ear through the grammatical structure; but, with that primary desideratum, the reader has also to consider what it is appropriate to do to bring out the form. This can properly vary with the style of a poem: line endings, for example, are heard more readily when they are marked by rhyme – as they always are in Chaucer. Intonation helps to point syntax, but also at times to decide implications of sense. Quite different ways of saying the same phrase or sentence may be acceptable as normal English intonation, though one may express better than another the appropriate sense in a given context. Intonation functions in part simply as a guide about syntax to the listener's ear – especially important when the syntax is complex. It is also an instrument of interpretation.

Tension between the demands of form and syntax can create the effect of passionate speech by giving a sense of energy both contained and bursting out. This depends on the listener being kept conscious of the underlying formal patterns against which the syntax is in revolt. Rearranging the layout of a stanza can show how syntactic shapes interact with the regularities of formal pattern. Reading should make audible both forms of structure.

So wolde god, that auctour is of kynde*, *nature
That with his bond loue of his vertue liste
To cerclen hertes alle and faste bynde,
That from his bond no wight the wey out wiste*; *might know
And hertes colde, hem wolde I that he twiste* *would wring
To make hem loue, and that hem liste* ay rewe* *it pleases them; *pity

On hertes sore, and kepe hem that ben trewe.
    (*Troilus and Criseyde*, III, 1765–71)

So woldë god, that auctour is of kynde,
That with his bond – loue – of his vertue
    liste to cerclen hertës alle
    and fastë bynde,
That from his bond no wight the wey out wiste;
And hertës colde, hem wolde I that he twiste to make hem loue,
    and that hem liste
        ay rewe on hertës sore,
        and kepe hem that ben trewe.

This stanza from *Troilus and Criseyde* – the last of a group supposedly heightened by a fiction of musical delivery (Troilus 'wolde synge') – follows from a series in which the regularities of formal shape enforce extended and elaborate patterns of the rhetoric (III, 1744–64). This preparation emphasizes by contrast that in this stanza the rhetorical shapes in part reinforce, but in part passionately overflow the formal pattern. The emphasis of rhythm is intensified by the music of alliteration ('loue . . . liste', 'wight . . . wey . . . wiste') and disturbed by the stressed syllables jammed together in apposition ('bond, loue'). Some phrases are both parallel and irregular – because they are of different lengths ('rewe . . . kepe . . .'), or the verb is in a symmetrically opposite position in the phrase ('cerclen . . . bynde'). Some parallels arise from and maintain a sense of the stanza structure ('with his bond . . . from his bond'; 'hertës colde . . . hertës sore'), but three times the syntax breaks through the line endings. Rhyme sounds then become involved with the less regular chime of assonance ('wiste . . . twiste . . . liste'). This rhyme assonance brings out the similarity of 'rewe' / 'trewe', balanced at the beginning and end of parallel phrases which draw together the gamut of lovers – the rejected (Troilus as he will be) and the accepted (Troilus as he here is). The irregular phrase lengths are complemented by irregular rhythm ('kepe hem that ben trewe'). All of these effects – of pattern enforced and of pattern broken – can be heard without analysis. Analysis simply brings out what reading attentive to the complementary demands of form and syntax will make audible – heightening and disturbance.

Simpler than either rhythm or syntax is pace. As with everything about reading aloud, there are few general rules. People often read too quickly: heightening and disturbance – or any other effect of sound – cannot be heard if the reader rushes. A reader must convey a sense that he or she is taking enough time to relish the words in all their aspects as structured sounds, and to think of and feel their meanings. Beyond that, much depends on the poem and the actual or assumed audience. A poem of action (narrative) can often be read more quickly than a poem of meditation (lyric). Poetry of argument and the spoken voice (Donne) may require more variation than poetry of song (Tennyson) – though all poetry requires variation, to emphasize central issues or to mark changes of direction; even various degrees of pause, related to overall sense and form, and immediate syntax and rhythm. It is important with variation of pace, and with pause, to maintain the fundamental feeling of an underlying rhythmic pulse. The effect should be like *tempo rubato* in music: the player maintains connection with the basic pulse while, for expressive purposes, but within limits, varying the pace. You may go further with this in dramatic than in non-dramatic poetry, because in dramatic poetry (narrative, as well as poetry written for the stage) there is more need to accommodate the inflections of a supposed speaking voice. With comic poetry, timing is particularly important because it points, and allows the listener to relish, humour – especially in live reading, where an audience's pleasure is heightened by being able to participate in shared delight at what is funny.

A reader has also to think about how to use his or her voice. The problem is that the reader needs to use his or her voice in part naturally, as it is used in the rest of life, as it aurally embodies characteristics of his or her thinking and feeling. This is key to connecting the poet's words with the reader's own emotional and intellectual life. Without this a reader cannot engage with a poem with full seriousness. Many people cannot do this readily because a poem is a shaped object. The difficulty is to find ways of using one's natural voice to cooperate with and project that: to relate one's natural voice to the degree of stylization of the poem; and to find some version of the full range of one's voice that can cooperate with the characteristic 'voice' of the poet – including the dramatic voices that the poet creates. Many people read with a narrower range of intonation and expressive inflections than they use in speaking, because in reading they cut down the range of expressive variation (of pitch, stress, pace) by which they are accustomed to express themselves in speech. There are, on the other hand, usual 'actorly' mistakes: treating a poem as an opportunity to display a self-consciously 'beautiful' voice, or supposing that poetry requires a voice infused with emotion. On the contrary, the voice is a vehicle and should not draw attention to itself; and the reader must not displace attention from the words by spicing them up with artificial additives. As T. S. Eliot has put it, 'So far as possible, the reciter should not dramatize. It is the words that matter, not the feeling about them.'[11]

Eliot was here discussing poetry that is philosophical or meditative. In his own reading of *The Waste Land* he made more concessions to the praise of Dickens' Sloppy (*Our Mutual Friend*) that he had once intended as a title for that many-voiced poem: 'he do the police in different voices.' Even at his most austere Eliot did not mean that a performer should read colourlessly; rather that the reader should trust the words, giving what Wordsworth calls an 'animated' realization of their formal and metrical arrangement. Reading should reveal the expressivity the poet has found in the language and built in to its organization, not apply expressivity from outside. There may be a great deal of colour present, but it should be the colours of the poem's words interacting with the colours of the reader's personality. To do this fully the reader has to live with a poem. Part of that 'living with' process is to read the poem repeatedly, working it into one's own voice, interiorizing a sense of its feelings and ideas. The poet Charles Tomlinson has remarked that reading aloud is 'a way of life' – meaning that to read poetry out loud well one needs to be accustomed to reading aloud in a variety of situations, intimate and formal, from bedtime story to lectern.

From this point of view the advice of a great French poet, Paul Valéry, is the epitome of error:

> In studying a piece of poetry to be spoken aloud, one should never take as a beginning or point of departure ordinary discourse or current speech, and then rise from the level of prose to the desired poetic tone; on the contrary, I believe one should start from song, put oneself in the attitude of the singer, tune one's voice to the fullness of musical sound, and from that point descend to the slightly less vibrant state suitable to verse. It seemed to me that this was the only way to preserve the musical essence of poems . . . The first condition for speaking verse well is an understanding of what it is not, and of how great a difference separates it from ordinary language. (Valéry 1958: 162–3)

Valéry's advice draws on French traditions of writing and performance that are markedly different from English ones. W. H. Auden wittily remarked that playing Racine is more like singing Wagner than acting Shakespeare, and that French classical tragedy is 'opera for the unmusical'.[12] The relation of much English poetry – including Chaucer's – to spoken English is closer than that of the classic traditions of French poetry to spoken French. With English poetry the view of Thomas Gray – 'the language of the age is never the language of poetry'[13] – has been aberrant. Wordsworth's account – 'a selection of the language really spoken by men'[14] – indicates the relation of poetic to spoken language to which English poetry has constantly returned. The way in which English poetry should be read – with a feeling for all the resources of the language as spoken – follows from that. But there must also be 'selection'. In verse drama, Yeats affirms ('Lapis Lazuli'), actors who understand their art 'do not break up their lines to weep'. So it is in reading all verse: the reader must find expressiveness, not in naturalistic effects at odds with form, but in a full realization of the complementary effects of the spoken voice and formal organization.

It is a usual aspect of training in musical performance that one memorizes: as a result of constant practice, a piece of music settles into the memory. Though you may continue to play from the score, memory helps with the concentrated participation in performance that holds an audience's attention because the performer is wholly immersed in the music. Similarly, the effect of reading aloud can be intensified by the reader having a poem somewhat in the memory (while reading from the text) – so as to guide the listener through the syntax, and so as to construct the poem's aural shapes in such a way as to guide the listener through its sequence of ideas and feelings. Gradual development of a poem in the memory is another aspect of living with it. It requires time and variety of circumstance, and a familiarity with the words themselves that is not necessarily analytic. As Wallace Stevens has it, 'In poetry you must love the words, the ideas and the images and rhythms with all your capacity to love anything at all.'[15] Loving involves not readily displacing the words themselves with ideas about them. Memory has a role in this, as Ted Hughes implied in calling an anthology of favourite poems *By Heart* (Faber, 1997): memorizing – not by repeated pounding of isolated fragments, but by repeated engaged reading – is an aspect of learning to love.

Chaucer apparently read aloud to an audience who listened and did not follow a text: the fifteenth-century manuscript of *Troilus and Criseyde* now in Corpus Christi College, Cambridge (MS 61) shows him doing this (see p. 12). He refers in his poems to audiences listening to readers (Criseyde, for example, is entertained by a reading of 'the geste / Of the siege of Thebes' [*Troilus*, II, 83–4]). His narrators, sometimes in the same poem, address both listeners who 'yheere' and readers who can 'turne over the leef' ('The Miller's Prologue', I, 3176–7). The *Canterbury Tales* assume oral delivery to an audience who intervene and respond. Evidently this cannot be read as directly reflecting historical circumstances (the fiction also assumes spontaneous utterance in verse), but it is significant that it represents listening to oral delivery as normal. However, Chaucer's contemporaries also read in something more like the usual modern situation – an individual reader alone with a book (manuscript). Chaucer's narrators are often bookish – which seems to mean they read privately. It may be that such readers did not read silently, or that silent reading was at least still somewhat unusual.[16] Whatever the case, Chaucer's contemporaries would have read imagining aural performance to a greater degree than a modern reader: they were accustomed to it. In so far as the historical situation is relevant, it gives added emphasis to the importance of reading aloud.

The sounds that Chaucer and his contemporaries made when they read aloud can be conjecturally reconstructed, and scholarly editions of Chaucer regularly include charts of vowel and consonant sounds of south-east midlands English in the late fourteenth century.[17] In brief, the sounds are more like modern French vowels and modern Scottish consonants; there were few silent letters (*k*night, *k*new; fo*l*k, ha*l*f), except in French loan words (*h*onour, si*g*ne); and in general, orthography reflected pronunciation more than in modern English. But historical phonology can take us only so far in working from written records to the spoken language. We cannot know precisely what range of sounds was found acceptable or comprehensible within a long dead speech community. We can know, from observing modern dialects, that a considerable range can be thought of as belonging within a single broad system; and variation in spoken forms is only likely to have been more common in a culture with no aural mass communication and relatively little in the way of institutions through which pronunciation would be standardized.

In any case, there are many characteristics of speech sounds about which written sources cannot give information, particularly expressive uses of pitch and stress – all that is meant by intonation. No native speaker of English can learn to sound like a living Russian without living among Russians. For non-native speakers, intonation almost never becomes entirely idiomatic, even for the standard patterns of the language, never mind for those that are individually and personally expressive to a native speaker of any linguistic sophistication. If, in reading poetry aloud, it is important that the reader use all the expressive resources of his or her individual voice, a native speaker of modern English can no more do that in reconstructed south-east midlands English of *c.*1400 than he or she can in contemporary Russian – rather less, in fact. South-east midlands English of *c.*1400 as it was spoken is more unknown to anyone now living than the French of Paris was to Chaucer's Prioress. Professor Nevill Coghill is a delightful reader of

Chaucer in reconstructed pronunciation. His voice and manner convey real understanding of the fundamental issues of Chaucer's poetry. But it is probable that if Chaucer could hear Coghill read he would wonder (his accent neither quite English nor quite French; his intonation sometimes curiously unidiomatic) where the professor had learned to speak English.

From the point of view of poetry, in any case, there is only one issue about Chaucer's pronunciation that is of radical importance: when and whether to pronounce final 'e'. This continually affects the rhythm. As in French, the reader should normally elide 'e' before a vowel and pronounce 'e' before a consonant; but unless Chaucer's rhythms were much rougher occasionally than they appear to have been usually, this was apparently not a hard and fast rule. The reader has to use his or her ear for rhythm to decide when it should be ignored. This, at least, seems more likely than that Chaucer had cloth ears – though perhaps some of his scribes did. It is improbable that final 'e' was not treated in whatever way would produce metrical regularity just because the usual rules of elision did not apply. Metrical regularity is the norm; the pronunciation necessary to produce it was possible; and other variable pronunciations to suit the metre were accepted.[18] (It is difficult always to get this right when you are reading an unfamiliar poem, because you sometimes cannot know that the rhythm is going to require an exceptional elided or pronounced 'e' until late in the line.)

Even in so far as reconstructed historical pronunciation is reliable, it does not follow that the contemporary reader should use it. Oral delivery of reconstructed pronunciation cannot be the same for a modern as for a fourteenth-century audience. Anybody now listening to Chaucer read aloud in reconstructed pronunciation will follow a text. If they do not they will frequently misunderstand, because many words in reconstructed pronunciation have the same sound as different words in contemporary pronunciation. Context will sometimes prevent misunderstanding – but sometimes it will not. For a modern audience, therefore, listening means following with the ear and eye together – a significantly different situation from that of Chaucer's contemporaries. Moreover, the sounds natural to Chaucer's audience are precisely unnatural to early twenty-first-century readers. The effect can be to make the poetry seem quaint, not fully serious. Despite the distortions involved, it may be that we reproduce the effect of Chaucer's poetry for its first audience better by speaking it as they did – that is, in pronunciation contemporary to us, as theirs was to them.

David Fuller

From Scylla to Charybdis. We may not know entirely what south-east midlands English c.1400 sounded like, and we cannot speak it as a living language; but it fitted. Modern pronunciation we know; it is the living form of the language; but it does not fit. Words that are entirely obsolete; words that now have a sense quite different from the sense they bore for Chaucer (so that it is actively misleading to make them sound the same as their modern non-equivalent); words the stress of which has changed (so that, whatever value you give their vowels and consonants, you must either distort their modern form or misrepresent Chaucer's rhythms); the frequent need to pronounce final 'e' or distort the rhythm – all these make for difficulty. Some of these problems arise when reading Shakespeare or Milton in modern pronunciation – but only some of them (words that are obsolete, words that have changed their meaning; words that have changed their stress or syllabic value); and all of them arise much less frequently.

The famous opening of the 'General Prologue' illustrates the problems. (The orthography here is altered to indicate the pronunciation of modern English in so far as that is compatible with preserving Chaucer's rhythms.)

When that April with his showrës soot	*sweet, fragrant
The drought of March hath piercèd to the root,	
And bathèd every vein in such liquor	
Of which virtue* engendered is the flower;	*power
When Zephyrus eke with his sweetë breath	
Inspirèd hath in every holt* and heath	*grove
The tender cropës, and the youngë sun	
Hath in the Ram* his halfë course y-run,	*Aries
And smallë fowlës maken melody,	
That sleepen all the night with open eye	
(So pricketh them Nature in their courages);	
Then longen folk to go on pilgrimages,	
And palmers for to seeken strangë strands*,	*shores
To fernë* hallows*, couth* in sundry lands;	*distant shrines; *known
And specially from every shirës end	
Of Engëland to Canterbury they wend,	
The holy blissful* martyr for to seek,	*blessed
That them hath holpen when that they were sick.	

(I, 1–18)

The simplest difficulty is that, to preserve Chaucer's rhythms, reading must incorporate archaic elements, especially the pronunciation of final 'e'. There is some freedom about what to do with changed stress patterns – how to pronounce 'liquor' where the shift of stress (from the second syllable to the first) means both that it does not fit the metrical structure and does not rhyme with 'flower' (monosyllabic to Chaucer ['flour'], disyllabic in modern Received Pronunciation). In both cases it is possible to find a version of modern pronunciation that minimizes the problems, but some such problem does occur in almost every line: words that have entirely dropped out of use (ferne, soot), words and forms that are archaic (eke, y-run, maken, sleepen, longen, seeken, holpen), words that have changed sense (inspired, couth), changed stress (liquor, Nature, courages), changed syllabic value (flower, Engëland), or changed in sound so that they are no longer full rhymes (liquor / flower; melody / eye). Lines that contain more than one of these features can be especially difficult to say – here particularly, 'So pricketh them Nature in their courages', with its two changes of stress (Nature, courages) and a shift of meaning (courages). Despite these difficulties, modern pronunciation does allow the reader to feel the connection of Chaucer's language with spoken English. The reader can therefore, within limits, use his or her own voice, and is potentially in command of aural shaping that is genuinely expressive.

Using either reconstructed or modern pronunciation involves some gains and some losses. But the two methods are not mutually exclusive. If one is persuaded by those who advocate historical reconstruction, one has to recognize that success can be no more than partial, and that to enjoy the pleasures of poetry and avoid the allure of quaintness the reader has to retain as far as possible a sense of connection with the living, spoken language. However, the best practical advice may be to observe the pronunciation of final 'e' where the rhythm requires it, to observe Chaucer's stress where stress in modern pronunciation has shifted (as one might in reading Shakespeare or Milton), and not to worry about shifts in the value of vowels and consonants, which cannot in any case be re-created with entire accuracy. The defect of this approach is an occasional sense of anachronism. Its virtues are that it avoids replacing the pleasures of poetry with the pleasures of antiquarianism and does not inhibit the reader's expressive use of idiomatic intonation and inflection.

If anyone can persuade that it is possible to deploy all the resources of your own voice when reading in the 'foreign' language of south-east midlands English *c*.1400 it is Nevill Coghill.[19] Coghill is the antitype of historical phonologists such as H. C. Wyld and Helge Kökeritz, whose recordings may exemplify correctly the sounds of vowels and consonants in so far as these can be known, but as for the Yeats prescription of 'music in the voice', theirs is exactly not 'a learned understanding of the sound' – that is, of poetry as poetry: of this it is learned ignorance. As narrator of 'The Nun's Priest's Tale' Coghill shows how to use a great range of expressive tones: he is wry about the virtues of farmhouse plain living, colourful for the description of the cock, Chanticleer, warm about the beauties of the hen, Pertelote, *faux naïf* for the beast-fable suppositions about talking animals, broadly comic for special effects (Chanticleer's clucking) and serious for the invocations of Saint Paul and God, using a weight of voice that persuades the listener that he knows what being serious really means. The British Council series of which Coghill's recordings are a part raises, however, a problem about whether the *Canterbury Tales*, and Chaucer's narrative poems more generally, should be distributed between different readers – as they are there. The texts themselves indicate a single narrator who performs the roles of all the characters. Distributing the roles tends to diminish the importance of the narrator, though the narrator's personality often interacts with the tale. In some of the *Canterbury Tales* the tale may be understood as part of the characterization of its narrator – the Knight, offering examples of courtly, refined and exalted feeling; the Miller offering the opposite; the Wife of Bath, concerned with women's power in sexual relationships; the Franklin, with examples of exalted behaviour in characters who are not aristocratic. One can overemphasize characterization of the narrator: it is not the primary aim of any tale. The central thematic focus of 'The Franklin's Tale' is love, and power in sexual relationships; 'The Nun's Priest's Tale' has no special relation to its teller. But Chaucer's fiction supposes a narrator who is all the characters, and though this has different importance in different works, where possible it is best to preserve this fiction in aural presentation. The Chaucer Studio recordings raise the same problem, which is compounded, in their case, by the variousness of the abilities of the readers between whom the group readings (about half the total) are distributed. Some are very good – A. C. Spearing as the narrator of 'The Franklin's Tale', Alan T. Gaylord in a solo reading of 'The Knight's Tale', Andrew Lynch reading selections from the *Legend of Good Women*. But not all are on this level, and some are distinctly below it. Few works distributed between several readers can be consistently enjoyed. Some readers are carefully prepared and fluent, but some are too concentrated on the difficulties of unfamiliar vowel and consonant sounds to shape the poetry for sense and feeling. Nevertheless, the Chaucer Studio recordings are particularly valuable: they are reliable, relatively easy to obtain and comprehensive (theirs, for example, is the only complete recording of *Troilus*); there are some interesting experiments (two different solo readings of 'The Prioress's Tale'; a solo and a group reading of 'The Tale of Sir Topas'); and the best are both lively and nuanced.

It is an interesting reflection on the supposed need for historically reconstructed pronunciation that there are virtually no readers who do not make mistakes: almost all, including the most accomplished, at times adapt the sound they are aiming for (the sound they produce elsewhere) towards the modern sound that has replaced it. Moreover, you can almost always hear, within reconstructed pronunciation, the form of contemporary dialect from which the reader starts. As is usual with the learning of any foreign language, the native language of the non-native speaker is embedded in the pronunciation of the language learned. Just as there is English French, American French, Australian French, so there is English, American and Australian south-east midlands English *c.*1400. That Jess Bessinger's American point of departure is obvious need bother only purists. He reads, as necessary, with gusto or with delicacy, is particularly good at pointing the relations of syntax and form when these are complex, and, unlike Coghill and the Chaucer Studio, he performs all the voices, maintaining the fiction of a unitary narrator.

The only complete recording of the *Canterbury Tales*, which also has the virtue of being relatively easily obtainable, is that of Trevor Eaton. Eaton is a practised reader, and he produces the unfamiliar sounds with great fluency. Like Bessinger, he too performs all the voices, in the cause of articulating which he departs as far as could be from the austere desiderata of T. S. Eliot. He precisely does not (as Eliot puts it) trust the words. Chaucer's irony may at times require a delivery that, without being flat, or failing to take opportunities the text implies for coloration, is interpretively neutral: when the poetry is purposefully ambiguous, for the reader to colour is actually to flatten the effect. But Eaton's desire to be lively leads him, on the contrary, to exaggerate, though with a similar style and expressive range whoever the character may be. I doubt whether most people would think these exaggerations acceptable if they were not protected from normal criteria of judgement by the fact that nobody has ever heard Chaucer's language spoken by (as it were) a native speaker. Eaton's extravagance demonstrates how reconstructed pronunciation can lead to an alienation from the language which means that as poetry it is not taken seriously. Eaton also sometimes reads too quickly, and so fails to maintain an adequate sense of the structure of the verse. And while he usually leads the ear through the syntax well in the well-known tales, the unfamiliarity of the less well-known sometimes shows in hesitations and stumblings. Overall Eaton misses what Coghill's range of tones so well registers, Chaucer's sophisticated blend of comedy and seriousness, a blend that depends on getting in viable relation innumerable local judgements about tone. As in the comedies of Shakespeare and Mozart, in Chaucer what is fundamentally serious is often presented with an ease and delicacy that only those who think of seriousness of matter as inseparable from seriousness of manner can mistake for lack of substance, but which it is an extraordinary challenge to the performer to register with the necessary combination and range of tones. It is beyond Eaton.

The only recordings that give one a chance to hear original texts in modern pronunciation are those made to accompany the modern-spelling editions of some *Canterbury Tales* by Michael Murphy. The editions are potentially of much greater interest in relation to reading Chaucer aloud than the tapes made to accompany them show, because, though the editions mark for pronunciation metrical final 'e', the recordings, by professional actors, do not carry out this instruction, and so seriously misrepresent the rhythms of Chaucer's verse. While this was apparently not Murphy's intention, it may be symptomatic of how difficult it is to read in modern pronunciation and retain the rhythms of the original.

Interestingly different realizations of some *Canterbury Tales* that make partial use of the original texts are the animated versions produced by Jonathan Myerson. Each of the nine tales performed is by a different animator and in a different style. Each tale is given in two versions, with selections from the original in modern English and in Middle English. In neither case are the dramatized readings particularly good, but the animations, which range from good to magnificent, are genuinely creative interactions with the texts that bring out in the new medium many central aspects of the poems. Pier Paolo Pasolini's *The Canterbury Tales* uses the stories of the Merchant, Friar, Cook, Miller, Wife of Bath, Reeve, Pardoner and Summoner. The script, characters and narratives are drawn from Chaucer more or less freely. Sex is central. The lechers subject to the Summoner's extortions are homosexuals spied on by the camera. The Pardoner's rioters are characterized by the highly varied pleasures of their brothel. Where Chaucer has some sex there is much; where he has much there is more. From images based on Bosch and Bruegel to a Chaplinesque clown, the film is a mixture of the medieval and modern more or less Chaucerian.

About judgements of the performance of poetry there is at bottom an element of the inescapably subjective: what personality does one hear in a voice, and how does one respond to it?[20] In so far as it tends to alienate a reader from the normal use of his or her full, natural expressive vocal range, historically reconstructed pronunciation probably distorts one's impressions. Nevertheless, when all that can be considered about the projection of meaning through form, rhythm, syntax and other quasi-objective elements of sound-structure has been said, there is always in relation to performance a judgement of taste that can only be rationalized within limits. The vocal tones of Trevor Eaton (for example) do not suggest to me capacious feeling and acute intelligence; the vocal tones of Nevill Coghill do. And that constitutes a part of my preference.

Not every critical account can be given an aural realization. But every aural realization has critical implications. As with all perfor-mance, one of the problems of listening to recordings is that the lis-tener receives interpretative choices readymade. Recorded performances should be used, then, as models for and adjuncts to one's own reading, particularly because reading aloud for oneself, whether alone or to an audience, is a great antidote to an alternative passivity – silent reading in which not articulating the words means one does not fully attend to them, or attends to them in only some of their aspects.

Chaucer is one of the greatest poets to have written in English. He should not be the province of the specialist. Specialist knowledge – linguistic and historical – always has its place. But specialist knowledge usurps too high a place if it tends to imply that what is most important in Chaucer cannot be understood and enjoyed other than with its help. Many of the poets who read Chaucer most creatively – Spenser (who saw him as an important source of his poetic language), Shakespeare (for whom he was a narrative source), Dryden (who translated him), Blake (whose 'Canterbury Pilgrims' was one of his most important engravings) – read him with no sense of the sound of south-east midlands English *c.*1400. Recording can make the linguistic knowledge of the specialist available to the non-specialist. Modern pronuncia-tion may more readily retain Chaucer for whatever general reader-ship English poetry still has. Both methods have losses and gains.

Whichever one adopts, to read Chaucer with pleasure requires above all what is common to all poetry: understanding of sophisticated linguistic soundscapes, and music in the voice.

See also chapter 2, MANUSCRIPTS AND AUDIENCE.

Notes

1 'Samhain: 1906. Literature and the Living Voice', *Explorations* (London: Macmillan, 1962), p. 212.

2 Preface, *Poems of 1815*; *The Prose Works of William Wordsworth*, ed. W. J. B. Owen and Jane Smyser, 3 vols (Oxford: Clarendon Press, 1974), vol. 3, p. 29.

3 Letter to Robert Bridges, 11 December 1886; *The Letters of Gerard Manley Hopkins to Robert Bridges*, ed. Claude Colleer Abbott (London: Oxford University Press, 1935), p. 246.

4 *The Poet's Tongue*, 1935; *The English Auden: Poems, Essays and Dramatic Writings, 1927–1939*, ed. Edward Mendelson (London: Faber, 1977), p. 327.

5 See Plato, *Ion*, sections 535–6.

6 'A Statement', in Jonathan Williams (ed.), *Descant on Rawthey's Madrigal: Conversations with Basil Bunting* (Lexington, Ky.: Gnomon, 1968) (no pagination).

7 Cf. T. S. Eliot on his own reading of *Four Quartets*: 'A poem . . . of any depth and complexity . . . should be capable of being read in many ways, and with a variety of emotional emphases . . . The chief value of the author's record is as a guide to the rhythms. Another reader, reciting the poem, need not feel bound to reproduce these rhythms' (recording sleeve note to HMV CLP 1115).

8 Cf. Coleridge on an actress, 'Miss Hudson, who pronounced the blank verse of Shakespeare, and indeed verse in general, better than I ever heard it pronounced . . . She hit the exact medium between the obtrusive Iambic march of recitation, and that far better yet still faulty style which . . . assuming that the actor cannot speak too like natural talking, destroys all sense of metre – and consequently, if it be metre, converts the language into a sort of Prose intolerable to a good ear.' Letter to Byron, 15 October 1815; *Collected Letters of Samuel Taylor Coleridge*, ed. Earl Leslie Griggs, 6 vols (Oxford: Clarendon Press, 1956–71), IV, p. 599.

9 On the tendency of the English pentameter to collapse into four beats see Northrop Frye, *Anatomy of Criticism* (Princeton, NJ: Princeton University Press, 1957), pp. 251–62.

10 Conversations with William Drummond, *Ben Jonson*, ed. C. H. Herford and Percy and Evelyn Simpson, 11 vols (Oxford: Clarendon Press, 1925–52), vol. 1, p. 133.

11   Ranjee Shahani, 'T. S. Eliot Answers Questions', *John O' London's Weekly*, LVIII.1369 (19 August 1949), p. 498; Eliot is speaking with reference to *Burnt Norton*, the first of his *Four Quartets*.
12   *The Dyer's Hand* (London: Faber, 1963), p. 25.
13   Letter to Richard West, 8 April, 1742; *Correspondence of Thomas Gray*, ed. Paget Toynbee and Leonard Whibley, 3 vols (Oxford: Clarendon Press, 1935), vol. 1, p. 192.
14   Preface to *Lyrical Ballads*; *Prose Works* (see note 2), vol. 1, p. 137.
15   'Adagia', *Opus Posthumous*, ed. Samuel French Morse (New York: Knopf, 1957), p. 161.
16   Alberto Manguel, *A History of Reading* (London: HarperCollins, 1996), pp. 41–53.
17   *The Complete Works of Geoffrey Chaucer*, ed. F. N. Robinson. 2nd edn (Boston: Houghton Mifflin, 1957), pp. xxx–xxxii; *Riverside Chaucer*, pp. xxvi–xxx.
18   Some words (often recent loan words that had not become entirely naturalized) could apparently be stressed on different syllables to suit the demands of the metre. The supposition of metrical regularity on which assumptions about variable accentuation and practices of elision are based is one of taste, not certain knowledge, as Robinson (1971) argues.
19   Details of all the recordings discussed are given in the bibliography.
20   For an attempt to see objective components of this, in the singing voice, see Roland Barthes, 'The Grain of the Voice', in *Image – Music – Text*, trans. Stephen Heath (London: Fontana, 1977), pp. 179–89.

References and Further Reading

Books and essays
CHAUCER'S PRONUNCIATION, HIS PROSODY, AND READING HIS POETRY ALOUD
Baum, Paull Franklin (1961). *Chaucer's Verse*. Durham, NC: Duke University Press.
Bowden, Betsy (1987). *Chaucer Aloud: The Varieties of Textual Interpretation*. Philadelphia: University of Pennsylvania Press. [With accompanying cassette.]
Bowden, Betsy (1988). *Listeners' Guide to Medieval English: A Discography*. New York: Garland.
Chaucer, Geoffrey (1894–7). *The Complete Works*, ed. W. W. Skeat. 6 vols, Oxford: Clarendon Press. [Versification is discussed mainly in vol. 6, pp. lxxxii–xcvii.]
Chaucer, Geoffrey (1987). *The Riverside Chaucer*, ed. Larry D. Benson. Oxford: Oxford University Press. [Contains a basic guide to Chaucer's versification by Norman Davis, pp. xxxviii–xli.]
Gaylord, Alan T. (1976). 'Scanning the Prosodists'. *Chaucer Review* 11, 32–82. Reprinted in Gaylord (ed.), *Essays on the Art of Chaucer's Verse*. New York: Routledge, 2001, pp. 79–129.

Gaylord, Alan T. (1990). 'Imagining Voices: Chaucer on Cassette'. *Studies in the Age of Chaucer* 12, 224–31.

Gaylord, Alan T. (1992). 'Reading Chaucer: What's Allowed in "Aloud"?' *Chaucer Yearbook* 1, 87–109.

Kökeritz, Helge (1954). *A Guide to Chaucer's Pronunciation*. Stockholm: Almquist and Wiksell. [Reprinted, Toronto: Medieval Academy of America, 1978.]

Lounsbury, Thomas Raynesford (1892). *Studies in Chaucer, his Life and Writings.* 3 vols. London: Osgood, McIlvaine. [In volume III, pp. 264–79 there is a witty and forcefully expressed argument for modern pronunciation.]

Murphy, Michael (1983). 'On Not Reading Chaucer Aloud'. *Mediaevalia* 9, 205–23.

Mustanoja, Tauno F. (1968). 'Chaucer's Prosody'. In Beryl Rowland (ed.), *A Companion to Chaucer Studies*. Toronto: Oxford University Press, pp. 58–84.

Robinson, Ian (1971). *Chaucer's Prosody: A Study of the Middle English Verse Tradition*. Cambridge: Cambridge University Press.

Southworth, James Granville (1954). *Verses of Cadence: An Introduction to the Prosody of Chaucer and his Followers*. Oxford: Blackwell.

Southworth, James Granville (1962). *The Prosody of Chaucer and his Followers: Supplementary Chapters to 'Verses of Cadence'*. Oxford: Blackwell.

THE SOUNDS AND RHYTHMS OF POETRY

Burke, Kenneth (1957). 'On Musicality in Verse'. In Burke, *The Philosophy of Literary Form: Studies in Symbolic Action*. Rev. edn, New York: Vintage. [First published in 1941.]

Carper, Thomas and Derek Attridge (2003). *Meter and Meaning: an Introduction to Rhythm in Poetry*. New York: Routledge.

Hobsbaum, Philip (1996). *Metre, Rhythm and Verse Form*. London: Routledge.

Leavis, F. R. (1986). 'Reading Out Poetry'. In Leavis, *Valuation in Criticism and Other Essays*, ed. G. Singh. Cambridge: Cambridge University Press, pp. 253–75.

Levi, Peter (1977). *The Noise Made by Poems*. London: Anvil.

Stevens, Wallace (1951). 'The Noble Rider and the Sound of Words'. In Stevens, *The Necessary Angel: Essays on Reality and the Imagination*. New York: Knopf, pp. 1–36.

Valéry, Paul (1958). 'On speaking verse'. In *Collected Works*, ed. Jackson Matthews. Vol. 7, *On the Art of Poetry*, trans. Denise Folliot; introd. T. S. Eliot. London: Routledge, pp. 159–66.

Winters, Yvor (1957). 'The Audible Reading of Poetry'. In *The Function of Criticism: Problems and Exercises*. Denver: Alan Swallow, pp. 79–100.

Audio and video resources

For full publication details of recordings to 1986 see Bowden, *Discography*, above.

*   currently available
+   available only in libraries

+ Bessinger, Jess B., Jr (reader). *The General Prologue; Prologue to The Parson's Tale; The Retraction.* Caedmon, 1962. Bessinger also recorded for Caedmon *The Parliament of Fowls* and other poems [short lyrics] (1967) and *The Miller's Tale* and *The Reeve's Tale* (1972).

+ British Council. *The General Prologue*, read by Nevill Coghill, Norman Davis and John Burrow. Argo, 1965. In the series The English Poets from Chaucer to Yeats. The series also included 'The Nun's Priest's Tale' and minor poems, read by Coghill, Norman and Lena Davis, and John Burrow (1966); selections from *Troilus and Criseyde*, Derek Brewer and various readers (1971); 'The Knight's Tale' (1976), and 'The Pardoner's Tale' (1976), both directed by Derek Brewer; and 'The Wife of Bath's Prologue and Tale', with Prunella Scales, directed by Derek Brewer (1978). The recordings, originally issued on LP, were reissued on cassette in 1982.

* Chaucer Studio. This ongoing series, begun in 1986, includes recordings of many of *The Canterbury Tales*, a complete recording of *Troilus and Criseyde*, and other works by Chaucer and by his contemporaries, with many different readers. The organization is assisted by the English Departments of the University of Adelaide and Brigham Young University in conjunction with the New Chaucer Society. The recordings, originally issued on cassette, are currently being reissued on CD. See http://english.byu.edu/chaucer/

* Eaton, Trevor (reader). *The Canterbury Tales*. Recordings of the complete *Canterbury Tales* made between 1986 and 1993 and issued on cassette by Pearl. Available from Pavilion Records, Sparrows Green, Wadhurst, East Sussex, TN5 6SJ, UK.

* Golden Clarion. Recordings of most of Chaucer's poetry, including the dream visions, selections from *Troilus and Criseyde*, and most of the *Canterbury Tales*, made between 1971 and 1986. The principal reader is Paul Piehler. These are currently available from Golden Clarion Literary Services, Marika Piehler, 232, East 12th Avenue, Vancouver, BC, V5T 2G9, Canada.

* Murphy, Michael (ed.), *Geoffrey Chaucer: The Canterbury Marriage Tales: A Reader-Friendly Edition* (the tales of the Wife of Bath, the Clerk, the Merchant, and the Franklin), the original words in modern spelling. Conal and Gavin: New York, 2000, with accompanying cassette.

* Murphy, Michael (ed.), *Geoffrey Chaucer: Canterbury Quintet: The General Prologue and Four Tales* (the tales of the Miller, the Wife of Bath [again], the Pardoner, and the Nun's Priest), Little Leaf Press and Conal and Gavin: New York, 2000, with accompanying cassette.

An almost complete edition of the *Canterbury Tales*, in modern spelling, with marginal glosses and annotation by Michael Murphy, is available at http://academic.brooklyn.cuny.edu/webcore/murphy/canterbury/

David Fuller

* Myerson, Jonathan (producer). *The Animated Canterbury Tales*. BBC Educational Publishing, 1998. Three videocassettes. Each cassette contains animated dramatizations of three tales with abbreviated texts. Each tale is given twice, once with the text in Middle English (derived entirely from Chaucer), once with the text in a free modernized form.
* Pasolini, Pier Paolo, *The Canterbury Tales* (1972), British Film Institute, BFIVD508, 1998.
* Spearing, A. C (reader). *The Merchant's Prologue and Tale*. Cambridge: Cambridge University Press. Cassette, 1976; CD, 1999.

Websites
<http://www.courses.fas.harvard.edu/~chaucer/>
    The Harvard Chaucer site.
<http://academics.vmi.edu/english/audio/audio_index.html>
    The Chaucer Metapage Audio Files.
Both offer guides to pronunciation with audio illustrations.

Index